"Natia Kalandarishvili-Mueller's book is an enlightening addition to the scholarship on international humanitarian law (IHL). In particular, her essential and precise clarification of the notion of 'effective control' is very much welcomed as it has been missing so far in the relevant literature. The lack of clarity on this key IHL and public international law concept has often put not only scholars and students, but also practitioners in a difficult position when it came to establish the applicability of IHL to certain situations of armed conflict. Dr Natia Kalandarishvili-Mueller's book is thus a must have for anyone interested in contemporary as well as more classic questions relating to military occupations."

– Dr Annyssa Bellal, *Senior Research Fellow and Strategic Adviser on International Humanitarian Law, Geneva Academy of International Humanitarian Law and Human Rights, Editor of the* War Report

"This book is an important contribution to the scholarship on the law of occupation. It offers a systematic and in-depth analysis of the role of control in establishing the beginning and ending of occupation, as well as the effect of control on substantive obligations. To this end, it presents and analyzes different conceptions of control that have been proposed in case law and doctrine. This leads to clear proposals concerning the appropriate standards to be applied in the framework of the law of occupation. As such, it is of value to both practitioners and scholars in the field of International Humanitarian Law."

– Marten Zwanenburg, *Professor of Military Law, Netherlands Defence Academy*

Occupation and Control in International Humanitarian Law

This book presents a systematic analysis of the notion of control in the law of military occupation. The work demonstrates that in present-day occupations, control as such occurs in different forms and variations. The polymorphic features of occupation can be seen in the way states establish control over territory either directly or indirectly, and in the manner in which they retain, relinquish, or regain it. The question as to what level and type of control is needed to determine the existence and ending of military occupation is explored in great detail in light of various international humanitarian law instruments. The book provides an anatomy of the required tests of control in determining the existence of military occupation based on the law. It also discusses control in relation to occupation by proxy and when and how the end of control over territory occurs so that military occupation is considered terminated. The study is informed by relevant international jurisprudence. It draws on numerous pertinent case studies from all over the world, various reports by different UN entities and other international organisations, as well as legal doctrine.

The book will be a valuable resource for academics, researchers, and practitioners working in the fields of international humanitarian law, international public law, and security studies.

Natia Kalandarishvili-Mueller is Professor of Public International Law at Tbilisi Open University, Georgia.

Routledge Research in the Law of Armed Conflict

Available titles in this series include:

International Law and Drone Strikes in Pakistan
The Legal and Socio-Political Aspects
Sikander Ahmed Shah

Islam and Warfare
Context and Compatibility with International Law
Onder Bakircioglu

The Concept of Military Objectives in International Law and Targeting Practice
Agnieszka Jachec-Neale

Cosmopolitan Ethics and Law on Autonomous Weapons in Modern Warfare
Ozlem Ulgen

A Guide to International Disarmament Law
Stuart Casey-Maslen and Tobias Vestner

Protection of Civilians and Individual Accountability
Obligations and Responsibilities of Military Commanders
in United Nations Peacekeeping Operations
Lenneke Sprik

Africa and International Criminal Justice
Radical Evils and the International Criminal Court
Fred Aja Agwu

Occupation and Control in International Humanitarian Law
Natia Kalandarishvili-Mueller

Occupation and Control in International Humanitarian Law

Natia Kalandarishvili-Mueller

LONDON AND NEW YORK

First published 2021
by Routledge
2 Park Square, Milton Park, Abingdon, Oxon OX14 4RN

and by Routledge
52 Vanderbilt Avenue, New York, NY 10017

Routledge is an imprint of the Taylor & Francis Group, an informa business

© 2021 Natia Kalandarishvili-Mueller

The right of Natia Kalandarishvili-Mueller to be identified as author of this work has been asserted by her in accordance with sections 77 and 78 of the Copyright, Designs and Patents Act 1988.

All rights reserved. No part of this book may be reprinted or reproduced or utilised in any form or by any electronic, mechanical, or other means, now known or hereafter invented, including photocopying and recording, or in any information storage or retrieval system, without permission in writing from the publishers.

Trademark notice: Product or corporate names may be trademarks or registered trademarks, and are used only for identification and explanation without intent to infringe.

British Library Cataloguing-in-Publication Data
A catalogue record for this book is available from the British Library

Library of Congress Cataloging-in-Publication Data
Names: Kalandarishvili-Mueller, Natia, author.
Title: Occupation and control in international humanitarian law / Natia Kalandarishvili-Mueller.
Description: Abingdon, Oxon ; New York, NY : Routledge, 2020. | Series: Routledge research in the law of armed conflict | Based on author's thesis (doctoral—University of Essex, 2018) issued under title: Occupation law and paradigms of control. | Includes bibliographical references and index.
Identifiers: LCCN 2020010997 (print) | LCCN 2020010998 (ebook) | ISBN 9780367476649 (hardback) | ISBN 9781003035732 (ebook)
Subjects: LCSH: Military occupation. | Humanitarian law.
Classification: LCC KZ6775 .K35 2020 (print) | LCC KZ6775 (ebook) | DDC 341.6/7—dc23
LC record available at https://lccn.loc.gov/2020010997
LC ebook record available at https://lccn.loc.gov/2020010998

ISBN: 978-0-367-47664-9 (hbk)
ISBN: 978-1-003-03573-2 (ebk)

Typeset in Galliard
by Apex CoVantage, LLC

This book is dedicated with gratitude to
Mother Mary

Contents

Foreword	xiii
Preface	xv
List of figures	xvi
List of abbreviations	xvii

Introduction	1

Overview 1
The notion of control 3
Structure of the book 12

1 Effective control in occupation law	13

1. Introduction 13
2. Establishing control 14
   2.1 Stepping back in time 14
      2.1.1 Authority and control 14
      2.1.2 Uprisings and effectivity 15
      2.1.3 Exercising authority 16
      2.1.4 Occupation duration 16
      2.1.5 The Oxford Manual of 1880 16
      2.1.6 The Hague 17
      2.1.7 De lege lata 20
   2.2 Common Article 2 GCs 21
   2.3 Article 1 AP I 1977 23
   2.4 Anatomy of the effective control test 24
      2.4.1 Military presence 28
      2.4.2 Consent 29
      2.4.3 Actual vs. potential control 32
      2.4.4 Effective control for qualifying a situation as an
         occupation 35

x   *Contents*

    3. Joint and shared control: control exercised by an MNF and
      UN endorsed control 38
      3.1 MNF control over territory 39
      3.2 UN operations 41
      3.3 The formula for ascertaining the responsibility of the UN
           and troop-contributing states 46
    Conclusions 52

2   Occupation by an intermediary   **53**
    1. Introduction 53
      1.1 Preliminary remarks 54
      1.2 Control over armed groups and subordinate governments/
           de facto authorities 55
    2. Control over an armed group: examples 57
      2.1 Croatia exercising control over the Croatian Defence
           Council (HVO) 57
      2.2 Uganda controlling the Congo Liberation Movement
           (MLC) 59
      2.3 Critical appraisal 61
    3. Control over de facto authorities: examples 66
      3.1 Crimea, Ukraine 67
      3.2 Cyprus 68
      3.3 Georgia 70
           3.3.1 The interrelationship of annexation and
               occupation 72
      3.4 Nagorno Karabakh 74
      3.5 Moldova 75
           3.5.1 Decisive influence 76
           3.5.2 Military presence and consent 78
      3.6 Critical appraisal 81
    4. IHL's own mechanism for control? 83
      4.1 Belonging to a party to the conflict under
           Article 4 GC III 83
      4.2 The potentiality of Article 29 GC IV 86
    Conclusion 87

3   Relinquishing control over territory   **90**
    1. Introduction 90
    2. Legal history 91
      2.1 From Brussels 1874 to The Hague 1907 91
           2.1.1 Brussels 91
           2.1.2 The Hague 92
      2.2 GC IV and relinquishing of control over territory 93

Contents xi

2.3 *Article 6 and the general close of military operations 95*

2.4 *Article 3 AP I 1977 and relinquishing control over the
territory 100*

2.5 *The needed test for relinquishing control in IHL 102*

3. *Forms of relinquishing control 104*

3.1 *Complete end of control over territory 105*

3.2 *Temporary and partial loss of control over parts of a
territory 106*

3.3 *The potential for regaining control 108*

3.4 *Control retained over territory after withdrawal: Gaza 112*

3.5 *The ending of indirect (effective) control/occupation
exercised by an intermediary 123*

3.6 *Remaining based on a UN SC mandate 125*

3.6.1 *The UN SC 125*

3.6.2. *Iraq and UN SC 1546 128*

Conclusion 132

4 The effect of control on substantive obligations   134

1. *Introduction 134*

2. *The occupying power's substantive obligations from the
perspective of IHL 135*

2.1 *Forms and degrees of control in GC IV 136*

2.2 *State obligations during the temporary or partial loss of
control over territory 141*

3. *Is control construed the same way in IHRL and occupation
law? 142*

3.1 *Authority and control over individuals 144*

3.2 *Control over territory 148*

3.3 *Degrees of IHRL obligations according to specific
contexts 159*

4. *A contextual approach to state obligations 162*

5. *IHL and IHRL inter-application 166*

Conclusion 170

Conclusion   172

Bibliography   177

1. *Primary sources 177*

International treaties and instruments 177

UN reports 178

UN human rights committee concluding observations 179

UN commission on human rights 179

Other international organisations 179

xii *Contents*

    Non-governmental organisation reports 181
    Historical sources 181
    Military manuals 182
  2. *Secondary sources 182*
    Books, articles, and chapters 182
    Internet and media sources 198

Table of cases   202
  1. *International tribunals 202*
    International Court of Justice (ICJ) 202
    International Criminal Court (ICC) 203
    International Criminal Tribunal for the Former Yugoslavia
    (ICTY) 203
    International Criminal Tribunal for Rwanda (ICTR) 203
    Special Court for Sierra Leone 204
    International military tribunals on WWII 204
    European Commission on Human Rights 204
    European Court of Human Rights (ECtHR) 204
    UN Human Rights Committee 205
    Inter-American Commission on Human Rights 205
    Inter-American Court of Human Rights 205
    Eritrea-Ethiopia Claims Commission 206
    Iran-United States Claims Tribunal 206
  2. *UN resolutions 206*
    Security council 206
    General assembly 207
  3. *National courts 207*
    Canada 207
    Belgium 207
    Greece 207
    Israel 207
    Japan 208
    United States Military Commission 208
    United Kingdom 208
    The Netherlands 208
  4. *Other relevant documents 208*
    National legislation 208
    Laws on admitting Crimea and Sevastopol to the Russian
    Federation, 21 March 2014 209
    National commissions 209
    Agreements and peace plans 209

Index   210

Foreword

The law of occupation does not always receive the attention it requires. In part, this is due to the public perception that situations of occupation are rare and limited to certain high-profile conflicts in the Middle East. This could hardly be further from the truth. International law pertaining to occupation is, in fact, triggered on a far more prevalent basis, and the need to clarify controversial elements of this legal framework is as acute as for any other branch of law dealing with conflict, force, and sovereignty. One of the reasons for the lack of awareness to the frequency of situations of occupation is that they do not all appear alike, and a significant number of occupations do not present themselves with images of the occupying state's military patrolling the streets of the occupied. Absent this most obvious picture of occupation, the determination of whether an occupation is actually taking place often boils down to determining complex questions of control – the subject of this book.

The notion of "control" masks a wide range of possibilities, and the term itself carries different meanings across the various branches of international law. This book makes a crucial contribution to the literature by analysing and elaborating upon the meaning of control in the context of the law of occupation, as opposed to the different approaches and concepts of control as they appear in other branches of law and used by a wide array of international legal institutions.

How control is established and subsequently relinquished are of course vital matters both covered carefully and in detail by this book, but equally – and in many conflicts, more – important are questions of identifying situations of occupation by intermediary. The book provides an excellent analysis of so-called occupations by proxy through the use of current and recent examples. By doing so, it provides valuable guidance in resolving some of the critical matters affected by the identification of the occupying power. Above all, it leads to the ability to determine responsibilities arising from control over another territory. Crucially, the book continues beyond this step and examines the question of the substantive obligations of an occupying state. Because of the potentially different approaches to control in occupation law and in the practice of international human rights bodies (as demonstrated in the opening sections of the book), there is a real risk of contradiction, or even a gap, in which a state might be considered in control of territory by one body of law but not the other. The implications of these differing

xiv *Foreword*

understandings of control for the scope of substantive obligations of states, and how they can be resolved in a coherent and practicable manner, is another important aspect of this work.

This book is based on the PhD thesis of Dr. Natia Kalandarishvili-Mueller, which I had the pleasure of supervising. An enormous amount of careful and rigorous research has been invested in this work, and the resulting analysis in this book makes a vital contribution to the field. All scholars and practitioners seeking to better understand the law of occupation would be well served by reading it.

Professor Noam Lubell,
University of Essex,
Wivenhoe, 2020

Preface

This book is based on my PhD thesis which I successfully defended at the University of Essex in late 2017. My interest in military occupation arose whilst working at the Office of the State Minister for Reintegration of Georgia (currently known as the State Ministry for Reconciliation and Civic Equality), where I held the position of Chief Legal Specialist (Adviser) in International Law, focusing on matters of international humanitarian law (IHL). In applying IHL, I could experience the complexity and uncertainty in delineating the integral elements of the notion of military occupation. This then led me to delve deeper into IHL in an academic manner. Hence, I set out to further study, identify, and distil the precise anatomy of the required level of control to establish military occupation and assess whether and when it ended. This was how the element of control became my primary object of interest.

Looking back, working on this book provided me with an exciting and rewarding time – both professionally and personally. First and foremost, I would like to express my deep gratitude to Professor Noam Lubell for having been my supervisor during my time in Essex. I also thank Professor Françoise Hampson and Dr. Daragh Murray for their feedback on parts of this research. I am also grateful to the Law Library of the University of Bern, especially Bernhard Dengg and Agathe Künzi, for having provided me a visiting researcher workplace. The Irish Centre for Human Rights, and especially Professors William Schabas and Ray Murphy, are thanked for a Doctorate Research Fellowship covering 2011–2012. I also thank the Routledge Taylor & Francis publishing team, especially Alison Kirk, for her support and the two anonymous reviewers for their constructive comments.

I would of course also like to thank my dear family: my parents and my brother, whose values, hard work and outlook have been a major inspiration for my life, personal, and professional development. My grandfather Konstantin and my father-in-law Bert are dearly remembered and thanked for their constant motivation and guidance. Finally, I thank my husband Sean for his unconditional dedication.

Any errors or omissions that may be found in this book fall under my sole responsibility.

Bern, February 2020

List of figures

2.1	The indirect effective control test (ICTY)	59
2.2	Occupation by intermediary (ICJ)	60
2.3	The decisive influence test (ECtHR)	78
2.4	Belonging to a party to the conflict (Article 4 GC III 1949)	85
2.5	Indirect effective control, hypothetical case	88
4.1	State agent authority and control over persons/individuals (ECtHR)	145
4.2	State obligations regarding protected persons (Article 4, GC IV 1949)	148
4.3	Territorial control and IHRL obligations	159
4.4	GC IV situational application and control (IHRL) over persons' particular rights	165
5.1	Control in public international law	173
5.2	Degrees of control	175

List of abbreviations

CPA	Coalition Provisional Authority
ECHR	European Convention of Human Rights
ECtHR	European Court of Human Rights
GA	General Assembly
GC	Geneva Convention
HCJ	High Court of Justice, Israel
HR	Hague Regulations
HVO	Croatian Defence Council
IAC	International Armed Conflict
ICC	International Criminal Court
ICCPR	International Covenant on Civil and Political Rights
ICESCR	International Covenant on Economic, Social and Cultural Rights
ICJ	International Court of Justice
ICL	International Criminal Law
ICRC	International Committee of the Red Cross
ICTR	International Criminal Tribunal for Rwanda
ICTY	International Criminal Tribunal for the Former Yugoslavia
IDF	Israel Defence Force
IHL	International Humanitarian Law
IHRL	International Human Rights Law
ILC	International Law Commission
MLC	Congo Liberation Movement
MNF	Multinational Force
NIAC	Non-International Armed Conflict
OCHA	United Nations Office for the Coordination of Humanitarian Affairs
PCIJ	Permanent Court of International Justice
PIL	Public International Law
POW	Prisoner of War
SC	Security Council
SCSL	Special Court for Sierra Leone
SR	State Responsibility
UN	United Nations
UNMIK	United Nations Mission in Kosovo
WWII	World War II

Introduction

Overview

Expanding territories through use of force can be cited among the most frequent phenomena in the context of conflict between states. Along this line, international law has progressed by starting to codify the law of war (known also as international humanitarian law, or IHL) as early as in the nineteenth century. After World War II (WWII), the creation of the United Nations (UN) brought the long awaited international obligation for states to refrain "in their international relations from the threat or use of force against the territorial integrity or political independence of any state."[1] Nevertheless, in the twentieth and still in the twenty-first century, states have continued to use force for various reasons: for lawful self-defence,[2] curbing civil uprisings on their own territory,[3] or claiming "legitimate territories" as theirs.[4] In short, armed conflicts both of an international (IAC) and a non-international (NIAC) character persist to plague modern reality.

States also strive to avoid the status of "military occupant", claiming not to be exerting the required degree of control over the territory in question. This might

---

1 Article 2(4) UN Charter.
2 T. Ruys, *Armed Attack and Article 51 UN Charter: Evolutions of Customary Law and Practice* (Cambridge: Cambridge University Press, 2010), at 15–19 and 127–249. See generally Y. Dinstein, *War, Aggression and Self-Defence* (5th edn., Cambridge: Cambridge University Press, 2011); F. H. Hinsley, *Sovereignty* (Cambridge: Cambridge University Press, 1986).
3 J. Holliday, *Middle East Security Report: The Struggle for Syria in 2011* (Institute for the Study of War, December 2011), at 12, available at www.understandingwar.org/sites/default/files/ Struggle_For_Syria.pdf (visited 2 November 2016); see also *Out of Sight, out of Mind: Deaths in Detention in the Syrian Arab Republic*, UN Human Rights Council A/HRC/31/CRP.1, 3 February 2016.
4 The recent example of Russia 'claiming back' Crimea can be thought of at this point, see further S. L. Myers and E. Barry, 'Putin Reclaims Crimea for Russia and Bitterly Denounces the West', *The New York Times*, 18 March 2014, available at www.nytimes.com/2014/03/19/ world/europe/ukraine.html?_r=0 (visited 2 November 2016); see also US Government Information, One Hundred Fifteenth Congress of the United States of America, An Act, H.R. 244, Countering Russian Influence and Aggression, Annexation of Crimea, at 571, available at www.congress.gov/115/bills/hr244/BILLS-115hr244enr.pdf (visited 6 May 2017).

2 Introduction

be due to the fact that "the concept of occupation has a pejorative connotation."[5] Moreover, the classification of a territory as occupied is a complex exercise due to different IHL sources not using clear wording and failing to provide what level and/or type of control is needed to determine the existence and ending of military occupation. Thus, Article 42 of the Convention (IV) Respecting the Laws and Customs of War on Land and Its Annex: Regulations Concerning the Laws and Customs of War on Land (Hague Regulations 1907 (HR 1907)) reads:

> Territory is considered occupied when it is actually placed under the authority of the hostile army.
> The occupation extends only to the territory where such authority has been established and can be exercised.[6]

Questions are therefore raised first and foremost about the concept of "authority" and the level of control required to establish military occupation. Attention should also be drawn to the fact that no explanation is given as to what ought to be construed under "actually placed under the authority". Furthermore, Common Article 2.2 to the Geneva Conventions of 1949 (GC I, II, III, and IV 1949) considers that: "The convention shall also apply to all cases of partial or total occupation of the territory of a High Contracting Party, even if the said occupation meets with no armed resistance."[7] Finally, Article 1 of Protocol Additional to the Geneva Conventions of 12 August 1949, and relating to the Protection of Victims of International Armed Conflicts of 8 June 1977 (AP I 1977), while restating the instrument's applicability to the same situations as envisaged by Common Article 2 GCs, adds situations of

> armed conflicts in which peoples are fighting against colonial domination and alien occupation and against racist regimes in the exercise of their right of self-determination as enshrined in the Charter of the United Nations.[8]

---

5 T. Ferraro, *Expert Meeting Occupation and Other Forms of Administration of Foreign Territory* (Geneva: ICRC, 2012), at 4, available at www.icrc.org/eng/assets/files/publications/icrc-002-4094.pdf (visited 2 November 2016).

6 Article 42 *Convention (IV) Respecting the Laws and Customs of War on Land and Its Annex: Regulations Concerning the Laws and Customs of War on Land*, The Hague, 18 October 1907 (HR 1907). See also Article 5 *The Convention for the Protection of Cultural Property in the Event of Armed Conflict with Regulations for the Execution of the Convention*, The Hague, 14 May 1954; Article 1 *First Protocol to the Convention for the Protection of Cultural Property in the Event of Armed Conflict*, The Hague, 14 May 1954; and Articles 3, 9, 21 and 44 *Second Protocol to the Hague Convention of 1954 for the Protection of Cultural Property in the Event of Armed Conflict*, The Hague, 26 March 1999.

7 Common Article 2 to the four Geneva Conventions of 1949, which are: *Convention (I) for the Amelioration of the Condition of the Wounded and Sick in Armed Forces in the Field; Convention (II) for the Amelioration of the Condition of Wounded, Sick and Shipwrecked Members of Armed Forces at Sea; Convention (III) Relative to the Treatment of Prisoners of War;* and *Convention (IV) Relative to the Protection of Civilian Persons in Time of War,* all at Geneva, 12 August 1949. Hereafter GC I, GC II, GC III, and GC IV.

8 Article 1 *Protocol Additional to the Geneva Conventions of 12 August 1949, and Relating to the Protection of Victims of International Armed Conflicts*, 8 June 1977 (AP I 1977).

Introduction 3

This article equally fails to provide an explanation of the notions used. More questions than answers, therefore, emerge: neither is a precise definition of a situation of occupation provided, nor are its constitutive elements presented. This book aims to do just that.

What is more, it also seems that there is no uniformity in the usage of terms by the international law scholarship with regards to defining "actually placed under the authority" either. Do "effective control"[9], "actual control,"[10] and simply "control"[11] all relate to the same legal phenomenon, i.e. "actually placed under the authority"?

To answer these and related queries, this book studies the notion of control in the law of military occupation, addressing in particular the following question: what does control denote and what are its implications for military occupation? Thus, the notion of control will be examined through the lens of the beginning and ending of military occupation. Approaching establishing occupation through identifying the necessary test of control over territory will be carried out in detail. Hence, a major contribution of this book is providing clarity on the concept of control on which military occupation rests. A second contribution of this book is that it offers control tests for establishing when occupation commences and when it ceases.

The notion of control

Before starting on this journey, it should be recalled that the notion of control is not only important for giving rise to situations of military occupation, but also plays a significant role in wider international law. Indeed, the element of control is used in multiple tests for multiple purposes. This creates confusion. More specifically, control surfaces in the law of state responsibility (SR), international humanitarian law (IHL), international criminal law (ICL), and international human rights law (IHRL) in different ways. Each branch of international law not only uses and positions control in different tests, but also with different thresholds. Different tribunals too have used different notions of control – and sometimes even the same tribunals, notably the ICJ or the ICTY, interpret and consider control in varied ways. As shall be seen, the control thresholds or tests found in the law of SR, IHL, and IHRL possess the most synergy with the element of control in occupation law. The following offers a brief synopsis of key legal formulations using the word *control*:

> *Complete dependency (SR)*: A test used by the ICJ for the purposes of establishing the responsibility of a state for internationally wrongful acts. The legal basis of this test is found in Article 4 of the ILC Articles on Responsibility

---

9 Y. Arai Takahashi, *The Law of Belligerent Occupation Continuity and Change in International Humanitarian Law* (Leiden; Boston: Martinus Nijhoff Publishers, 2009), at 6.

10 M. Bothe, 'Occupation, Belligerent', in R. Bernhardt (ed.), *Encyclopedia of Public International Law*, Vol. 3 (Amsterdam: Elsevier, 1997) 763–768, at 764.

11 M. Sassòli and A. B. Bouvier, *How Does Law Protect in War?*, Vol. 1 (2nd edn., Geneva: ICRC, 2006), at 187.

4   *Introduction*

of States for Internationally Wrongful Acts (2001). Basic elements are de jure and de facto organs over which the state in question has *total control.* The object of state control is a person or entity.[12]

Decisive influence: Test used by the ECtHR to establish the extraterritorial application of states' human rights responsibilities based on the relationship between the state party of the Convention and local de facto authorities. The legal basis of this test is the notion of jurisdiction as enshrined in the ECHR. The basic element is military, economic, and political support given by the outside state to the de facto authorities.[13]

---

12 See further *Case Concerning Military and Paramilitary Activities in and Against Nicaragua (Nicaragua v. United States of America)*, Judgment of 27 June 1986, § 86, §§ 109–110, available at www.icj-cij.org/files/case-related/70/070-19860627-JUD-01-00-EN.pdf; *Case Concerning Application of the Convention on the Prevention and Punishment of the Crime of Genocide (Bosnia and Herzegovina v. Serbia and Montenegro)*, Judgment of 26 February 2007, § 386, §§ 388–389, §§ 391–393, available at www.icj-cij.org/files/case-related/91/091-20070226-JUD-01-00-EN.pdf (both visited 28 January 2020); *Yeager v. Islamic Republic of Iran (1987)*, Iran-United States Claims Tribunal Reports, Vol. 17 (Cambridge: Grotius, 1988), at 101–102. See further A. Pellet, 'The Definition of Responsibility in International Law', in J. Crawford, A. Pellet and S. Olleson (eds.), *The Law of International Responsibility* (Oxford: Oxford University Press, 2010) 3–16, at 4; F. Messineo, 'Attribution of Conduct', in A. Nollkaemper and I. Plakokefalos (eds.), *Principles of Shared Responsibility in International Law* (Cambridge: Cambridge University Press, 2014) 60–97, at 66; I. Brownlie, *System of the Law of Nations: State Responsibility* (Oxford: Clarendon Press, 1983), at 142; S. Talmon, 'The Various Control Tests in the Law of State Responsibility and the Responsibility of Outside Powers for Acts of Secessionist', *Legal Research Paper Series, University of Oxford* (May 2009) 1–25, at 5 (footnote 29); A. J. J. De Hoogh, 'Articles 4 and 8 of the 2001 ILC Articles on State Responsibility, the Tadić Case and Attribution Acts of Bosnian Serb Authorities to the Federal Republic of Yugoslavia', *72 British Yearbook of International Law* (2001) 255–292, at 255; D. Momtaz, 'Attribution of Conduct to the State: State Organs and Entities Empowered to Exercise Elements of Governmental Authority', in J. Crawford, A. Pellet, and S. Olleson (eds.), *The Law of International Responsibility* (Oxford: Oxford University Press, 2010), 237–246, at 239; P. Palchetti, 'De Facto Organs of a State', *Max Planck Encyclopedia of Public International Law* (2010), § 2, available at http://opil.ouplaw.com/view/10.1093/law:epil/9780199231690/law-9780199231690-e1394?prd=EPIL (visited 2 December 2016); M. Leigh, 'Yeager v. Islamic Republic of Iran', *82 American Journal of International Law* (1988) 353–362, at 355; S. Rosenne (ed.), *The International Law Commission's Draft Articles on State Responsibility* (Dordrecht: Martinus Nijhoff Publishers, 1991), at 1–34; J. Crawford, *The International Law Commission's Articles on State Responsibility: Introduction, Text and Commentaries* (Cambridge: Cambridge University Press, 2005), at 82; J. Crawford and S. Olleson, 'The Nature and Forms of International Responsibility', in M. D. Evans (ed.), *International Law* (Oxford: Oxford University Press, 2010) 441–471, at 452. See further L. Condorelli and C. Kress, 'Rules of Attribution: General Considerations', in J. Crawford, A. Pellet, and S. Olleson (eds.), *The Law of International Responsibility* (Oxford: Oxford University Press, 2010) 221–236; C. Kress, 'L'Organe de facto en droit international public: réflexions sur l'imputation à l'état de l'acte d'un particulier à la lumière des développements récents', 105 *Revue Générale de Droit International Public* (2001) 93–144.

13 *Ilaşcu and Others v. Moldova and Russia*, ECtHR (2004) (App. no. 48787/99) § 392; *Ivanţoc and Others v. Moldova and Russia*, ECtHR (2011) (App. no.

Effective control (ICL): In international criminal law, effective control is used to ascertain command responsibility (Article 28 ICC Statute) in a military or civilian hierarchy. It aims to establish the responsibility of the superior over the actions of persons lower down the chain of command.[14]

23687/05) § 115–120; *Catan and Others v. the Republic of Moldova and Russia*, ECtHR (2012) (App. nos. 43370/04, 8252/05 and 18454/06) § 122; *Mozer v. The Republic of Moldova and Russia*, ECtHR (2016) (App. No. 11138/10) § 110.

14 See further France et al. v. Goering et al. (1946) 22 IMT 203; (1946) 13 ILR 203 41 *American Journal of International Law* 172 (1946), at 221: "Crimes against international law are committed by men, not by abstract entities, and only by punishing individuals who commit such crimes can the provisions of international law be enforced."; *Trial of General Tomoyuki Yamashita* (Case No. 21) (IV Law Reports of Trials of War Criminals, United States Military Commission, Manila, 8 October–7 December 1945), at 35, available at www.loc.gov/rr/frd/Military_Law/pdf/Law-Reports_Vol-4.pdf (visited 2 December 2016); see generally G. Mettraux, *The Law of Command Responsibility* (Oxford; New York: Oxford University Press, 2009); Judgment, *Kunarac* (IT-96-23-T and IT-96-23/ 1-T), Trial Chamber, 22 February 2001, § 397; Judgment, *Hadžihasanović* (IT-01-47-A), Appeals Chamber, 22 April 2008, §§ 20–21; Judgment, *Kajelijeli* (ICTR-98-44A-A), Appeals Chamber, 23 May 2005, § 84–85; Judgment, *Kajelijeli* (ICTR-98-44A-T), Trial Chamber, 1 December 2003, §773–774; Judgment, *Nahimana* (ICTR-99-52-A), Appeals Chamber, 28 November 2007, §625, § 787; Judgment, *Delalić, Mucić, Delić, and Landžo* (IT-96-21-T), Trial Chamber Judgment, 16 November 1998, § 647; Judgment, *Delalić, Mucić, Delić, and Landžo* (Celebici Case) (IT-96-21-A), Appeals Chamber, 20 February 2001, § 195 and §303. See also High Command Trial, *The United States of America v. Wilhelm von Leeb et al.*, Judgment of 27 October 1948, US Military Tribunal Nuremberg, § 543, available at http://werle.rewi.hu-berlin.de/High%20Command%20Case.pdf (visited 2 December 2016): this case introduces the 'should have known' element. Also Judgment, *Halilović* (IT-01-48-A), Appeals Chamber, 16 October 2007, §§ 214–216; The Prosecutor v. Jean-Pierre Bemba Gombo (ICC-01/05–01/08), Pre-Trial Chamber II, 15 June 2009, §§ 412–413; note § 413: "the term 'effective authority' may refer to the modality, manner or nature, according to which, a military or military like commander exercise 'control' over his forces or subordinates."; The Prosecutor v. Jean-Pierre Bemba Gombo (ICC-01/05–01/08 66/364), Trial Chamber III, 21 March 2016, § 183, §§188–190; Judgment, *Kordić and Čerkez* (IT-95-14/2-T), Trial Chamber, 26 February 2001, § 418: "actual authority however will not be determined by looking at formal positions only. Whether de jure or de facto, military or civilian, the existence of a position of authority will have to be based upon an assessment of the reality of the authority of the accused."; Judgment, *Orić* (IT-03-68-A), Appeals Chamber, 3 July 2008, § 91. See also Judgment, *Perišić* (IT-04-81-T), Trial Chamber, 6 September 2011, § 138: "Superior responsibility [. . .] also includes responsibility [. . .] for military troops who have been temporarily assigned to a military commander [. . .] if the troops were under the effective control of that commander at the time when the acts [. . .] were committed. [. . .] The superior does not need to know the exact identity of those subordinates who committed the crimes, to be held responsible." *Hostages Case*, US Military Tribunal, Judgment of 19 February 1948, Nuremberg, § 1256; *Trial of Wilhelm List et al.*, United States Military Tribunal Nuremberg, 8 July 1947 to 19 February 1948 (Case No. 47), at 71, available at www.loc.gov/rr/frd/Military_Law/pdf/Law-Reports_Vol-8. pdf (visited 2 December 2016). For civilian command responsibility see Y. Ronen, 'Superior Responsibility of Civilians for International Crimes Committed in Civilian Settings', 43 *Vanderbilt Journal of Transnational Law* (2010) 314–356, at 346–349; W. A. Schabas, *International Criminal Law* (4th edn., Cambridge: Cambridge University Press, 2012), at

6   *Introduction*

Effective control (IHRL): Control over territory, used by human rights bodies (e.g. Human Rights Committee, ECtHR or IACtHR) to establish the extraterritorial application of states' human rights responsibilities.[15]

231–235; *Josef Altstötter et al.*, US Military Tribunal Nuremberg (The Justice Cases), Judgment of 4 December 1947, especially § 993–994, available at http://werle.rewi.hu-berlin. de/Justice%20Case%20Judgment.pdf (visited 2 December 2016). Also holding military and civilian commanders responsible for war crimes committed by their subordinates is upheld by IHL, see Rule 152: Command Responsibility for Orders to Commit War Crimes (applicable IAC/NIAC), IHL Database, Customary IHL, ICRC, available at https://ihl-databases. icrc.org/customary-ihl/eng/docs/v1_rul_rule152 (visited 5 April 2019); and Rule 153: Command Responsibility for Failure to Prevent, Repress or Report War Crimes (applicable IAC/NIAC), IHL Database, Customary IHL, ICRC, available at https://ihl-databases.icrc. org/customary-ihl/eng/docs/v1_rul_rule153 (visited 5 April 2019); Judgment, *Aleksovski* (IT-95–14/1-T), Trial Chamber, 25 June 1999, § 78; Judgment, *Musema* (ICTR-96–13-A), Trial Chamber, 27 January 2000, §135; Judgment, *Bagilishema* (ICTR-95–1A-A), Appeals Chamber, 3 July 2002, §§51–55; Judgment, *Kayishema* (ICTR-95–1-T), Trial Chamber, 21 May 1999, §§ 479–483; Judgment, *Bagosora et al.* (ICTR-98–41-T) Trial Chamber I, 18 December 2008, §§2030–2031; Judgment, *Aleksovski* (IT-95–14/1-A), Appeals Chamber, 24 March 2000, § 76; Judgment, *Fofana and Kondewa* (SCSL-04–14-T), Trial Chamber, 2 August 2007, §§238–241; Judgment, *Brima et al.* (SCSL-04–16-T) Trial Chamber, 20 June 2007, §§782–790; Judgment, *Akayesu* (ICTR-96–4-T), Trial Chamber, 2 September 1998, § 491; Judgment, *Gacumbitsi* (ICTR-2001–64-A), Appeals Chamber, 7 July 2006, §144; I. Bantekas, S. Nash, and M. Mackarel (eds.), *International Criminal Law* (New York: Cavendish, 2001), at 108; see also B. Bing Jia, 'The Doctrine of Command Responsibility in International Law With Emphasis on Liability for Failure to Punish', XLV *Netherlands International Law Review* (1998) 325–347, at 328–347; J. A. Williamson, 'Some Considerations on Command Responsibility and Criminal Liability', 90 *International Review of the Red Cross* (2008) 303–317, at 306–307; G. R. Vetter, 'Command Responsibility of Non-Military Superiors in the International Criminal Court', 25 *The Yale Journal of International Law* (2000) 90–143, at 99; I. Bantekas, *Principles of Direct and Superior Responsibility in International Humanitarian Law* (Manchester: Manchester University Press, 2002), at 80.

15 See generally General Comment No. 31 (80), *Nature of the General Legal Obligation Imposed on State Parties to the Covenant*, UN Doc. CCPR/C/21/Rev.1/Add.13, 29 March 2004, § 10. See also *Working Paper on the Relationship Between Human Rights Law and International Humanitarian Law*, United Nations, Economic and Social Council, E/CN.4/Sub.2/2005/14 (2005); UN Human Rights Committee, *Concluding Observations: Cyprus*, CCPR/C/79/add.88, 6 April 1998, §3; *Loizidou v. Turkey*, ECtHR (preliminary objections) (1995) (15318/89) § 56 and § 62; UN Human Rights Committee, *Concluding Observations: Sudan*, UN Doc. CCPR/C/79/Add.85, 19 November 1997, § 3–4; *Cyprus v. Turkey*, ECommHR (Appl. nos. 6780/74 and 6950/75) (1975) § 136; *Concluding Observations of the Human Rights Committee: Lebanon*, UN Doc. CCPR/C/79/Add.78, 5 May 1997, § 5; *State Obligations in Relation to the Environment in the Context of the Protection and Guarantee of the Rights to Life and to Personal Integrity: Interpretation and Scope of Articles 4(1) and 5(1) in Relation to Articles 1(1) and 2 of the American Convention on Human Rights*, IACtHR, Advisory Opinion of 15 November 2017, §§73–78; *Franklin Guillermo Aisalla Molina (Ecuador v. Colombia)*, Report no. 112/10 (2011) § 91; F. Coomans and M. T. Kaminga, 'Comparative Introductory Comments on the Extraterritorial Application of Human Rights Treaties', in F. Coomans and M. T. Kamminga (eds.), *Extraterritorial Application of Human Rights Treaties* (Antwerp; Oxford: Intersentia, 2004), at 1–7; R. Wilde, 'Triggering State Obligations Extraterritorially: The Spatial Test in Certain Human Rights Treaties', 40 *Israel Law Review* (2007) 503–526, at 508–509 and 515–523.

Effective control (SR): (1) The ICJ uses it for the purposes of establishing the responsibility of a state for internationally wrongful acts. The legal basis of this test is found in Article 8 of the ILC Articles on Responsibility of States for Internationally Wrongful Acts (2001). Basic elements are persons or a group of persons whose specific operations and acts the state has effective control over.[16] (2) The ICTY uses it to establish whether an individual is a de facto state agent based on the Article 8 of ILC Articles on Responsibility of States for Internationally Wrongful Acts (2001), where it has to be shown that a state in question issued specific instructions to the person to commit the wrongful act.[17] (3) Also used to establish the responsibility of international organisations pursuant to Article 7 of the Draft Articles on the Responsibility of the International Organizations.[18]

Effective overall control (IHRL): Test used by the ECtHR to establish the extraterritorial application of states' human rights responsibilities. The legal basis of this test is the notion of jurisdiction as enshrined in the ECHR. The basic elements of this test are: (1) the presence of a foreign state's large army on the territory in question; and (2) the subordination of local authorities to that foreign state through such presence. This entails the foreign state's responsibility for the actions and policies of the subordinate local administration/de facto authorities. The object of state control is the local subordinate administration/de facto authority.[19]

Normative control: Governs a relationship between an international organisation and a state, based on the former's values and judgments. Typically, normative control takes the form of explicit authorisations as understood by Article 17 §2 of the Draft Articles on the Responsibility of the International Organizations (acts "committed *because* of that authorization").[20]

Overall control (SR/IHL): A test developed by the ICTY for the purposes of establishing (a) state responsibility and (b) foreign state participation in a prima facie NIAC. The legal basis for both is Article 8 of the ILC Articles

---

16 Nicaragua case, *supra* note 12, § 115; see also § 116; Genocide case, *supra* note 12, §§ 396–397, § 400, §§405–406; T. Ferraro and L. Cameron, 'Article 2: Application of the Convention', in ICRC (ed.), *Commentary on the First Geneva Convention* (Cambridge: Cambridge University Press, 2016) 68–125, at 99, footnote N 124: "effective control linked to every single operation is almost impossible to prove because it requires a level of proof that will unlikely be reached [. . .] the attribution test based on 'total control and dependence' [. . .] makes the test for attribution even stricter."

17 Judgment, *Tadić* (IT-94–1-A), Appeals Chamber, 15 July 1999, §§117–118, see also §118, § 132 and § 137.

18 Article 7 ILC Draft Articles on the Responsibility of the International Organizations (2011).

19 *Loizidou v. Turkey*, ECtHR (Judgment) (1996) (App. no. 15318/89) § 56. 'Effective overall control' was also mentioned in Djavit v. Turkey, ECtHR (2003) (Appl. no. 25781/94) §18–23; Cyprus v. Turkey, ECtHR (2001) (25781/94) § 77. For a different definition of this test, see M. Milanović, *Extraterritorial Application of Human Rights Treaties: Law, Principles, and Policy* (Oxford: Oxford University Press, 2011), at 136–141.

20 Article 17 ILC Articles on the Responsibility of the International Organizations (2011).

8 *Introduction*

on Responsibility of States for Internationally Wrongful Acts (2001). It pertains to organised and/or armed groups and operates via financial support, training assistance, and the general planning and supervision of military activities.[21]

Protected persons: Status accorded by Article 4 GC IV 1949 to civilians who "at a given moment and in any manner whatsoever, find themselves, in case of a conflict or occupation, in the hands of a Party to the conflict or Occupying Power of which they are not nationals."[22] Here, control is exerted by a state over persons because they may either happen to be present or live in an area which is under the control of a party to an armed conflict *or* a military occupant.

State agent authority and control test: (1) Control over persons, establishing a state's jurisdiction extraterritorially (e.g. in detention centres); or (2) control over persons' particular rights, establishing a state's jurisdiction extraterritorially (e.g. the right to life when passing through a checkpoint or climbing a flagpole).[23]

---

21 Tadić, *supra* note 17, § 115, § 117, § 120–122, § 131. On the overall control test being suitable for establishing state responsibility and conflict classification, see T. Ferraro and L. Cameron, 'Article 2', *supra* note 16, at 99; A. Cassese, 'The Nicaragua and Tadić Tests Revisited in Light of the ICJ Judgment on Genocide in Bosnia', 18 *The European Journal of International Law* (2007) 649–668, at 655–667; M. Spinedi, 'On the Non-Attribution of the Bosnian Serbs' Conduct to Serbia', 5 *Journal of International Criminal Justice* (2007) 829–838, at 832–833. See, however, K. Mačák, *Internationalised Armed Conflicts in International Law* (Oxford: Oxford University Press, 2018), at 43–47. See also Genocide case, *supra* note 12, § 404: "Insofar as the 'overall control' test is employed to determine whether or not an armed conflict is international [. . .] it may well be that the test is applicable and suitable; the Court does not however think it appropriate to take a position on the point in the present case, as there is no need to resolve it for purposes of the present Judgment. On the other hand, the ICTY presented the 'overall control' test as equally applicable under the law of State responsibility for the purpose of determining – as the Court is required to do in the present case – when a State is responsible for acts committed by paramilitary units, armed forces which are not among its official organs. In this context, the argument in favour of that test is unpersuasive." See additionally International Law Commission Study Group on Fragmentation, *Fragmentation of International Law: Difficulties Arising from the Diversification and Expansion of International Law*, UN GA A/CN.4/L.682, 13 April 2006, at 32; R. Higgins, 'A Babel of Judicial Voices', 55 *The International and Comparative Law Quarterly* (2006) 791–804, at 795; B. Simma, 'Universality of International Law from the Perspective of Practitioner', 20 *The European Journal of International Law* (2009) 265–297, at 280.

22 Article 4 GC IV 1949.

23 See further Sergio Euben Lopez Burgos v. Uruguay, Communication No 12 12/52, UN Doc. (1981) A/36/40, 176, §§ 2.2–2.3, §12.2; *Lilian Celiberti de Casariego v. Uruguay*, Communication No. 56/1979, U.N. Doc. CCPR/C/OP/1 at 92 (1984) §§ 10.1–10.3. See further *Chitat Ng v. Canada*, HRC 5 November 1993, UN Doc. A/49/40; *Kindler v. Canada*, HRC 31 July 1993, UN Doc A/48/50, 138; *Mabel Pereira Montero v. Uruguay*, Communication No. 106/1981, U.N. Doc. CCPR/C/OP/2 at 136 (1990); UN Human Rights Committee Concluding Observations on the Seventh Periodic Report of the Russian Federation, CCPR/C/RUS/CO/7, 28 April 2015; UN Human Rights Committee

Introduction 9

Ultimate control and authority: A form of responsibility attribution used by the ECtHR in Behrami and Behrami v. France and Saramati v. France, Germany and Norway. Used to distinguish the UN Security Council's "retained ultimate authority and control" from the "effective command of the relevant operational matters" by NATO.[24]

Finally, it should also be briefly mentioned that there is an ongoing tension[25] between the tests of complete dependency (SR), effective control (SR), and

---

Concluding Observations: Israel, CCPR/C/79/Add.93, 18 August 1998; UN Human Rights Committee Concluding Observations: Israel, CCPR/C/ISR/CO13, 29 July 2010; UN Human Rights Committee Concluding Observations: Uganda, CCPR/CO/80/UGA, 4 May 2004; Öcalan v. Turkey, ECtHR (2005) (App. no. 46221/99) § 91; Sanchez Ramirez v. France, Decision of 24 June 1996 on the Admissibility of the Application (Decision of the European Commission of Human Rights) (App. no. 28780/95); Al-Skeini and Others v. the United Kingdom, ECtHR (2011) (App. no. 55721/07) § 137; Issa and Others v. Turkey, ECtHR (2004) (App. no 31821/96) § 55, § 79 and § 82; Drozd and Janousek v. France and Spain, ECtHR (1992) (App. no. 12747/87) § 91; Coard vs. United States, IACHR (Case 10.951, Report no. 109/99) (1999) § 37; Inter-American Commission on Human Rights, *Precautionary Measure 259/02 – Detainees Held by the United States in Guantanamo Bay, Cuba* (13 March 2002): "No Person Under the Authority and Control of a State, Regardless of His or Her Circumstances, Is Devoid of Legal Protection for His or Her Fundamental and Non-Derogable Human Rights.", available at http://hrlibrary.umn.edu/cases/guantanamo-2003.html (visited 23 July 2017);
Banković et al. v. Belgium et al., ECtHR (Grand Chamber Decision as to the Admissibility of) (2001) (App. no. 52207/99) § 46; Solomou and Others v. Turkey, ECtHR (2008) (App. no. 36832/97) § 71, §§ 73–74 and § 79; Pad and Others v. Turkey, ECtHR (2007) (App. no. 60167/00) (as to the admissibility of application) § 54; Isaak v. Turkey, ECtHR (2008) (App. no. 44587/98) § 110–120; Andreau v. Turkey, ECtHR (2009) (App. no. 45653/99) § 41–51; Alejandre Jr and Others v. Republica de Cuba (Brothers to the Rescue) 11.589, Report no. 86/99 OEA (1999) §25 and §53; *Human Rights Committee, Concluding Observations on the Fourth Report of the United States of America, UN CCPR/C/USA/CO/4,* 23 April 2014, § 22; *Jaloud v. The Netherlands,* ECtHR (App. no. 47708/08) (2014) § 152.

24 Behrami and Behrami v. France and Saramati v. France, Germany and Norway, ECtHR (2007) (App. no. 71412/01) § 140.

25 See International Law Commission Study Group on Fragmentation, *Fragmentation of International Law, supra* note 21, at 32; R. Higgins, 'A Babel of Judicial Voices', *supra* note 21, at 795; B. Simma, 'Universality of International Law from the Perspective of Practitioner', *supra* note 21, at 280; See generally M. Milanović and V. Hadzi-Vidanovic, 'A Taxonomy of Armed Conflict', in N. White and C. Henderson (eds.), *Research Handbook on International Conflict and Security Law: Jus ad Bellum, Jus in Bello and Jus Post Bellum* (London: Edward Elgar Publishing, 2013) 256–314; S. Verhoeven, 'International and Non-international Armed Conflicts', *Institute for International Law*, Working Paper No. 107, K.U. Leuven Faculty of Law (2007) 3–22; T. Meron, 'Classification of Armed Conflict in the Former Yugoslavia: Nicaragua's Fallout', 92 *The American Journal of International Law* (1998) 236–242; D. Schindler, *The Different Types of Armed Conflicts According to the Geneva Conventions and Protocols* (Alphen aan den Rijn: Sijthoff & Noordhoof, 1979); S. Vité, 'Typology of Armed Conflicts in International Humanitarian Law: Legal Concepts and Actual Situations', 91 *International Review of the Red Cross* (2009) 69–94; H.-P. Gasser, 'Internationalised Non-International Armed Conflicts: Case Studies of Afghanistan,

10 Introduction

overall control (SR/IHL) as developed by the ICJ and the ICTY to, respectively, establish state responsibility and classify a prima facie NIAC as an IAC.[26] The question is why should overall control (SR/IHL) be given precedence over complete dependency (SR) and effective control (SR)?[27] On the one hand, applying the complete dependency test (SR) for establishing state responsibility raises the bar to generate the required evidence substantiating the state's participation in a certain armed conflict unrealistically high.[28] Ultimately, this would also allow states to evade their international legal responsibility not only under the law of state responsibility, but also under IHL.

On the other hand, while the effective control test (SR) is less stringent than the complete dependency (SR) test, it nevertheless ignores the fact that a state may use armed groups to undertake actions "that are intended to damage, or in the event do damage, other states."[29] Furthermore, it appears that effective control (SR) is better suited to establish the responsibility of a state for the actions of a single private individual. When a state is tasking an individual, it may order him/her to perform either a one-time action or a series of

---

Kampuchea and Lebanon', 33 *The American University Law Review* (1983) 145–161; J. Pejic, 'Status of Armed Conflicts', in E. Wilmshurst and S. Breau (eds.), *Perspectives on the ICRC Study on Customary International Humanitarian Law* (Cambridge: Cambridge University Press, 2007) 77–100; C. Greenwood, 'International Humanitarian Law and the Tadić Case', 7 *The European Journal of International Law* (1996) 265–283; M. Milanović, 'State Responsibility for Acts of Non-State Actors: A Comment on Griebel and Plücken', 22 *Leiden Journal of International Law* (2009) 307–324; K. Huszti Orban, *The Concept of Armed Conflict in International Humanitarian Law*, PhD Thesis, Graduate Institute of International and Development Studies, 2014.

26 Initially, the ICTY Trial Chamber considered that the conflict in Bosnia-Herzegovina after 19 May 1992 was of a non-international character. However, in order to determine whether the grave breaches regime applied the ICTY Appeals Chamber needed to re-examine the classification of the conflict and found it to be an IAC. To this end, the ICTY analysed whether the acts of the VRS could be attributed to Serbia (i.e. the former FRY). Because IHL itself is silent on this link, the ICTY had to look at the attribution mechanism in the law of state responsibility, i.e. the attribution to a state of acts of an armed group which is not that state's de jure organ. On what grounds, that is, through what relationship does such an attribution arise? The ICTY Appeals Chamber upheld the Trial Chamber in finding of fact that the armed conflict prior to 19 May 1992 was an IAC, but whether the armed conflict after 19 May 1992 continued to be an IAC or degenerated into a NIAC was dependent on whether Bosnian Serb forces (in whose hands the Bosnian victims in this case found themselves) could be considered de jure or de facto organs of a foreign power, namely the FRY. See further Judgment, *Tadić* (IT-94-1-A), Appeals Chamber, 15 July 1999, § 84, § 86–87, §§97–162. See also K. Kirss, 'Role of the International Court of Justice: Example of the Genocide Case', 3 *ACTA SOCIETATIS MARTENSIS* (2007/2008) 143–164, at 152.

27 See M. Sassòli and L. M. Olson, 'The Judgment of the ICTY Appeals Chamber on the Merits in the Tadić Case', 839 *International Review of the Red Cross* (2000) 733–769, at 740.

28 A. Cassese, 'The Nicaragua and Tadić Tests Revisited', *supra* note 21, at 665. See also T. Ferraro and L. Cameron, 'Article 2', *supra* note 16, at 99.

29 A. Cassese, 'The Nicaragua and Tadić Tests Revisited', *supra* note 21, at 654.

Introduction 11

actions. And it is only logical that such an act is based on effective control (SR), since individual actions necessitate specific instructions. In the context of armed groups, however, overall control (SR/IHL) may suffice to consider non-state actors as state agents.[30]

In sum, the overall control (SR/IHL) test is more realistic to be satisfied, more robust in its application,[31] and consequently affords better protection pursuant to IHL. Henceforth, the book proceeds on this basis. In Chapter 2, the analysis of the overall control (SR/IHL) test suitability is continued on this premise, particularly when discussing the indirect effective control phenomenon in the context of military occupation.

In the opinion of this author, the same test – that of overall control (SR/IHL) – should be used for establishing state responsibility and classifying armed conflicts in the event of foreign intervention (including military occupation) into a NIAC. Adopting *one test* avoids the fragmentation of the concept of responsibility, as state responsibility is engaged through state action and participation.[32]

In times of armed conflicts, the relationship between the belligerents is regulated by IHL, which chiefly aims to render protection to those who are affected. When states engage in armed conflicts, they are usually performing certain actions via their de jure organs (for instance armed forces), thereby assuming full responsibility for the latter's acts or omissions. Similarly, when states are participating in an armed conflict via non-state actors/armed groups, there is no justification not to consider that state to be responsible for any acts or omissions carried out by them.[33] This is so because a state ought to be held "legally responsible for acts which are really its own".[34] Considering states to be responsible only for the actions of their de jure but not their de facto organs or other actors that they control would, therefore, fragment the concept of state responsibility.

---

30 T. Ferraro, 'The ICRC's Legal Position on the Notion of Armed Conflict Involving Foreign Intervention and on Determining the IHL Applicable to This Type of Conflict', 97 *International Review of the Red Cross* (2015) 1227–1252, at 1250.

31 A. Cassese, 'The Nicaragua and Tadić Tests Revisited', *supra* note 21, at 661 and 665.

32 M. Spinedi, 'On the Non-Attribution of the Bosnian Serbs' Conduct to Serbia', *supra* note 21, at 832–833. However, see I. van der Heijden, 'Other Issues Relating to the Treatment of Civilians in Enemy Hands', in A. Clapham, P. Gaeta, and M. Sassòli (eds.) *The 1949 Geneva Conventions (A Commentary)* (Oxford: Oxford University Press, 2015) 1241–1268, at 1253. See additionally International Law Commission Study Group on Fragmentation, *Fragmentation of International Law*, supra note 21, at 31–33; M. Koskenniemi and P. Leino, 'Fragmentation of International Law? Postmodern Anxieties,' 15 *Leiden Journal of International Law* (2002) 553–579, at 564–567 and 575–576.

33 M. Spinedi, 'On the Non-Attribution of the Bosnian Serbs' Conduct to Serbia', *supra* note 21, at 835.

34 D. Akande, 'Classification of Armed Conflicts: Relevant Legal Concepts', in E. Wilmshurst (ed.), *International Law and Classification of Conflicts* (Oxford: Oxford University Press, 2012) 32–79, at 60. However, note that Akande favours the threshold of effective control (SR); ibid.

12 *Introduction*

Structure of the book

The book is structured into four chapters and a conclusion. Chapter 1 details the complexities of establishing control over territory in IHL through the HR 1907, the GCs 1949, and AP I 1977. It examines control exercised without intermediary, that is, solely through a state's own armed forces. Chapter 2, dedicated to indirect (effective) control, or occupation by an intermediary, investigates a type of control that states employ to avoid the status of military occupant. This chapter also investigates the ECtHR's concept of decisive influence as a form of indirect effective control, sufficient to deem a state a military occupant under IHL, and concludes with probing whether IHL possess its own mechanism of control over armed group X via which a territory can be considered occupied. Chapter 3 analyses relinquishing control over territory for determining the end of occupation. Overall, six forms of relinquishing control over territory pursuant to occupation law are identified. Chapter 4, finally, deals with states' substantive obligations pursuant to IHL and IHRL based on the level and type of control exercised by a state at a specific point in time. The chapter concludes with a brief discussion of the inter-application of IHL and IHRL. The book's Conclusion summarises the main findings of the work and answers the question posed above on control and its implications for military occupation.

1 Effective control in occupation law

1. Introduction

In 2007, the ICRC initiated a project on occupation law "to analyse whether, how and to which extent occupation law might need to be reinforced, clarified or developed."[1] It further indicated that "some have challenged occupation law on the basis it was ill-suited for the polymorphic features of contemporary occupations".[2] While the project culminated in an extensive report entitled 'Occupation and Other Forms of Administration of Foreign Territory',[3] questions remain as to what exactly constitutes the test of establishing control over territory for the purposes of military occupation. In other words, what is it that makes a state an occupant? And what "polymorphic features of contemporary occupations" may there be?

Throughout this book, it will be seen that control over territory can take various forms and play out at different levels, that it can be exercised directly or indirectly, and that it can include one or more actors – a state, its armed forces, several states, an international organisation, or an armed group. This chapter centres on effective control exercised by states directly and consists of two sections.

Section one looks at the level of control needed to determine the start of occupation based on the *travaux préparatoires* for the Hague Regulations 1907 (HR 1907), Geneva Conventions 1949 (GCs 1949), and Additional Protocol I of 1977 (AP I 1977). This will clarify the different elements of the control test. Such a method is based on and supported by Article 32 VCLT, which indicates the preparatory work of a treaty to be an important source of clarification of key terms.[4] The first section also deals with the difference between actual and potential control.

---

1 ICRC, *Contemporary Challenges to IHL – Occupation: Overview*, available at www.icrc.org/eng/war-and-law/contemporary-challenges-for-ihl/occupation/overview-occupation.htm (visited 27 April 2014).
2 Ibid.
3 T. Ferraro, *Expert Meeting Occupation and Other Forms of Administration of Foreign Territory* (Geneva: ICRC, March 2012).
4 Article 32, *Vienna Convention on the Law of Treaties*, 1969, available at http://untreaty.un.org/ilc/texts/instruments/english/conventions/1_1_1969.pdf (visited 4 April 2019).

14 *Effective control in occupation law*

Section two explores the concept of joint control, which is a form of direct control involving more than one state's armed forces – for example control exercised by a multinational force (MNF). The section finishes with assessing the possibility of the UN itself being an occupant and analyses the concept of UN SC-endorsed control.

2. Establishing control

2.1 Stepping back in time

For a long time, there was no consensus over the concept and content of occupation in the laws of war. One particular divide can be found between the concepts developed by the Brussels and Hague conferences, on the one hand, and the Oxford Manual (1880), on the other. The different elements around which the pre-1949 understanding of occupation centred were authority and control, uprising and effectivity, exercising authority, and occupation duration.

2.1.1 Authority and control

The analysis begins with the Brussels Conference.[5] In summer 1874, the delegates of 15 European states met to examine the draft of an international agreement concerning the laws and customs of war, wherein one section was entitled 'On Military Authority over the Territory of the Hostile State'. The Conference adopted a Russian draft with only minor alterations, yet not all governments were willing to accept the document as binding. Consequently, it was not ratified. The Conference nevertheless marked an important step towards IHL codification.[6] It notably constitutes the first attempt at providing a definition of military occupation and its integral elements, specifically regarding the level of control.

Accordingly, military occupation is associated with state A's hostile military forces' unwelcomed presence on and control over state B's territory. The underlying element, and the backbone of such control, are a state's military forces, i.e. its troops, through which it is able to show force and ultimately secure control over the territory. In fact, the International Declaration Concerning the Laws and Customs of War (Brussels Declaration of 1874) put this very requirement at the forefront of its definition of occupation:

> A territory belonging to one of the belligerents is considered as occupied when it is actually placed under the authority of the hostile army. The

---

Note, however, that Article 31 (General Rule of Interpretation) of the same instrument takes precedence.

5 'Project of an International Declaration Concerning the Laws and Customs of War', Brussels, 27 August 1874, available at www.icrc.org/ihl/INTRO/135 (visited 3 December 2017).

6 Ibid.

occupation only extends to those territories where this authority is established and lasts only so long as it can be exercised.[7]

It is noteworthy that the word *control* was neither explicitly mentioned nor discussed in greater detail. However, control's omnipresence is felt when exploring the Conference records via the notion of *authority*. These records, as a result, provide a rather flawed and uneven conceptualisation of the level of control required. Nonetheless, if territory "actually placed under the authority of the hostile army" signifies territory under the *control, power*, and *discretion* of an adversary state's military forces, quite simply the word *authority* has been substituted for *control* – without defining either. Still, despite the absence of the term *control* from that formulation, it is found to be firmly instilled in the notion of power.[8]

2.1.2 Uprisings and effectivity

Conference delegates viewed uprisings as a major challenge to the occupant's control over territory. Only being able to deal away with insurrections suggested that the control possessed by the occupant over territory was effective. Authority had to be exercised[9] and territories which contrived to free themselves from this authority ceased to be under occupation.[10] Hence, disallowing uprisings by the local population was key, otherwise the occupant was shorn of its authority.[11]

What is significant here is that the number of troops was not deemed to be important, provided both the local population and the ousted sovereign succumbed to the military strength of the occupant.[12] There were contrary views, too. For instance, the Dutch delegate regarded it necessary that "the occupier must always be in sufficient force to put down an insurrection should one break out."[13] Yet, *being in sufficient force* does not mean the armed forces of the occupant have to be constantly present on the territory in specific numbers. In fact, this can also be understood as a mere potentiality: The population of the occupied territory has to constantly feel that any attempt on their part to eject the occupant *would* be put down and suppressed by virtue of the occupant's military force. It was also understood that the occupant had the right to protect its control over the territory and thus suppress an insurrection.[14]

---

7 'Correspondence Respecting the Proposed Conference at Brussels on the Rules of Military Warfare', *United Kingdom Parliamentary Papers*, Miscellaneous No. 1 (1875) at 202.
8 Ibid., at 236.
9 Ibid.
10 Ibid.
11 Ibid., at 236–237.
12 Ibid., at 237.
13 Ibid.
14 Ibid.

16   *Effective control in occupation law*

2.1.3 Exercising authority

The Conference records also furnish a glimpse of the occupant actually exercising its authority (i.e. control). If the occupier was *in a position* to exercise its authority, the occupation was a reality; the moment this power no longer existed, occupation ceased.[15] From this it may be inferred that the occupant should not only possess sufficient military personal and equipment to have taken control over the territory, but also to sustain it without any difficulties. Its powers have to be real and sufficient, something which however is difficult to practically ascertain.[16]

The occupant's power can also be established gradually.[17] For an occupant's authority to be practically established, there had to be no threat coming from the population of the occupied territory.[18] This further indicates that control over territory is established by the occupant to such an extent that any opposition from the side of the occupied territory is, or at least can be, rapidly dealt away with.

2.1.4 Occupation duration

Delegates also briefly touched upon occupation duration, linking it to the duration of the occupant's control. This is seen in Baron Jomini's thought: "occupation lasts as long as it is practically carried out",[19] denoting that as long as control of a territory lasts, occupation continues.

In sum, while the Brussels Conference records provide a convoluted picture of the notion of occupation, with little agreement on fundamental issues such as the number of troops required or the level of control needed, the delegates' explanations still have to be duly taken note of as they "threw light on the sense"[20] of military occupation at that time.

2.1.5 The Oxford Manual of 1880

The next instrument, more to the point in dealing with the notion of occupation and offering more clarity, was drawn up by the International Law Institute. The 1880 Manual of the Laws and Customs of War at Oxford (Oxford Manual) offers the following:

> Territory is regarded as occupied when, as the consequence of invasion by hostile forces, the State to which it belongs has ceased, in fact, to exercise its ordinary authority therein, and the invading State is alone in a position

---

15 Ibid., at 259.
16 Ibid., at 237.
17 Ibid., at 237–238.
18 Ibid., at 238.
19 Ibid., at 237.
20 Ibid., at 239.

to maintain order there. The limits within which this state of affairs exists determine the extent and duration of the occupation.[21]

Compared to the Brussels text, this definition is distinguished by the ousted sovereign *ceasing to exercise its authority*, as well as by the invading state being *in a position to maintain order* on the territory in question. The control requirement is mirrored in these two conditions as it is impossible to secure control over territory without first ousting the sovereign. The ability by the invader's military to control the territory should trump the military capacity of the former sovereign. Maintaining order then must be understood as the occupant being in charge of the territory in lieu of the displaced sovereign. A hostile force possessing a high degree of military power becomes a prerequisite for the occupant's authority in this regard.

The mentioned conditions all pertain to a high degree of control, henceforth called *effective control* (OL). The last sentence of the 1880 definition restates the requirement of such control to be exercised by the occupant, as without such there would be no occupation – thus, the moment an occupant stops exercising such control, occupation is over (see also Chapter 3).

The other point in this definition that needs to be addressed is the formulation "in a position", which did not figure in the Brussels Declaration. The question is whether this can be read as including a potential of control which is *not* exercised by the occupant, for example because it chooses not to? In other words, what happens if a sovereign is ousted and only an invading army could – but does not – exercise authority? Should this be linked to the duty to maintain law and order? Or to the occupant setting up a military administration apparatus in the territory? These concerns will be addressed later.

2.1.6 The Hague

In 1899, the international community assembled again, this time in The Hague, to revise the 1874 Brussels text – and the issue of occupation was discussed anew. The Hague delegates did not adopt the Oxford Manual's definition,[22] instead reverting back to 1874.[23] Yet more precision was brought to understanding the *level* of control required for establishing military occupation. This time, three elements stand out from the deliberations among delegates: establishing occupation/control (as opposed to authority and control in Brussels), the occupant's military presence

---

21 Article 41, *The Laws of War on Land* (Oxford, 9 September 1880), also known as the Oxford Manual.
22 D. Appel Graber, *The Development of the Law of Belligerent Occupation, 1863–1914: A Historical Survey* (New York: Colombia University Press, 1949), at 59.
23 J. Brown Scott and Carnegie Endowment for International Peace, *The Proceedings of the Hague Peace Conferences, Translation of the Official Texts: The Conference of 1899*, Second Commission: Second Sub-commission, Seventh Meeting, 8 June 1899 (London: Oxford University Press, 1920) 509–512, at 512.

18   *Effective control in occupation law*

and access to the occupied territory (as opposed to exercising authority), and the status of the legal authorities (as opposed to uprisings, effectivity, and occupation duration). All three demonstrate what the delegates prioritised in defining military occupation.

The discussions commenced with examining the perception of an occupant's power and considering when occupation was established. Again, as in Brussels, neither the term *control* nor its required threshold were explicitly and unequivocally specified. For this reason, the meaning of control must be read between the lines of the delegates' reasoning. For instance, the German participant proposed to delete the second paragraph of the Brussels definition, as it was

> necessary to provide for the case in which a belligerent has effectively established his authority in a territory, but in which communications between the army or the occupying bodies and the other forces of the belligerent are interrupted and in which uprisings occur in that territory and are momentarily successful.[24]

Another delegate, considering this amendment too extensive in scope, thought that occupation could be recognised only when "the authority of the belligerent is actually established."[25] However, what it signified was not explained. What is unambiguous is that, for the delegates in The Hague, the existence of military occupation was more clearly based on the requirement of the occupant's army being present on and controlling the territory than in Brussels. This meant that the occupant had overcome the powers of the ousted sovereign – exactly what the Oxford Manual had proposed.

An explanation for maintaining control over territory, from a military perspective, was given through emphasising that securing the lines of communication was important and the presence of large numbers of the occupant's army was an essential condition, since the military was the main tool via which control was established and maintained.[26] The notion of *lines of communication* indicates that in establishing them, the occupant already controlled some territory.[27]

---

24 Ibid., at 509.

25 Ibid., 509–510.

26 *Actes de la Conférence de Bruxelles 1874* (Paris: Librairie des publications législatives, 1874), at 105. Gilinksy (ibid.) also reminded the assembly of the explanation that was adopted by the Brussels Conference in 1874: "We may consider occupation as established when a part of the occupying army has secured its positions and its line of communications with the other bodies. This being done, it is in a position to cope with the army of the occupied country and the uprisings of the population."

27 C. von Clausewitz, *On War* (translated by Col. J. John Graham, London: N. Trübner, 1873), Book 5: Military Forces, Chapter 16, available at www.clausewitz.com/readings/OnWar1873/BK5ch16.html#a (visited 3 December 2016); see also C. James, *An Universal Military Dictionary* (4th edn., London: T. Egerton, 1816), at 439: "In military strategy, that line which corresponds with the line of operation and proceeds from the base point."

Effective control in occupation law 19

On this account, then, access to the occupied territory is more important than the extent of one's presence there. This stands in stark contrast to the majority view of delegates at Brussels, when military presence alone seemed to determine control over territory.

Overall, the conference delegates explained control based on their own experience. However, while they advanced different conceptualisations of control over territory, one commonality remained: firm control by the army over territory was needed to claim that a situation amounted to occupation. Even if such control was challenged from within the occupied territory, provided the occupant's army dealt away with it, occupation continued. The key was thus to possess the power to do so.[28]

Only a minority of delegates considered that stripping the legal authorities of their powers over the invaded territory indicated that the territory was placed under the occupant's control.[29] Barring the legal authorities from carrying out their professional duties, and more generally hindering the work of the state apparatus, are undeniably signs of an enemy's effective control over the territory. However, this was itself predisposed on having military troops on the ground.

The previously reproduced thoughts were all voiced by military experts of that time. However, lawyers had a different regard of occupation and the needed threshold of control. Those partaking in the Conference generally demanded more clarity, arguing that when "authority" was not of sufficient strength to sustain itself, it was not "established" in the territory and that territory was in no true sense "occupied".[30] It transpires that for them, ample military force was a *sine qua non* for establishing occupation. It was the first element, which would then gradually give rise to the other elements of occupation.[31] This in turn means the occupant has to strive to stabilise its power over the territory.[32] And occupation would receive recognition only when the occupied territory's government authorities were expelled and the commander of the occupying army was able to make its authority respected.[33]

The requirement of control is therefore identified not only in ensuring respect for one's powers, but also in the ability of the occupant to maintain possession of the territory.[34] Exercising *sole* control over territory was also advocated;[35] the

---

28 *Actes de la Conférence de Bruxelles 1874, supra* note 26, at 511.

29 Ibid., at 511.

30 W. I. Hull, *The Two Hague Conferences* (Boston: Ginn and Company, 1908), at 246.

31 W. E. Hall, *A Treatise on International Law* (Oxford: The Clarendon Press, 1924), at 482–500.

32 W. E. Birkhimer, *Military Government and Martial Law* (Kansas City, MO: Franklin Hudson Publishing Company, 1914), para. 35.

33 Ibid.

34 Ibid., para. 43.

35 H. S. Maine, *International Law* (Boston: Adamant Media Corporation/Elibron Classics, 2005), at 108.

20 *Effective control in occupation law*

true test of military occupation was exclusive possession:[36] The authority of the regular government was to be supplanted by the invading one and nobody else.[37] As will be seen later (section 2.4), all of this can be interpreted to mean effective control (OL) over territory.

2.1.7 De lege lata

All these considerations of the notion of occupation and its needed level of control are implied and read between the lines of Article 42 HR 1907. This article is couched in Section III, HR 1907, which by its mere title, 'Military Authority over the Territory of the Hostile State', hinges on a military force:

> Territory is considered occupied when it is actually placed under the authority of the hostile army.
>
> The occupation extends only to the territory where such authority has been established and can be exercised.

This article has never been subjected to any modification and acquired customary law status.[38] It creates the impression that a clear concept of occupation is spelled out in IHL. Nonetheless, upon closer scrutiny this impression fades away as the word *considered* does not signify something definite, and the formulation *actually placed under the authority* lacks clarity, too, as has just been demonstrated. For instance, the French text of Article 42 seems to advance a factual test:

> Un territoire est considéré comme occupé lorsqu'il se trouve placé de fait sous l'autorité de l'armée ennemie.
>
> L'occupation ne s'étend qu'aux territoires où cette autorité est établie et en mesure de s'exercer.

The wording "de fait" appears somewhat inaccurately translated as "actually" instead of "in fact" or de facto. Taking this into account, what does *actually/in fact placed under the authority* signify? Does it mean effective control (OL)? What is the level of control necessary to qualify a situation as one of military occupation? And how does effective control in Article 42 HR 1907 manifest itself? Having found no conclusive answers from the delegates' deliberations, it is thought the element of control required for the purposes of military occupation continues

---

36 Ibid.

37 Ibid., at 109. Also D. Appel Graber, *The Development of the Law*, *supra* note 22, at 57–59.

38 International Military Tribunal, 'Nuremberg, Trial of the Major War Criminals Before the International Military Tribunal', Vol. I (1947), at 254; *Case Concerning Legal Consequences of the Construction of a Wall in the Occupied Palestinian Territory*, Advisory Opinion of 9 July 2004, § 78, § 89 available at www.icj-cij.org/en/case/131 (visited 15 July 2017); *Case Concerning Legality of the Threat or Use of Nuclear Weapons*, Advisory Opinion of 8 July 1996, §§ 82–83, available at www.icj-cij.org/en/case/95 (visited 15 July 2017).

Effective control in occupation law 21

its life in Common Article 2 GCs as well as in Article 1 AP I 1977. Since the forms and degrees of control triggering the application of GC IV will be dealt with in Chapter 4, we next consider Common Article 2 GCs.

2.2 Common Article 2 GCs

Common Article 2 GCs determines the scope of application of the GCs, but fails to clearly define not only international armed conflicts, but also military occupation. The level of control needed for the latter to come about is implicit only:

> In addition to the provisions which shall be implemented in peacetime, the present Convention shall apply to all cases of declared war or of any other armed conflict which may arise between two or more of the High Contracting Parties, even if the state of war is not recognized by one of them.
>
> The Convention shall also apply to all cases of partial or total occupation of the territory of a High Contracting Party, even if the said occupation meets with no armed resistance.[39]

During the diplomatic conference of 1949 when the four GCs were drawn up, delegates were preoccupied with other issues such as the reciprocity of parties engaged in an IAC, whether the regulation of NIAC should be envisaged in Common Article 2 GCs, and the status of internal uprisings. The delegates were also engaged in adopting protective mechanisms for civilians, the lack of which had resulted in the atrocities committed during WWII. No room was thus left for tackling the complexities of determining occupation anew or giving it any further clarifications. Article 42 HR 1907 already existed, and the Nuremberg Tribunal considered this instrument to be of customary nature; thus, "sovereignty" and "occupation of territory" seemed to be well-defined ideas of international law.[40]

From the records of the 1949 conference, it can be discerned that paragraphs 1 and 2 of Common Article 2 GCs "did not give rise to any amendments and were adopted according to the Stockholm text".[41] Given the scarcity of information on the level of control needed to consider territory occupied, the Pictet

---

39 Common Article 2 to Geneva Convention I, II, III, IV of 1949.

40 'International Military Tribunal (Nuremberg), Judgment and Sentences', 41 *The American Journal of International Law* (1947) 172–333, at 248–249; *Final Record of the Diplomatic Conference of Geneva of 1949*, Vol. II B (Bern: Federal Political Department, 1979), at 75, available at www.loc.gov/rr/frd/Military_Law/pdf/Dipl-Conf-1949-Final_Vol-2-B.pdf (visited 3 December 2016). During the discussions about the protecting power's and the detaining power's obligations at the diplomatic conference, "Mr. Sokirkin (Union of Soviet Socialist Republics) pointed out that the expression 'freedom to negotiate' was ambiguous, whereas in the first version of the French amendment the words 'sovereignty' and 'occupation of territory' were well-defined ideas in international law"; ibid.

41 Ibid., at 108; see also the *Seventeenth International Red Cross Conference Report* (Stockholm, August 1948), at 71–72 and 95, available at www.loc.gov/rr/frd/Military_Law/pdf/RC_XVIIth-RC-Conference.pdf (visited 3 December 2016).

22 *Effective control in occupation law*

Commentary to the GCs fills that gap and reflects about occupation under the realm of Common Article 2 GCs. It states that paragraph 2 "does not refer to the cases in which territory is occupied during the hostilities",[42] since "in such cases the convention will have been in force since the outbreak of hostilities or since the time war was declared",[43] but that it "only refers to cases where the occupation has taken place without a declaration of war and without hostilities".[44] This suggests that while effective control (OL) over territory might be achieved via full-fledged military hostilities amongst warring parties, the scenario envisaged by para. 2 of Common Article 2 GCs can also be achieved short of armed hostilities and confrontation. Interestingly, Pictet considers the wording of the second paragraph to be "not very clear" and suggests a simultaneous examination of paragraphs 1 and 2, as the last "was intended to fill the gap left by paragraph 1".[45]

This "gap" can be explained through the example of Czechoslovakia at the outbreak of WWII, when the Germans invaded and occupied it without armed resistance.[46] Had there been only paragraph 1 of Common Article 2 GCs, the GC IV would not have applied, as that paragraph only applies to armed conflicts and occupations occurring *during* an armed conflict. Only paragraph 2 extends the GC's application to *all* cases of partial or total occupation. Similarly, in 2014 the Russian military established control over the Ukrainian territory of Crimea without having met any armed resistance.[47] This case equally amounts to occupation in light of Common Article 2 para. 2 GCs and will be dealt with in Chapter 2.

The absence of any elaboration in Common Article 2 GCs on occupation and, importantly, on determining the level of control needed for it to come about, indicates that the criteria of Article 42 HR 1907 subsist in it, even if in an expanded manner. According to Common Article 2 GCs, occupation can happen not only through use of force but also without, while Article 42 seems to confine itself to instances of occupation coming about by virtue of fully-fledged armed hostilities only. Still, the required level of control over territory for occupation to be established is the same as in Article 42 HR 1907, namely effective control (OL), which will be dealt with in greater detail in section 2.4.

---

42 J. Pictet (ed.), *Commentary of 1958, Convention (IV) Relative to the Protection of Civilian Persons in Time of War Geneva, 12 August 1949*, Article 2 (Geneva: International Committee of the Red Cross, 1958), at 21.

43 Ibid.

44 Ibid.

45 Ibid., at 22.

46 T. Snyder, *Bloodlands: Europe Between Hitler and Stalin* (New York: Basic Books, 2012), at 114.

47 'Ukraine Says It Will Not Fight Russia Over Crimea', *The Telegraph*, 12 March 2014, at www.telegraph.co.uk/news/worldnews/europe/ukraine/10692122/Ukraine-says-will-not-fight-Russia-over-Crimea.html (visited 3 December 2016).

2.3 Article 1 AP I 1977

Article 1 AP I 1977 defines the scope of the application of AP I 1977, but without any additional information on occupation or the level of control needed for the purposes of establishing occupation:[48]

> This Protocol, which supplements the GCs of 12 August 1949 for the protection of war victims, shall apply in the situations referred to in Article 2 common to those Conventions.
>
> The situations referred to in the preceding paragraph include armed conflicts in which peoples are fighting against colonial domination and alien occupation and against racist *régimes* in the exercise of their right of self-determination, as enshrined in the Charter of the United Nations and the Declaration on Principles of International Law concerning Friendly Relations and Co-operation among States in accordance with the Charter of the United Nations.

Paragraph 3 gives grounds to develop two points. First, Article 1 AP I 1977 enhances the GCs and does not abolish them. Second, it also applies to situations envisaged under Common Article 2 GCs, thus adhering to their idea of occupation and its necessary elements as developed in Article 42 HR 1907. This reasoning is further solidified by the Diplomatic Conference records being silent on what could have been considered as occupation according to the then-existing understanding.[49] Instead, lengthy discussions ensued amongst the delegates on the issue of self-determination, i.e. armed struggles for self-determination waged by a people as part of an international armed conflict.[50] On the other hand, clues can be drawn from paragraph 4, which reaches out to cover armed conflicts in time of colonialism and alien occupation. The question then arises as to what could connect instances of military occupation to cases of colonialism and alien occupation. The Commentary to Article 1 AP I 1977 states that colonial domination frequently occurred and the "alien occupation" in this article covered cases of partial or total occupation of a territory "which has not yet been fully formed as a State".[51]

---

48 Article 1 of Protocol Additional to the Geneva Conventions of 12 August 1949, and relating to victims of International Armed Conflicts (Protocol I) 1977 (Article 1 AP I 1977).

49 *Official Records of the Diplomatic Conference on the Reaffirmation and Development of International Humanitarian Law Applicable in Armed Conflicts (Geneva, 1974–1977)*, Vol. VIII (Bern: Federal Political Department, 1978), at 17–51, available at www.loc.gov/rr/frd/Military_Law/Geneva-Conventions_materials.html (visited 15 December 2016).

50 Ibid.

51 Y. Sandoz, C. Swinarski and B. Zimmerman (eds.), *Commentary on the Additional Protocols of 8 June 1977 to the Geneva Conventions of 12 August 1949* (ICRC: Martinus Nijhoff Publishers, 1987) § 112, at 54.

24 *Effective control in occupation law*

Hence, the elements of colonial domination and alien occupation of territory are essentially identical to those of Article 42 HR 1907: An army asserts control over a territory, thereby hindering the process of state formation or self-determination (e.g. through the election of a new government or a constituent assembly). A difference, nevertheless, lies with the *status* of the territory, that is the territory might not (yet) be recognised as (part of) a sovereign state, although this does not exclude it from being considered as occupied. Widely known instances of such cases are the Palestine Territories (discussed in Chapter 3) and Western Sahara.[52]

2.4 Anatomy of the effective control test

We are now in a position to define effective control (OL) and its integral elements. While Article 42 HR 1907 does not use the term *control*, nor define what type of control is needed for occupation to come about, there is a certain uniformity in the usage of the term by contemporary international law scholars with regards to the *level of control necessary for establishing occupation*. This level of control is labelled "effective", and legal scholarship weighs in heavily on its threshold.[53]

However, providing a definition of the exact amount of control that will objectively be effective is an "imponderable problem"[54] and may prove to be challenging in practice. Article 42 HR 1907 displays both explicit and implicit criteria to be met for its application. The *explicit elements* are (a) an army hostile to the sovereign that is (b) physically present on the territory of that sovereign and (c) that territory being actually placed under the authority (i.e. control) of the hostile army. The *implicit elements* are (a) the absence of any other power on the

---

52 S. Casey-Maslen (ed.), *The War Report 2012* (Oxford: Oxford University Press, 2013), at 63; See generally *Western Sahara Advisory Opinion of 16 October*, available at www.icj-cij.org/en/case/61; 'Western Sahara Remains on the UN Listing as a Non-Self-Governing Territory Since 1963', available at www.un.org/en/decolonization/pdf/Western%20Sahara%20 2015%20profile_15Dec2015.pdf (both visited 15 July 2017); 'Special Committee on the Situation with Regard to the Implementation of the Declaration on the Granting of Independence to Colonial Countries and Peoples', working paper, *Western Sahara* (18 January 2016), A/AC.109/2016/17; UN Secretary General Ban Ki-Moon said during a press conference that Western Sahara remained occupied by Morocco, see Secretary-General's Remarks to Press with Foreign Minister of Algeria, 6 March 2016, available at www.un.org/sg/en/content/sg/press-encounter/2016-03-06/secretary-generals-remarks-press-foreign-minister-algeria (visited 3 December 2016); *Report of the Secretary-General on the Situation Concerning Western Sahara*, UN SC S/2016/355, 19 April 2016.

53 Y. Dinstein, *The International Law of Belligerent Occupation* (Cambridge: Cambridge University Press, 2009), at 39; H.-P. Gasser, 'From Military Intervention to Occupation of Territory: New Relevance of International Law of Occupation', in H. Fischer et al. (eds.), *Krisensicherung und Humanitärer Schutz – Crisis Management and Humanitarian Protection: Festschrift für Dieter Fleck* (Berlin: Wissenschaftsverlag, 2004) 139–159, at 154; M. J. Kelly, 'Iraq and the Law of Occupation: New Tests for an Old Law', 6 *Yearbook of International Humanitarian Law* (The Hague: T.M.C. Asser Press, 2003) 127–165, at 130; O. Ben-Naftali, A. M. Gross and K. Michaeli, 'Illegal Occupation: Framing the Occupied Palestinian Territory', 23 *Berkley Journal of International Law* (2005) 551–614, at 563–564.

54 Y. Dinstein, *The International Law of Belligerent Occupation, supra* note 53, at 43.

territory that can challenge this control (the sovereign has been ousted or is at least divested of any governmental powers to control the territory), and (b) the presence to the hostile force being unconsented to by the sovereign power of that territory.

This anatomy is based on reading in between its lines, as Article 42 HR 1907 "is not at all precise, but is as precise as a legal definition of such kind of fact as occupation can be."[55] For the purposes of illustrating the quandary and legal discrepancy attached to the control element in military occupation, in addition to establishing the required level of control for the purposes of occupation, the expression *actually placed under the authority* should first of all be deciphered.

The word *actually* (or *actual*) means something existing in reality or as a matter of fact. The commencement of occupation is thus "essentially a question of fact".[56] This necessitates that there should be more than a proclamation that possession of the territory has been taken (or that one is intending to take possession). That the main forces of a country have been defeated does not automatically mean occupation begins.[57] The emphasis here is on equating the word *actual* with *factual*. Furthermore, differentiating between the *mere proclamation of occupation* and *exercising occupation* suggests that the authority of the occupant has to be truly established.

Two other factual conditions that have to be met are, "first, the legitimate government should, by the act of the invader, be rendered incapable of publicly exercising its authority within the occupied territory; [and,] secondly, the invader should be in a position to substitute his own authority for that of the legitimate government".[58] The legitimate sovereign relinquishes its authority over both the territory and its inhabitants and submits to the invader. The cessation of local resistance, as a consequence of surrender, defeat, or withdrawal, as well as the submission of inhabitants all point to the fact that occupation has commenced.[59] The exercise of unhindered control over territory is therefore central to situations of occupation:

> Un territoire est considéré comme occupé lorsqu'il se trouve placé de fait sous l'autorité de l'armée ennemie, même si celle-ci ne rencontre aucune résistance militaire. L'occupation ne s'étend qu'aux territoires où cette armée est établie et en mesure d'exercer son autorité.[60]

---

55 L. Oppenheim, *International Law: A Treatise, Disputes, War and Neutrality,* Vol. 2 (London; New York: Longmans Green, 1921), at 207–208.

56 Canada, National Defence, *The Law of Armed Conflict at the Operational and Tactical Levels,* Office of the Judge Advocate General (2001), § 1203, 1.

57 Ibid., § 1203, 2.

58 Ibid., § 1203, 4; see also the UK Ministry of Defence, *The Manual of the Law of Armed Conflict* (Oxford: Oxford University Press, 2004), § 11.3, at 275.

59 Canada, National Defence, *The Law of Armed Conflict, supra* note 56, § 1203, 5.

60 République Française, Ministère de la Défense, *Manuel De Droit De Conflits Armés* (Paris: Ministère de la Défense, 2012), at 88, available at www.cicde.defense.gouv.fr/IMG/pdf/20130226_np_cicde_manuel-dca.pdf (visited 3 December 2016).

26 *Effective control in occupation law*

Yet there may be areas with pockets of resistance or parts of the territory that are temporarily controlled by the sovereign state's armed forces. However, this does not mean that the territory is not occupied, provided the resistance in these places does not render the occupier unable to exercise control over the remainder of the occupied territory.[61]

Heed should also be paid to the fact that although occupation does not take effect just because a country's main forces have been defeated, since it "depends on whether authority is actually being exercised over the civilian population",[62] there is no necessity for troops to be permanently stationed throughout the entire area. It is, instead, sufficient that the sovereign forces have withdrawn, the inhabitants are disarmed, that measures are taken to protect their life, property, and order, and that in case of necessity troops are available to enforce authority in the area.[63]

But how to ascertain whether authority is actually *exercised over the civilian population*? In my understanding, this means that the occupant leaves civilians no prospects to challenge its power, consequently ruling out an uprising, in addition to establishing a curfew on all civilian movement. interning them, or even refusing them the right to leave.[64] Such an interpretation is supported by the wording of Article 43 HR 1907, especially in its original French version:

> L'autorité du pouvoir légal ayant passé de fait entre les mains de l'occupant, celui-ci prendra toutes les mesures qui dépendent de lui en vue de rétablir et d'assurer, autant qu'il est possible, l'ordre et la vie publique en respectant, sauf empêchement absolu, les lois en vigueur dans le pays.[65]

Note that "ordre et la vie publique" (literally: public order and life) is wider than the English "public order and safety".[66] What is more, the first sentence of this article depicts an occupant establishing effective control by having *taken away* the powers of the ousted sovereign. By reason of such action, the occupant is in control in lieu of the ousted sovereign and is obligated, due to such control, to provide for the occupied territory and its population not only regarding basic

---

61 *The US Department of Defense Law of War Manual* (Office of General Counsel Department of Defense, June 2015), at 746.
62 UK Ministry of Defence, *The Manual of the Law*, *supra* note 58, at § 11.3.2., at 276.
63 Ibid.
64 Article 42, Article 48 GC IV 1949; see also C. Bruderlein, 'Protection, Occupation and International Humanitarian Law in the Occupied Palestinian Territory: A Critical Appraisal', 28 *Humanitarian Exchange* (Humanitarian Practice Network) (2004) 5–9, at 9.
65 The English version of the text reads: "The authority of the legitimate power having in fact passed into the hands of the occupant, the latter shall take all the measures in his power to restore, and ensure, as far as possible, public order and safety, while respecting, unless absolutely prevented, the laws in force in the country."
66 M. Sassòli, 'Legislation and Maintenance of Public Order and Civil Life by Occupying Powers', 16 *The European Journal of International Law* (2005) 661–694, at 663–664; see also M. Siegrist, *The Functional Beginning of Belligerent Occupation* (Geneva: The Graduate Institute Publications, 2011), at 65.

needs but also through ensuring public order and safety.[67] Rendering the invaded sovereign incapable of exercising its power should then be interpreted not only as the invader being present on the territory, but also as the invader having the possibility (which might not be used) to substitute the vanquished sovereign's authority with its own.

However, setting up a military administration is not a *sine qua non*, as a military force effectively capturing the territory is sufficient for occupation:[68]

> Application of Chapter 3 of the Hague Regulations and application of the parallel provisions of the Fourth Geneva Convention are not conditional upon the set-up of a special organizational system taking the form of military government. The obligations and powers of a military force which stem from its effective seizure of territory exist and come into being due to the very fact of military seizure of the territory, i.e., even if the military force only effects control via its ordinary combat units.[69]

Hence, what matters is that no one else exercises control over territory.

In sum, the notion of effective control (OL) for the purposes of military occupation is not *per se* mentioned in IHL; instead, "it reflects an idea developed in the legal discourse pertaining to occupation to describe the circumstances and conditions under which one could determine the existence of a state of occupation under IHL."[70] Military occupation hinges on control that is actual, firm and unchallenged. Thus, *actually placed under the authority* crystallises as nothing other than effective control (OL), composed of the following cumulative elements: the military presence of state A on state B's territory; this presence being unconsented to by state B; and state A's ability to exercise authority over state B's territory where the latter cannot exercise any governmental powers and/or territorial control.

---

67 See for example *Humanitarian Law in Armed Conflicts (Manual)* (The Federal Ministry of Defence of the Federal Republic of Germany, VR II 3, 1992), at § 527: A "force invading hostile territory will not be able to substantiate its occupational authority unless it is capable of enforcing directions issued to the civilian population." Where such a control is not established, according to the manual, the territory is not occupied, that is for example over battle areas – areas still embattled and not subject to permanent occupational authority (area of invasion, withdrawal area); ibid., at § 528.

68 However, see the Russian Federation Legislation Database (definition of Military Occupation) (Военная Оккупация, Законодательная база Российской Федерации), available at http://zakonbase.ru/dictJur/2587 (3 December 2016). The Russian view of territory being occupied is paralleled to territorial administrative control. According to the source, control that makes the territory occupied, based on the applicability of Article 42 HR 1907, GC IV, Article 1 AP I 1977, is of factual and administrative nature that gives the army both the right and the obligation to restore civilian life in and public order of the occupied territory to the extent possible.

69 High Court of Justice, Israel (HCJ) 102/82 *Tzemel v. Minister of Defence* (1982) 37 (3) PD 365, at 373.

70 T. Ferraro, *Expert Meeting, supra* note 3, at 17, footnote N 3.

28 *Effective control in occupation law*

2.4.1 *Military presence*

Can a Gaza-type situation as currently the case be considered as a military occupation pursuant to IHL, even though there is no Israeli military force permanently present on that territory? More generally, regardless of whether an army has withdrawn (thereby ending, or not, its military occupation: see Chapter 3) or never entered in the first place – is military presence still a qualifying necessity pursuant to Article 42 HR 1907, Common Article 2 GCs, and Article 1 AP I 1977?

The situation in Gaza shows that control can engulf just the civilian aspects of life without a military presence on the ground – through threatening to cut the power and water and limit food supplies and the flow of goods and persons in and out of the territory. This amounts to so-called remote control. Gisha, therefore, argues that the IHL on occupation should be interpreted in light of technological developments and changes in the use of force[71] and that the "legal test for occupation has always been the fact of control – not the means by which it is exercised."[72]

However, this view was not supported by the deliberations of experts during the work on the ICRC Report.[73] A majority concluded that the presence of foreign armed forces remains a prerequisite for the establishment of occupation.[74] Hence, "occupation could not be established or maintained solely through power exercised from beyond the boundaries of the occupied territory."[75]

It was also stressed that solely controlling the airspace would not satisfy the requirement of "effective control" and that only effective control on land would characterise military occupation within the meaning of IHL.[76] Also, having troops on the ground would not mean effective control necessitated their presence on each square meter of the territory.[77]

A majority of experts also thought that the test for occupation should not be who among belligerents has the military ability to enforce its will, but rather which of them possessed the military capability as a result of their presence in a given area to impose their authority (hence, preventing their opponent from doing so), and ultimately be in effective control of that area.[78] In my view, however, the establishment of authority by the occupier presupposes the deployment of its forces into

---

71 Gisha – Legal Centre for Freedom of Movement, 'Disengaged Occupiers: The Legal Status of Gaza', *Position Paper* (2007) at 69 ff., available at www.gisha.org/userfiles/file/Report%20for%20the%20website.pdf (visited 3 December 2016).

72 Ibid., at 76.

73 T. Ferraro, *Expert Meeting, supra* note 3, at 17.

74 Ibid.

75 Ibid.

76 Ibid; see however G. von Glahn, *The Occupation of Enemy Territory: A Commentary on the Law and Practice of Belligerent Occupation* (Minneapolis, MN: Lund Press Inc., 1957), at 28–29.

77 Ibid.; see also *The US Department of Defense Law of War Manual, supra* note 61, at 746.

78 T. Ferraro, *Expert Meeting, supra* note 3, at 18–19.

Effective control in occupation law   29

enemy area and the ability to exercise related military control over it. The two depend on one another.[79] This also becomes evident in the way that IHL instruments formulate the obligations of an occupant (see Chapter 4).[80]

That military presence remains a prerequisite for the beginning of occupation can also be seen in the ICJ's reasoning. While, in the Wall case, the ICJ considered Israel to be an occupying power without practically analysing Article 42 HR 1907,[81] in Armed Activities on the Territory of Congo the ICJ did apply the latter. The Court had to consider whether Uganda was an occupant in those parts of Congolese territory where its troops were present.[82] The ICJ stated that in order to determine

> an "occupying Power" in the meaning of the term as understood in the jus in bello, the Court must examine whether there is sufficient evidence to demonstrate that the said authority was *in fact established and exercised by the intervening State in the areas in question*. In the present case, the Court will need to satisfy itself that the Ugandan armed forces in the DRC *were not only stationed* in particular locations, but *also that they had substituted* their own authority for that of the Congolese Government. In that event, any justification given by Uganda for its occupation would be of no relevance; nor would it be relevant whether or not Uganda had established a structured military administration of the territory occupied.[83]

The remaining shortcomings detected in this reasoning will be addressed later (see section 2.4.3 on actual vs. potential control). For the time being, suffice it to highlight that the ICJ views physical military presence on a territory as essential for exercising effective control (OL) over territory for the purposes of occupation law.

2.4.2 Consent

The phenomenon of consent in IHL, and particularly in occupation law, is a largely unexplored matter. Yet it occupies a central role due to its capacity to qualify a territory as occupied (absence of consent) or not (presence of genuine consent).[84] In this regard, Sassòli rightly noted that in "the Westphalian system,

---

79 T. Ferraro, 'Determining the Beginning and End of an Occupation Under International Humanitarian Law', 94 *International Review of the Red Cross* (2012) 133–163, at 144.
80 Ibid.; for instance, ensuring law and order, seizing the properties, providing for the hygiene and medical needs.
81 *Legal Consequences of the Construction of a Wall in the Occupied Palestinian Territory, supra* note 38, § 73.
82 *Case Concerning Armed Activities on the Territory of the Congo (Democratic Republic of the Congo v Uganda)*, Judgment of 19 December 2005, § 166, available at www.icj-cij.org/en/case/116 (visited 15 July 2017).
83 *Ibid.*, § 173 (emphasis added).
84 V. Koutroulis, *Le début et la fin de l'application du droit de l'occupation* (Paris: Pedone, 2010), at 76–89.

30 *Effective control in occupation law*

the consent of a State is a factor which carries significant legal consequences".[85] At this stage of the book, the focus will remain on the *absence* of consent, while the presence of genuine consent will be dealt with in Chapter 3 when discussing relinquishing control over territory and occupation ending. The absence of consent in effective control (OL) is married to the element of military presence. Article 42 HR 1907 uses the wording "hostile army", which clearly denotes the army's unwelcomed presence. Absence of consent becomes "a precondition for occupation"[86] and key element of the effective control (OL) test.

But what happens if the territory occupied does not have sovereign authorities, its status under international law is unclear, and/or it has not (yet) attained statehood? When there is no one who can actually consent, at least on the official governmental level, consent is missing by default. Consent could instead be given by the people who inhabit the territory. They are the ones who should actually decide on the political future and status of their territory. Nevertheless, in Western Sahara for example a referendum in which the Sahrawi people could choose to be independent or integrate with Morocco has yet to take place.[87] Thus, and as discussed earlier in relation to Article 1 AP I 1977, given a foreign state's military presence there, such a territory must be considered occupied since the people have been prevented from consenting. By contrast, if such consent were to be given, foreign military presence would cease to amount to military occupation: the "existence of consent is simply incompatible with the institution of belligerent occupation."[88]

In the context of military occupation, consent can take various forms: unwelcomed, welcomed, engineered, or coerced. The element of consent was also discussed during the preparatory work of the ICRC Report. Importantly, the experts referred to "engineered consent" through which states intervening in a foreign territory would safeguard that the presence of their troops appears to have the consent of the concerned state,[89] with the view to avoid the deprecatory status of occupant. Assessing the genuineness and validity of consent is, therefore, a crucial task.[90]

Another form of consent is coerced consent. The framework for assessing the validity of coerced consent, as well as welcomed consent in general, should be interpreted in accordance with the law of treaties, since IHL does not provide criteria to assess this component of occupation.[91] Article 52 VCLT states, "a treaty is void if its conclusion has been procured by the threat or use of force in

---

85 M. Sassòli, 'Legislation and Maintenance', *supra* note 66, at 690.
86 T. Ferraro, *Expert Meeting*, *supra* note 3, at 21.
87 SC Res. 690 (1991) MINRUSO (United Nations Mission for Referendum in Western Sahara); *Report of the Secretary-General on the situation Concerning Western Sahara*, UN SC S/2019/787, 2 October 2019; *Report of the Secretary-General on the Situation Concerning Western Sahara*, UN SC S/2016/355, 19 April 2016; *Report of the Secretary-General on the Situation Concerning Western Sahara* S/2015/246, 10 April 2015.
88 T. Ferraro, 'Determining the Beginning and End', *supra* note 79, at 153.
89 T. Ferraro, *Expert Meeting*, *supra* note 3, at 21.
90 Ibid.
91 Ibid.

Effective control in occupation law   31

violation of the principles of international law embodied in the Charter of the United Nations."[92]

There is also a question over who has the authority to speak on behalf of the state (and its people) – the president, the prime minister, the foreign minister, or any member of the government? Finally, one must distinguish between the absence of military opposition to the foreign troops' presence and formal consent given by a local governmental authority.[93] The entity competent to issue consent on behalf of a state or engage in any dealings about the political status of the territory needs to be deduced from the domestic law of that state.[94] Thus, the head of state is often presumed to be the highest authority towards the outside. For example, in the case of the 2008 Russian-Georgian war, the Georgian president signed off on a deal with the help of then EU president Mr. Sarkozy, pledging Georgia would obey the Six Point Plan. Crucially, however, the Georgian president refused to consent to Russia's continued military presence on Georgian soil.[95]

The unconsented character of belligerent occupation clearly distinguishes it from pacific occupation.[96] The latter type is considered by Benvenisti to occur due to an "agreement between the sovereign State and the pacific occupant whereby the former grants the latter, and the latter assumes, powers and responsibilities to maintain public order over a part of its territory and its population."[97] Examples of such occupations are the post-Franco-Prussian War (1870–71) agreements of France temporarily approving the occupation of its territories by Germany or the occupation of Rhineland after World War I.[98] However, pacific occupation is a doubtful phenomenon for the purposes of IHL applicability, as it amounts to a consensual, welcomed presence.

On the whole, consent has the power to tip the balance in qualifying a situation as occupation. For example, the withdrawal of Congolese consent to the presence of Uganda's military troops "lay at the root of the Judgment"[99] of the

---

92 Article 52 *Vienna Convention on the Law of Treaties*, 1969.

93 T. Ferraro, *Expert Meeting*, *supra* note 3, at 22.

94 A. Watts, 'Heads of State', *Max Planck Encyclopedia of Public International Law* (2010), § 3, available at http://opil.ouplaw.com/view/10.1093/law:epil/9780199231690/law-9780199231690-e1418 (visited 5 December 2016).

95 J. Swaine, 'Russia and Georgia "Agree in Principle" to Nicolas Sarkozy Backed Peace Plan', *The Telegraph*, 13 August 2008, available at www.telegraph.co.uk/news/worldnews/europe/georgia/2550129/Russia-and-Georgia-agree-in-principle-to-Nicolas-Sarkozy-backed-peace-plan.html (visited 5 December 2016).

96 Y. Dinstein, *The International Law of Belligerent Occupation*, *supra* note 53, at 35. See also G. Schwarzenberger, *The Law of Armed Conflict: International Law as Applied by International Courts and Tribunals* (London: Stevens & Sons, 1968), at 184.

97 E. Benvenisti, 'Occupation, Pacific', *Max Planck Encyclopedia of Public International Law* (2009), § 4, available at http://opil.ouplaw.com/view/10.1093/law:epil/9780199231690/law-9780199231690-e360?prd=EPIL (visited 5 December 2016).

98 Ibid.

99 Y. Dinstein, *The International Law of Belligerent Occupation*, *supra* note 53, at 42; *Case Concerning Armed Activities on the Territory of the Congo*, *supra* note 82, § 292.

32 *Effective control in occupation law*

ICJ in the case of *DRC v. Uganda*.[100] Similarly, in the case of South West Africa (today Namibia), the GA in its Resolution 2145 (XXI) (1966) declared that South Africa did not duly administer the territory according to the conferred mandate. South Africa, therefore, had no right to administer it any longer, and the territory came under UN responsibility.[101] In other words, the UN GA (and not the state) withdrew the mandate of South Africa to be present on that territory. Withdrawing the mandate in the context of de-colonisation is functionally equivalent to withdrawing consent to a state's presence on the territory. The ICJ, too, decreed that South Africa had to withdraw from the territory and terminate Namibia's occupation.[102]

2.4.3 *Actual vs. potential control*

When it comes to exercising authority, an important inconsistency emerges. The key to this inconsistency lies in the difference between actual and potential forms of control. Article 42 HR 1907 creates uncertainty by using two different wordings: first, in para. 1, "territory [. . .] actually placed under the authority of the hostile army", and then, in para. 2, "territory where such authority [. . .] can be exercised", thus pitting *actual authority* and *can be exercised* against each other.[103]

The difference between actual and potential control was also examined by the experts working on the ICRC Report. Three main issues were highlighted: "the nature of the authority, the necessity – or otherwise – of substantiating such authority, and the legal significance of sharing authority between the occupying power and local government."[104] The experts were unanimous in agreeing that "authority" should refer to the notion of governmental functions, because occupation had to do with the political direction of the territory.[105] What the invited experts disagreed with, and rightly so, was the approach taken by the ICJ in the *Democratic Republic of Congo (DRC) v. Uganda* case, where the Court thought it had to be proved that the "Ugandan armed forces in the DRC were not only stationed in particular locations but also that they had substituted their own authority for that of the Congolese Government."[106]

Hence, the Court had introduced a cumulative test, fitting only some situations and creating the impression that it had succumbed to the misperception that a formal administration was necessary for occupation to commence. The

---

100 *Case Concerning Armed Activities on the Territory of the Congo, supra* note 82, §§ 50–54.
101 GA Res. 2145 (XXI) (1966); see also F. Carroll, *South West Africa and the United Nations* (Lexington, KY: University of Kentucky Press, 1967), at 21–29.
102 *Legal Consequences for States of the Continued Presence South Africa in Namibia (South West Africa) Notwithstanding Security Council Resolution (276) (1970)*, Advisory Opinion of 21 June 1971, § 118–119, available at www.icj-cij.org/en/case/53 (visited 15 July 2017).
103 A. Roberts, 'What Is Military Occupation?', 55 *British Yearbook of International Law* (1984) 249–305, at 300.
104 T. Ferraro, *Expert Meeting, supra* note 3, at 19.
105 Ibid.
106 *Case Concerning Armed Activities on the Territory of the Congo, supra* note 82, § 173.

Effective control in occupation law   33

wording "had substituted their own authority for that of the [. . .] Government", however, is rather vague.[107] This could indeed mean to not only incapacitate the former sovereign to exercise its authority by virtue of one's own military presence, but also to set up a new military/civilian administration on the territory. However, this directly conflicts with the other part of the paragraph, where the ICJ considers that to be irrelevant, provided control was actually exercised.[108]

The experts, working on the ICRC report, considered the exercise of actual authority by foreign forces to be "too narrow", emphasising that upholding *actual* over *potential* control would create "more legal black holes", ultimately resulting in a protection gap for the individuals caught up in such areas.[109] Hence, "a test based on the *ability* of enemy foreign forces to exert authority over a specific area"[110] was preferred and supported – in other words, paragraph 2 Article 42 HR 1907. Such a test has a twofold significance: first, to render futile any attempts by the occupying power to evade responsibilities to govern the occupied territories, e.g. by refusing to set up a (provisional) civil administration; and second, to hinder the occupant state to evade its duties under occupation law through establishing a government by proxy, which would exercise governmental functions on its behalf.[111] Chapter 2 examines proxy occupation in more detail.

Furthermore, the ICJ's "substitution of the occupant's authority for that of the territorial power" was not supported by all the judges, notably not by Kooijmans. In his separate opinion, he considered such an approach to lead to an "unwarranted narrowing of the criteria of the law of belligerent occupation as these have been interpreted in customary law since 1907."[112]

The "substitution of authority" also appears to be illustrated differently by the US and the UK military manuals.[113] The UK manual uses "in the position to substitute",[114] while the US speaks of "must substitute its authority for that of the territorial State".[115] The UK manual, therefore, seems to render better protection to civilians.

---

107 T. Ruys and S. Verhoven, 'DRC v. Uganda: The Applicability of International Humanitarian Law and Human Rights Law in Occupied Territories', in R. Arnold and N. Quénivet (eds.), *International Humanitarian Law and Human Rights Law* (Leiden: Martinus Nijhoff Publishers, 2008) 155–195, at 165.
108 *Case Concerning Armed Activities on the Territory of the Congo, supra* note 82, § 173.
109 T. Ferraro, *Expert Meeting, supra* note 3, at 19.
110 Ibid.
111 Ibid.
112 *Case Concerning Armed Activities on the Territory of the Congo (Democratic Republic of the Congo v. Uganda)*, Judgment of 19 December 2005, Separate Opinion of Judge Kooijmans § 44; also, according to this judge (§ 45), "military occupation presupposes a hostile invasion, resisted or un-resisted, as a result of which the invader has rendered the invaded government incapable of exercising its authority, and [secondly] that the invader is in a position to substitute its own authority for that of the former government" (§46); see also T. Ferraro, 'Determining the Beginning and End', *supra* note 79, at 151.
113 UK Ministry of Defence, *The Manual of the Law, supra* note 58, at § 275.
114 Ibid.
115 *The US Department of Defense Law of War Manual, supra* note 61, at 747.

34 *Effective control in occupation law*

While the ICRC's approach is commendable, the question remains what should be understood under the *ability* of foreign forces to exert authority over a specific area. I believe this ability to be linked to state A's military forces being present on the territory of state B and, by virtue of such presence, to incapacitate the latter from exercising its governmental authority. This can happen in the form of taking over certain geographical areas and completely isolating them from state B's governmental reach. This means that the hostile army of state A holds on to and controls the "nerve centre of governmental authority"[116] of state B, i.e. its vital infrastructure and power-exercising centres such as military bases, airports, harbours, and key roads. The result of all this is to bar the sovereign state from exercising its authority, thereby maintaining discretion over any action connected to territorial administration. Thus, the presence of the occupant's military force is a sign of vast abilities for its further action(s). The activities of Russia in Crimea are a useful example of this.[117]

Lastly, the matter of sharing authority between the occupant and the occupied territory's government or local authorities should be examined. During the ICRC report deliberations, one expert thought that "occupation necessitated having exclusive and unique authority over the occupied territory".[118] Other experts were of the view that sharing authority was the very rationale underlining the concept of occupation, that is "the allocation of responsibilities between governments, which helped to fill the vacuum of authority that developed when a legitimate government had been displaced by force."[119] In this regard, it is important to identify "who was the ultimate and overall bearer of responsibility in occupied territory."[120] Having determined this, "occupation law would allow for a vertical, but not a horizontal, sharing of authority."[121]

Such vertical sharing of authority[122] rests on a hierarchical relationship between the occupying power and the local authorities, where the occupying power "maintains a form of control" over the local authorities "through a top down approach in the allocation of responsibilities."[123] Horizontal sharing of power, in turn, is demonstrated by a sort of competition between the hostile troops and the local authorities, raising questions about the ability of the former to impose their will on the latter and, consequently, also about the existence of effective control (OL) over territory.[124]

Vertical authority is implied in the provisions of GC IV, such as Articles 6§3 (the occupant's obligations concerning protected persons), 47 (inviolability of the rights of protected persons), 50 (children), or 56 (hygiene and public health). In

---

116 *Case Concerning Armed Activities on the Territory of the Congo (Democratic Republic of the Congo v. Uganda)*, Separate Opinion of Judge Kooijmans, *supra* note 112, § 46.
117 See also Chapter 3 of this book.
118 T. Ferraro, *Expert Meeting*, *supra* note 3, at 20.
119 Ibid., at 20.
120 Ibid.
121 Ibid.
122 R. Kolb, *Theory of International Law* (Bloomsbury: Hart Publishing, 2016), at 62–63.
123 T. Ferraro, *Expert Meeting*, *supra* note 3, at 20, footnote N 7.
124 Ibid.

fact, Articles 50 and 56 explicitly mention "national and local authorities", stating the latter's cooperation with the occupant. On the other hand, Article 47 merely mentions "authorities". However, Article 55 (provision of food and medical supply to the protected persons) could indeed be an example of implied vertical authority, as it does not directly refer to the local authorities. Power sharing, then, should not affect the occupant's authority, nor interfere with its security and military operations, and must stem from the occupant's "genuine will and not from its inability to displace the legitimate government and/or its surrogates."[125] In other words: the occupant should allow such a vertical relationship. However, this would only assist, never supplant, the occupant in discharging its duties. This stance was also taken by the Supreme Court of Israel in *Tsemel v. Minister of Defence*:

> the occupying military force may determine to what degree it exercises its powers of civil administration through its direct delegates and which areas it leaves in the hand of the former government, whether local or central government officials. Permitting the activities of such governmental authorities does not per se detract from the factual existence of effective military control over the area and the consequences that ensue therefrom under the laws of war.[126]

However, this usually happens in rare cases only. Such is, in sum, the majority position in IHL.[127] The application of IHL may be undermined in a situation where the foreign state refuses to exercise some of its duties and at the same time keeps the territorial state from exercising its obligations under IHL, leading to a "protection gap"[128] where one state should, but does not, and the other state cannot, but would want to, fulfil its obligations.

2.4.4 *Effective control for qualifying a situation as an occupation*

Occupation is a question of fact. The ICTY Trial Chamber in Naletilić provided factually verifiable examples of what "under the authority of the occupying power actually established" could mean:[129]

1   The occupying power must be in a position to substitute its own authority for that of the occupied authorities, which must have been rendered incapable of functioning publicly;

---

125 Ibid.
126 High Court of Justice, Israel (HCJ) 102/82, Tsemel v. Minister of Defence, 37 (3), P.D. (1983), at 373–374.
127 See, however, D. Shraga, 'Military Occupation and UN Transitional Administrations: The Analogy and Its Limitations', in M. G. Cohen (ed.), *Promoting Justice, Human Rights and Conflict Resolution Through International Law: Liber Amicorum* (Leiden: Martinus Nijhoff Publishers, 2007) 479–498, at 481.
128 T. Ferraro, *Expert Meeting, supra* note 3, at 19.
129 Judgment, *Mladan Naletilić and Vinko Martinović* (IT-98–34-T), Trial Chamber, 31 March 2003, § 217.

36 *Effective control in occupation law*

2 The enemy's forces have surrendered, been defeated, or withdrawn. In this respect, battle areas may not be considered occupied territory. However, sporadic local resistance, even if successful, does not affect the reality of occupation;

3 The occupying power has a sufficient force present, or the capacity to send troops within a reasonable time to make the authority of the occupying power felt;

4 A temporary administration has been established over the territory; and/or

5 The occupying power has issued and enforced directions to the civilian population.[130]

While the first example shows potential control, illustration four demonstrates actual control in the form of setting up a new territorial administration. All in all, the provided examples suggest that not all occupations are identical, as different forms materialise at different times and in different places. For example, the occupant can set up a military or civilian administration. However, when Russia occupied Crimea, it did not do either, instead using the existing Crimean regional authorities to assert control (see Chapter 2).[131] By contrast, Israel installed a military government in the West Bank, the Gaza Strip, the Golan Heights, and the "Solomon Area" shortly after the 1967 ceasefire.[132] But in 1981, Military Order No. 947 established a civilian administration to supply and implement public services in the West Bank.[133]

Further, the ICTY Trial Chamber averred the customary nature of Article 42 HR 1907,[134] distinguishing two types of control: *effective* and *overall control*, reaffirming that Article 42 HR embodies nothing other than effective control (OL):

> The overall control test, submitted in the Blaškić Trial Judgment, is not applicable to the determination of the existence of an occupation . . . there is an essential distinction between the determination of a state of occupation and that of the existence of an international armed conflict. The application of the overall control test is applicable to the latter. A further degree of control is required to establish occupation.[135]

According to the parlance of international law, this further degree of *overall control* (SR/IHL) would be *effective control* (SR), as there can be no in-between

---

130 Ibid.

131 Europa Publications (ed.), *The Territories of Russian Federation 2016* (17th edn., London: Routledge, 2016), at 318.

132 N. Raphaeli, 'Military Government in the Occupied Territories: An Israeli View', 23 *Middle East Journal* 2 (Spring 1969) 177–190, at 178.

133 Israel Military Order No. 947 Concerning the Establishment of a Civilian Administration, www.israellawresourcecenter.org/israelmilitaryorders/fulltext/mo0947.htm; and Order Regarding the Establishment of a Civilian Administration (Judea and Samaria) (Order No. 947) 5742–1981.

134 Judgment, *Mladan Naletilić and Vinko Martinović, supra* note 129, §§ 215–216.

135 Ibid., at § 214: "Occupation is defined as a transitional period following invasion and preceding the agreement on the cessation of the hostilities."

Effective control in occupation law   37

situation. At least this is what the ICJ seems to have favoured for the purposes of establishing state responsibility.[136] However, for the purposes of occupying territory in IHL, effective control (OL) is indispensable. Moreover, the *authority of the occupying power actually established* embodies principles of factuality and effectivity. I therefore suggest that for the purposes of qualifying a situation as military occupation, effective control (OL) is comprised of three cumulative elements:

1   State A's military forces are physically present on the territory in question, with this presence not being consented to by the territorial government;
2   The government of the territory has been totally or partially overcome by state A's military presence and, by virtue of such presence, cannot exercise its governmental powers (this covers both occupation following hostilities and occupation after no armed resistance); and
3   State A's military forces are in such a position that they *can* exercise authority over the total territory or parts of it. The condition to being considered an occupant is thus not to have a military or civilian administrative apparatus. Instead, the armed forces present on the territory of state B are in principle able to set up such a body.

At what stage does the authority of the occupying power actually start? Does it envisage ensuring law and order as soon as the occupant's armed forces set foot on the ground? For instance, should the US have prevented the rampage and looting of museums in Baghdad which happened immediately after the Iraq invasion?[137] Numerous valuables were stolen and as it appears such actions were not prevented by the US or its coalition partners. Baghdad fell to the US army on 9 April 2003.[138] Thefts took place between 7 and 12 April, with staff attempting to hold back looters until US forces arrived on 16 April.[139]

---

136   *Case Concerning Application of the Convention on the Prevention and Punishment of the Crime of Genocide (Bosnia and Herzegovina v. Serbia and Montenegro)*, Judgment of 26 February 2007, at § 406, available at www.icj-cij.org/files/case-related/91/091-20070226-JUD-01-00-EN.pdf; see also *Case Concerning Application of the Convention on the Prevention and Punishment of the Crime of Genocide (Bosnia and Herzegovina v. Serbia and Montenegro)*, Judgment of 26 February 2007, Dissenting Opinion of Vice President Al-Khasawneh § 37–39, disagreeing with this stance (§ 39), available at www.icj-cij.org/files/case-related/91/091-20070226-JUD-01-01-EN.pdf (both visited 15 July 2017).

137   On the looting of the museum in Baghdad, see M. Bogdanos and W. Patrick, *Thieves of Baghdad* (New York: Bloomsbury, 2005); 'Liberation and Looting in Iraq', *Human Rights Watch*, 13 April 2003, available at https://www.hrw.org/news/2003/04/13/liberation-and-looting-iraq-0 (visited 5 May 2020).

138   Human Rights Watch, *Off Target: The Conduct of the War and Civilian Casualties in Iraq* (section 'Synopsis of the Air War') (December 2003), available at www.hrw.org/reports/2003/usa1203/index.htm (visited 5 December 2016); 'The Fall of Baghdad', *The New York Times*, 10 April 2003, available at www.nytimes.com/2003/04/10/opinion/the-fall-of-baghdad.html (visited 5 December 2016).

139   The Iraq Museum, *About the Museum*, available at www.iraqmuseum.org/pages/about-the-museum/ (visited 5 December 2016); M. Bogdanos and W. Patrick, *Thieves of Baghdad, supra* note 137, at 14–16.

38 *Effective control in occupation law*

The authority of the occupying power, in my view, comes into effect when the government of the territory is no longer exercising its governmental functions and when the occupant's forces, by virtue of their established control, can deal away not only with pockets of resistance, but also react to such looting and plundering. However, the occupant's forces may not be in a position to ensure law and order – or, in this case, protect the cultural property of the occupied state – immediately, since the territorial state may collapse faster than the occupant is able to firmly establish its effective control (OL). In the case at hand, even once the active combat phase was over, the US had to engage Article 43 HR 1907 only once there were enough ground troops on the territory to do so.

According to Schmitt, precisely dating the commencement of occupation is difficult as "an entire State need not be occupied before occupation rights and duties attach."[140] US military detachments could have been tasked by the occupying forces' commander to patrol and help maintain order in some parts of Iraq but not (yet) on the streets of Baghdad, although the Iraqi government and military structures were rapidly collapsing[141] and there was no one who could guarantee law and order other than the incoming US Coalition Forces. Chapter 4 discusses in greater detail the so-called functional application of state obligations; for example, when already in the initial stages of an invasion a state is bound by certain rules of GC IV.

3. Joint and shared control: control exercised by an MNF and UN endorsed control

Examples of effective control (OL) exercised jointly by military forces, that is, where more than one entity is involved, include Iraq or the UN's presence in Kosovo, Timor, and Somalia. Two questions arise: firstly, who is deemed to be an occupant amongst the multinational force (MNF) and on what grounds? Secondly, is occupation law also applicable to actions of the UN, i.e. may the UN also be called an occupying power – and if so, by what criteria – or only the force-contributing states?

A distinction should therefore be made between effective control (OL) exercised over territory X by an MNF and effective control (OL) wielded over territory X by a UN mission. With regards to the former, there may or may not be a UN SC endorsement of their deployment. For example, in the case of the US-led Coalition invasion of Iraq in 2003, no UN SC endorsement was given;[142] whereas the SC authorised member states "to use all necessary means . . . to restore international peace and security"[143] when in 1990 Iraq had invaded and occupied

---

140 M. N. Schmitt, 'Iraq (2003 Onwards)', in E. Wilmshurst (ed.), *International Law and the Classification of Conflicts* (Oxford: Oxford University Press, 2012) 356–386, at 365.

141 Ibid.

142 Ibid.

143 SC Res. 678 (1990); see also R. S. Lowry, *The Gulf War Chronicles* (New York: iUniverse, Inc., 2003), at 6–10.

Effective control in occupation law 39

Kuwait. Such a military operation was authorised by the UN SC but conducted by national contingents operating under national command and control. For the purposes of this book, which is concerned with control in occupation law and therefore *jus in bello*, the legality of authorising a multinational contingent to use force is not pursued further. The two types of missions are therefore considered together but remain different from UN missions proper, i.e. UN military operations established by the UN SC and conducted under UN command and control (e.g. the UN Protection Force in Yugoslavia, UNPROFOR, or the UN Operations in Somalia, UNOSOM).[144]

An MNF exercising effective control (OL) over territory is investigated first, followed by UN missions. It should nevertheless be stated that the fundamental question from the point of view of occupation law is identical for both, namely whether there is effective control (OL) over territory and lack of consent by the host state to the troops' presence. Where the two may differ is with regards to who ultimately bears the responsibility for IHL norms of occupation law.

3.1 MNF control over territory

An MNF is composed of more than one state's armed forces "which are allied to each other, and are perhaps under a unified command system".[145] A US Joint Chiefs of Staff publication defines multinational operations as carried out by armies of two or more nations, usually within the structure of a coalition or alliance.[146] One example is the US-led invasion of Iraq in spring 2003.[147] The US and the UK spoke of the "liberation" of Iraq, rather than of aggression and occupation,[148] but UN SC Resolution N 1483 (2003), in its preamble, referred to them as occupying powers.[149] This suggests that the SC did not create occupation, but that it recognised an occupation already existed.[150]

Resolution 1483 in its preamble further stated: "*Noting further* that other States that are not occupying powers are working now or in the future may work under the Authority [. . .]".[151] This refers to states which provided support to the Coalition Provisional Authority (CPA), but whose engagement did not amount to exercising effective control (OL) over any part of the territory of

---

144 C. Greenwood, 'International Humanitarian Law and United Nations Military Operations', 1 *Yearbook of International Humanitarian Law* (1998) 3–34, at 4.
145 A. Roberts, 'What Is Military Occupation?', *supra* note 103, at 289.
146 US Department of Army Joint Publication 3–16, *Multinational Operations*, 16 July 2013, available at www.fas.org/irp/doddir/dod/jp3-16.pdf (visited 15 July 2017), at I-1.
147 K. Dörmann and L. Colassis, 'International Humanitarian Law in the Iraq Conflict', 47 *German Yearbook of International Law* (2004) 293–342.
148 Ibid., at 297.
149 SC Res. 1483 (2003).
150 A. Roberts, 'The End of Occupation: Iraq', 54 *International and Comparative Law Quarterly* (2005) 27–48, at 32.
151 SC Res. 1483, *supra* note 149.

40 *Effective control in occupation law*

Iraq.[152] In addition, it indicated that states contributing forces to Iraq would not incur the responsibilities and "the odium that came with being labelled an occupier".[153] The CPA was set up right after the US and its allies had invaded Iraq. Based on SC Resolution 1483 and the laws of war, the CPA took over the executive, legislative, and judicial powers of Iraq between 21 April 2003 and 28 June 2004.[154]

It has to be noted that if one carries out tasks under the command or instruction of an occupying power, the status of an occupant is also conferred upon states which comply, particularly when such tasks are crucial to the way in which the authority "executes its role as an Occupying Power and carries out its administrative responsibilities."[155] Within the context of occupying powers acting and governing in a coalition, the occupying powers "will bear the brunt of joint responsibility for what is happening within the area subject to their combined effective control."[156] When coalition partners divide the occupied territory into zones, each occupying power administering its own area "will assume sole responsibility commensurate with the span of its respective effective control."[157]

The question then arises as to the grounds on which the troops *not* from the US or the UK could be considered occupants. Are they fully bound by HR 1907 and GC IV? The situation is complex as there are multiple actors involved, with various tasks, such as carrying out patrolling missions, detentions of persons protected by GC IV, or manning mobile checkpoints.[158] The ICRC found a way out of this conundrum by focusing solely on what the different contingents were actually doing on the ground. It thus differentiated states according to their functions and duties, centring on those that actually provided combat personnel but excluding states that merely provided engineers or medical staff.[159] The ICRC then examined whether the national contingents in question had been assigned responsibility for, and were exercising effective control (OL) over, a portion of Iraqi territory.[160] If that was the case, the ICRC considered such states to be occupying powers. In a situation where states were exercising control over protected persons and interacted with them, they would have to respect the law

---

152 K. Dörmann and L. Colassis, 'International Humanitarian Law', *supra* note 147, at 303.
153 A. Roberts, 'The End of Occupation', *supra* note 150, at 33.
154 Coalition Provisional Authority Regulation Number 1, available at www.iraqcoalition.org/regulations/20030516_CPAREG_1_The_Coalition_Provisional_Authority_.pdf (visited 5 December 2016).
155 L. Lijnzaad, 'How Not to Be an Occupying Power: Some Reflections on UN Security Council Resolution 1483 and the Contemporary Law of Occupation', in L. Lijnzaad, J. van Sambeek, and B. Tahzib-lie (eds.), *Making the Voice of Humanity Heard* (Leiden: Martinus Nijhoff Publishers, 2004) 291–306, at 298.
156 Y. Dinstein, *The International Law of Belligerent Occupation*, *supra* note 53, at 48–49.
157 Ibid; see also UK Ministry of Defence, *The Manual of the Law*, *supra* note 58, section 11.3.3.
158 K. Dörmann and L. Colassis, 'International Humanitarian Law', *supra* note 147, at 304.
159 J.-P. Lavoyer, 'Jus in Bello: Occupation Law and the War in Iraq', 98 *Proceedings of the American Society of International Law* (2004) 117–124, at 122.
160 Ibid.

Effective control in occupation law 41

of occupation, too. And if the armed forces of any state became involved in hostilities, they would even have to abide by IHL irrespective of their occupant status.[161]

3.2 UN operations

MNFs operating under UN aegis and with a UN mandate (both for peace-enforcement or peacekeeping purposes) have, over the past years, become of broad interest due to the multifaceted nature of such operations.[162] This mostly concerns integrated missions and their deployments into violent environments (both IACs and NIACs). Such missions are also tasked to administer a territory.[163] Due to this fact, identifying the legal framework applicable to such instances is needed.[164] Does IHL apply to such forces and, if so, under what conditions?[165] Can UN forces be considered occupants? These questions have been the subject of much consideration, but clarity is still lacking.

The essence and spirit of the UN is anti-war; it is thus difficult to imagine that the UN too may become a military occupant. There are indeed views not favouring the application of occupation law to it. Some consider that the UN can never be party to a conflict, nor a power within the understanding of the GCs, as UN peacekeepers are impartial, objective, and neutral, "their sole interest in the conflict being the restoration and maintenance of international peace and security".[166] Furthermore, peacekeeping forces act pursuant to a mandate conferred upon them by the SC and with the concerned government's consent.[167]

Thus the Belgium Military Court, for example, in the case related to Belgian peacekeeping actions in Somalia, opined that the situation in Somalia in

---

161 Ibid.
162 T. Ferraro and L. Cameron, 'Article 2: Application of the Convention', in ICRC (ed.), *Commentary on the First Geneva Convention* (Cambridge: Cambridge University Press, 2016), 68–125, at 88, Footnote N 81.
163 S. R. Ratner, 'Foreign Occupation and International Territorial Administration: The Challenges of Convergence', *The European Journal of International Law* (2005) 695–719, at 698; see also ICRC, *Multinational Forces* (Overview), 29 October 2010, available at www.icrc.org/eng/war-and-law/contemporary-challenges-for-ihl/multinational-forces/overview-multinational-forces.htm (visited 5 December 2016).
164 Ibid., at 705.
165 T. Ferraro, 'The Applicability and Application of International Humanitarian Law to Multinational Forces', 95 *International Review of the Red Cross* (2013) 561–612, at 562.
166 D. Shraga, 'The United Nations as an Actor Bound by International Humanitarian Law', 5 *International Peacekeeping* 2 (1998) 64–81, at 67.
167 Ibid. However, no legal definition of either peacekeeping or peace enforcement exists, see P. I. Labuda, 'Peacekeeping and Peace Enforcement', *Max Planck Encyclopedia of Public International Law* (2015) § 1, §§ 6–14, available at https://opil.ouplaw.com/view/10.1093/law:epil/9780199231690/law-9780199231690-e364 (visited 8 February 2020); R. Murphy, *UN Peacekeeping in Lebanon, Somalia and Kosovo* (Cambridge: Cambridge University Press, 2007), at 8–9; T. Ferraro and L. Cameron, 'Article 2: Application of the Convention', *supra* note 162, at 89.

42 *Effective control in occupation law*

1993 could not be considered an IAC because peacekeeping forces could not be regarded as a party to a conflict nor, *a fortiori*, occupants.[168] It was also put forth that because UN forces were engaged on behalf of the international community, IHL did not apply to them and they were exempt from the belligerent status.[169] At most, IHL should apply differently or, as a matter of policy, only electively (e.g. laxer rules on the use of force).[170]

However, this standpoint runs counter to the spirit of the *jus ad bellum* and *jus in bello* separation and the principle that IHL application is dependent on facts, irrespective of the mandate or status allotted to a party to the conflict, in this case a UN MNF. This matters for two reasons: first, just because the deployment of a force is consented to by the host state does not mean that consent will remain valid indefinitely. For example, once the UN MNF uses force in self-defence, consent to its presence may be withdrawn. Further, when a peacekeeping force is deployed, a SOFA (status of forces agreement) or SOMA (status of mission agreement) is signed between the UN and the receiving state, covering general aspects of the MNF's presence and including aspects such as the scope of their activities and the jurisdiction they submit to.[171] It then might happen that a withdrawal of consent to the peacekeepers' presence occurs, as in the case of United Nations Emergency Force I in Egypt in 1967.[172] Second, whether IHL applies to UN MNFs hinges entirely on the circumstances prevailing in the field, irrespective of the international mandate assigned to them by UN SC and whether legal conditions of Common Articles 2 and 3 of GCs are met.[173]

The 1999 bulletin on the 'Observance by United Nations Forces of International Humanitarian Law' caused further uncertainty, stating that IHL applied "in peacekeeping operations when the use of force is permitted in self-defence".[174] Ferraro terms this formulation "misleading", since it could be interpreted as triggering

---

168 Cour Militaire Belge, *Jugement concernant des Violations du Droit Humanitaire commises en Somalie et au Rwanda*, Nr. 54 A.R. 1997, 20 Novembre 1997 Journal des Tribunaux, 14 Avril 1998, pp. 286–289.

169 T. Ferraro, 'The Applicability and Application of International Humanitarian Law to Multinational Forces', *International Law Programme Discussion Summary*, 20 November 2014, at 2, available at www.chathamhouse.org/sites/files/chathamhouse/field/field_docume nt/20141120IHLMultinationalForces.pdf (visited 5 December 2016); T. Ferraro, 'The Applicability and Application of International Humanitarian Law to Multinational Forces', 95 *International Review of the Red Cross* (2013) 561–612, at 563–564.

170 Ibid.

171 United Nations Peacekeeping Law Reform Project, *UN Peacekeeping and the Model Status of Forces Agreement* (University of Essex, School of Law, 2010), at 15–17, available at www. essex.ac.uk/plrp/documents/model_sofa_peliminay_report_august_2010.pdf (visited 5 December 2016).

172 Peace and Security Section (in cooperation with the Department of Peacekeeping Operations) Middle East UNEF-1, Completed Peacekeeping Operations, 2003, available at www. un.org/en/peacekeeping/missions/past/unef1backgr2.html (visited 5 December 2016).

173 T. Ferraro, 'The Applicability and Application', *supra* note 169, at 565.

174 United Nations, Secretary-General's Bulletin, *Observance by United Nations Forces of International Humanitarian Law*, ST/SGB/1999/13, 6 August 1999, at § 1.1.

IHL application as soon as force is used for self-defence purposes,[175] when in fact IHL application is triggered the very moment the criteria of its applications are met.[176] But while it might be clear for the purposes of Common Article 2.1 and 3 GCs,[177] it is not clear whether UN MNFs can be considered occupiers since they do not fit the criteria of Article 42 HR 1907, which uses the term "hostile army".

In general, operations of international organisations administering territories are seldom referred to as occupations, irrespective of the fact that often a significant civilian and military presence is needed to undertake many of the activities of occupying forces in terms of control and governance.[178] There seems to be no uniform stance on the issue of whether the UN may be an occupant either.[179] UN operations themselves are known for their conceptual muddling-through and line-blurring between the concepts of peacekeeping, peace-building, peace-making, and peace enforcement, which are often used interchangeably, although they cover different operations.[180] Shraga and Zacklin, for instance, detect a blurring of the distinction between peacekeeping and peace enforcement, raising the question of the applicability of IHL to peacekeeping operations.[181] The traditional peacekeeping mission comprises a force deployed by the UN into a war-affected country to limit the (effects of the) violent conflict occurring there. The requirements for a peace-*keeping* mission are the consent of the host state, impartiality, and minimal use of force.[182] UN peace-*enforcement* operations, however, do not need a host state's consent.[183] Also, they are based on a strong Chapter 7 mandate

---

175 T. Ferraro, 'The Applicability and Application', *supra* note 169, at 578.
176 Ibid., at 575–579.
177 Whether AP II 1977 applies to multinational forces is unclear due to the stringent test expounded by Article 1 of this instrument. Notably AP II applies only to cases of NIAC unfolding on the territory of the contracting party.
178 S. R. Ratner, 'Foreign Occupation and International Territorial Administration', *supra* note 163, at 696.
179 See for instance P. I. Labuda, 'Peacekeeping and Peace Enforcement', *supra* note 167, § 48; S. Wills, 'Occupation Law and Multi-National Operations: Problems and Perspectives', 77 *British Year Book of International Law* (2006) 256–332, at 320–325; M. J. Kelly, *Restoring and Maintaining Order in Complex Peace Operations* (The Hague: Kluwer Law International, 1999), at 172–181; see further M. Sassòli, 'Protection of Civilians in the Mandates of Military Operations: Legal and Operation Considerations: Interview', *Professionals in Humanitarian Assistance*, 21 January 2015, available at https://phap.org/thematic-notes/2015/january/interview-prof-marco-Sassòli-protection-civilians-mandates-military-op (visited 5 December 2016).
180 P. F. Diehl, *Peace Operations* (London: Policy Press, 2008), at 3.
181 D. Shraga and R. Zacklin, 'L'applicabilité du DIH aux Opérations de Maintien de la Paix de Nations Unies: Questions Conceptuelles et Pratiques', in *Symposium sur l'action humanitaire et les opérations de maintien de la paix*, Rapport, CICR Genève, 1995, at 43.
182 P. F. Diehl, *Peace Operations*, *supra* note 180, at 6.
183 T. D. Gill, 'Legal Characterisation and Basis for Enforcement Operations and Peace Enforcement Operations Under the Charter', in T. D. Gill and D. Fleck (eds.), *The Handbook of the International Law of Military Operations* (2nd edn., Oxford: Oxford University Press, 2015), 95–109, at 96–99; D. Murray et al., *Practitioner's Guide to Human Rights Law in Armed Conflict* (Oxford: Oxford University Press, 2016), at 260.

44 *Effective control in occupation law*

addressing serious human rights violations and threats against international peace and security.[184]

The changing nature of UN missions and referencing to UN Chapters 6 and 7 suggest that situations on the ground may at times be of a combined nature, requiring SC actions under both chapters. In this light, the UN presence in Kosovo, under Chapter 7 (UNMIK),[185] or in Cambodia (UNTAC), under Chapter 6,[186] raises the question of the applicability of the law of occupation to UN forces in terms of their rights and duties as well as of the legal protection this regime extends to the civilian population.[187]

One possibility is to consider these missions as instances of international territorial administration. The actors in such administrations and in situations of occupation are usually different: in the former, it is an international organisation, while in the latter it is commonly held to be a state. Nevertheless, the two share a major commonality – exerting control over territory through armed forces. In this regard, for Wilde the relationship between an international territorial administration and military occupation has a general institution in international public policy, "international trusteeship", and covers a relationship of administrative control by States or international organisations over a territorial unit.[188] Occupations thus vary with respect to both their causes and legal bases: states either occupy territory during or after armed conflict, using force in self-defence, pursuant to UN authority, or aggressively and without UN authorisation. In the last case, the act of using force would typically be regarded as illegal.[189] However, neither of this affects occupation as such because of the fundamental principle, as mentioned earlier, of the *jus ad bellum* and *jus in bello* separability.[190]

The element of consent should not be forgotten either. When a territory is placed under UN MNF authority or UN administration, the rules of IHL on

---

184 B. F. Klappe, 'The Law of International Peace Operations', in D. Fleck (ed.), *The Handbook of International Humanitarian Law* (3rd edn., Oxford: Oxford University Press, 2014) 611–646, at 615.

185 SC Res. 1244 (1999).

186 SC Res. 745 (1992); see more generally F. M. Buerger, 'Analysis of UN Peacekeeping in Cambodia' (Naval War College, November 1994), available at www.dtic.mil/dtic/tr/fulltext/u2/a283479.pdf (visited 5 December 2016).

187 T. Ferraro, 'The Applicability of the Law of Occupation to Peace Forces', in G. L. Beruto (ed.), *International Humanitarian Law, Human Rights and Peace Operations* (International Institute of Humanitarian Law, Sanremo, 4–6 September 2008) 133–167, at 136.

188 R. Wilde, *International Territorial Administration: How Trusteeship and the Civilising Mission Never Went Away* (Oxford: Oxford University Press, 2008), at 356–357; see also S. R. Ratner, 'Foreign Occupation and International Territorial Administration', *supra* note 163, at 697.

189 S. R. Ratner, 'Foreign Occupation and International Territorial Administration', *supra* note 163, at 698.

190 M. Zwanenburg, 'United Nations and International Humanitarian Law', *Max Planck Encyclopedia of Public International Law* (2015) § 23, available at http://opil.ouplaw.com/view/10.1093/law:epil/9780199231690/law-9780199231690-e1675 (visited 5 December 2016).

occupied territories do not apply if consent has been given.[191] Nevertheless, the ICRC considers that for the applicability of the law of occupation, it makes no difference whether an occupation has received UN SC approval, what its aim is, or indeed whether it is called an *invasion, liberation, administration*, or *occupation*, as solely the facts on the ground establish its application.[192]

In this way, wherever effective control (OL) over territory is exercised by an international organisation and there is no consent by the territorial state, under Article 42 HR 1907, Common Article 2 GCs, and Article 1 AP I 1977 the relevant rules of IHL should apply to UN operations, too.[193] What therefore matters are the UN forces' actions, and the responsibilities they perform, by virtue of which they are exercising effective control (OL), and not so much whether the UN perceives itself as the source of authority in the area of operation.[194]

The absence of consent is an integral element in qualifying the UN as an occupant. This is because, firstly, the nature of occupation as seen before is non-consensual. Secondly, the UN, like any other actor in a situation of occupation (i.e. a state, and even the UN is composed of member states[195]), may keep the territorial government from exercising its authority. This would also extend to a scenario where there is no government and the UN MNF would be the only one to exercise territorial control. If there remains a doubt that consent was extended genuinely, its legality should be assessed (see also section 2.4.2).

The counter-position to this could argue that occupation law only applies in IACs, and that the UN cannot be a party to such an armed conflict simply because it is a supra-national and not a national actor, and therefore not "bound by the same rules as their enemies."[196] Yet UN SC Res. No. 1327 clearly states:

> the need for any provisions for a peacekeeping operation to meet minimum conditions, including [. . .] compliance with the rules and principles of international law, in particular international humanitarian, human rights and refugee law.[197]

---

191 M. Sassòli, A. A. Bouvier, and A. Quintin, *How Does Law Protect in War?*, Vol. 1 (3rd edn., Geneva: ICRC, 2011), at 381; see further C. Emanuelli, *Les Actions Militaires de l'Onu et le Droit International Humanitaire* (Montreal: Wilson et Lafleur Itée, 1995), at 40, where the author attaches the possibility of UN forces being an occupant to Chapter 7 of the UN Charter, where Article 42 excludes the consent of the state. See also C. Greenwood, 'International Humanitarian Law and United Nations Military Operations', *supra* note 144, at 10–12.

192 ICRC, *Occupation and International Humanitarian Law: Questions and Answers*, Resource Centre, 4 August 2008, available at www.icrc.org/eng/resources/documents/misc/634kfc.htm (visited 5 December 2016)

193 ICRC, *Multinational Forces* (Overview), *supra* note 163.

194 T. Ferraro, 'The Applicability of the Law of Occupation to Peace Forces', *supra* note 187, at 146.

195 D. Shraga, 'The United Nations', *supra* note 166, at 67.

196 M. Sassòli, A. A. Bouvier and A. Quintin, *How Does Law Protect in War?*, *supra* note 191, at 381.

197 UN SC Res.1327 (2000); see also S. Vité, 'L'applicabilité du droit de l'occupation militaire aux opérations des organisations internationales', *Current Challenges to the Law of*

46   *Effective control in occupation law*

Yet somehow the transformative aspect of a UN mandate would run counter to the legal obligation of preserving the status quo of an occupied territory's institutions and laws.[198] However, to the extent that UN missions are confined to enforcing peace and nothing more, there is no *a priori* contradiction with the law of military occupation, which equally speaks of maintaining law and order and ensuring the safety and well-being of the local population.[199] This amounts to the same purpose as enforcing and then keeping peace in a loose sense. Hence, that a UN enforcement operation "ousting a legitimate sovereign and administering a territory in accordance with the Hague Regulations and the Fourth Geneva Convention, should not, in theory, be excluded."[200]

All this suggests that one needs to assess whether UN missions, both peace-keeping and peace-enforcing, fulfil the following:[201]

1   The UN mission has to be stationed on a territory without the consent of the "receiving" state;
2   The governmental authorities have been rendered partially or completely incapable to perform their functions due to the presence of the UN mission, or were initially incapable (e.g. in failed states); and
3   The UN mission is capable of exercising governmental functions in lieu of the affected state.[202]

This brings us to the issue of the various states contributing their armed forces to a UN mission.[203] The question then arises whether each state contributing such a contingent can be considered an occupant or whether the UN alone carries that status.[204]

3.3   *The formula for ascertaining the responsibility of the UN and troop-contributing states*

Article 7 of the ILC Articles on the Responsibility of International Organisations sets forth the criteria for the attribution of responsibility for the conduct of state

---

     Occupation: Proceedings of the Bruges Colloquium, 20–21 October 2005, 93–100, at 95; B. F. Klappe, 'The Law of International Peace Operations', *supra* note 184, at 618 ff.

198   S. Vité, 'L'applicabilité du droit de l'occupation militaire', *supra* note 197, at 98; on transformative occupation more generally, see A. Carcano, *Transformation of Occupied Territory in International Law* (Leiden: Brill/Martinus Nijhoff Publishers, 2015); and G. Fox, 'Transformative Occupation and the Unilateralist Impulse', 94 *International Review of the Red Cross* (2012) 237–266.

199   D. Shraga, 'The United Nations', *supra* note 166, at 69.

200   Ibid., at 70.

201   T. Ferraro, 'The Applicability of the Law of Occupation to Peace Forces', *supra* note 187, at 154.

202   T. Ferraro, *Expert Meeting*, *supra* note 3, at 33–34.

203   Article 43 UN Charter; see also Article 44 UN Charter.

204   S. R. Ratner, 'Foreign Occupation and International Territorial Administration', *supra* note 163, at 701–703; C. Greenwood, 'International Humanitarian Law and United Nations Military Operations', *supra* note 144, at 18–19.

organs, or agents of another international organisation, that are placed at the disposal of an international organisation. Their conduct "shall be considered under international law an act of the latter organization if the organization exercises effective control over that conduct."[205]

The crux of the analysis of this article is again "effective control", but this time connecting a specific conduct to an international organisation – or not, in which case it would be the troop-contributing state or organisation which is responsible.[206] Pursuant to this article, the seconded organ remains to a certain degree an organ of the seconding state or organisation. For instance, when a state places its military force at the disposal of the UN, it preserves disciplinary powers and criminal jurisdiction over the members of the national contingent.[207] The attribution of the responsibility for the conduct to the seconding actor or to the receiving international organisation is based on the kind of control exercised over the specific conduct of the organ or agent placed at the receiving organisation's disposal.[208] In other words, who is exercising effective control over a specific conduct clarifies which entity – the contributor or the recipient – is responsible for it.[209] In combination with effective control (OL) over the territory, answering the responsibility question determines who is the occupant.

The main problem relates to determining the meaning of *effective control* in this context.[210] Here, control does not concern the issue whether a certain conduct is attributable at all to a state or an international organisation, but rather to which entity conduct has to be attributed: the contributing state, organisation, or the receiving organisation.[211] In other words, one of the two is inevitably bound to be exercising effective control over the actions of the troops. The advantage of such an approach is that it narrows the search for responsibility to only two options: the sending state or the receiving international organisation. However, which of the two still has to be identified, and the mechanism via which this is done is effective control. The question now is whether *this* effective control is the

---

205 Article 7 ILC Draft Articles on the Responsibility of International Organisations (2011).
206 B. Montejo, 'The Notion of "Effective Control" Under the Articles on the Responsibility of International Organisations', in M. Ragazzi (ed.), *Responsibility of International Organisations* (Leiden: Martinus Nijhoff Publishers, 2013), 389–404, at 403.
207 *Draft Articles on the Responsibility of International Organisations, with Commentaries* (United Nations, 2011), at 20; see also S. R. Ratner, 'Foreign Occupation and International Territorial Administration', *supra* note 163, at 701. On the issue of international personnel taking part in peace support operations, see F. Hampson, 'Administration of Justice, Rule of Law and Democracy, Economic and Social Council', E/CN.4/Sub.2/2005/42, 7 July 2005.
208 *Draft Articles on the Responsibility of International Organisations, supra* note 207, at 20.
209 Ibid., at 21.
210 P. Palchetti, 'The Allocation of Responsibility for Internationally Wrongful Acts Committed in the Course of Multinational Operations', 95 *International Review of the Red Cross* (2013) 727–742, at 732.
211 *Draft Articles on the Responsibility of International Organisations, supra* note 207, at 21.

48 *Effective control in occupation law*

same as understood in the law of state responsibility (SR). To answer this, the facts on the ground should be assessed.

However, once the IHL threshold applicability has been crossed for the purposes of occupation, when ascertaining UN or the troop-contributing states' responsibility, one should not examine UN occupation in a manner in which only the contributed troops *or* the UN appointed administration exercise(s) control over the actions of the troops. Certain acts may well occur outside the command and control of the UN, and/or under the control of the troop-contributing state. The words of the ILC Special Rapporteur Gaja suggests that effective control in this regard may shift the responsibility accordingly:

> This implies that, with regard to a United Nations peacekeeping force, while in principle the conduct of the force should be attributed to the United Nations, effective control of a particular conduct may belong to the contributing State rather than the United Nations.[212]

Matters became even more complicated when the ECtHR – in *Behrami and Behrami v. France* and *Saramati v. France, Germany and Norway* – interpreted effective control to mean "ultimate authority and control" as opposed to "effective command of the relevant operational matters".[213] The ECtHR found that the UN SC had retained such ultimate authority and control whereas "the operational command" was delegated to NATO, who in turn established KFOR.[214] This delegation rested on UN SC Resolution 1244 and was borne out by five factors:[215]

1 Chapter 7 allowing the UN SC to delegate to states and international organisations;
2 The relevant power being a delegable power;
3 Delegation being prior and made explicit in the Resolution;
4 Limiting delegation via setting out the objectives, roles, and responsibilities; and
5 The leadership of the military presence being required, by Resolution 1244, "to report to the UNSC so as to allow the UNSC to exercise its overall authority and control".[216]

---

212 G. Gaja, *Eighth Report on the Responsibility of International Organisations*, UN Doc. A/CN.4/640, 14 March 2011, at 13.
213 Behrami and Behrami v. France and Saramati v. France, Germany and Norway, ECtHR (2007) (App. no. 71412/01) § 140; see also A. Orakhelashvili, 'Human Rights Protection During Extra-territorial Military Operations: Perspectives on International and English Law', in N. White and C. Henderson (eds.), *Research Handbook on International Conflict and Security Law: Jus ad Bellum, Jus in Bello and Jus Post Bellum* (London: Edward Elgar Publishing, 2013) 598–637, at 601.
214 Ibid., § 133.
215 Ibid., § 134.
216 Ibid.

In short, the Court viewed the UN SC to have retained general, i.e. overall authority and control over the entire mission, thus broadening the scope of its responsibility so that the impugned action was attributable to the UN, as opposed to effective control, which would mean controlling a certain action in a material time.

The UN expressed its opposition to this view by firmly upholding the ILC Articles on the Responsibility of International Organisations. The UN Secretary General regarded it "understood that the international responsibility of the United Nations will be limited in the extent of its effective operational control."[217] In other words, UN responsibility would arise based on control strictly relating to a concrete operation, premised, in my view, on the rationale that *one's actions generate one's responsibility.* The UK's Lord Bingham, too, in the Al-Jedda case concerning UK troop actions in Iraq within the context of the MNF there, upheld the effective control test when inspecting UN responsibility: "It cannot realistically be said that US and UK forces were under the effective command and control of the UN, or that UK forces were under such command and control when they detained the appellant."[218]

Thus, when the ECtHR dealt with *Al-Jedda v. United Kingdom*, it seems to have altered its previous approach by adopting the effective control criterion of Article 7 (then Article 5):

> the Court considers that the United Nations Security Council had neither effective control nor ultimate authority and control over the acts and omissions of troops within the Multinational Force and that the applicant's detention was not, therefore, attributable to the United Nations.[219]

But the Court's dictum is still not clear enough. Note that effective control does not stand alone; instead, the formulation – "nor ultimate authority and control" – is repeated from Behrami and Saramati. One therefore wonders why the Court did not fully abandon the latter formulation and what it could possibly mean.

A possible interpretation as to where this test is anchored is Article 17.2 ILC Articles on the Responsibility of International Organisations (2011).[220] Here, under specific conditions, an organisation bears responsibility for having authorised a state to commit an act that is unlawful if committed by the organisation. For Palchetti, Article 17 rests on the idea that since the organisation, by its authorisation, exercised a form of "normative control" over the state, it has to

---

217 *Report of the Secretary General on the United Nations Interim Administration Mission in Kosovo,* S/2008/354, 12 June 2008, § 16; see also B. Montejo, 'The Notion of "Effective Control" ', *supra* note 206, at 402.

218 R (on the Application of Al-Jedda) (FC) (Appellant) v. Secretary of State for Defence (Respondent) Opinion of Lord Bingham of Cornhill, House of Lords, Session 2007–08, *on appeal from:[2006] EWCA Civ 327* § 23.

219 *Al-Jedda v. United Kingdom,* ECtHR (2011) (App. no. 27021/08) § 84.

220 P. Palchetti, 'The Allocation of Responsibility', *supra* note 210, at 738–739.

50 *Effective control in occupation law*

bear the consequences of its contribution to the wrongful act. In this way, some common characteristics with the *ultimate control and authority test* applied by the ECtHR emerge, as they both appear to rely on the "normative control" exercised by the organisation rather than effective control.[221] Consequently, how to define normative control? The following explanation may be offered: normative[222] control is a form of control that governs the relationship between an international organisation and a state, based on the former's values and judgments. Typically, normative control takes the form of explicit authorisations as understood by Article 17.2 (acts "committed *because* of that authorization").[223]

It is submitted here that some of the confusion is caused by disregarding the hypothesis of *concrete actions generating responsibility*. If one engages in a certain act, it is only logical that the carrying out of the act is controlled, to a certain extent and via a certain level of control, by an actor. If this action is sought to be successful, a *see-through approach* has to be taken so that the act actually materialises – in other words, the act in question has to be controlled effectively. The result would then be that both lawful and unlawful actions generate responsibility. One possible way to view and explain the *ultimate control and authority test* is to regard it in a way that if it were not for effective control, ultimate control would not materialise. Put differently, because effective control (SR) existed during the action, ultimate control over and thus for the action comes to life. One triggers the other.

While the criterion of effective control (SR) is gaining ground in practice, its application by national courts may add additional factors, raising the bar further in its interpretation. At least this is what can be inferred from *Nuhanović*, where the Hague Court of Appeal employed not only the understanding of effective control embodied in Article 7, but viewed this threshold to also encompass an obligation extending to both the UN and states to prevent certain actions from actually happening:

> Significance should be given not only to the question whether the conduct constituted the execution of a specific instruction, issued by the United Nations or the State, but also to the question whether, if there was no such specific instruction, the United Nations or the State had the power to prevent the conduct concerned.[224]

Nada v. Switzerland, while not concerned with multinational peace operations, may equally be considered as the ECtHR's attempt to set the record straight

---

221 Ibid., at 739.
222 Normative is defined as "expressing value judgments or prescriptions as contrasted with stating facts"; see Collins Dictionary, available at www.collinsdictionary.com/dictionary/english/normative (visited 5 December 2016).
223 Ibid.
224 The Hague Court of Appeal, Nuhanović v. Netherlands, Appeal Judgment, 5 July 2011, ILDC 1742 (NL 2011) § 5.9.

Effective control in occupation law 51

regarding the created uncertainty. The intervening French government argued that the measures taken by a UN member to implement SC resolutions under Chapter 7 of the UN Charter were attributable to the United Nations – very much as in Behrami and Saramati, where the impugned acts and omissions of KFOR, whose powers had been delegated to it by the Security Council under Chapter 7 of the Charter, as well as those of UNMIK, a subsidiary organ of the United Nations set up under the same chapter, were directly attributable to the UN.[225] However, the Court did not endorse this stance, opining instead that measures imposed by SC resolutions are implemented at national level, in this case by Switzerland; after all, the applicant's request for exemption from the ban on entry into Swiss territory related to the *national implementation*. The alleged violations of the ECHR were, therefore, attributable to Switzerland alone.[226]

To conclude, if the question about UN responsibility should be established for a specific act involving a UN mission and their contributing states within an occupation context, the following should be assessed: Were the forces of country X placed at the disposal of the UN as part of a UN force? Did the UN exercise effective control (SR) over the conduct of these forces? Can the specific conduct of X's forces be attributed to the UN rather than to country X? Did the UN have effective command and control over the conduct of X's forces when the action was carried out, e.g. issuing directions during the materialisation of the act or through the involvement of UN personnel?[227]

Moreover, should the question arise as to who among the troop-contributing states wielded effective control (OL) over the territory, then what the different contingents were actually doing at the specific time should be examined. In this regard, differentiating between coalition members according to their functions and duties is important. When it, therefore, comes to situations of occupation, UN occupation rests on effective control (OL) over territory where more than one entity is involved: the UN as well as troop-contributing states. In addition, because the UN has international legal personality, it may be in control of certain aspects of the mission, such as the governance of the territory or appointing officials. Nevertheless, while states contribute their troops to the mission, they still have their own officers and troop commanders accountable to them, and a number of their decisions have to be taken in consultation with their home governments before embarking on a task. For some actions, therefore, the UN would be responsible, while for others, the contributed troops. In short, one should always look at the actual actions and tasks carried out, and whoever is fulfilling a task is exercising effective control as understood by both the law of state responsibility and the Draft Articles on the Responsibility of International

---

225 Nada v. Switzerland, ECtHR (2012) (App. no. 10593/08) § 120.
226 Ibid., § 121.
227 This formula is based on R (on the Application of Al-Jedda) (FC) (Appellant) v. Secretary of State for Defence (Respondent), Opinion of Lord Bingham of Cornhill, § 22.

52　*Effective control in occupation law*

Organisations. At the end of the day, both share the same understanding of effective control (SR).[228]

Conclusions

This chapter has clarified the necessary test for establishing control over territory for the purposes of military occupation in IHL. The wording in Article 42 HR 1907, "actually placed under the authority", was shown to mean effective control (OL),[229] which in turn consists of the following, cumulative elements:

1　State A's military forces are physically present on the territory in question. Such a presence is not consented to by the original territorial government;
2　The original government of the territory has been totally or partially overcome by state A's military presence and, because of such a presence, cannot exercise its governmental powers; and
3　State A's military forces are in a position to, that is they *can*, exercise authority over the total or parts of a territory. However, there is no need to actually set up military or civilian administrative apparatus on the ground, although this must remain a possibility *in principle*.[230]

Examining instances of MNF control – UN SC endorsed or not – over territory as well as UN operations has revealed that there can be more than one occupant. International organisations such as the UN may obtain such a status, depending on whether they exercise effective control (OL) as just defined over a portion of the territory. Finally, the way in which the responsibility of the UN or one or more troop-contributing state(s) can be established is through assessing who exercised effective control (SR) over a specific action pursuant to Article 7 of the ILC Articles on the Responsibility of International Organisations.

228　See also Chatham House, *International Law Discussion Group on Legal Responsibility of International Organisations in International Law*, 10 February 2011, at 4, available at www.chathamhouse.org/sites/files/chathamhouse/public/Research/International%20 Law/il100211summary.pdf (visited 5 December 2016).
229　See Sargsyan v. Azerbaijan, ECtHR (2015) (App. no. 40167/06) § 94; Chiragov and Others v. Armenia, ECtHR (2015) (App. no 13216/05) § 96.
230　See, however, H. Cuyckens, *Revisiting the Law of Occupation* (Leiden: Brill/Martinus Nijhoff Publishers, 2018), at 25 where only two conditions are advanced: "(1) the occupying power has rendered the former government incapable of publicly exercising its authority in the area; and (2) the occupying power is in a position to substitute its own authority for that of the legitimate power in the occupied territory."

2 Occupation by an intermediary

1. Introduction

This chapter explores a type of control that states started to rely upon in view of avoiding the status of military occupant: *controlling a territory through an intermediary, i.e. via de facto local authorities or an armed group.* Such type of control is identified as indirect effective control and the ensuing situation as "long arm occupation".[1] This chapter thus explores the control of a state over an armed group or a local authority for the purposes of military occupation and *not* the control of that armed group or de facto authority over territory.

Whenever an armed group controls a given territory and fights a state without any involvement of an outside state, there is a NIAC and no laws of military occupation apply.[2] However, if another state has overall control (SR/IHL) over that armed group, the conflict may in fact be an IAC[3] and there could be a situation of military occupation. Would the HR 1907 and GC IV then also be applicable to the actions of the armed group and/or the de facto authorities? It is therefore essential to determine what status the outside state has, whether the armed group is its agent, and whether consequently the whole situation amounts to an occupation. Following on from this, a further enquiry emerges as to whether certain IHL instruments contain their own test of control over the armed group through which territory is occupied. To answer that, the final section of this chapter examines Article 4 GC III ("belonging to a party to the conflict") and Article 29 GC IV ("by its *agents*").

---

1 T. Ferraro (ed.), *Expert Meeting Occupation and Other Forms of Administration of Foreign Territory* (Geneva: ICRC, 2012), at 23.
2 Y. Dinstein, *Non-International Armed Conflicts in International Law* (Cambridge: Cambridge University Press, 2014), at 222.
3 T. Ferraro, 'The ICRC's Legal Position on the Notion of Armed Conflict Involving Foreign Intervention and on Determining the IHL Applicable to This Type of Conflict', 97 *International Review of the Red Cross* (2015) 1227–1252, at 1249.

54 *Occupation by an intermediary*

1.1 Preliminary remarks

During a NIAC,[4] states are often fearful that their sovereignty is violated by the dissident armed forces they are fighting gaining international recognition.[5] States have never regarded IAC and NIAC as being on the same footing. The use of force within state boundaries is inherent in the concept of the modern state, which bars groups within that state from conducting war against other factions or the government.[6] In international law, the recognition of belligerency of an armed group by a state opposing it transforms a NIAC into an IAC.[7] The possibility of a non-state armed group becoming an occupant *strictu sensu*, in times of a NIAC, was spurned by the Special Court of Sierra Leone.[8] It concluded that the rights and duties of occupying powers under IHL did not regulate the Revolutionary United Fronts' actions in the Kailahun District, or in any other district, during the NIAC that existed in Sierra Leone.[9] In other words, the "legal architecture of belligerent occupation does not fit NIACs, since neither areas seized by insurgents nor those retained or recovered by the Government can be regarded as occupied territories in the sense of IAC *jus in bello*".[10]

However, outside control exercised by an intervening state over an intermediary may indeed give rise to occupation. The question is what level of control: effective (SR) or overall (SR/IHL)? There is no unified stance on this question and divergent views are expressed. Sassòli and Benvenisti, for instance, side with effective control (SR),[11] while Ferraro argues for overall control (SR/IHL).[12]

---

4 S. Sivakumaran, *The Law of Non-International Armed Conflict* (Oxford: Oxford University Press, 2012), at 529; L. Moir, *The Law of Internal Armed Conflict* (Cambridge: Cambridge University Press, 2002), at 24–29; L. Zegveld, *The Accountability of Armed Opposition Groups in International Law* (Cambridge: Cambridge University Press, 2002), at 141; A. Roberts and S. Sivakumaran, 'Law Making by Non-State Actors: Engaging Armed Groups in the Creation of International Humanitarian Law', 37 *Yale Journal of International Law* (2012) 108–152, at 132–134; M. Sassòli, 'Taking Armed Groups Seriously: Way to Improve Their Compliance with International Humanitarian Law', 1 *Journal of International Humanitarian Legal Studies* (2010) 5–51, at 12.

5 R. Bartels, 'Timelines, Borderlines and Conflicts', 873 *International Review of the Red Cross* (2009) 35–67, at 47–54.

6 M. Sassòli, A. A. Bouvier, and A. Quintin, *How Does Law Protect in War?*, Vol. 1 (3rd edn., Geneva: ICRC, March 2011), at 323.

7 Y. Dinstein, *The International Law of Belligerent Occupation* (Cambridge: Cambridge University Press, 2009), at 34; H. Wilson, *International Law and the Use of Force by National Liberation Movements* (Oxford: Clarendon Press, 1988), at 27; see additionally N. Bhuta, 'The Role International Actors Other Than States Can Play in the New World Order', in A. Cassese (ed.), *Realising Utopia: The Future of International Law* (Oxford: Oxford University Press, 2012) 61–75.

8 Judgment, *Sesay, Kallon and Gbao* (SCSL-04-15-T), Trial Chamber I, 2 March 2009, § 988.

9 Ibid. §§ 982–988.

10 Y. Dinstein, *Non-International Armed Conflicts, supra* note 2, at 222.

11 M. Sassòli, 'The Concept and the Beginning of Occupation', in A. Clapham, P. Gaeta, and M. Sassòli (eds.), *The 1949 Geneva Conventions: A Commentary* (Oxford: Oxford University Press, 2015) 1390–1419, at 1400; E. Benvenisti, *The International Law of Occupation* (Oxford: Oxford University Press, 2013), at 62.

12 T. Ferraro, 'Determining the Beginning and End of an Occupation Under International Humanitarian Law', 885 *International Review of the Red Cross* (2015) 133–163, at 158; also

Occupation by an intermediary 55

Indirect effective control is also applied to scenarios where a state exercises effective control over the territory of another state not through its own armed forces, but indirectly, as a result of "effective authority" or "decisive influence" exercised over a subordinate local administration.[13]

It thus becomes indispensable to define precisely what renders state A a military occupant when state B lost control of its territory to a de facto authority or an armed group. Is an armed presence of that state necessary for this purpose? What level and type of control is needed by state A over the de facto authority and/or the armed group on the territory of state B? The term *decisive influence*, introduced by the ECtHR in the case of Ilaşcu, also requires clarification.

1.2 Control over armed groups and subordinate governments/de facto authorities

States have often used armed groups and subordinate governments to channel their interests in the aftermath of military interventions and during situations of military occupation. The latter practice was employed for example during WWII, when Nazi Germany installed collaborationist regimes throughout Europe.[14] These regimes were referred to as *puppet governments*, for instance the Vichy government under Philippe Pétain (1940–44) in France[15] or the Hellenic State (1941–1945) in Greece.[16]

In international law, labelling a government a puppet regime signifies that it is divested from exercising any legitimate authority. The appellation must "be reserved to extreme cases of external dependency."[17] In times of military occupation, the external dependency of a puppet government may more easily be noticeable, as it is often the occupant's very creation and instrument.[18] The Greek

---

T. Ferraro, 'The ICRC's Legal Position', *supra* note 3, at 1249; see additionally R. Kolb et S. Vité, *Le droit de l'occupation militaire: perspectives historiques et enjeux juridiques actueles* (Bruxelles: Bruylant, 2009), at 180–181: "in the case of exercising indirect authority, via global or effective control of an intermediary, it is not excluded that certain obligations arising from the law of occupation might be applicable selectively, at least indirectly" (own translation).

13 D. Murray et al., *Practitioners' Guide to Human Rights Law in Armed Conflict* (Oxford: Oxford University Press, 2016), at 72; see also UK Ministry of Defence, *The Manual of the Law of Armed Conflict* (Oxford: Oxford University Press, 2004), § 11.3.1, at 276.

14 On WWII, see A. Beevor, *The Second World War* (London: Phoenix, 2013); T. D. Snyder, *Bloodlands: Europe Between Hitler and Stalin* (New York: Basic Books, 2012).

15 N. Atkin, *Pétain* (London; New York: Routledge, 2014), at 131–156.

16 M. Mazower, *Griechenland unter Hitler* (Frankfurt am Main: Fischer, 2016), at 42; see also Y. Durand, *Le Nouvel ordre européen nazi (1938–1945)* (Paris: Éditons Complexe, 1990).

17 G. Nolte, 'Intervention by Invitation', *Max Planck Encyclopedia of Public International Law* (2010), § 18, available at http://opil.ouplaw.com/view/10.1093/law:epil/9780199231690/law-9780199231690-e1702?prd=EPIL (visited 3 January 2017).

18 K. Marek, *Identity and Continuity of States in Public International Law* (Geneva: Droz, 1968), at 114.

56 *Occupation by an intermediary*

Criminal Court of Heraklion in Crete in 1945 referred to such governments as mere organs of the occupant.[19]

Constituting "mere organs of the occupant" indicates that such de facto governments are under the *total control*, carrying out orders of the occupying state and acting according to the latter's will. In such cases, the responsibility of the occupant should be ascertained based on Article 4 of the ILC Articles on the Responsibility of States.

Clear-cut cases of total dependency in times of military occupation could be expected to be extinct, due not least to the emergence of the obligation by states to respect each other's sovereignty and not interfere with internal matters. Instead, as mentioned earlier, states covertly intervene, using de facto authorities and/or armed groups. A recent example are the alleged "serious violations of the Covenant in the Donbas region of Ukraine by forces over which the State party [Russia] appears to have considerable influence which may amount to effective control."[20]

Such interferences also present a challenge for establishing situations of military occupation. In this respect, the ICRC Report submitted that a state would be an occupant pursuant to IHL when it enforced overall control over de facto local authorities or other organised groups that have effective control over a territory or part thereof.[21] However, the report is not clear on how to apply this overall control test. Should it be understood as in Tadić, determining the nature of the armed conflict involving foreign intervention, or as controlling the territory in an overall, general manner with fewer troops stationed on the territory?

In Tadić, the ICTY Appeals Chamber advanced that unquestionable evidence was needed to demonstrate a state had overall control (SR/IHL) over a group:

> if [. . .] the controlling State is not the territorial state where the armed clashes occur or where at any rate the armed units perform their acts, more extensive and compelling evidence is required to show that the State is genuinely in control of the units or groups not merely by financing and equipping them, but also by generally directing or helping plan their actions.[22]

The Chamber also deemed that in case a foreign state had territorial aspirations, the link between an armed group and that state would be easier to prove:

> Where the controlling State in question is an adjacent State with territorial ambitions on the State where the conflict is taking place, and the controlling

---

19 Judgment, *In re G.* (Criminal Court of Heraklion) (Crete) (1943–1945) 12 AD 437 Case No 151) cited in K. Marek, *Identity and Continuity of States*, *supra* note 18, at 114; Col. R. A. Picciotti, 'Problems of Occupied Nations After the Termination of Occupation', 33 *Military Law Review* (1966) 25–57, at 33.

20 Human Rights Committee, *Concluding Observations on the Seventh Periodic Report of the Russian Federation*, CCPR/C/RUS/CO/7, 28 April 2015, § 6 (International Covenant on Civil and Political Rights).

21 T. Ferraro, *Expert Meeting*, *supra* note 1, at 23.

22 Judgment, *Tadić* (IT-94-1-A), Appeals Chamber, 15 July 1999, § 138.

State is attempting to achieve its territorial enlargement through the armed forces which it controls, it may be easier to establish the threshold.[23]

This book uses overall control (SR/IHL) both for assessing state responsibility and conflict classification under IHL (see Introduction). The subsequent analysis of the case law will further argue for the suitability and practicability of the overall control (SR/IHL) test for the purposes of establishing proxy occupation. Section 2 discusses outside state control over an armed group, whereas section 3 deals with control over de facto authorities.

2. Control over an armed group: examples

2.1 Croatia exercising control over the Croatian Defence Council (HVO)

The ICTY's Trial Chamber in Tadić considered that the relationship between de facto organs or agents and a foreign power included those circumstances where the foreign power occupied or operated within a certain territory solely through the acts of the local de facto organs or agents.[24] In Rajić, the prosecution argued that when Stupni Do was overrun by forces of the Croatian Defence Council (HVO) under the command of Ivica Rajić, and subsequently came under their control, the property of Stupni Do became protected because it was Bosnian property under the control of HVO forces, who in turn were to be regarded as part of the state on the opposite side, namely Croatia.[25] The Trial Chamber held that as the Bosnian Croats controlled the territory surrounding the village of Stupni Do, Croatia could be regarded as in control of the area in question.[26] Thus, when Stupni Do was invaded by HVO forces, the Bosnian village came under the control of Croatia as part of an IAC. Also, the property of Stupni Do became protected for the purposes of the grave breaches provisions of GC IV.[27]

The Trial Chamber furthered this reasoning in Blaškić, regarding the occupied territory as part of Bosnia and Herzegovina (BiH), within the enclaves dominated by the HVO, namely Vitez, Busova, and Kiseljak. In these enclaves, Croatia was an occupying power through the overall control (SR/IHL) it had over the HVO, the support it gave, and the close ties it maintained with it.[28] Using the same reasoning that applies to establishing the international nature of a conflict, "the overall control exercised by Croatia over the HVO means that at the time of its destruction, the property of the Bosnian Muslims was under the control of

---

23 Ibid., § 140.
24 Opinion and Judgment, *Tadić* (IT-94–1-T), Trial Chamber, 7 May 1997, § 584.
25 Review of the Indictment Pursuant to Rule 61 of the Rules of Procedure and Evidence, Rajić, Trial Chamber, 13 September 1996, § 38.
26 Ibid. § 42.
27 Ibid.
28 Ibid.

58 *Occupation by an intermediary*

Croatia and was in occupied territory."[29] Nevertheless, Sassòli regards this reasoning to be leading to an "absurd result":[30] Croatia had become an occupant in parts of Bosnia where it had never directed an armed group, and the HVO was itself assembled from (local) Bosnian Croats.[31] Also, HVO fighters had to comply with the rules applicable to an occupying power while "operating on territory inhabited by Bosnian Croats, including when carrying out activity on their own initiative while fighting against the Bosnian Government."[32]

In Naletilić, however, the ICTY Trial Chamber disagreed with the stance advanced in Blaškić. It held that the overall control (SR/IHL) test developed in Blaškić was not applicable when determining the existence of military occupation, since effective control (OL) was needed. This would be so because there is an essential distinction between determining a situation of occupation, on the one hand, and establishing the international nature of an armed conflict, on the other. While the overall control test would be suitable for the latter purpose, a further degree of control was required for the former.[33] Sassòli views such a "further degree of control" to be in need of additional clarification. For him, it remained unclear "whether effective control was required and, if so, whether the effective control must be exercised by the foreign state over the group, or alternatively by the group or the foreign state over the territory in question."[34]

The problem is that the ICTY did not examine whether there might have been an occupation by an intermediary. Based on what *kind* of control did the property of the Bosnian Muslims come under the control of the HVO and, through it, of Croatia? While Croatia was not itself in control of the territory, the HVO was. Hence, not the test of territorial control is of primary interest here. Instead, what matters is the *connection* between the overall control (SR/IHL) of Croatia over the HVO and, *at the same time*, the latter's effective control (OL) over territory. Neither the first nor the second element alone is sufficient to bring about a situation of occupation by an intermediary. Only the presence of both relationships of control at the same time does,[35] as shown in Figure 2.1.

The ICTY Appeals Chamber in Prlić et al.[36] confirmed that "Croatia through the HVO had actual authority over the relevant municipalities."[37] In so doing, the Appeals Chamber upheld the suitability of the overall control

---

29 Judgment, *Blaškić* (IT-95–14-IT), Trial Chamber, 3 March 2000, § 149.
30 M. Sassòli, 'The Concept and the Beginning of Occupation', *supra* note 11, at 1399.
31 Ibid.
32 Ibid.
33 Judgment, *Naletilić and Martinović* (IT-98–34-T), Trial Chamber, 31 March 2003, § 214.
34 M. Sassòli, 'The Concept and the Beginning of Occupation', *supra* note 11, at 1399.
35 ICRC Commentary of 2016, Convention I for the Amelioration of the Condition of the Wounded and Sick in Armed Forces in the Field (1949) Article 2: Application of the Convention, § 331 and § 332, available at https://ihl-databases.icrc.org/applic/ihl/ihl.nsf/Comment.xsp?action=openDocument&documentId=BE2D518CF5DE54EAC1257F7D0036B518 (visited 3 January 2017).
36 Judgment, *Prlić et al.* (IT-04–74-A), Appeals Chamber, 29 November 2017, Vol. 1.
37 Ibid., §334.

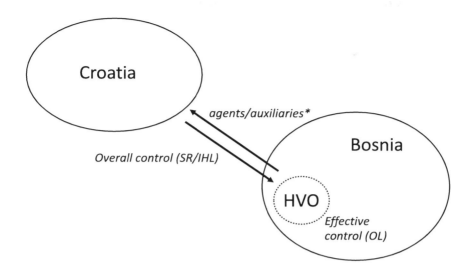

*ICRC Commentary of 2016, Geneva Convention I 1949, §140.

Figure 2.1 The indirect effective control test (ICTY)

Note: HVO = Croatian Defence Council

test (SR/IHL) against the submission of the accused (Petković) to rely on the effective control test (SR) instead.[38]

2.2 Uganda controlling the Congo Liberation Movement (MLC)

Another very relevant example concerns the ICJ's stance in *DRC v. Uganda*.[39] The DRC had requested that the ICJ adjudicate, amongst others, that the Republic of Uganda – by virtue of engaging in military and paramilitary activities against the DRC, by occupying its territory, and by actively extending military,

---

38 Ibid., § 308; The overall control test was also applied by the ICC when it had to determine the character of the armed conflict in the Central African Republic, see The Prosecutor v. Jean-Pierre Bemba Gombo (ICC-01/05-01/08 66/364), Trial Chamber III, 21 March 2016, § 130, § 302, § 654–656; see also The Prosecutor v. Thomas Lubanga Dyilo (Decision on the Confirmation of Charges) (ICC-01/04-01/06), Pre-Trial Chamber I, 29 January 2007, § 211: "the overall control test will be used to determine whether armed forces are acting on behalf of the first State."

39 See generally L. Arimatsu, 'The Democratic Republic of the Congo 1993–2010', in E. Wilmshurst (ed.), *International Law and the Classification of Conflicts* (Oxford: Oxford University Press, 2012) 146–203.

60 *Occupation by an intermediary*

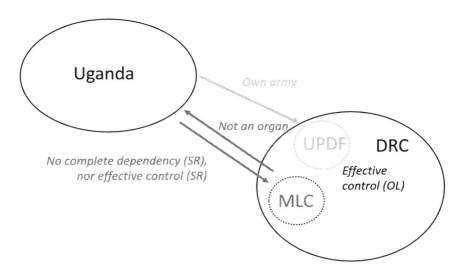

Figure 2.2 Occupation by intermediary (ICJ)

Note: DRC = Democratic Republic of Congo, UPDF = Uganda Peoples' Defence Forces, MLC = Congo Liberation Movement

logistic, economic, and financial support to irregular forces – had violated the principle of non-interference, including providing assistance to the parties of a civil war operating on the territory of another state.[40]

However, the ICJ saw no credible evidence that would have proven that Uganda had spawned the Congo Liberation Movement (MLC). It did not consider the MLC "an organ" of Uganda, as per Article 4 of the ILC Articles on Responsibility of States, nor an entity exercising elements of governmental authority on its behalf, as per Article 5 of that same instrument. The ICJ further examined whether the MLC's conduct took place "on the instructions of, or under the direction or control of" Uganda (Article 8 ILC Articles). Again, it found no evidence for this. The ICJ, therefore, applied both the complete dependency (SR) and effective control (SR) tests to the armed group – only to conclude that neither was met in this case, as shown in Figure 2.2.

In addition, while the DRC referred to the Ugandan officers' "indirect administration" through various Congolese rebel factions and the supervision by Ugandan officers of local elections in the territories controlled by Uganda Peoples' Defence Forces (UPDF), according to the ICJ the DRC did not provide specific

---

40 *Case Concerning Armed Activities on the Territory of the Congo (Democratic Republic of the Congo v Uganda)*, Judgment of 19 December 2005, §24 and §28, available at www.icj-cij.org/en/case/116 (visited 15 July 2017).

Occupation by an intermediary 61

evidence such authority was in fact exercised by the Ugandan armed forces in any areas other than Ituri. And although Uganda admitted that as of 1 September 1998 it exercised "administrative control" at Kisangani Airport, no proof was shown by the DRC which would have allowed the ICJ to characterise the presence of Ugandan troops stationed there as constituting military occupation. The ICJ also did not endorse the DRC's claim that Uganda was an occupying power in areas outside Ituri, which were controlled and administered by Congolese rebel movements: the evidence presented did not give rise to the view that these groups were "under the control" of Uganda.[41]

Thus, for the ICJ an outside state's responsibility for acts of armed groups that do not belong to its own armed forces is only triggered based on the complete dependency (SR) or effective control (SR) tests. While the ICJ did not dismiss the possibility of a state exercising control over territory through armed groups, to give rise to military occupation the necessary test is not overall control (SR/IHL) as advanced by the ICTY.

It thus seems that when the ICJ has to determine the existence of intermediary occupation, the effective control (SR) test is used for establishing state responsibility, whereas the effective control (OL) test is used for establishing whether an armed group controls the territory. In other words, when the ICJ deals with armed groups that do not belong to a state party to the conflict and when the responsibility of said state has to be established, the situation either falls under Article 4 or under Article 8 of the ILC Articles on Responsibility of States. Only if either of these two tests is met, and if the group over which control is wielded has effective control (OL) over the territory in question, can the respective state be considered an occupant.

2.3 Critical appraisal

In sum, while the ICTY employs the overall control (SR/IHL) test to both establish state responsibility and classify armed conflicts,[42] the ICJ uses the complete dependency (SR) and effective control (SR) tests to establish state responsibility in international law.[43] Therefore, the message that the ICJ conveys is that there

---

41 Ibid., §177, also § 160.

42 See primarily Judgment, *Tadić* (IT-94–1-A), Appeals Chamber, 15 July 1999, § 120–122, § 131; see A. Cassese, 'The Nicaragua and Tadić Tests Revisited in Light of the ICJ Judgment on Genocide in Bosnia', 18 *The European Journal of International Law* (2007) 649–668, at 663–664.

43 *Case Concerning Military and Paramilitary Activities in and Against Nicaragua (Nicaragua v. United States of America)*, Judgment of 27 June 1986, § 109–110, § 115, available at www.icj-cij.org/files/case-related/70/070-19860627-JUD-01-00-EN.pdf (visited 14 January 2020); *Case Concerning Application of the Convention on the Prevention and Punishment of the Crime of Genocide (Bosnia and Herzegovina v. Serbia and Montenegro)*, Judgment of 26 February 2007, § 400, § 403, § 406, available at www.icj-cij.org/files/case-related/91/091-20070226-JUD-01-00-EN.pdf (visited 15 July 2017); see also *Case Concerning Application of the Convention on the Prevention and Punishment of the Crime*

62   *Occupation by an intermediary*

are two different tests, one for conflict classification and another for state responsibility purposes (see Introduction). However, such a stance is problematic, for several reasons.

Firstly, if one follows the logic of the ICJ, even though there may be strong factual evidence to suggest that state A is involved in the armed conflict on the territory of state B through armed group X, state A would still not be responsible for the actions of that group. Put differently, having two separate tests could mean that state A is involved in a certain international conflict but would not be responsible for the actions carried out by armed group X, as the group is neither completely dependent on the state nor does the state possess effective control (SR) over it.

Secondly, another problem possibly arising is that when using a less stringent test for conflict classification purposes, i.e. overall control (SR/IHL) as put forth by the ICTY, that same overall control test is also employed for establishing state responsibility. So while there would be a single test both for establishing state responsibility and classifying a conflict, ascertaining state responsibility would be done through *a lower* threshold of control – contrary to what the ICJ had advanced. This raises the question of how international law understands state responsibility and attribution *per se*. In the Genocide case, what the ICJ advanced was that the Tadić and Nicaragua tests had been developed for two different situations, thereby separating conflict classification and state responsibility (see Introduction).[44] However, what the ICJ seems to have omitted from its analysis is that, in practice, when one begins to classify an armed conflict, a party to the conflict is identified based on its actions, because with its actions it actually participates in the armed conflict. This way, in light of military occupation, if one considers that for attributing state responsibility there is a separate test, this could mean that an occupying power is simply not responsible for acts that it engaged in on the territory it controlled whilst being an occupant. In maintaining this view, the more appropriate test to establish the occupant's responsibility – effective control (SR) or overall control (SR/IHL) – should be selected. Choosing overall control (SR/IHL) would lower the bar for establishing state responsibility and attribution. Yet, there still would *be* a bar which would ultimately pave the way to qualifying a situation as one of military occupation or not.

The opponents of the overall control (SR/IHL) test could argue that a danger is thus created in that *every* NIAC might end up being regarded as an occupation, or that even acts which are *not* committed by a state are attributed

---

of Genocide (Bosnia and Herzegovina v. Serbia and Montenegro)*, Judgment of 26 February 2007, Dissenting Opinion of Vice President Al-Khasawneh § 37–39, disagreeing with this stance (§ 39), available at www.icj-cij.org/files/case-related/91/091-20070226-JUD-01-01-EN.pdf (visited 14 January 2020).

44 See especially *Case Concerning Application of the Convention on the Prevention and Punishment of the Crime of Genocide (Bosnia and Herzegovina v. Serbia and Montenegro)*, Judgment of 26 February 2007, §§ 405–406, available at www.icj-cij.org/files/case-related/91/091-20070226-JUD-01-00-EN.pdf (visited 15 July 2017).

Occupation by an intermediary 63

to it. Nevertheless, one should not forget that if an armed group does not exercise effective control (OL) over territory, there is no such danger. At the same time, it still has to be demonstrated that the state does in fact exercise overall control (SR/IHL) over the armed group. The alternative to what is advanced here would be that, in order to establish intermediary/proxy occupation, the responsibility of state A for the actions of armed group X is only triggered through effective control (SR) as formulated by the ICJ. This would avoid the risk of turning every NIAC with some sort of foreign intervention into an IAC; additionally, attributing all acts committed by an armed group to the outside state is circumvented. Yet this would ultimately allow that state to escape its obligations under international law by creating and using "groups of individuals to undertake actions that are intended to damage, or in the event do damage, other states".[45]

The supporters of the effective control (SR) test should also perhaps query what happens when a state exerts effective control (SR) intermittently, whilst the proxy maintains effective control (OL) over the territory. In my understanding, for the test to be fully met, the outside state should sustain effective control (SR) over the proxy's each and every action continually and unfailingly. This may be difficult to maintain, as it may very well happen that effective control (SR) over the armed group is not constantly wielded but exercised only periodically. For example, when flight MH17 was downed in Ukrainian air space, pro-Russian separatists were widely held responsible. Moscow in turn said that a Ukrainian military jet or a missile launched from Ukrainian government-controlled territory was to blame.[46] Evidence then emerged pursuant to which a pro-Russian

---

45 A. Cassese, 'The Nicaragua and Tadić Tests', *supra* note 42, at 654.
46 L. Hardin and S. Walker, 'Flight MH17 Downed by Russian-Built Missile Dutch Investigators Say', *The Guardian*, 13 October 2015, available at www.theguardian.com/world/2015/oct/13/mh17-crash-report-plane-partially-reconstruced-blames-buk-missile-strike (visited 3 January 2017); see also *Application of the International Convention for the Suppression of the Financing of Terrorism and of the International Convention on the Elimination of All Forms of Racial Discrimination (Ukraine v. Russian Federation)*, Order of 19 April 2017, § 1, § 16, §§ 25–31, §66–67, §§ 75–77, available at www.icj-cij.org/files/case-related/166/166-20170419-ORD-01-00-EN.pdf (visited 4 April 2019): On 16 January 2017, Ukraine filed in the ICJ Registry an application instituting proceedings against Russia, alleging violations of the International Convention for the Suppression of the Financing of Terrorism of 9 December 1999 (ICSFT) and the International Convention on the Elimination of All Forms of Racial Discrimination of 21 December 1965 (CERD). With regards to ICSFT, Ukraine contended that in its eastern part of the territory, since the spring of 2014, Russia had systematically supplied 'illegal armed groups' such as Donetsk People's Republic (DPR), the Luhansk People's Republic (LPR), the Partisans of the Kharkiv People's Republic, and other associated groups and individuals with heavy weaponry, money, personnel, training, and by giving other support. Ukraine also argued that such assistance had been used not only to support combat against the Ukrainian authorities, but also to conduct terrorist attacks against civilians, within the meaning of Article 2, paragraph 1 (a) and (b) of the ICSFT, including downing of Flight MH17. See also *Application of the International Convention for the Suppression of the Financing of Terrorism and of the International Convention on the*

64 *Occupation by an intermediary*

separatist officer claimed the plane had been shot accidentally by a mixed team of anti-Ukrainian separatists and Russian military personnel.[47] The Ukrainian government later issued an audiotape of a phone conversation between an alleged pro-Russian rebel and an alleged Russian intelligence office right after the plane crash in which the former told the latter of the circumstances of the accident.[48] A lawsuit was also filed in a Chicago court, accusing Mr. Igor Girkin (former commander of the pro-Russian separatist forces in Eastern Ukraine, also known as "Strelkov") of orchestrating the shooting down, in addition to alleging that the Kremlin was complicit in the act.[49]

For some, this example does not pass the bar of the effective control test (SR); hence, Russia's responsibility is not triggered, although it was involved at least somehow. In other words, Russia could have created, financed, and equipped the armed group, as well as developed its overall strategy and directed every other action – but because it did not issue specific instructions for downing *this* plane, it would not be responsible. For others, Russia militarily equipping and financing the armed group and generally planning its activities is enough to establish that Russia had overall control (SR/IHL) over the anti-Ukrainian rebel forces; hence, Russia would be responsible. It also has to be pointed out that even within states, when de jure organs are given orders, they may not be reporting on the progress of their actions at each and every moment; not even *they* are controlled on a constant basis during such time as an act in question is occurring.

So in arguing for the adequacy of the effective control (SR) test for the purposes of proxy occupation, one should be aware that this level of control has to be firmly maintained over the proxy's actions, leaving no room for merely sporadic exercises. But states could deliberately avoid exerting control over intermediaries to such an extent that ultimately effective control (SR) is not met. The danger is that they will keep their control over the proxy somewhere just below the threshold of effective control (SR), retaining however substantial influence and leverage over the armed group. In this way, states do not have to fear for their responsibility to be engaged.

Neither Sassòli[50] nor Benvenisti[51] clearly state why effective control (SR) is a suitable test for establishing intermediary/proxy occupations. Both suggest that

---

Elimination of All Forms of Racial Discrimination (Ukraine v. Russian Federation), Judgment 8 November 2019, § 64, § 113, § 121, available at https://www.icj-cij.org/files/case-related/166/166-20191108-JUD-01-00-EN.pdf (visited 1 June 2020).

47 'Leaked MH17 Draft Report Blames Pro Russian Rebels', *Radio Free Europe* (2015), available at www.rferl.org/content/mh17-draft-report-points-to-pro-russian-rebels-ukraine/27130860.html (visited 3 January 2017).

48 Ibid.

49 D. Millward, 'MH17: Russian Separatist Leader Sued for $900 Million by Crash Victims', *The Telegraph*, 16 July 2015, available at www.telegraph.co.uk/news/worldnews/europe/ukraine/11742865/MH-17-Russian-separatist-leader-sued-for-900-million-by-crash-victims.html (visited 3 January 2017).

50 M. Sassòli, 'The Concept and the Beginning of Occupation', *supra* note 11, at 1400.

51 E. Benvenisti, *The International Law of Occupation*, *supra* note 11, at 62.

because military occupation is determined based on effective control (OL) over territory, the relationship between the outside state and the proxy should rest on effective control (SR), too. But is this so because occupation and state responsibility are based on stringent tests and overall control is a weaker test, therefore the latter is unsuitable? Or is it because, during occupation, a state has to control all the armed forces' actions?

In sum, the debate boils down to our understanding of effective control (SR).[52] If we follow the ICJ's original thinking based on the Nicaragua and Genocide cases, it amounts to state control over an armed group's *specific* operations and acts. However, it is submitted here that determining whether a situation is an occupation is already part of the broader conflict classification exercise. It now seems accepted that overall control (SR/IHL) as spelled out in Tadić can turn a NIAC into an IAC.[53] If one employs the effective control (SR) test solely to ascertain proxy occupations while regarding the overall control (SR/IHL) test to be suitable for such conflict transformation, the proponents of effective control (SR) turn a blind eye to a possible rift in the system of conflict classification, suggesting military occupation not to be part thereof. When a third state possesses overall control (SR/IHL) over an armed group, as developed in Tadić, and when this armed group then controls the territory as understood in occupation law, the situation should be labelled one of occupation. Due to the fact that effective control (OL) is not employed for identifying the international nature of an armed conflict, and because overall control (SR/IHL) is not used for ascertaining situations of occupation, marrying the two seems to follow the virtue of the exigencies of the situation on the ground.[54] Ultimately, this avoids a protection gap in the application of GC IV, i.e. even when there is control involved via proxies a state cannot shun its responsibilities under IHL.[55]

---

52 K. Schmalenbach, 'International Responsibility for Humanitarian Law Violations by Armed Groups', in H. Krieger (ed.), *Inducing Compliance with International Humanitarian Law* (Cambridge: Cambridge University Press, 2015) 470–503, at 477–486; S. Darcy, *Judges, Law and War: The Judicial Development of International Humanitarian Law* (Cambridge: Cambridge University Press, 2014), at 96; K. Kirss, 'Role of the International Court of Justice: Example of the Genocide Case', 3 *ACTA SOCIETATIS MARTENSIS* (2007/2008) 143–164, at 154–156.

53 ICRC, *Violence and the Use of Force* (Geneva: ICRC, July 2011), at 33; see also T. Ferraro, 'The ICRC's Legal Position', *supra* note 3, at 1249.

54 See, however, K. Mačák, *Internationalised Armed Conflicts in International Law* (Oxford: Oxford University Press, 2018), at 230: "the better approach is to separate the question of conflict qualification (determined by a test akin to the 'overall control' test propounded by the ICTY) from the question of the identification of the occupying power (determined by a case-by-case consideration of the facts on the ground and the degree of operational autonomy of the individual actors)." See also ibid., at 229.

55 ICRC Commentary of 2016, Convention (I) for the Amelioration of the Condition of the Wounded and Sick in Armed Forces in the Field, *supra* note 35, § 140.

3. Control over de facto authorities: examples

Two types of de facto authorities exist: de facto regimes and de facto states. The former are entities exercising a certain level of authority over a territory within a state,[56] coupled with a certain political structure and organisational capacity.[57] Such an entity aims to represent the territory it controls in the capacity of its official government.[58] Its aim is to be recognised as the official government, leaving the state and its territory intact.[59] The qualifier *de facto* means that the power it holds is actually illegal. An example of such an instance is the Ivorian election crisis in 2010, when Laurent Gbagbo refused to concede electoral defeat to former Prime Minister Alassane Ouattara.[60] The latter's electoral victory was strongly backed by the international community,[61] making the administration of Gbagbo a de facto regime, in turn.

A de facto state, on the other hand, is a geographical and political entity that has the features of a state but is not recognised and remains illegitimate in the international community's eyes.[62] Its main aim is the legitimisation of the secession from its parent state, thus acquiring independent statehood.[63] For example, while Kosovo has attained recognition by many members of the international community,[64] the TRNC, Abkhazia, South Ossetia, Transdniestria, and Nagorno Karabakh are not internationally recognised. Yet all of them claim to have successfully and legitimately seceded from their respective parent state.[65] Except

---

56 M. Schoiswhol, 'De Facto Regimes and Human Rights Obligations – The Twilight Zone of Public International Law', 6 *Austrian Review of International and European Law* (2001) 45–90, at 50; See also T. Baty, 'So-Called "De Facto Recognition"', 5 *Yale Law Journal* (1922) 469–488, at 472. See generally J. Nijman, *The Concept of International Legal Personality: An Inquiry Into History and Theory of International Law* (The Hague: T.M.C. Asser Press, 2004); D. Thürer, 'The "Failed State" and International Law', 836 *International Review of The Red Cross* (1999), available at www.icrc.org/eng/resources/documents/article/other/57jq6u.htm (visited 3 January 2017).

57 J. van Essen, 'De Facto Regimes in International Law', 28 *Merkourios – Utrecht Journal of International and European Law* 74 (2012) 31–49, at 32.

58 Ibid.

59 Ibid., at 33.

60 United Nations Operation in Côte d'Ivoire (UNOCI), Post-Election Crisis, available at www.un.org/en/peacekeeping/missions/unoci/elections.shtml (visited 3 January 2017).

61 J. van Essen, 'De Facto Regimes in International Law', *supra* note 57, at 33.

62 Ibid.; see also S. Pegg, *International Society and the De Facto State* (Brookfield, VT: Ashgate, 1998) at 26; J. A. Frowein, 'De Facto Regime', *Max Planck Encyclopedia of Public International Law* (2013) §§1–12, available at http://opil.ouplaw.com/view/10.1093/law:epil/9780199231690/law-9780199231690-e1395 (visited 3 January 2017).

63 J. van Essen, 'De Facto Regimes in International Law', *supra* note 57, at 33.

64 Republic of Kosovo, Ministry of Foreign Affairs, 'International Recognitions of the Republic of Kosovo', available at www.mfa-ks.net/?page=2,224 (visited 3 January 2017); see also R. Wilde, 'Kosovo (Advisory Opinion)', *Max Planck Encyclopedia of Public International Law* (2011) §§ 1–29, available at http://opil.ouplaw.com/view/10.1093/law:epil/9780199231690/law-9780199231690-e1307?prd=EPIL (visited 3 January 2017).

65 S. Casey-Maslen (ed.), *The War Report 2012* (Oxford: Oxford University Press, 2013).

Occupation by an intermediary   67

for Kosovo, all these examples also implicate an outside state and are widely referred to as occupied territories.[66] For this reason, the question addressed next is whether these instances constitute situations of military occupation and, if so, on what legal basis. Examining these cases helps identify the way in which indirect effective control operates in practice – or, in other words, how overall control (SR/IHL) is wielded by state A over a de facto authority who has effective control (OL) over territory in state B.

3.1 Crimea, Ukraine[67]

In February 2014, Russian troops without insignia (known as "little green men" or "polite people"[68]) took over Crimea's Supreme Council, asserting control over key sites across the peninsula such as Simferopol International Airport and military bases. After this takeover, the Crimean parliament held an emergency session and under dubious circumstances installed a new government.[69] On 11 March 2014, the regional parliament adopted the Declaration of Independence of Crimea with the clear aim that Crimea and the city of Sevastopol would

---

66 Ibid., at 29–37, 42–46 and 50–54.
67 See generally C. Walter, 'Postscript: Self-Determination, Secession, and the Crimean Crisis 2014', in C. Walter, A. von Ungern-Sternberg, and K. Abushov (eds.), *Self-Determination and Secession in International Law* (Oxford: Oxford University Press, 2014) 293–331. On Crimean secession and its integration into Russia, see A. Peters, 'The Crimean Vote of March 2014 as an Abuse of the Institution of the Territorial Referendum', in C. Calliess (ed.), *Staat und Mensch im Kontext des Völker und Europarechts: Liber Amicorum für Torsten Stein* (Baden-Baden: Nomos, 2015) 255–280; E. Milano, 'The Non-Recognition of Russia's Annexation of Crimea: Three Different Legal Approaches and One Unanswered Question', *Questions of International Law* (2014), available at www.qil-qdi.org/the-non-recognition-of-russias-annexation-of-crimea-three-different-legal-approaches-and-one-unanswered-question/ (visited 3 January 2017); R. Emmott, 'Putin Warns Ukraine Against Implementing EU Deal Letter', *Reuters*, 23 September 2014, available at www.reuters.com/article/us-ukraine-crisis-trade-idUSKCN0HI1T820140923 (visited 3 January 2017); 'Vladimir Putin Describes Secret Meeting When Russia Decided to Seize Crimea', *Agence France-Presse/The Guardian*, 9 March 2015, available at www.theguardian.com/world/2015/mar/09/vladimir-putin-describes-secret-meeting-when-russia-decided-to-seize-crimea (visited 3 January 2017); 'Prime Minister of Crimea Declared Crimea Would Support New Elected Ukrainian President', *Radio Svoboda*, 24 February 2014, available at https://web.archive.org/web/20140224032704/www.radiosvoboda.org/content/article/25274524.html (visited 3 January 2017); 'У парламенті Криму заявили, що не планують відділятись від України' (Crimean Parliament Stated They Did Not Plan to Separate from Ukraine), *Ukraynskaya Pravda*, available at www.pravda.com.ua/news/2014/02/26/7016360/ (visited 3 January 2017).
68 V. Shevchenko, 'BBC Monitoring "Little Green Men" or "Russian Invaders"', *BBC*, 11 March 2014, available at www.bbc.com/news/world-europe-26532154 (visited 3 January 2017).
69 A. de Carbonnel, 'How the Separatists Delivered Crimea to Moscow', *Reuters*, 12 March 2014, available at www.reuters.com/article/us-ukraine-crisis-russia-aksyonov-insigh-idUSBREA2B13M20140312 (visited 3 January 2017).

68   Occupation by an intermediary

become part of Russia.[70] The referendum on joining Russia was held just five days later. On 27 March, the UN General Assembly in its Resolution 68/262 (by 100 votes to 11 with 58 abstentions) rejected the results of that referendum, regarding it invalid for constituting the basis for any alteration of the status of the Autonomous Republic of Crimea and the city of Sevastopol.[71] Nevertheless, in mid-April 2014 the Russian president appointed an interim head of Crimea,[72] and currently Crimea is governed by the "Head of the Russian Republic of Crimea".[73] Sevastopol and the Republic of Crimea are now regarded as the 84th and 85th subjects of the Russian Federation.[74]

3.2 Cyprus

The second relevant example is Cyprus. The island has been divided since 1974, when Turkey invaded the north in response to a military coup on the island backed by the Greek government.[75] Cyprus was subsequently partitioned, with the northern third inhabited by Turkish Cypriots and the southern two-thirds by Greek Cypriots.[76] On 15 November 1983, the northern area of Cyprus constituted itself into the Turkish Republic of Northern Cyprus (TRNC),[77] recognised only by Turkey.[78] The latter is believed to be maintaining over 40,000 troops there.[79]

---

70 'Declaration of Independence of the Autonomous Republic of Crimea and Sevastopol', *Voltaire Network*, 11 March 2014, available at www.voltairenet.org/article182723.html (visited 3 January 2017).

71 GA Res. 68/262, 27 March 2014; A. Peters, 'The Crimean Vote', *supra* note 67, at 278–281.

72 A. Nikolsky, 'Putin Signed Order Appointing Aksyanov as Interim Head of Crimea', *Russian News Agency*, 15 April 2014, available at http://tass.ru/en/russia/727839 (visited 3 January 2017).

73 Article 61 Конституция Республики Крым, 11 апреля 2014 года (Article 61 Constitution of the Crimean Republic, 11 April 2014), available at http://rk.gov.ru/rus/info.php?id=623228 (visited 3 January 2017); see also Article 65 of the Constitution of the Russian Federation of 1993 as amended by 21 March 2014, available at http://constitution.kremlin.ru/#article-65 (visited 3 January 2017).

74 Ibid.; see also OSCE PA, Tbilisi Declaration and Resolutions, Political Affairs and Security, 1–5 July 2016, at 4, available at www.oscepa.org/documents/all-documents/annual-sessions/2016-tbilisi/declaration-24/3371-tbilisi-declaration-eng/file (visited 3 January 2017); see also Constitution of Ukraine of 1996 (amended by 21 February 2014), Articles 37, 85 and Article 136, available at http://iportal.rada.gov.ua/uploads/documents/29523.pdf (visited 3 January 2017).

75 S. Casey-Maslen (ed.), *The War Report 2012*, *supra* note 65, at 35.

76 Ibid.

77 SC Res. 541 (1983) considered the TRNC declaration invalid and called for its withdrawal; see also SC Res. 550 (1984).

78 F. Hoffmeister, 'Case Study on Cyprus', in A. von Arnauld, N. Matz-Lück, and K. Odendhal (eds.), *100 Years of Peace Through Law: Past and Future* (Berlin: Duncker and Humbolt, 2015) 113–131, at 118–119.

79 S. Evripidou, 'Turkish Troop Numbers Upped in North', *Cyprus Mail*, 2 July 2013, available at http://cyprus-mail.com/2013/07/03/turkish-troop-numbers-upped-in-north/

Occupation by an intermediary   69

In Loizidou, the ECtHR considered that the responsibility of a party to the Convention could arise

> when as a consequence of military action – whether lawful or unlawful – it exercises effective control of an area outside its national territory. The obligation to secure, in such an area, the rights and freedoms set out in the Convention derives from the fact of such control, whether it be exercised directly, through its armed forces, or through a subordinate local administration.[80]

The Court later added it was not necessary to determine whether Turkey actually exercised *detailed* control over the policies and actions of the (subordinate) TRNC authorities. This could mean that overall control (SR/IHL) by the outside country over the intermediary would have sufficed. However, the Court came up with a seemingly new term, "effective overall control", which as we will see later does not constitute a new type of control but is equivalent to the previously discussed indirect effective control:[81]

> It is obvious from the large number of troops engaged in active duties in Northern Cyprus [. . .] that her [Turkey's] army exercises *effective overall control* over that part of the island. Such control, according to the relevant test and in the circumstances of the case, entails her responsibility for the policies and actions of the 'TRNC'.[82]

The ECtHR explicitly referred to "the occupied area of northern Cyprus"[83] already during the deliberations on the establishment of the facts in the Loizidou case. In other words, the ECtHR may have identified a form of occupation, based on cloaked control. While the Court did not provide a definition of the *effective overall control* test, it is submitted here that, due to the actors involved, it should be understood as developed by the ICTY. In other words, without the support of state A extended to the de facto authorities (the overall control (SR/IHL) of state A over de facto authorities), the latter would not be in a position to exercise effective control (OL) over the territory belonging to state B. In this case specifically, numerous facts suggest that it was only due to the Turkish military

---

(visited 3 January 2017). See also A. Aristotelous, 'What Will Be the Strategy of Akinci?', *Cyprus Centre for Strategic Studies*, 8 May 2015, available at http://strategy-cy.com/ccss/index.php/el/anaysis-gr/item/276-pia-stratigiki-tha-akoloyuesei-o-akinci-watill-be-the-strategy-of-acinci (visited 3 January 2017).

80 Loizidou v. Turkey, ECtHR (1995) (App. No. 15318/89) § 62.

81 Loizidou v. Turkey, ECtHR (Judgment on Merits) (1996) (App. no. 40/1993/435/514) § 56.

82 Ibid., § 56. See also Djavit v. Turkey, ECtHR (2003) (App. no. 25781/94) §§ 18–23; Demades v. Turkey, ECtHR (2003) (App. no. 16219/90) §§ 36–37; Adali v. Turkey, ECtHR (2005) (App. no. 38187/97) section A.

83 Loizidou v. Turkey, *supra* note 81, § 16; see also SC Res. 541 (1983), SC Res. 550 (1984).

70 *Occupation by an intermediary*

involvement that the TRNC came into existence.[84] The ECtHR corroborated this in *Cyprus v. Turkey.*

> Having effective overall control over northern Cyprus, its responsibility cannot be confined to the acts of its own soldiers or officials in northern Cyprus but must also be engaged by virtue of the acts of the local administration which survives by virtue of Turkish military and other support.[85]

The other question is whether the ICRC and the ECtHR, albeit coining two different terms – *indirect effective control* and *effective overall control* – conceptualised them identically. Upon closer scrutiny this seems indeed to be the case, since both *indirect effective control* and *effective overall control* when seen in light of occupation law concern the same objects and possess the same content: a state purporting to veil its control over foreign territory via the control over an intermediary (in this case, a local de facto authority). The ICRC and the ECtHR also converge on the aspect that control by the outside state over the de facto authority need not be based on effective control (SR). What creates confusion are the different names given to the same phenomenon, notably when the lawyer is confronted with the task of classifying a situation in view of these two tests so as to determine the applicable law. It would be preferable that for these types of circumstances one test existed with one and the same name only.

In sum, in both the Loizidou and Cyprus cases, the ECtHR suggests that control by an outside state over a de facto authority means overall control (SR/IHL), encompassing not only supplying it with weapons and finances and the general planning of its operations, but also deciding on the wider aspects of the territory, including its political future.

3.3 Georgia

Another well-known case concerns Georgia, whose two breakaway regions, Abkhazia and South Ossetia, equally possess close links with Russia. While ethnically driven, both regions have sought secession and independence from Georgia.[86]

---

84 N. Skoutaris, *The Cyprus Issue: The Four Freedoms in a Member State Under Siege* (Oxford; Portland, OR: Hart Publishing, 2011), at 28–31.
85 Cyprus v. Turkey, ECtHR (2001) (App. no. 25781/94) § 77. See also T. Ferraro, *Expert Meeting, supra* note 1, at 23.
86 C. Waters, 'South Ossetia', in C. Walter, A. von Ungern-Sternberg, and K. Abushov (eds.), *Self-Determination and Secession in International Law* (Oxford: Oxford University Press, 2014) 175–190; and F. Mirzayev, 'Abkhazia', in C. Walter, A. von Ungern-Sternberg, and K. Abushov (eds.), *Self-Determination and Secession in International Law* (Oxford: Oxford University Press, 2014) 191–213; V. M. Artman, 'Annexation by Passport', *Aljazeera America*, 14 March 2014, available at http://america.aljazeera.com/opinions/2014/3/ukraine-russia-crimeapassportizationcitizenship.html; D. McElroy, 'South Ossetia Police Tell Georgians to Take a Russian Passport, or Leave Their Home', *The Telegraph*,

Occupation by an intermediary 71

On 8 August 2008, after fighting between South Ossetian armed forces and Georgian troops had erupted, Russia entered the Georgian territory the same day, employing ground and air forces as well as the Black Sea Fleet, in the process also attacking targets on Georgian territory beyond South Ossetia.[87]

On 12 August 2008, the Russian forces occupied a number of locations on the territory of Georgia.[88] On 14 August, then-French president Nicolas Sarkozy drew up a peace agreement and submitted it to Georgia's and Russia's presidents. The document envisaged "the withdrawal of Russian military forces to the lines they held before hostilities broke out."[89] However, the 2011 'Implementation Review: Six Point Ceasefire Agreement between Russia and Georgia', prepared by the National Committee on American Foreign Policy and the Institute for the Study of Human Rights, claimed that Russia not only failed to withdraw, but even expanded its hold on territory beyond the pre-war conflict zones. More particularly, it established troop presence in 51 villages it had not controlled before the war, deployed new weapons systems, singed 49-year lease agreements with automatic five-year renewals in Gudauta and Tskhinvali, and built bases in South Ossetia and Abkhazia which are manned by regular army troops, border guards, and Russian Secret Service personnel.[90]

---

30 August 2008, available at www.telegraph.co.uk/news/worldnews/europe/georgia/2651836/South-Ossetian-police-tell-Georgians-to-take-a-Russian-passport-or-leave-their-homes.html (all visited 3 January 2017); GA Res 62/249, 15 May 2008.

87 *Independent International Fact-Finding Mission on the Conflict in Georgia*, Vol. II (September 2009), at 210, available at www.mpil.de/files/pdf4/IIFFMCG_Volume_II1.pdf (visited 3 January 2017); see also *Council of Europe, Consolidated Report on the Conflict in Georgia* (October 2017–March 2018), 11 April 2018, available at https://rm.coe.int/consolidated-report-on-the-conflict-in-georgia-october-2017-march-2018/16807b81cc (visited 20 December 2019); 'General Assembly Adopts Text on Status of Georgia's Refugees, Internally Displaced, Calling Upon Geneva Participants to Intensify Efforts', GA 12151 (4.06.2019), available at www.un.org/press/en/2019/ga12151.doc.htm (visited 20 December 2019); UN General Assembly, 'Status of Internally Displaced Persons and Refugees from Abkhazia, Georgia, and the Tskhinvali Region/South Ossetia, Georgia', 21 May 2019, A/73/880, §§ 15–36, available at https://undocs.org/en/A/73/880 (visited 20 December 2019).

88 Ibid., at 211.

89 'Georgia: The 6 Point Plan', 14 August 2008, Embassy of France in Washington D.C., 8 September 2008, § 5 available at http://franceintheus.org/spip.php?article1101 (visited 3 January 2017); see also Council of Europe and the Conflict in Georgia, CM/Del/Dec(2017)1285/2.1, 1285th Meeting 3 May 2017, § 3 available at https://search.coe.int/cm/Pages/result_details.aspx?ObjectID=090000168070ec0b (visited 5 May 2017); US Government Information, One Hundred Fifteenth Congress of the United States of America, An Act, H.R. 244, *Occupation of the Georgian Territories of Abkhazia and Tskhinvali Region/South Ossetia*, at 572, available at www.congress.gov/115/bills/hr244/BILLS-115hr244enr.pdf (visited 6 May 2017).

90 D. L. Phillips, 'Implementation Review: Six Point Ceasefire Agreement Between Russia and Georgia', *The National Committee on American Foreign Policy*, August 2011, at 10, available at www.ncafp.org/2016/wp-content/uploads/2011/08/implementation-review-russia-and-georgia-aug2011.pdf (visited 3 January 2017).

72 *Occupation by an intermediary*

In addition to this, South Ossetian and Abkhaz separatist forces have enjoyed the strong military, political, and financial support of the Russian Federation.[91] In November 2014, Russia and Abkhazia signed a Treaty on Alliance and Strategic Partnership.[92] The document incorporates Abkhazia into Russia's military, economic, social, and legal space. It also creates a common security and defence system for the armed forces of Russia and Abkhazia in the form of joint defence and border protection forces and unifies the standards of warfare management and law enforcement. The provisions further include the harmonisation of the breakaway region's legislation with that of Russia and with the standards of the Eurasian Economic Union. In March 2015, Russia and South Ossetia equally signed a Treaty on Alliance and Integration[93] containing the same provisions as the treaty with Abkhazia. Clearly, then, the relationship between the two territories and Russia rests on tight control, if not even indistinguishable from the full incorporation of the territories as in the Crimean example. The government of Georgia regards both these treaties as amounting to Russian annexation of Georgian territory.[94]

3.3.1 *The interrelationship of annexation and occupation*

The cases of Ukraine and Georgia necessitate a few remarks on the interrelationship between occupation and annexation. Annexation means the forcible acquisition of territory by one state at the expense of another; it often presupposes the effective occupation of the territory in question with the clear intention to take possession.[95] Formerly, when a state conquered territory, it also took title to the territory.[96] This is no longer the case in today's international law, as Article 2.4 of the UN Charter suggests that the acquisition of territory by force is illegal.[97] Annexation of territory

---

91 'Tension's Rise in Georgia's Breakaway Regions', *Radio Free Europe*, 26 August 2013, available at www.rferl.org/a/georgia-breakaway-abkhazia-south-ossetia/25086522.html (visited 3 January 2017).

92 'Moscow, Sokhumi Sign Treaty on "Alliance and Strategic Partnership"', Civil.Ge, 24 November 2014, available at www.civil.ge/eng/article.php?id=27845 (visited 3 January 2017).

93 Кавказский Узел, Договор между Российской Федерацией и Республикой Южная Осетия о союзничестве и интеграции, available at www.kavkaz-uzel.eu/articles/259096 (visited 3 January 2017).

94 See 'Statement of the President of Georgia on Signing the So-Called "Treaty on Alliance and Integration" Between the Russian Federation and the Occupational Regime of Tskhinvali', available at www.president.gov.ge/en/PressOffice/News?9351 (visited 3 January 2017).

95 R. Hofmann, 'Annexation', *Max Planck Encyclopedia of Public International Law* (2013), § 1, available at http://opil.ouplaw.com/view/10.1093/law:epil/9780199231690/law-9780199231690-e1376?prd=EPIL (visited 3 January 2017).

96 N. A. Maryan Green, *International Law: Law of Peace* (London: Macdonald and Evans, 1982), at 168; L. Oppenheim, 'The Legal Relations Between and Occupying Power and the Inhabitants', 33 *The Law Quarterly Review* (1917) 363–370, at 364.

97 M. N. Shaw, *International Law* (6th edn., Cambridge: Cambridge University Press, 2010), at 502; S. Rosenne, *The Perplexities of Modern International Law* (Leiden: Brill/Martinus Nijhoff Publishers, 2004), at 109–140, and at 242–248.

Occupation by an intermediary   73

thus arises from a serious breach of international law[98] and may be defined as the unlawful acquisition of territory via threat or use of force.

Accordingly, the UN has called upon the international community not to recognise[99] the annexation of East Jerusalem by Israel,[100] nor of the Golan Heights,[101] and equally condemned the Iraqi annexation of Kuwait.[102] The ICJ, too, when dealing with the Wall case, noted that the wall's trajectory included the majority of Israeli settlements in the occupied Palestinian territory, including East Jerusalem.[103] The Court therefore opined

> that the construction of the wall and its associated régime create a 'fait accompli' on the ground that could well become permanent, in which case, and notwithstanding the formal characterization of the wall by Israel, it would be tantamount to de facto annexation.[104]

Examining annexation through the prism of IHL makes clear that when annexation of territory occurs, occupation persists. In fact, in the context of de facto authorities effectively controlling territory, annexation denotes effective control (OL) where not only these de facto authorities are totally submitted to the will of the annexor, but where the latter also exercises effective control (OL) over the territory directly, thereby obliterating the intermediary proxy. This can also be inferred from Article 47 GC IV:

> Protected persons who are in occupied territory shall not be deprived, in any case or in any manner whatsoever, of the benefits of the present Convention by any change introduced, as the result of the occupation of a territory, into the institutions or government of the said territory, nor by any agreement concluded between the authorities of the occupied territories and the Occupying Power, nor by any annexation by the latter of the whole or part of the occupied territory.[105]

---

98 N. Kalandarishvili-Mueller, 'The Status of the Territory Unchanged: Russia's Treaties with Abkhazia and South Ossetia, Georgia', *Opinio Juris*, 20 April 2015, available at http://opiniojuris.org/2015/04/20/guest-post-the-status-of-the-territory-unchanged-russias-treaties-with-abkhazia-and-south-ossetia-georgia/ (visited 3 January 2017).

99 On non-recognition, see S. Talmon, 'The Duty Not to Recognise as Lawful a Situation Created by the Illegal Use of Force or Other Serious Breaches of a Jus Cogens Obligation: An Obligation Without Real Substance?', in C. Tomuschat and J-M. Thouvenin (eds.), *The Fundamental Rules of the International Legal Order Jus Cogens and Obligations Erga Omnes* (Leiden: Brill/Martinus Nijhoff Publishers, 2006) 99–125, at 100–120.

100 SC Res. 478 (1980).

101 UN Commission on Human Rights, *Human Rights Resolution 2005/8: Human Rights in the Occupied Syrian Golan*, 14 April 2005, E/CN.4/RES/2005/8 § 4.

102 SC Res. 662 (1990).

103 *Case Concerning Legal Consequences of the Construction of a Wall in the Occupied Palestinian Territory*, Advisory Opinion, 9 July 2004, § 119, available at www.icj-cij.org/en/case/131 (visited 15 July 2017).

104 Ibid., § 121.

105 Article 47 Geneva Convention (IV) Relative to the Protection of Civilian Persons in Time of War (12 August 1949).

74   *Occupation by an intermediary*

The Pictet Commentary to Article 47 regards an occupying power to be bound by the GC IV "even when, in disregard of the rules of international law, it claims during a conflict to have annexed all or part of an occupied territory."[106] Thus, annexation of the occupied territory is prohibited: the occupant cannot take the title, which de jure the displaced sovereign continues to hold.[107] Therefore, "any unilateral annexation of an occupied territory – in whole or in part – by the Occupying Power would be legally stillborn".[108]

The Georgian example prior to the de facto authorities' treaties with Russia rested on indirect effective control (i.e. proxy occupation), while based on these treaties Russia is now exercising effective control (OL) over the territories in question directly and openly. In Crimea, too, initially territorial control was asserted by Russia indirectly, through proxies, but after the area's ambiguous self-determination result Russia fully incorporated the peninsula.[109] However, from an IHL point of view, all these territories continue to be occupied.

3.4 Nagorno Karabakh

Our next example is Nagorno Karabakh, a territory of Azerbaijan.[110] In February 1992, an armed conflict erupted between Armenian and Azerbaijani forces, including also the forces of Nagorno Karabakh.[111] Armenian troops helped the Nagorno Karabakh rebels occupy the mountainous Nagorno Karabakh enclave (10 percent of Azerbaijan's total territory) as well as another 10 percent of Azerbaijani territory surrounding Karabakh on the east, south, and west.[112]

---

106 J. Pictet (ed.), *Commentary of 1958, Convention (IV) Relative to the Protection of Civilian Persons in Time of War Geneva, 12 August 1949*, Article 47 (Geneva: International Committee of the Red Cross, 1958), at 276.

107 Y. Dinstein, *The International Law of Belligerent Occupation, supra* note 7, at 49.

108 Ibid., at 50; *Declaration of Guidelines on the Recognition of New States in Eastern Europe and in the Former Soviet Union*, 16 December 1991, available at www.dipublico.org/100636/declaration-on-the-guidelines-on-the-recognition-of-new-states-in-eastern-europe-and-in-the-soviet-union-16-december-1991/ (visited 3 January 2017).

109 Laws on admitting Crimea and Sevastopol to the Russian Federation, 21 March 2014 available at http://en.kremlin.ru/events/president/news/20625; see also *Ceremony Signing the Laws on Admitting Crimea and Sevastopol to the Russian Federation*, The Kremlin, Moscow, 21 March 2014, available at http://en.kremlin.ru/events/president/news/20626 (both links visited 3 January 2017).

110 A. Y. Melnyk, 'Nagorny-Karabakh', *Max Planck Encyclopedia of Public International Law* (2013), § 1, available at http://opil.ouplaw.com/view/10.1093/law:epil/9780199231690/law-9780199231690-e2073?prd=EPIL (visited 3 January 2017); H. Krüger, 'Nagorno-Karabakh', in C. Walter, A. von Ungern-Sternberg, and K. Abushov (eds.), *Self-Determination and Secession in International Law* (Oxford: Oxford University Press, 2014) 214–232, at 215–216; Human Rights Watch, *Azerbaijan: Seven Years of Conflict in Nagorno Karabakh*, 8 December 1994, at 1–3, available at www.hrw.org/sites/default/files/reports/AZER%20Conflict%20in%20N-K%20Dec94.pdf (visited 3 January 2017).

111 S. Casey-Maslen (ed.), *The War Report 2012, supra* note 65, at 30–31.

112 Human Rights Watch, *Azerbaijan, supra* note 110, at 157, Appendix A.

Occupation by an intermediary 75

Since 1994, Nagorno Karabakh and seven surrounding administrative districts have been under the control of Armenia proper and Nagorno Karabakh Armenians.[113] Armenia is the "guarantor and supporter of security for the population of the Nagorno-Karabakh Republic and the course of development it has chosen".[114] Both the UN SC and the GA regard Azerbaijan's territory as occupied by Armenia.[115] A GA Resolution from 2008, for instance, demanded "the immediate, complete and unconditional withdrawal of all Armenian forces from all the occupied territories of the Republic of Azerbaijan".[116]

This case, too, amounts to a situation of military occupation. Such a conclusion is premised on the fact that while the armed forces of Armenia are present on the territory in question, the de facto authorities of Nagorno Karabakh are under the overall control (SR/IHL) of that state. The de facto authorities seem to be stripped of their independence in decision making, in addition to Armenia organising, coordinating, and planning the military and political actions of the entity. All the previously reproduced facts attest to this. In turn, the de facto entity ensures the effective control (OL) of the territory in question, thereby barring the ousted sovereign, Azerbaijan, to exercise its authority there.

3.5 Moldova

Finally, Russia is also considered to be occupying Transdniestria, a territory of Moldova.[117] It is believed that some 2,500 Russian troops are stationed there.[118] According to Human Rights Watch, Transdniestria and its de facto authorities have long enjoyed Russia's military support.[119] The ECtHR equally concluded that the Moldavian Republic of Transdniestria (MRT)

> set up in 1991–92 with the support of the Russian Federation, vested with organs of power and its own administration, remains under the *effective authority*, or at the very least *under the decisive influence*, of the Russian Federation, and in any event that it survives by virtue of the military, economic, financial and political support given to it by the Russian Federation.[120]

---

113 A. Bellal (ed.), *The War Report: Armed Conflict in 2014* (Oxford: Oxford University Press, 2015), at 61–66; H. Krüger, *The Nagorno Karabakh Conflict: A Legal Analysis* (Heidelberg: Springer, 2010), at 93–94.

114 *The Military Doctrine of the Republic of Armenia*, Preface, Ministry of Defence of Armenia, 2015, available at www.mil.am/media/2015/07/825.pdf (visited 3 January 2017).

115 SC Res. 822 (1993), SC Res. 853 (1993), SC Res. 874 (1993), SC Res. 884 (1993); GA Res. 62/243, 14 March 2008.

116 Ibid., GA Res. 62/243, 14 March 2008. See also T. Ferraro, *Expert Meeting, supra* note 1, at 23.

117 S. Casey-Maslen (ed.), *The War Report 2012, supra* note 65, at 50–54.

118 Ibid., at 53.

119 *War or Peace? Human Rights and Russian Military Involvement in the 'Near Abroad'*, Human Rights Watch Report, 1 December 1993, available at www.hrw.org/legacy/reports/1993/russia/ (visited 3 January 2017).

120 *Ilaşcu and Others v. Moldova and Russia*, ECtHR (2004) (App. no. 48787/99) § 392 (emphasis added).

76 *Occupation by an intermediary*

Pursuant to the Court, it is of little consequence that since May 1998 no agents of the Russian Federation have participated directly in the events complained about by the applicants.[121] The applicants still came within the jurisdiction of the Russian Federation for the purposes of Article 1 ECHR, and Russia's responsibility was triggered.[122] It seems that for the ECtHR, exercising effective control is a factual matter, attached to the military presence of the state. However, other indicators may also be relevant for the Court, such as the extent to which its military, economic, and political support for the local subordinate administration provides it with influence and control over the region.[123]

In *Catan and Others v. the Republic of Moldova and Russia*, the ECtHR maintained its findings of the Ilaşcu judgment that during 2002–2004, the MRT was able to continue its existence and resist Moldovan and international efforts to resolve the conflict and bring democracy and the rule of law to the region only thanks to Russian military, economic, and political support.[124] Hence, Russia's military presence and the MRT's high level of dependency on Russian support both indicate "that Russia exercised effective control and decisive influence over the MRT's administration".[125] One can, however, observe a slightly different wording in the Court's dictum in the most recent case of *Mozer v. the Republic of Moldova and Russia*, where "Russia continues to exercise effective control and a decisive influence over the MRT authorities".[126] While in Ilaşcu the Court spoke of "or" and in Catan of "and", in Mozer it employed "and a" decisive influence.

3.5.1 Decisive influence

Let us deal with the formulation "decisive influence", used by the ECtHR in the cases dealing with the MRT, a little further. The question is why the Court did not use the term "occupation" and instead opted for "effective authority" and "under the decisive influence". One possibility is that the ECtHR was trying to use non-IHL terminology, since it was not called to adjudicate on IHL. However, one may still wonder whether decisive influence is a variant of indirect effective control.

To begin with, it cannot be stated that all forms of influence over de facto authorities, and by extension territory, may be regarded as occupation. In fact, *decisive influence* conveys the impression that it rests on a low(er) threshold of control, where one does not need to establish effective control (OL) over territory.

---

121 Ibid., § 393.
122 Ibid., § 394; see also Ivanţoc and Others v. Moldova and Russia, ECtHR (2011) (App. no. 23687/05) § 115–120.
123 Al-Skeini and Others v. the United Kingdom, ECtHR (2011) (App. no. 55721/07) § 139.
124 Catan and Others v. the Republic of Moldova and Russia, ECtHR (2012) (App. nos. 43370/04, 8252/05 and 18454/06) § 122.
125 Ibid., § 122.
126 Mozer v. The Republic of Moldova and Russia, ECtHR (2016) (App. No. 11138/10) § 110.

Occupation by an intermediary 77

This would mean that decisive influence does not amount to a day-to-day control of territory. It is rather something that does not necessitate too much control, although control is still exerted when taking major decisions. In the case of Northern Cyprus, for example, when Turkey invaded the territory, during the early stages of its presence Turkey wielded effective control (OL) over the territory. But over time the TRNC authorities gained a certain level of freedom in taking decisions, albeit on a small scale. To date, Northern Cyprus and its authorities have remained heavily dependent on Turkey's finances and troops, and Turkey simply considers the territory "as its child".[127] In the case of Transdniestria, too, its de facto authorities possess a certain level of freedom in taking small-scale decisions, yet they largely remain under the sway of Russia, relying notably on her finances and troops.[128]

While effective control (OL) denotes the status of an occupant, "decisive influence" is far from being lucid and not defined by conventional IHL and IHRL. The difficulty is that when dealing with something that does not have a definition in law, there is no right or wrong answer. There may only be an answer that is coherent and practical versus answers that are incoherent and impractical. But, at the end of the day, in IHL one should look at the facts on the ground and apply the law accordingly. In this manner, Mirzayev[129] and Bowring,[130] in the context of the case of Ilaşcu, equate decisive influence with effective control (OL) over territory. In other words, Russia is occupying Transdniestria on the basis of effective control (OL) over territory. But while I agree that Transdniestria is occupied, I disagree with their explanation of the type of control. The synonyms of "influence" are control, power, authority, and direction; while "decisive" means something crucial, significant, and critical. Hence, the formulation amounts to not just *any* influence. It is rather a type of influence that has an impact. Decisive influence in this case, therefore, can only mean the capacity of state A to exercise crucial, critical power, control, and authority over entity X in state B. Effective control (OL) over territory, in turn, is exercised by that entity.

The de facto authorities in places such as the TRNC, Transdniestria, Abkhazia, South Ossetia, and Nagorno Karabakh all cloak the control of a foreign state over the territory of another state, i.e. Cyprus, Moldova, Georgia, and Azerbaijan, respectively. I therefore consider that the ECtHR, in the various cases having to do with Transdniestria, implicitly opined that the situation was one of occupation through middlemen, albeit using different wording. This in turn points to the possibility that a state can wield control over parts of the territory in various forms

---

127 F. Taştekin, 'Northern Cyprus Demands Respect from Turkey', *Turkey Pulse*, 28 April 2015, available at www.al-monitor.com/pulse/originals/2015/04/turkey-greece-cypriot-baby-grow-up.html# (visited 3 January 2017).

128 J. Malling, 'The Value of a Frozen Conflict', *Le Monde Diplomatique*, March 2015, available at http://mondediplo.com/2015/03/04transnistria (visited 3 January 2017).

129 F. Mirzayev, 'Abkhazia', *supra* note 86, at 208–209.

130 B. Bowring, 'Transnistria', in C. Walter, A. von Ungern-Sternberg, and K. Abushov (eds.), *Self-Determination and Secession in International Law* (Oxford: Oxford University Press, 2014) 157–174, at 158.

78 *Occupation by an intermediary*

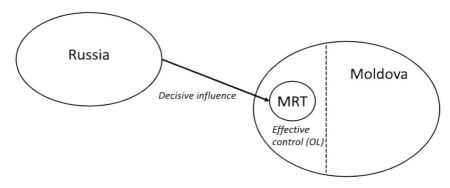

Figure 2.3 The decisive influence test (ECtHR)
Note: MRT = Moldavian Republic of Transdniestria

and degrees. It can control different aspects of the life on the territory, which together amount to a form of control sufficient for establishing military occupation. It is thus submitted here that decisive influence amounts to overall control (SR/IHL) as used by the ICRC in the indirect effective control test. Figure 2.3 displays how the decisive influence test is met in the case of Transdniestria.

3.5.2 *Military presence and consent*

Some might counter that the previously-discussed cases are not situations of occupation from the perspective of IHL. Since outside states do not maintain large military presences there, in addition to being welcomed by the inhabitants of the territory, two criteria seem not to be met. However, is a large military presence really required for classifying such situations as occupation? What about the local population welcoming the presence of the foreign state, in addition to sharing a common ethnicity?

Let us first assume there is an intervening state whose population has a different ethnicity than the population of the sovereign state, but the same as the group that is opposing that sovereign. The latter might be a weak but nevertheless internationally recognised state. The group may not be heavily armed, i.e. possess full military capacity, and yet manage to expel the local authorities of the state through the military support of the foreign state whose ethnicity it shares. This state then sends approximately 1,000 armed soldiers into this breakaway region. Such a number amounts to a relatively small presence. The population of the territory does not oppose the forces and the de facto authorities explicitly welcome them. The de facto authorities may or may not have the consent of the local population. Consent to be present on the territory is not given by the sovereign, but rather by the de facto authorities in question. According to

Occupation by an intermediary 79

international law, are the de facto authorities entitled to give such consent? Or do the people living on the territory have to consent to the presence of the foreign state's troops?

These questions bring us to consider the issue of self-determination in international law. Self-determination may be defined as the right of a people living on a certain territory to determine its own affairs, be that in cultural, social, economic, political, and/or legal terms.[131] The problem is that there is no uniform definition of who constitutes "the people",[132] nor are the exact circumstances of resorting to self-determination identified. While self-determination reflects both a principle and a right in international law,[133] it should not be exercised in contravention of state sovereignty and territorial inviolability.[134]

There are two forms of self-determination, internal and external.[135] *Internal* self-determination encompasses the right of all segments of a population to influence the constitutional and political structure of the system in which they live.[136]

131 Article 8 Conference on Security and Cooperation in Europe, Final Act (Helsinki, 1975); Article 1 International Covenant on Civil and Political Rights (1966); Article 1 International Covenant on Economic, Social, and Cultural Rights (1966); M. N. Shaw, *International Law*, *supra* note 105, at 251–257 and especially at 289–293; see also P. Malantczuk, *Akehurst's Modern Introduction to International Law* (7th edn., London: Routledge, 1997), at 326. On whether self-determination has a *jus cogens* nature or not, no uniform stance can be observed in the international legal community; see D. Thürer and T. Burri, 'Self-Determination', *Max Planck Encyclopedia of Public International Law* (2008) § 45, available at http://opil.ouplaw.com/view/10.1093/law:epil/9780199231690/law-9780199231690-e873 (visited 6 December 2017); M. Saul, 'The Normative Status of Self-Determination in International Law: A Formula for Uncertainty in the Scope and Content of the Right?', 11 *Human Rights Law Review* (2011) 609–44, at 634–41; see also *Case Concerning East Timor (Portugal v. Australia)*, Judgment of 30 June 1995, § 29, available at www.icj-cij.org/en/case/84 (visited 5 December 2017).
132 I. Jennings, *The Approach to Self-Government* (Cambridge: Cambridge University Press, 1958), at 56: "On the surface it seemed reasonable: let the people decide. It was in fact ridiculous because the people cannot decide until somebody decides who are the people."
133 J. Summers, *Peoples and International Law* (2nd edn., Leiden: Brill/Martinus Nijhoff Publishers, 2013), at 71–73.
134 The Secretary General of the UN stated that: "as far as the question of secession of a particular section of a Member State is concerned, the United Nations attitude is unequivocal. As an international organisation, the United Nations has never accepted and does not accept and I do not believe it will ever accept a principle of secession of a part of a Member State." U. Thant, 'Secretary General's Press Conferences', 34 *UN Monthly Chronicle* (1970) at 36.
135 L. C. Buchheit, *Secession: The Legitimacy of Self-determination* (New Haven, CT: Yale University Press, 1978), at 14; M. Pomerance, *Self-Determination in Law and Practice* (The Hague: Martinus Nijhoff Publishers, 1982), at 37–42.
136 L. C. Buchheit, *Secession*, *supra* note 135, at 14; C. J. Borgen, 'States and International Law: The Problems of Self-Determination, Secession, and Recognition', in B. Cali (ed.), *International Law for International Relations* (Oxford: Oxford University Press, 2009) 191–212, at 207.

80 *Occupation by an intermediary*

It may be interpreted to support human rights and multiparty democracy[137] and can take various forms, from simple cultural autonomy to the canton system in Switzerland.[138] *External* self-determination, on the other hand, means that a group is entitled to constitute itself as a nation-state or to integrate into or federate with another, already existing state.[139]

Sadly, the circumstances which would pronounce the conditions for external self-determination, i.e. secession, were not dealt with by the ICJ in its advisory opinion on the Accordance with International Law of the Unilateral Declaration of Independence in Respect of Kosovo. Rather, the ICJ examined whether or not Kosovo's unilateral declaration of independence was in accordance with international law.[140] However, the Canadian Supreme Court views external self-determination as a step of last resort and applicable only in particular situations.[141] These were spelled out as follows:

> the international law right to self-determination only generates, at best, a right to external self-determination in situations of former colonies; where a people is oppressed, as for example under foreign military occupation; or where a definable group is denied meaningful access to government to pursue their political, economic, social and cultural development. In all three situations, the people in question are entitled to a right to external self-determination because they have been denied the ability to exert internally their right to self-determination.[142]

---

137 J. Summers, *Peoples and International Law, supra* note 133, at 343.

138 See generally C. Dominicé, 'The Secession of the Canton of Jura in Switzerland', in M. G. Kohen (ed.), *Secession: International Law Perspectives* (Cambridge: Cambridge University Press, 2006) 453–469.

139 S. Senese, 'External and Internal Self-Determination', 16 *Social Justice* (Human Rights and Social Rights: Views) (1989) 19–25, at 19.

140 *Accordance of International Law of the Unilateral Declaration of Independence in Respect of Kosovo*, Advisory Opinion, 22 July 2010, § 49–56 and § 82–83, available at www.icj-cij.org/en/case/141 (visited 15 July 2017). In this case, the ICJ did not refer to the dimensions of internal and external self-determination; however, see further Separate Opinion of Cançado Trindade, at 125–218 and 197, § 184, and Separate Opinion of Judge Yusuf, at 219–227 and 222–223, § 9–10; see generally S. E. Meller, 'The Kosovo Case: An Argument for a Remedial Declaration of Independence', 40 *Georgia Journal of International and Comparative Law* (2012) 834–866. See also *Legal Consequences of the Separation of the Chagos Archipelago from Mauritius in 1965*, Advisory Opinion, 25 February 2019, § 144, available at www.icj-cij.org/files/case-related/169/169-20190225-01-00-EN.pdf (visited 4 April 2019), where the ICJ considered "that the right to self-determination, as a fundamental human right, has a broad scope of application. However, to answer the question put to it by the General Assembly, the Court will confine itself, in this Advisory Opinion, to analysing the right to self-determination in the context of decolonization."

141 Reference re Secession of Quebec, Supreme Court of Canada (1998) 2. SCR 217, 1998 CanLII 793 (SCC) § 126.

142 Ibid., §138. See also Y. Ronen, 'A Century of the Law of Occupation', 17 *Yearbook of International Humanitarian Law* (The Hague: T.M.C. Asser Press, 2014) 169–186, at 182.

Linking (external) self-determination to military occupation underlines the tension between the principle of the legality of the regime operating on a territory and the continuation of effective control (OL) over that same territory. In other words, so that consent is regarded valid, not only must it not be engineered, but it also has to be extended by the recognised government (not a de facto regime) of the recognised state (not a de facto state).[143] The alternative argumentation, namely for consent to be the legitimate expression of external self-determination by a "people" that was denied internal self-determination, would mean to welcome the very forces that "oppress" them in this case, the military occupant.

Thus, if the 1,000 soldiers are welcomed by those who live on the territory, while arguably no big number of troops would further be needed, and while the people do not oppose this type of presence and are even content about it, it may still be the case that the people are not entitled to extend such a welcome. *A fortiori*, nor is the de facto authority entitled to extend such consent. Pursuant to IHL, the situation on the ground would then still be one of occupation since consent by the legitimate government is lacking.

3.6 Critical appraisal

Unlike armed groups, de facto authorities possess state-like features and some may even be recognised internationally, however controversial this might be. For example, the so-called Republic of Abkhazia has been recognised only by Venezuela, Nicaragua, and Russia.[144] When it comes to occupations based on indirect effective control, this chapter has argued that both armed groups and de facto authorities can be regarded as proxies of the outside state, provided that this state exercises overall control (SR/IHL) over them and that they in turn exercise effective control (OL) over territory.

Yet it may also be advanced that some de facto authorities are mere puppet regimes in that they are created, staffed, maintained, and disposed of by an outside state, to the extent that they are de facto organs under Article 4 ILC Articles on Responsibility of States[145] (see also section 2.3). Such a type of relationship should rest on complete dependency (SR). The advantage of this approach is that one would not need to show that each and every act of that organ has been specifically ordered by the outside state, since automatically the state would be responsible for all acts of the de facto authorities. Such a proposition would then need to provide evidence of the complete dependency (SR) of the puppet

---

143 E. Benvenisti, *The International Law of Occupation*, *supra* note 11, at 67; see also F. J. Hampson, 'Afghanistan 2001–2010', in E. Wilmshurst (ed.), *International Law and Classification of Conflicts* (Oxford: Oxford University Press, 2012) 242–279, at 245.

144 See Ministry of Foreign Affairs, Republic of Abkhazia, available at http://mfaapsny.org/en/apsny/historyofabkhazia.php (visited 26 May 2017).

145 D. Akande, 'Classification of Armed Conflicts: Relevant Legal Concepts', in E. Wilmshurst (ed.), *International Law and Classification of Conflicts* (Oxford: Oxford University Press, 2012) 32–79, at 59; see also Genocide case, *supra* note 44, § 393.

82 *Occupation by an intermediary*

regime on the outside state. Generating evidence of such dependency, nevertheless, would be difficult, to say the least.

A second alternative is to adhere to the requirement of effective control (SR) by the outside state over the de facto authorities. Sassòli for example considers the supporters of the overall control (SR/IHL) test to base their arguments on the ECtHR's reasoning in the Loizidou case, where Turkey's overall control over the TRNC authorities was sufficient to find Turkey responsible for the latter's human rights violations, stating however that

> the difference between this and the question discussed here – whether IHL of military occupation applies – is that human rights obligations had to be complied with by the authorities of the 'Turkish Republic of Northern Cyprus' [. . .] on their own territory, while the IHL of military occupation must only be applied in a foreign territory. It is therefore entirely conceivable that it is sufficient that a state has overall control over unrecognised authorities in another state to make it responsible for their human rights violations, while to make IHL of military occupation applicable, it needs effective control over conduct triggering such applicability.[146]

Yet the ECtHR primarily ascertained Turkey's human rights responsibility through the prism of jurisdiction, which materialised through the actions of the TRNC and the fact that Turkey maintained forces there.[147] In other words, if there was no Turkish *military* involvement in Northern Cyprus, the TRNC would never even have come into existence. This component expresses a close affinity to IHL.

Moreover, while I agree that the IHL of military occupation applies on foreign territory only, the issue here is precisely that: Northern Cyprus was never regarded as Turkish territory by the international community.[148] Northern Cyprus, therefore, constitutes a territory foreign to that of Turkey. Consequently, the latter's responsibility for IHRL violations was established not on "own territory", but extraterritorially. When the ECtHR regarded Northern Cyprus to be occupied, it arguably may have kept these points in mind. It thus seems the Court advanced overall control – or, in its own parlance, *effective overall control* – precisely for such situations of proxy occupation. While some shortcomings in the analysis of the ECtHR are visible as it developed this test, the core question is whether the

---

146 M. Sassòli, 'The Concept and the Beginning of Occupation', *supra* note 11, at 1400.

147 Loizidou v. Turkey, ECtHR (Judgment on Merits), *supra* note 81, § 56; Cyprus v. Turkey, ECtHR, *supra* note 85, § 77.

148 SC Res. 541 (1983); SC Res. 550 (1984) refers to Northern Cyprus as the "legally invalid 'Turkish Republic of Northern Cyprus'" and in § 3 reiterates the call on all the states not to recognise it; see also Permanent Representation of the Republic of Cyprus to the European Union, 'The Cyprus Question', 29 November 2016, available at www.mfa.gov.cy/mfa/PermRep/PermRep_Brussels.nsf/page32_en/page32_en?OpenDocument (visited 3 January 2017).

Occupation by an intermediary 83

extraterritorial application of human rights and the law of military occupation base themselves on the same test. I shall address this in Chapter 4.

4. IHL's own mechanism for control?

4.1 Belonging to a party to the conflict under Article 4 GC III

The purpose of Article 4 GC III is to grant POW status to certain categories of persons who have fallen into the power of an adversary. Section A (2) includes persons that are not part of the armed forces of the state *strictu sensu*:

> Members of other militias and members of other volunteer corps, including those of organized resistance movements, belonging to a Party to the conflict and operating in or outside their own territory, even if this territory is occupied.

The possible test of control that is contained in this section, i.e. in the formulation *belonging to a Party to the conflict*, is examined next. Since Article 4 does not define this expression, it is important to interpret what "belonging to" means.

In Tadić, the prosecution contended that the alleged perpetrator of crimes had to be "sufficiently linked to a Party to the conflict" so as to come under the jurisdiction of Article 2 ICTY Statute. It further advanced that the "showing of a demonstrable link between the VRS and the FRY or VJ" was sufficient for this purpose. This link could be proven by showing a general form of control, which was found in the GCs.[149] Determining whether certain armed forces were sufficiently related to a high contracting party via the rules relating to state responsibility would lead to absurd results.[150] The Appeals Chamber addressed the question from the perspective of IHL, setting out to consider the conditions under which armed forces may be assimilated to organs of a state other than that on whose territory they operate.[151] Under GC III, militias or paramilitary groups or units can be regarded as combatants/POWs if they form "part of the armed forces" of a party to the conflict (Article 4A(1)) or "belong to a Party to the conflict" (Article 4A(2)) and satisfy the other four requirements (a) through (d) listed in that Article.[152]

According to the Chamber, one of the logical consequences of this article was that if in an armed conflict paramilitary units "belong" to a state other than the one against which they are fighting, the conflict is international. Thereby

---

149 Tadić, *supra* note 22, § 88.
150 Ibid., § 89.
151 Ibid., § 91. See also A. Cassese, 'The Nicaragua and Tadić Tests', *supra* note 42, at 655–656.
152 J. Pictet (ed.), *Commentary to the Geneva Convention (III) Relative to the Treatment of Prisoners of War (12 August 1949)*, Article 4 (Geneva: ICRC, 1960), at 57–58.

84 *Occupation by an intermediary*

serious violations of the GCs might be classified as "grave breaches".[153] For the ICTY Appeals Chamber, the requirement "belonging to a Party to the conflict" was far from clear. The rationale in this provision was that during WWII it was agreed that states should be legally responsible for the conduct of irregular forces they sponsored.[154] So that the irregulars were categorised as combatants, it was required that a party to an IAC "controlled" them. This type of control would result in a "relationship of dependence and allegiance of these irregulars vis-à-vis that Party to the conflict. These then may be regarded as the ingredients of the term 'belonging to a Party to the conflict'."[155] The ICTY Appeals Chamber, therefore, considered that in Article 4 the requirement of "belonging to a Party to the conflict" was an implicit referral to a control test.[156]

The Pictet Commentary also makes it explicit that paragraph A2 of Article 4 was based on WWII experience, particularly with resistance movements fighting against occupation regimes. Nevertheless, this does not mean that other categories, such as armed groups, are excluded. However, the Commentary does not explain the meaning of *belonging to a party to the conflict*. It solely speaks of the fact that the resistance movements must be fighting on behalf of a party to the conflict[157] and that

> it is essential that there should be a 'de facto' relationship between the resistance organization and the party to international law which is in a state of war, but the existence of this relationship is sufficient. It may find expression merely by tacit agreement, if the operations are such as to indicate clearly for which side the resistance organization is fighting.[158]

In this manner, for some "belonging" just calls for a form of acceptance, either expressly or tacitly, on the part of the state and individuals concerned, that the latter are fighting on behalf of the former.[159] For Melzer "it appears essential that [the armed groups] conduct hostilities on behalf and with the agreement of"[160] the party to the conflict.

It is nevertheless submitted here that there is rarely a "belonging to" without some form of control by the one who is belonged to over the one who belongs.

---

153 Tadić, *supra* note 22, § 92.
154 Ibid., § 93.
155 Ibid., § 94; See also S. Watts, 'Who Is a Prisoner of War?' in A. Clapham, P. Gaeta, and M. Sassòli (eds.), *The 1949 Geneva Conventions: A Commentary* (Oxford: Oxford University Press, 2015) 890–910, at 897–898.
156 Tadić, *supra* note 22, § 95.
157 Convention (III) Relative to the Treatment of Prisoners of War, Geneva, 12 August 1949; J. Pictet (ed.), *Commentary to the Geneva Convention (III)*, Article 4, *supra* note 152, at 56.
158 Ibid.
159 K. Del Mar, 'The Requirement of "Belonging" Under International Humanitarian Law', 21 *The European Journal of International Law* (2010) 105–124, at 112.
160 N. Melzer, *Interpretive Guidance on the Notion of Direct Participation in Hostilities Under International Humanitarian Law* (Geneva: ICRC, 2009), at 23.

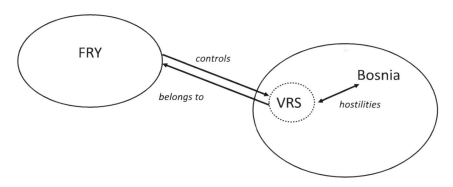

Figure 2.4 Belonging to a party to the conflict (Article 4 GC III 1949)

Note: FRY = Federal Republic of Yugoslavia (Serbia and Montenegro); VRS = army of the Serbian Republic of Bosnia and Herzegovina/Republika Srpska

The question, however, is what degree of control such a relationship rests on. Is it effective (SR) or overall control (SR/IHL)? For Akande, the de facto relationship appears to be a looser test even than the "overall control" test because already tacit agreement suffices.[161] However, the de facto relationship between the outside state and the armed group signals a form of control that is not at all loose. In fact, the formulation *fighting on behalf of a party to the conflict* encompasses two meanings: in the interests and as a representative of.[162]

Hence, an armed group that "belongs" to an outside state is not only fighting in the interests of that state, but is also under a certain degree of control by it, as shown in Figure 2.4 for Bosnia. For example, the state may instruct the group when and how to perform certain actions. Furthermore, when an armed group "belongs to a party to the conflict", it is bound to this state by ties of dependence or allegiance, and it may follow the state in its ideology and pursue the same aim. Based on such a belonging, the armed group may thus be considered a de facto organ of the state.

The way I view "belonging to a party to the conflict" is that the group is receiving general directions from the state and, based on these, the group is fighting the adversary state. A de facto relationship, while it signifies a factual, existing relationship between the state and the armed group, indicates that it might not amount to a day-to-day control from the side of the state, nor to control exercised specifically over each detail of the operation or task, but rather control

---

161 D. Akande, 'Classification of Armed Conflicts', *supra* note 145, at 61.
162 S. Watts, 'Who Is a Prisoner of War?', *supra* note 155, at 898; Oxford Dictionary, definition of 'behalf' in English, available at https://en.oxforddictionaries.com/definition/behalf (visited 3 January 2017).

86 *Occupation by an intermediary*

exercised in a general manner. This type of control amounts to overall control (SR/IHL) as advanced by the Tadić Appeals Chamber.

For the purposes of military occupation, the test can therefore be spelled out in the following manner: if an armed group which exercises effective control (OL) over territory belongs to a party to the conflict, overall control (SR/IHL) is exerted by the state over the armed group. Again, such a link would avoid the protection gap in the application of GC IV.

4.2 The potentiality of Article 29 GC IV

The other possible basis in IHL that could make state A an occupant via armed group X engaged in an armed conflict with state B is found in Article 29 GC IV:

> The Party to the conflict in whose hands protected persons may be, is responsible for the treatment accorded to them by its agents, irrespective of any individual responsibility which may be incurred.[163]

In her dissenting opinion in Tadić, Judge McDonald viewed this article useful for classifying a prima facie NIAC as an IAC, particularly regarding situations of military occupation via armed groups.[164] According to the Pictet Commentaries, by means of "a general formula" this article defines the persons who by their acts give rise to the responsibility of a certain state.[165] One should thus take notice of the word *agent*, as it may be construed to be including everyone who is in the service of a state, including an armed group, provided the criteria of Articles 4 or 8 ILC Articles on Responsibility of States are met (see also Introduction).

What should again be examined is the relationship between that outside state and the agent: does the former control the latter? And if so, what type of control? The Pictet Commentary to Article 29 GC IV purports to explain these aspects:

> The term "agent" must be understood as embracing everyone who is in the service of a Contracting Party, no matter in what way or in what capacity . . . and so covers a wider circle than the definition in the Fourth Hague Convention [. . .] the word "agent" limits the scope of the provision to those persons alone who *owe allegiance* to the Power concerned. [. . .] The nationality of the agents does not affect the issue [. . .] as it means that the occupying authorities are responsible for acts committed by their locally recruited agents of the nationality of the occupied country [. . .] *what is important is to know where the decision leading to the unlawful act was made, where the*

---

163 Article 29, GC IV 12 August 1949.

164 Trial Chamber, Prosecutor v. Dusko Tadić, Separate and Dissenting Opinion of Judge McDonald Regarding the Applicability of Article 2 of the Statute, 7 May 1997, §§ 31–34.

165 J. Pictet (ed.), *Commentary of 1958, Convention (IV) Relative to the Protection of Civilian Persons in Time of War Geneva, 12 August 1949*, Article 29 (Geneva: ICRC, 1958), at 211.

intention was formed and the order given. If the unlawful act was committed at the instigation of the Occupying Power, then the Occupying Power is responsible; if, on the other hand, it was the result of a truly independent decision on the part of the local authorities, the Occupying Power cannot be held responsible.[166]

Like "belonging to", "allegiance" thus does not exist without some form of control. Allegiance denotes loyalty, duty, and obligation as well as obedience.[167] Because agents show allegiance to the state, that state controls them to a certain level. Again, it is necessary to establish the level of control in this situation. Therefore, the participation of the state in planning the actions of the armed group has to be examined and/or whether the state was in control of the actions of the armed group when they carried them out.

This is even more so the case when the Pictet Commentary invites us to pay attention to whether an act was committed on the instigation of the occupant. An occupant instigating an act would mean that it causes, actuates, or encourages its materialisation. This resembles the overall control (SR/IHL) formula in Tadić. Reconciling this test with military occupation is based on ascertaining whether an armed group *owes allegiance* to the foreign state and whether that armed group exercises effective control (OL) over territory.[168] Just as with "belonging", this avoids a protection gap in the application of GC IV.

Conclusion

This chapter has analysed occupation by an intermediary. The following example shows the way in which overall control (SR/IHL) triggers military occupation.

Let us assume a situation where state A occupies state B's western territories through its own army (see Figure 2.5). This amounts to the classic understanding of military occupation (see Chapter 1). In parallel, state B is engaged in a NIAC with armed group X in the north of its territory. That group has ties to the occupying power, state A. So that group X is considered a de facto agent of state A, the latter should wield overall control (SR/IHL) over it. In other words, state A should provide armed group X with financial, military, and operational support

---

166 Ibid., at 211–212 (emphasis added).
167 Oxford Dictionary, Definition of '*allegiance*' in English, available at https://en. oxforddictionaries.com/definition/allegiance (visited 3 January 2017).
168 T. Gal, 'Unexplored Outcomes of Tadić: Applicability of the Law of Occupation to War by Proxy', 12 *Journal of International Criminal Justice* (2014) 59–80, at 66: "Accepting that the agent of the occupying state can be a non-state armed group, there is still a need to examine whether a non-state armed groups can exercise the degree of territorial control required by Geneva Convention IV. One can refer by analogy to Article 1 (1) of the 1977 Protocol II Additional to the 1949 Four Geneva Conventions [. . .] Relying on Article 1 (1) of the 2nd Protocol and its Commentary, one can deduce that non-state armed groups can in fact exercise control over the territory."

88 *Occupation by an intermediary*

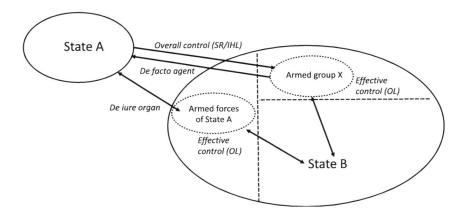

Figure 2.5 Indirect effective control, hypothetical case

and generally participate in, organise, coordinate, and/or plan its military operations. By contrast, no detailed control over each and every action of the group is needed. It bears mentioning that the situation in the north of state B would not automatically be classified as one of occupation. For this to happen, armed group X additionally needs to exercise effective control (OL) over the territory there.

Our classic understanding of effective control (OL) over territory has thus developed in several ways. The actors that exercise it do not necessarily have to be de jure organs of the occupying state so long as the armed groups and/or puppet governments are under that state's *overall* control (SR/IHL) and it is them, in turn, who exercise *effective* control (OL) over territory. Still, it is the state that carries the status of occupant, not the armed group.

Indirect effective control is therefore composed of three aspects:

1   Two actors: a foreign state, on the one hand, and an armed group and or de facto local authorities (neither of which is the legitimate government) present on the territory in question, on the other;
2   The relationship between the two should rest on *overall control* (SR/IHL), with the actions of the armed group/de facto authorities being attributable to the state in question and the state using them as its pawn; and
3   The armed group or de facto authorities have to have *effective control* (OL) over a territory or its part as envisaged by Article 42 HR 1907, Common Article 2 GCs, and Article 1 AP I 1977.

The notion of decisive influence was also addressed in this chapter. It was interpreted as a situation of occupation where state A exercised crucial, critical power and hence overall control (SR/IHL) over group X in state B, the group in turn exercising effective control (OL) over the territory. Finally, the chapter discussed IHL's own mechanism of control, anchored in Article 4A(2) GC III and Article 29 GC IV. Both could serve as a mechanism for classifying armed conflicts involving foreign state intervention as IACs and therefore lead to establishing proxy occupations. The level of control alluded to by the notions of belonging and agents, respectively, was said to correspond to overall control (SR/IHL).

3 Relinquishing control over territory

1. Introduction

When and how does the end of control over territory occur so that military occupation is considered terminated?[1] IHL fails to provide clear guidelines and appropriate tests in this regard.[2] What is more, the process of occupation ending may be different from its beginning (see Chapter 1). While the constitutive elements remain identical – hostile military forces, lack of consent, effective control over territory, and an ousted sovereign – the *sequence* by which they come about may be different.[3]

At the same time, there are different forms of relinquishing control over territory, entailing different combinations of the mentioned elements. For example, the complete loss of effective control (OL) over territory may occur either voluntarily, by the army of the hostile state deciding to withdraw, or unwillingly, by being pushed out. By contrast, establishing effective control (OL) never happens unwillingly. The question also arises whether once established, effective control (OL) can only be maintained through the physical presence of a military force, or whether it can also be upheld without boots on the ground.

---

1 G. von Glahn, *The Occupation of Enemy Territory: A Commentary on the Law and Practice of Belligerent Occupation* (Minneapolis, MN: Lund Press Inc., 1957), at 257; H. Cuyckens, *Revisiting the Law of Occupation* (Leiden: Brill/Martinus Nijhoff Publishers, 2018), at 59–60.

2 ICRC, *31st International Conference of the Red Cross and Red Crescent, International Humanitarian Law and the Challenges of Contemporary Armed Conflicts*, Geneva, October 2011 (EN 31IC/11/5.1.2), at 27: "IHL instruments do not provide clear standards for determining when an occupation starts and terminates", available at https://app.icrc.org/e-briefing/new-tech-modern-battlefield/media/documents/4-international-humanitarian-law-and-the-challenges-of-contemporary-armed-conflicts.pdf (visited 5 January 2017).

3 E.g. T. Ferraro (ed.), *Expert Meeting Occupation and Other Forms of Administration of Foreign Territory* (Geneva: ICRC, 2012), at 28; see also *Commentary of 2016, Convention (I) for the Amelioration of the Condition of the Wounded and Sick in Armed Forces in the Field*, Geneva 12 August 1949, Article 2, § 306, available at www.icrc.org/applic/ihl/ihl.nsf/Comment.xsp?action=openDocument&documentId=BE2D518CF5DE54EAC1257F7D0036B518 (visited 5 January 2017).

Relinquishing control over territory 91

This chapter therefore deepens our understanding of *how* and *when* occupation ends and what role effective control (OL) plays in this context. It discusses the interplay of the various constitutive elements of occupation whilst ending and delineates a possible hierarchy among them. More specifically: what happens when the occupant is no longer militarily present – yet still exerts control over the territory and its inhabitants? And how to deal with situations when the occupant manages to procure consent for remaining on the territory?

The ending of occupation is examined primarily pursuant to the criteria contained in Article 42 HR 1907, Article 6 GC IV 1949, and Article 3 AP I 1977. Still, there is yet another threshold of control for the purposes of ending the application of GC IV, which in turn generates a state's substantive obligations (discussed in Chapter 4).[4] As with occupation starting (Chapter 1), the analysis of relinquishing control in a military occupation context begins by examining the drafting history of the respective IHL instruments, in line with Article 32 VCLT.[5]

2. Legal history

2.1 From Brussels 1874 to The Hague 1907

2.1.1 Brussels

The Brussels Declaration of 1874 makes no mention of when or how occupation may end. The key therefore lies in analysing Article 1, paragraph 2 of this historic text, which reads that "occupation extends only to the territory where such authority has been established and can be exercised."

In examining the proceedings, it becomes apparent that the delegates, when reflecting on the notion of occupation and its commencement, inadvertently also dealt with the issue of occupation ending. This is primarily seen in the factor of a possible uprising, which would debilitate the capability of the occupant to exercise power, i.e. obstruct it to effectively control the territory. The notion of effectivity was used synonymously with the possibility to exercise authority without any restrictions, since "territories which contrive to free themselves from this authority cease to be occupied."[6] It was also stressed that the authority had

---

4 See generally, E. Benvenisti, 'The Law on the Unilateral Termination of Occupation', 93 *Tel Aviv University Law Faculty Papers* (2008) 1–12, available at http://law.bepress.com/cgi/viewcontent.cgi?article=1099&context=taulwps (visited 5 January 2017).

5 Article 32, *Vienna Convention on the Law of Treaties*, 1969, available at http://untreaty.un.org/ilc/texts/instruments/english/conventions/1_1_1969.pdf (visited 4 April 2019). Note, however, that Article 31 (General Rule of Interpretation) of the same instrument takes precedence.

6 UK House of Commons, 'Correspondence Respecting the Proposed Conference at Brussels on the Rules of Military Warfare', *United Kingdom Parliamentary Papers*, Miscellaneous No. 1 (1875) at 236.

92 *Relinquishing control over territory*

to be visible during insurrections, so occupation ending was associated to a successful uprising.[7] Control became the main indicator for assessing the end of occupation.[8]

Similarly, the Oxford Manual 1880 does not lay out any specific article determining the end of occupation. Like for the Brussels text, the key lies in analysing Article 41. Particularly its last sentence provides a relevant clue; however, it cannot be understood if not read within the context of the entire article:

> Territory is regarded as occupied when, as the consequence of invasion by hostile forces, the State to which it belongs has ceased, in fact, to exercise its ordinary authority therein, and the invading State is alone in a position to maintain order there. The limits within which this state of affairs exists determine the extent and duration of occupation.[9]

In other words, as long as the occupant exercises authority and for as long as effective control (OL) enables the occupant to maintain order, occupation has not (yet) ended. Occupation ends only once such control fails to be exerted.

2.1.2 The Hague

The 1899 and 1907 Hague Conferences also did not go further in defining the end of occupation. A reading of the delegates' deliberation concerning Article 1 of the 1874 Brussels Declaration (currently Article 42 HR 1907) suggests that territory is no longer occupied if the hostile army's control over the territory is lost via a successful uprising by the respective inhabitants. According to the majority view, the occupier must always be in sufficient strength to repress an outbreak, since "he proves his occupation by this act",[10] and an army only establishes an occupation when "its positions and lines of communication are secured by other corps. If the territory frees itself from the exercise of this authority it ceases to be occupied."[11]

During the deliberations of both the 1874 Brussels Declaration and the Hague Regulations of 1899 and 1907, the question of the duration of occupation remained equally unaddressed. No clause was specified that would determine the temporal frame. A lengthy occupation was not even contemplated.[12] During the 1874 discussions, the fact that determining the duration of an occupation was difficult was equally noted. On one occasion a reference was made to a lengthy occupation in connection to taxes[13] – without any further clarifications, however.

---

7 Ibid., at 237.
8 Ibid., at 259.
9 Article 41, *The Laws of War on Land*, Oxford, 9 September 1880.
10 UK House of Commons, *Correspondence, supra* note 6, at 160.
11 Ibid.
12 Ibid., at 161.
13 Ibid.

2.2 GC IV and relinquishing of control over territory

Let us now turn to GC IV to explore the way in which it addresses the control element as regards the ending of military occupation.[14] GC IV is the only Convention of 1949 containing specific provisions on the general cessation of its application.[15]

The analysis starts with Article 6 of GC IV. At first sight, the article solely deals with residual or continued obligations of the occupant. However, Article 6 in fact also contains answers to questions regarding the end of occupation. It uncovers a close link between the process of occupation ending and the ending of the application of the convention. Residual obligations are only briefly dealt with at the end of this chapter, and in more detail in Chapter 4. Our focus here is with the *ratione temporis* of Article 6 GC IV, which reads:

> The present Convention shall apply from the outset of any conflict or occupation mentioned in Article 2.
>
> In the territory of Parties to the conflict, the application of the present Convention shall cease on the general close of military operations. In the case of occupied territory, the application of the present Convention shall cease one year after the general close of military operations; however, the Occupying Power shall be bound, for the duration of the occupation, to the extent that such Power exercises the functions of government in such territory, by the provisions of the following Articles of the present Convention: 1 to 12, 27, 29 to 34, 47, 49, 51, 52, 53, 59, 61 to 77, 143. Protected persons whose release, repatriation or re-establishment may take place after such dates shall meanwhile continue to benefit by the present Convention.

Paragraph two raises two important questions: what does "one year after the general close of military operations" signify for the purposes of military occupation? And how to comprehend "however, the Occupying Power shall be bound, for the duration of the occupation, to the extent that such Power exercises the functions of government in such territory"?

The Pictet Commentary to this article provides a somewhat one-sided explanation, applicable to limited cases only. It explains that, in the preliminary stages of the drafting process of the Convention, it was thought the GC IV would

---

14 On the relationship between the HR 1907 and the GCs 1949, see Article 154 GC IV and the accompanying commentary: J. Pictet (ed.), *Commentary of 1958, Convention (IV) Relative to the Protection of Civilian Persons in Time of War Geneva, 12 August 1949*, Article 154 (Geneva: ICRC, 1958), at 614: " the Hague Regulations codify the laws and customs of war and are intended above all to serve as a guide to the armed forces, whereas the Fourth Convention aims principally at the protection of civilians."

15 Ibid., at 59.

94 *Relinquishing control over territory*

only cease to apply "when the occupation itself was at an end";[16] this is what the draft text adopted by the Stockholm Conference advanced. However, during the deliberations, some delegations pointed out that if the occupation were to continue for a long time after the general cessation of hostilities, a moment would come when the application of the Convention was no longer befitting, particularly if most of the governmental and administrative responsibilities carried out by the occupant had been passed on to the authorities of the occupied territory.[17]

At that time, i.e. in 1949, the conference delegates were thinking of the cases of Germany and Japan. Thus, it was decided that in the occupied territory, the convention would be fully applicable for one year, after which the occupant would only be bound by it "in so far as it continued to exercise governmental functions."[18] Pictet, too, considers the one-year rule reasonable since when hostilities cease, stringent measures against the civilian population will no longer be justified.[19] While Pictet's thinking about not needing stringent measures may seem appropriate, full protective measures were left unconsidered since only the articles extending certain minimal guarantees remained applicable.

Whether the selection of articles is sufficient for extending an adequate protection to protected persons after the one-year rule in Article 6 has lapsed will largely depend on the needs of the local population and the duration of the occupation regime itself. Certainly, an occupation lasting more than a year would necessitate additional rules to the benefit of protected persons. The rules provided may not sufficiently respond to the different needs of the population if an occupation lasts, for example, more than five years. The problem with the given articles is that they only deal with certain rights of protected persons that are very much basic in their nature. And the longer occupation lasts, the more the shortcomings of the IHL regime emerge,[20] as there will be a need for other rights to fully apply to the

---

16 Ibid., at 62.

17 Ibid.

18 Ibid., at 63.

19 Ibid.

20 M. Sassòli and A. A. Bouvier, *How Does Law Protect in War?*, Vol. 1 (2nd edn., Geneva: ICRC, 2006), at 186; N. Lubell, 'Challenges in Applying Human Rights Law to Armed Conflict', 87 *International Review of the Red Cross* (2005) 737–754, at 751–753. See further F. J. Hampson, 'The Relationship Between International Humanitarian Law and Human Rights Law from the Perspective of a Human Rights Treaty Body', 871 *International Review of the Red Cross* (2008) 549–572, at 557–560; N. Lubell, 'Parallel Application of International Humanitarian Law and International Human Rights Law: An Examination of the Debate', 40 *Israel Law Review* (2007) 648–660, at 651–654; C. Droege, 'The Interplay Between International Humanitarian Law and International Human Rights Law in Situations of Armed Conflict', 40 *Israel Law Review* (2007) 310–355, at 327–330. See additionally R. Wilde, 'Triggering State Obligations Extraterritorially: The Spatial Test in Certain Human Rights Treaties', 40 *Israel Law Review* (2007) 503–526, at 510–511; R. K. Goldman, 'Extraterritorial Application of the Human Rights to Life and Personal Liberty, Including Habeas Corpus, During Situations of Armed Conflict', in

benefit of protected persons, for example Article 74 AP I 1977 dealing with the reunion of dispersed families as a result of the armed conflict. Also not covered are refugees and their protection (Articles 44–45 GC IV), the right to leave of non-nationals of the occupied power (Article 48 GC IV), the extensive provisions regarding children's rights and their right to education (Article 50 GC IV), or even the duty of the occupant to maintain the public health and hygiene of the territory (Article 56 GC IV).

2.3 Article 6 and the general close of military operations

Article 6 also advances that the general close of military operations, i.e. the termination of hostilities, moves an occupation closer to its actual end. Paragraph 3 conveys the impression that when hostilities are over, occupation is over, too. In fact, such an impression should not arise because of paragraphs 1 and 2 of the same article. As such, an occupation's end should not be viewed to be dependent on hostilities coming to an end. If it were so, this would flatly contradict the fact that effective control (OL) over territory is needed in the understanding of Article 42 HR 1907, Article 2 Common GCs, and Article 1 AP I 1977 to qualify a situation as one of occupation. For a situation of occupation is defined precisely by the fact there are *no* ongoing hostilities, as they would hinder effective control (OL) over territory.

Also, in actual reality hostilities may or may not lead to a situation of occupation. If there is no effective control (OL) exerted over the territory and active hostilities amongst the belligerents continue, an IAC ensues and the IHL on the conduct of hostilities applies. There may also be cases, not to be confused with the foregoing, when during military occupation hostilities erupt between the occupant and a resistance movement.[21] This by itself would not change the fact that the territory is occupied, provided that effective control (OL) by the occupant over the territory is maintained. This will depend on the kind, intensity, and duration of the hostilities.[22] In other words, it is advanced here that what matters is whether effective control (OL) is still exercised by the state in question.

R. Kolb and G. Gaggioli (eds.), *Research Handbook on Human Rights and Humanitarian Law* (London: Edward Elgar Publishing, 2013) 104–124, at 114–115. See generally N. Lubell, *Extraterritorial Use of Force Against Non-State Actors* (Oxford: Oxford University Press, 2010); M. Milanović, *Extraterritorial Application of Human Rights Treaties: Law, Principles, and Policy* (Oxford: Oxford University Press, 2011); K. Da Costa, *The Extraterritorial Application of Selected Human Rights Treaties* (Leiden: Martinus Nijhoff Publishers, 2013).

21 On the legality of armed resistance in times of military occupation see M. Longobardo, *The Use of Armed Force in Occupied Territory* (Cambridge: Cambridge University Press, 2018), at 135–149.

22 G. Gaggioli (ed.), *The Use of Force in Armed Conflicts* (Geneva: ICRC, 2013), at 18–23.

96 *Relinquishing control over territory*

The analysis is linked to the following question: when does the "conduct of hostilities model" come into play in times of military occupation? During the discussions on the ICRC Report, experts thought that "active hostilities must be observable in occupied territory in order for the IHL rules on the conduct of hostilities to become applicable."[23] The discussions then revolved around the armed violence between the occupant's forces and those of the adversary government that were connected to the original IAC leading to the occupation[24] and the classification of the armed conflict in the context of military occupation. During the original IAC, rules on the conduct of hostilities would be activated.[25] In fact, any degree of armed violence involving both sides would justify resorting to these rules.[26] And once occupation was established, hostilities and other acts of violence directed towards the occupant could emanate from armed groups which do not formally belong to the occupied state. Then, if the threshold for determining a NIAC (Article 3 Common)[27] is met, the rules on the conduct of hostilities apply.[28]

Two additional points must be raised on this. First, Article 6 GC IV is worded in a way that creates a certain misunderstanding. It should in fact not make any reference to hostilities at all, since when there is a situation of occupation, there should be no active hostilities (excluding sporadic acts of violence or uprisings that may be dealt with by the occupant quickly; see also section 3.2). Hence, the exercise of effective control (OL) by the occupant is neither challenged nor lost. Second, if armed confrontations erupt on the occupied territory between the occupant's forces and an organised armed group or civilians (in both cases not affiliated with the occupied state), the question then is: which rules apply? Those on the conduct of hostilities, as soon as the threshold of a NIAC is crossed; or those on the use of force stemming from a law enforcement mode (derived mainly from IHRL); or both in parallel but directed at different actors?[29]

---

23 T. Ferraro, *Expert Meeting, supra* note 3, at 121.

24 Ibid., including forces that are affiliated militias or other resistance movements satisfying the criteria of Article 4 (A) (2) GC III 1949.

25 Ibid.

26 Ibid.

27 Ibid., at 122: "The Conduct of Hostilities Model would therefore apply only when the groups opposed to the occupying power displayed a form of organization enabling them to conduct concerted military operations and when the violence committed by them reached a certain level of intensity. The use of these criteria was justified by the fact that this kind of confrontation would constitute a 'new' armed conflict unconnected to the one that led to the occupation, since the parties challenging the occupying power's effective control would not be identical even if they claimed, as they often do, to fight on behalf or in support of the occupied state."

28 Ibid.

29 Ibid., 122–124; see further G. Gaggioli, *The Use of Force, supra* note 22, at 1: "It is not entirely clear in international law which situations in the context of an armed conflict are governed by the conduct of hostilities paradigm and which are covered by the law enforcement paradigm. [. . .] For example, in a non-international armed conflict, when a State is using force against fighters, it may be considered as simultaneously conducting hostilities

Relinquishing control over territory 97

It is submitted here that military occupation presumes the application of the law enforcement model, simply because occupation does not include active hostilities.[30] However, if violence between an armed group not affiliated with the state whose territory is occupied and the occupant meets the threshold of a NIAC, the conduct of hostilities mode becomes applicable.[31] Whether that equals the loss of control over territory and consequently the end of occupation is dependent on the armed group wrestling away effective control (OL) from the occupying state.

The drafting period of GC IV further reveals that Article 6 (then Article 4) generated a debate on whether the termination of hostilities should be construed as the end of an armed conflict or not, while the ending of occupation was not elaborated upon. For the delegates, the latter seemed to be clear and was to be regulated through the HR 1907.[32] Overall, it seemed that the US delegation was in favour of the application of the Convention as long as the conditions provided for in the Convention existed.[33] The UK viewed Article 42 and 43 HR 1907 to constitute "generally accepted principles", whereby the occupant "should not exceed those limits", while prolonging obligations until a peace treaty was concluded would have meant going much too far.[34] The delegate from Monaco believed the article under consideration to be well defined, as Conventions were drawn up for wartime – therefore, only a peace treaty could end a conflict.[35] The Italian delegate, in turn, regarded "end of hostilities" not to mean "the signing of a peace treaty" but rather as the "termination of military operations".[36]

The conference delegates avoided tackling the principles already defined in the HR 1907. They did not regard the issue of military occupation's ending as problematic. Moreover, they did not distinguish between, and seem to have been confused by, instances of *the ending of hostilities* and the *termination of*

---

and maintaining law and order (since fighters are also frequently criminals under domestic law). Similarly, situations of civilian unrest (such as riots) may arise while combat operations against the adversary are taking place. Sometimes the two situations of violence may even intermingle, for instance when fighters are hiding among rioting civilians or demonstrators. In such cases, it may become difficult to distinguish fighters from rioting civilians and to identify the relevant applicable paradigm." See also ibid., at 25.

30 D. Murray et al., *Practitioners' Guide to Human Rights Law in Armed Conflict* (Oxford: Oxford University Press, 2016), at 91 and 99.

31 M. Longobardo, *The Use of Armed Force, supra* note 21, at 236, and more generally at 229–240.

32 Final Record of the Diplomatic Conference of Geneva of 1949, Vol. II: Section A, Summary Records of 51 Meetings, Committee III, Civilians, Third Meeting (Bern: Federal Political Department, 1949), at 623–624.

33 Ibid., at 624.

34 Ibid.

35 Ibid.: "The present occupation of Germany was an entirely different case. While it was not desirable to dwell upon the point, it was nevertheless essential that Article 4 should be applicable to protected persons after the end of hostilities and the occupation, so long as those persons remained under conditions which called for such protection."

36 Ibid., at 625.

98 *Relinquishing control over territory*

occupation. In sum, it is unclear why the delegates at the diplomatic conference viewed occupation ending to be so clearly spelled out by the HR 1907.

Yet clearly the delegates were concerned about the responsibilities of the occupant. How long would they persist? Thus, delegates were largely concerned with the *duration* of occupation. Matters seem to have cleared up once the explanation provided by the International Committee of the Red Cross (ICRC) representative, Mr. Pilloud, was heard; he was asked to shed light on the intentions of the authors of Article 4 (i.e. Article 6 GC IV) when using the word "or" between the expressions "close of hostilities" and "of occupation".[37] He explained that the clause had been condensed and that a "distinction must be made between the application of the Convention in national territory and in occupied territory. In national territory, the Convention would cease to be applicable at the end of hostilities, whereas in occupied territory it would cease at the end of the occupation."[38] However, to our great disappointment, as this would have given more clarity to Article 6, the ICRC's clarification was not included. It is thought to be incorporated only by the way in which the GC IV is structured, i.e. through dividing the rules into those applying in *own* and those applying in *occupied territory*. The end of hostilities and occupation ending are two different factual occurrences. The delegates were primarily concerned with instances of prolonged occupation,[39] their thinking prompted by the cases of Germany and Japan during WWII.[40]

Be that as it may, Article 6 gives rise to debates and causes misperception, primarily because of the one-year rule. Article 6(3) is regarded to be in contrast with the provisions of HR 1907, which apply as long as the occupation lasts.[41] The GC IV appears to be departing from this rule and "even complicating the

---

37 Ibid. Also, the text of the article discussed (then Article 4) read as follows: "The present Convention shall be applied from the outset of all conflicts covered by Article 2. Its application shall cease at the close of hostilities or of occupation, except as regards the protected persons whose release, repatriation or reestablishment may take place subsequently and who until such operations are terminated, shall enjoy the benefits of the present Convention", see *The Draft Revised or New Conventions for the Protection of War Victims*, XVII International Red Cross Conference (Stockholm, August 1948), at 155, available at www.loc.gov/rr/frd/Military_Law/pdf/RC_Draft-revised.pdf (visited 5 January 2017).

38 Final Record of the Diplomatic Conference of Geneva of 1949, *supra* note 32, at 625.

39 Further on prolonged occupation, see generally I. Scobbie, 'International Law and the Prolonged Occupation of Palestine', United Nations Roundtable on Legal Aspects of the Question of Palestine, The Hague (20–22 May 2015), available at http://papers.ssrn.com/sol3/papers.cfm?abstract_id=2611130 (visited 5 January 2017); A. Roberts, 'Prolonged Military Occupation: The Israeli-Occupied Territories Since 1967', 84 *The American Journal of International Law* (1990) 44–103.

40 See O. Ben-Naftali, '"A La Recherche Du Temps Perdu": Rethinking Article 6 of the Fourth Geneva Convention in the Light of the Legal Consequences of the Construction of a Wall in the Occupied Palestinian Territory Advisory Opinion', 38 *Israel Law Review* (2005) 211–229, at 215.

41 R. Kolb and R. Hyde, *An Introduction to the International Law of the Armed Conflict* (Oxford; Portland, OR: Hart Publishing, 2008), at 103.

law".[42] When the ICJ opined on the Wall case, it also seems to have misread the law and confused the matter additionally by concluding that long-term occupations reduce the responsibilities of the occupant vis-à-vis the civilian population:

> A distinction is also made in the Fourth Geneva Convention between provisions applying during military operations leading to occupation and those that remain applicable throughout the entire period of occupation. . . . Since the military operations leading to the occupation of the West Bank in 1967 ended a long time ago, only those Articles of the Fourth Geneva Convention referred to in Article 6, paragraph 3, remain applicable in that occupied territory. These provisions include Articles 47, 49, 52, 53 and 59 of the Fourth Geneva Convention.[43]

Imseis terms the ICJ's interpretation of Article 6 GC IV "the most serious substantive error committed by the Court on IHL issues [. . .] relating to its beginning and end of its application to occupied territories".[44] The difficulty is that the ICJ unnecessarily narrowed the meaning of "military operations" to only those having led to occupation, although no such qualifying statement exists in the GC IV.

Instead, the phrase "after the general close of military operations" should be compared with the formulation in Article 118 GC III: "after the cessation of active hostilities". This is so because "the general close of military operations may occur after the cessation of active hostilities", as "no doubt, the cessation of active hostilities can precede a treaty of peace."[45] Moreover, as long as no peace treaty has entered into force, even if military operations are believed to be closed at a specific time, they may start anew and trigger the renewed application of GC IV.[46]

To summarise this section, it could not be identified clearly when in the case of occupied territory GC IV would stop to apply. The impracticable nature of Article 6 was demonstrated, incapable of dealing with protracted occupations. Moreover, setting a time limit artificially constrains the application of IHL and has the potential to disregard the existing facts, i.e. continuation of effective control (OL) over territory. Such was also the view of the ICRC delegate,

---

42 Ibid., at 104.

43 *Case Concerning Legal Consequences of the Construction of a Wall in the Occupied Palestinian Territory*, Advisory Opinion, 9 July 2004, § 125–126, available at www.icj-cij.org/en/case/131 (visited 15 July 2017). Although the experts during the deliberations on the ICRC Report on Occupation agreed that "the ICJ's statement on this article was incorrect for the purposes of IHL, they contended that – as a consequence – its validity could not be completely disregarded and its desuetude not yet established"; T. Ferraro, *Expert Meeting*, *supra* note 3, at 77.

44 A. Imseis, 'Critical Reflections on the International Humanitarian Aspects of the ICJ Wall Advisory Opinion', 99 *The American Journal of International Law* (2005) 102–118, at 105.

45 Y. Dinstein, *The International Law of Belligerent Occupation* (Cambridge: Cambridge, University Press, 2009), at 282.

46 Ibid.

100 *Relinquishing control over territory*

Mr. Pilloud. Thus, so long as occupation persists, that is for as long as the occupant exercises effective control (OL), the GC IV should apply. An analysis of Article 3 AP I 1977, following this section, supports this claim.

2.4 Article 3 AP I 1977 and relinquishing control over the territory

Article 3 AP I 1977 regulates the beginning and end of the application of that instrument and may be viewed as an attempt to remedy the confusion created by Article 6 GC IV. Whether this Article is of customary nature remains to be ascertained by practice.[47] Article 3(b) reads that:

> the application of the Conventions and of this Protocol shall cease, in the territory of Parties to the conflict, on the general close of military operations and, in the case of occupied territories, on the termination of the occupation.

Unlike Article 6 GC IV, Article 3 AP I 1977 does not confuse situations of military operations with military occupations. It clearly keeps them apart. The Commentary on the Additional Protocols on this part of the article confirms this by explaining "military operations" to mean movements, manoeuvres, and actions of any kind, carried out by the armed forces to fight their adversaries.[48] And the formulation "on the general close of military operations", according to the Commentary, conforms to the expression used in Article 6 GC IV.[49] This time the Commentary more clearly articulates that the latter formulation is at "the time of a general armistice, capitulation or just when the occupation of the

---

47 On the Customary Status of AP rules, see generally T. Meron, *Human Rights and Humanitarian Norms as Customary Law* (Oxford: Oxford University Press, 1989); The Honorable F. Pocar, 'To What Extent Is Protocol I Customary International Law?', 78 *International Law Studies* (2002) 337–351; C. Greenwood, 'Customary Law Status of the 1977 Geneva Protocols', in A. J. M. Delissen and G. J. Tanja (eds.), *Humanitarian Law of Armed Conflict: Challenges Ahead* (Dordrecht: Martinus Nijhoff Publishers, 1991) 93–114; G. Abi-Saab, 'The 1977 Additional Protocols and General International Law: Some Preliminary Reflections', in A. J. M. Delissen and G. J. Tanja (eds.), *Humanitarian Law of Armed Conflict: Challenges Ahead* (Dordrecht: Martinus Nijhoff Publishers, 1991) 115–126. Note: According to Ben-Naftali, while Israel remains a persistent objector of some AP I rules, such an objection does not seem to extend to Article 3 (b): "The argument that Article 6 of the Fourth Geneva Convention limits the Convention's scope of applicability was never raised before the Israeli Courts, and indeed the Israeli High Court of Justice had applied provisions that would have otherwise become inapplicable in light of the language of Article 6. This practice characterizes other prolonged occupations, thereby lending support to the proposition that Article 3(b) of Protocol I enjoys customary status"; O. Ben-Naftali, '"A La Recherche Du Temps Perdu"', *supra* note 40, at 216–217.

48 Y. Sandoz, C. Swinarski and B. Zimmerman (eds.), *Commentary on the Additional Protocols of 8 June 1977 to the Geneva Conventions of 12 August 1949* (ICRC: Martinus Nijhoff Publishers, 1987), at 67.

49 Ibid.

Relinquishing control over territory   101

whole territory of a Party is completed, accompanied by the effective cessation of all hostilities, without the necessity of a legal instrument of any kind."[50]

From the perspective of military occupation coming to an end, this article too does not clearly provide a test when and how occupation is over. The expression "on the termination of the occupation" indicates that there is no time limit given as to when occupation may be over and that its ending is dependent on the moment the occupant desists exercising effective control (OL). In implying that the duration of occupation (the elements of *ratione temporis*) is dependent on the occupant exercising effective control (OL) over territory, it reaffirms that the termination of occupation is a factual matter. This further suggests that the 1949 Conventions and AP I 1977 stop applying when effective control (OL) is no longer wielded by the occupant. The Commentary to this provision explains that the termination of occupation "may occur a long time after the beginning of that occupation, and can come about in various ways, de facto or de jure, depending on whether it ends in the liberation of the territory or in its incorporation into one or more of its states with the right of the people or peoples of that territory to self-determination."[51]

During the Diplomatic Conference, Article 3(b) AP I 1977 was largely well received. For the Cypriot delegate, it constituted a forward development of IHL by expanding its application.[52] The insertion of the word "conventions" was intended to ensure that the provisions concerning the beginning and ending of the application of the two protocols and the four conventions would coincide, otherwise discrepancies could have arisen.[53] I consider this Article to draw the line between a situation of military operation and the termination of occupation, reconfirming that these two were contemplated as separate factual occurrences. For as long as the territory remains under military occupation, the rules of IHL must be fully respected by the occupant. This is what permeates the logic of Article 3 AP I 1977. In sum, the wording of the entire Article 3 AP I 1977 implies that the test of occupation termination is necessarily based on the elements of Article 42 HR 1907 and Common Article 2 GCs. This is primarily because AP I 1977 does not replace Article 42 HR 1907, nor does it supply a new test. Additional information is still detected with regards to conceptualising the ending of occupation, for the wording "on the termination of the occupation" indicates that the territory remains occupied for as long as it is under the effective control (OL) of the

---

50 Ibid., at 67–68.

51 Ibid.

52 Official Records of the Diplomatic Conference on the Reaffirmation and Development of International Humanitarian Law Applicable in Armed Conflicts (Geneva, 1974–1977), Vol. VI, at 60 (the Cypriot Delegate).

53 Official Records of the Diplomatic Conference on the Reaffirmation and Development of International Humanitarian Law Applicable in Armed Conflicts (Geneva, 1974–1977), Vol. VIII, at 67 (Delegate of the Arab Republic of Egypt).

102 *Relinquishing control over territory*

hostile army,[54] thereby adopting a broader approach than Article 6 GC IV and its one-year rule.

2.5 *The needed test for relinquishing control in IHL*

Military manuals provide additional clarification for distilling the necessary test. More specifically, the aspect of the *transfer* of effective control (OL) from the occupant to the old or a new power stands out. What is additionally interesting is that these manuals do not share a uniform stance, nor one test regarding when or how occupation ends.

The Canadian Military Manual states that occupation can be terminated in at least three ways: the occupying power may withdraw from the territory; it may be ejected from it; or a part or all of the occupied territory may be annexed by the occupant.[55] Furthermore, occupation does not terminate until a state exercises its authority over the area as part of its own territory.[56] This implies that the transfer of effective control (OL) over territory is possible only to a sovereign. However, the UK Military Manual considers a transfer of effective control to *anyone* except the former occupant; it further stipulates that occupation ends when the occupant is driven out or evacuates the area. Thus, occupation will end "when effective control transfers to a different authority, such that the territory ceases to be under the authority of external military forces."[57] The UK manual also does not consider a rebellion of inhabitants or the occasional success of guerrilla or resistance movements to bring occupation to a close.[58] The US Law of War Manual stipulates that a state ceases to be an occupant when it no longer governs the occupied territory, or when a hostile relationship stops to exist between the occupied territory and the occupant.[59] This confirms the previously-said: occupation lasts for as long as effective control (OL) is wielded by the occupant.

Another question is what degree of control can determine the ending of occupation? Assessing the required level of control for the ending of occupation is considered to be a factual matter.[60] Let us now revert to Article 42 HR 1907,

---

54 R. Kolb and R. Hyde, *An Introduction to the International Law, supra* note 41, at 103.

55 Canada, National Defence Joint Doctrine Manual (B-GJ-005–104/FP-021) (Issued on Authority of the Chief of Defence Staff) (2001–08–13), § 1204.1 at 12–2. It should be noted, however, that annexation of territory constitutes a breach of international law; see Chapter 2, section 3.3.1.

56 Ibid., § 1204.2 at 12–2.

57 UK Ministry of Defence, *The Manual of the Law of Armed Conflict* (Oxford: Oxford University Press, 2004), § 11.7 at 277.

58 Ibid., § 11.7.1 at 277.

59 *Department of Defense Law of War Manual*, Office of General Counsel, Department of Defense (Washington, DC: Department of Defense, June 2015), at 750.

60 Program on Humanitarian Policy and Conflict Research (Policy Brief), 'Legal Aspects of Israel's Disengagement Plan Under International Humanitarian Law', Harvard University, 2010, at 9, available at http://hhi.harvard.edu/publications/

Relinquishing control over territory   103

as the end of an occupation should in effect be determined by the same two conditions that trigger occupation law's application: the control of territory by hostile armed forces and their possibility to exercise authority over the local population.[61] The threshold of control required for assessing the ending of military occupation then is nothing other than complete abandonment of effective control (OL) over the territory. The test for determining the ending of occupation consists of the same elements as those used for determining the establishment of control over territory in the first place: physical presence of foreign troops, their ability to enforce authority over the territory instead of the local governmental power, and absence of the local government's consent to such a presence.

However, the main difference lies in the fact that effective control (OL) over territory has to be fully relinquished by the former occupant in a way that *some other* authority is able to step in and control the territory. But whether that other authority – which can either be the ousted sovereign or a new legitimate power – actually takes over control over the territory is irrelevant for occupation as such to have ended. This does not exclude a scenario in which the occupant peacefully hands over territorial control to the previous sovereign or to a new authority (for example via self-determination as envisaged by PIL, see section 3.5.2 in Chapter 2).

Nor does it mean the former occupant is exempt from certain post-occupation obligations. What matters is that the former occupant fully exempts itself from any form of control over that new power (if there is one). It should not interfere and allow the new power to govern and fully exercise governmental powers over the area and its inhabitants. Of course, it is possible that when a state withdraws from the territory and there is no new power in place, a power vacuum ensues[62] with only rivalling armed groups left for vying over controlling the territory. In this case, while occupation has ended, a transfer of power over the territory has not taken place. However, nothing in the law of military occupation suggests that the occupant is obligated to ensure such a transfer.[63]

Alternatively, in case state A obtains consent for its military forces to remain on the territory of state B or parts thereof, occupation has equally ended – provided such a presence is based on the genuine consent (as per Article 25 VCLT) issued by the ousted sovereign or the authority that has come into power. Hence, state A's forces are no longer hostile and the previous sovereign

---

legal-aspects-israels-disengagement-plan-under-international-humanitarian-law-ihl   (visited 5 January 2017).

61 D. Thürer and M. Maclaren, ' "Jus Post Bellum in Iraq": A Challenge to the Applicability and Relevance of International Humanitarian Law', in K. Dicke et al. (eds.), *Weltinnenrecht Festschrift für Jost Delbrük* (Berlin: Dunker and Humblot, 2005) 1–30, at 21, available at www.ivr.uzh.ch/dam/jcr:00000000-528e-0b9e-ffff-ffff93869fca/FSDelbrueck.pdf   (visited 5 January 2017).

62 Y. Ronen, 'Post-Occupation Law', in C. Stahn, J. S. Easterday, and J. Iverson (eds.), *Jus Post Bellum* (Oxford: Oxford University Press, 2014) 428–446, at 435.

63 C. Stahn, *The Law and Practice of International Territorial Administration* (Cambridge: Cambridge University Press, 2008), at 119.

or the new power exercises effective control over the territory and its inhabitants instead. Occupation, therefore, ends if at least *one* of the following three conditions is met:

1 State A's military forces are no longer physically *present* on the territory (they have either willfully left or been forcefully ejected);
2 State A's military forces are not in a position or willfully do not *exercise authority* over the total or parts of the territory of state B anymore; or
3 State A's military forces are no longer *hostile* to state B, as their presence is consented to by the latter.

Do these elements stand in a hierarchy? The answer to this query is negative, since the three elements can work perfectly well in isolation from each other to end occupation: either lack of consent disappears by obtaining it, or effective control (OL) over the territory vanishes by withdrawing one's army and/or by handing over the authority.

On the face of it, this test may seem straightforward. But applying it in practice, and especially to contemporary instances of occupation, can be difficult. This is so because often an occupant does not fully give up control over territory and finds a way to still exercise it. For example, its armed forces physically withdraw from a territory but retain elements of control over it through the air space and maritime zones, like in the case of Gaza (see section 3.4). Or, after having invaded a territory, an occupant establishes a puppet government and through it wields control (see Chapter 2).

3. Forms of relinquishing control

Two readings of the ending of occupation that both depend on the level of control, namely the actual and potential control tests, have been advanced:

> Under the test of actual control, occupation ends when the occupant no longer exercises its authority in the occupied territory. Under the test of potential control, occupation ends when the occupant is no longer capable of exercising its authority.[64]

However, both these tests lack clarity. How to conceive of "potential control" or being "no longer capable of exercising its authority"? Should both be understood as no longer having the capacity to reoccupy the territory? Or should it be construed in the same way that Article 42 HR 1907 envisages the potential for exercising control, that is when a hostile army is present on the territory and can, according to its discretion, set up a military administration?

---

64 E. Benvenisti, 'The Law on the Unilateral Termination of Occupation', *supra* note 4, at 4.

We can identify at least six forms of relinquishing control over territory that states have employed when they claimed occupation did not exist anymore. These six are discussed in turn.

3.1 Complete end of control over territory

This type of occupation ending takes place when there is no more control over the territory wielded by the occupant as defined by Article 42 HR 1907, Common Article 2 GCs, and Article 1 AP I 1977. It might be triggered by the fact that the occupant vacates the territory and leaves, and/or by the hostile forces being pushed out by the sovereign's forces, a new governmental authority or a third party (e.g. by the coalition forces who pushed Iraq out of Kuwait[65]), or by an uprising. This type of relinquishing control is easiest to identify, as the key element of effective control (OL), namely military presence, is no longer given.

The complete loss of control may also take place gradually, that is, in a prolonged fashion and/or geographically uneven. This happens when the occupant keeps some territories under a tight grip but others not. It can result from a selective approach by the occupant on where to wield its effective control. However, occupation as such is not over until the complete withdrawal of troops has taken place. An example of troops "phasing out" is the Soviet Union's dis-occupation of Afghanistan,[66] leaving behind a protracted civil war with devastating impact.[67] The military withdrawal had been outlined in the Pakistani-Afghan 'Agreement on the Interrelationships for the Settlement of the Situation Relating to Afghanistan':

> In accordance with the timeframe agreed upon [. . .] there will be a phased withdrawal of the foreign troops which will start on the date of entry into force. [. . .] One half of the troops will be withdrawn by 15 August 1988 and the withdrawal of all troops will be completed within nine months. [. . .] The phased withdrawal of the foreign troops will start and be completed within the timeframe envisaged in paragraph 5.[68]

---

65 J. Kostiner, *Conflict and Cooperation in the Gulf Region* (Wiesbaden: VS Verlag für Sozialwissenschaften, 2009), at 116–119 and 260; W. Kälin, *Report on the Situation of Human Rights in Kuwait Under Iraqi Occupation*, UN Commission on Human Rights, EC/N 4/1992/26, 16 January 1992, available at http://hr-travaux.law.virginia.edu/content/report-situation-human-rights-kuwait-under-iraqi-occupation-prepared-walter-kälin-special (visited 5 January 2017); see generally H. A. Hassan, *The Iraqi Invasion of Kuwait* (London: Pluto Press, 1999).

66 G. Feifer, *The Great Gamble: The Soviet War in Afghanistan* (New York: Harper Perennial, 2009), at 238–241.

67 Human Rights Watch, *World Report 1989: Afghanistan*, available at www.hrw.org/reports/1989/WR89/Afghanis.htm#TopOfPage (visited 5 January 2017).

68 *Agreements on the Settlement of the Situation Relating to Afghanistan* (Geneva Accords), SC Res. S/19834 (1988), available at http://peacemaker.un.org/sites/peacemaker.un.org/files/AF_880414_AgreementsSettlementoftheSituationRelatingAfghanistan%28eng%29.pdf (visited

106 *Relinquishing control over territory*

3.2 Temporary and partial loss of control over parts of a territory

A temporary and partial loss of control over parts of a territory occurs when the occupant's effective control (OL) is challenged by an uprising, insurgency, or some other armed force. Such an instance does not *per se* mean that the rest of the territory is no longer occupied. In order that the territory over which the occupant lost its effective control (OL) is still considered occupied, the occupant must successfully curb the uprising and regain effective control (OL). Depending on the will and military might of the occupant, this can take some time. The uprising should be substantial and must *disable* the occupant to exert effective control. Small-scale uprisings or hit-and-run operations that can easily be put down do not mean that, where they occur, occupation ends.

Out of these two forms of loss of control, a merely temporary loss exhibits fewer problems for the occupant, since it envisages regaining effective control (OL) in a short timeframe. An example is the uprising on 19 April 1943 in the Warsaw Ghetto after the German troops and police had entered the ghetto to deport its surviving inhabitants. The Germans suppressed the insurrection by 16 May 1943, leaving the area in complete ruins.[69] By contrast, the partial loss of control over territory is usually connected to a longer period of time and repeated efforts to re-establish control over territory. A case in point are the events surrounding the Coalition Forces in Fallujah,[70] notably the initial US-led invasion of Iraq in April 2003 and the two instances of trying to re-establish control over Fallujah.

After having asserted effective control (OL) over Baghdad, in April 2003 the Coalition Forces occupied Fallujah. The residents resented the troops patrolling the area as well as their other actions.[71] Facts attest that the Coalition Forces lost effective control (OL) over Fallujah after its initial occupation, though not all at once. The initial occupation phase of Iraq was not marked by Fallujah posing a threat to the hostile forces' control. Nevertheless, according to the US Army National Ground Intelligence Center, on 28 April 2003 a large Iraqi crowd protesting the Coalition's takeover of a school turned violent and 15 Iraqis were killed.[72] Violence against the Coalition continued well into fall 2003, causing the

---

5 January 2017); D. Cordovez and S. S. Harrison, *Out of Afghanistan: The Inside Story of the Soviet Withdrawal* (New York: Oxford University Press, 1995), at 396; see also UNGOMAP, *Afghanistan/Pakistan Background*, UNGOMAP (2002), available at www.un.org/en/peacekeeping/missions/past/ungomap/background.html (visited 5 January 2017).

69 Holocaust Encyclopedia, *Warsaw Ghetto Uprising*, 2 July 2016, available at www.ushmm.org/wlc/en/article.php?ModuleId=10005188 (visited 5 January 2017); A. Beevor, *The Second World War* (London: Weidenfeld and Nicolson, 2012), at 298–299.

70 W. C. Martel, *Victory in War* (Cambridge: Cambridge University Press, 2007), at 263.

71 Human Rights Watch Report, *Violent Response: US Army in al-Fallujah* (16 June 2003), available at www.hrw.org/report/2003/06/16/violent-response/us-army-al-falluja (visited 5 January 2017).

72 I. Fisher, 'US Troops Fire on Iraqi Protestors, Leaving 15 Dead', *The New York Times*, 29 April 2003, available at www.nytimes.com/2003/04/29/international/worldspecial/29CND-IRAQ.html?pagewanted=all (visited 5 January 2017).

US forces to change garrison locations to a series of camps outside Fallujah.[73] At the same time, the infiltration of foreign fighters into Fallujah began.

The culmination of these events was the slaying of four American Blackwater contractors, on 31 March 2004. Secretary of Defence Rumsfeld, Commander Abizaid, and Coalition Provisional Authority (CPA) Chief Bremer then decided that a military response was needed immediately, as "Fallujah had become a symbol of resistance that dominated international headlines."[74] Thus, "Operation Vigilant Resolve" (also dubbed "first battle of Fallujah") was launched on 4 April 2004 in direct response to the Blackwater incident to deal with the insurgency.[75] But the advance of the Coalition Forces was met with harsh resistance.[76] This first battle ended on 30 April 2004, when the US mandated the "Fallujah Brigade" composed of Iraqi soldiers to take over the city under US command.[77]

The resistance was never at bay and a second onslaught was thus prepared by the Coalition Forces. On 8 November 2004, operation "Phantom Fury" began.[78] Stiff resistance was encountered by US Marines and the other components of the Coalition Forces. The mosques served the resistance as command and control centres. This second battle of Fallujah continued until 26 November,[79] and only by the end of December 2004 was Fallujah cleared for civilian return.[80]

What to make of this case in terms of temporary loss of control? After the initial American invasion of Iraq, within one year's time, local resistance to the occupation in Fallujah was strong and consolidating control had become increasingly difficult. The Coalition was thus not in effective control (OL) of the entire area as understood in Article 42 HR 1907, Common Article 2 GCs, and Article 1 AP I 1977. Based on the above it is even difficult to advance that Fallujah was *ever* really occupied by the Coalition Forces between 28 April 2003 and 26 November 2004. This does *not* mean that other parts of Iraq were not under the Coalition Force's occupation; according to Common Article 2 GCs, territory can be under partial or total occupation. In other words, occupation extends to whichever part of the territory a hostile force is capable of exerting effective control (OL) over, provided there is no armed resistance to such a control. By contrast, given successful resistance pockets it would be futile to claim the territory there to be under effective control (OL). Hence, all appears to depend on the *moment* in which the occupant successfully curbs an uprising, thereby regaining and maintaining effective control (OL). In Fallujah, this moment occurred only in late 2004.

---

73 US Army National Ground Intelligence Centre (NGIC), *Complex Environments: Battle of Fallujah 1, April 2004*, NGIC, 31.03.2006, at 4, available at www.expose-the-war-profiteers.org/archive/government/2006/20060331.pdf (visited 5 January 2017).

74 Ibid.

75 V. L. Foulk, *The Battle for Fallujah* (Jefferson, NC: McFarland and Company, 2007), at 21–22.

76 Ibid.

77 Ibid., at 44.

78 Ibid., at 212–213.

79 Ibid., at 224.

80 Ibid., at 225–226.

108 *Relinquishing control over territory*

3.3 The potential for regaining control

The potential for regaining control as a form of relinquishing control over territory was raised as a form of its own since the occupant is "no longer capable of exercising its authority".[81] This explanation suggests that all possible avenues for the occupant to exercise its authority no longer exist, manifested primarily in the ousted sovereign regaining its original territorial control, thereby impeding the former occupant to wield control over the territory. Alternatively, it may also mean that the former occupant no longer has any interest in re-occupying the territory.

However, I primarily consider the potential for regaining control to mean the former occupant's military capacity to re-assert its effective control (OL) over territory any time after its partial withdrawal. In this scenario, the armed forces have partially vacated the territory, leaving behind – based on the consent of the returned sovereign or a new government – a military garrison or large military base that is in principle capable of asserting effective control (OL) over a part or the whole of the territory. If consent to the presence of the garrison is then withdrawn by the territorial administration, and if the garrison's armed force asserts effective control (OL) over a part or all of the territory, military occupation begins anew.

The potential for regaining control can be exemplified by the situation in the West Bank. Israel effectively seized the West Bank from Jordan in the 1967 Six-Day War.[82] As a result of that war, Israel occupied the West Bank and Eastern Jerusalem[83], the Sinai Peninsula, the Gaza Strip, and Golan Heights.[84] Although UN Security Council Resolution 242 called for a withdrawal of Israel from those

---

81 E. Benvenisti, 'The Law on the Unilateral Termination of Occupation', *supra* note 4, at 4. See also M. Milanović, *Extraterritorial Application of Human Rights Treaties: Law, Principles, and Policy* (Oxford: Oxford University Press, 2011), at 142–144.

82 See generally S. M. Akram and M. Lynk, 'Arab-Israeli Conflict', *Max Planck Encyclopedia of Public International Law* (2011), available at http://opil.ouplaw.com/view/10.1093/law:epil/9780199231690/law-9780199231690-e1246 (visited 5 January 2017).

83 B. Rubin, 'Israel Occupied Territories', *Max Planck Encyclopedia of Public International Law* (2009) § 11, available at http://opil.ouplaw.com/view/10.1093/law:epil/9780199231690/law-9780199231690-e1301 (visited 5 January 2017): "In 1980 the Knesset adopted the Basic Law: Jerusalem, Capital of Israel, which provides that '[u]nified Jerusalem is the capital of Israel', hence there is no doubt that Israel regards the annexed area as its own territory." See also E. Lauterpacht, *Jerusalem and the Holy Places* (London: The Anglo-Israeli Association, 1968/1980); M. Hirsch, D. Housen-Couriel and R. Lapidoth, *Whither Jerusalem* (The Hague: Martinus Nijhoff Publishers, 1995).

84 B. Rubin, 'Israel Occupied Territories', *supra* note 83, §§ 1–3; see also US Department of State, 'Israel and the Occupied Territories', available at www.state.gov/j/drl/rls/hrrpt/2001/nea/8262.htm (visited 5 January 2017).

Relinquishing control over territory 109

territories,[85] the West Bank – including East Jerusalem[86] – is until today regarded as occupied by Israel.[87]

Nevertheless, some views from Israel consider this situation not to amount to an occupation,[88] upholding instead the "missing reversioner" theory.[89] The Levy Report, whose panel was formed by Prime Minister Netanyahu and headed by former Supreme Court Justice Edmond Levy,[90] echoed this theory.[91] This not only contradicts the opinion of the international community as seen earlier, but

85 SC Res. 242 (1967), see also SC Res. 446 (1976), SC Res. 465 (1980), SC Res. 484 (1980) and SC Res. 2334 (2016). The ICJ in the Wall case opined that: "The territories situated between the Green Line [. . .] and the former eastern boundary of Palestine under the Mandate were occupied by Israel in 1967 during the armed conflict between Israel and Jordan. Under customary international law, these were therefore occupied territories in which Israel had the status of occupying Power. Subsequent events in these territories [. . .] have done nothing to alter this situation. All these territories (including East Jerusalem) remain occupied territories and Israel has continued to have the status of occupying Power." *Case Concerning the Legal Consequences of the Construction of a Wall in the Occupied Palestinian Territory*, supra note 43, § 78, §§ 75–77, and §§ 90–101.

86 *Israeli Settlements in the Occupied Palestinian Territory, Including East Jerusalem, and the Occupied Syrian Golan*, UN Doc. A/71/355, 24 August 2016, §3; *Human Rights Situation in Palestine and Other Occupied Arab Territories*, Human Rights Council 34th session, A/HRC/34/L. 41/Rev.1, 24 March 2017; see also 'B'Tsalem – The Israeli Information Center for Human Rights in the Occupied Territories', *47 Years of Temporary Occupation*, available at www.btselem.org/download/201406_47_year_long_temporary_occupation_eng.pdf (visited 5 January 2017).

87 *Israeli Settlements in the Occupied Palestinian Territory, supra* note 86, § 5, § 10–11; see also Amnesty International, *Israel and the Occupied Palestinian Territories: 2015/2016 Annual Report*, available at www.amnesty.org/en/countries/middle-east-and-north-africa/israel-and-occupied-palestinian-territories/report-israel-and-occupied-palestinian-territories/ (visited 5 January 2017); *Case Concerning the Legal Consequences of the Construction of a Wall in the Occupied Palestinian Territory, supra* note 43, §§ 90–101.

88 J. Goldberg, 'The West Bank: If It's Not Occupation, Then What Is It?', *The Atlantic*, 9 July 2012, available at www.theatlantic.com/international/archive/2012/07/the-west-bank-if-its-not-occupation-then-what-is-it/259562/ (visited 5 January 2017).

89 I. Scobbie and S. Hibbin, *The Israeli-Palestine Conflict in International Law: Territorial Issues* (The U.S./Middle East Project, 2009), at 102; see also Y. Z. Blum, 'The Missing Reversioner: Reflections on the Status of Judea and Samaria', 3 *Israel Law Review* (1968) 279–301, at 288; see generally M. Shamgar, 'The Observance of International Law in the Administered Territories', 1 *Israel Yearbook on Human Rights* (1971) 263–266.

90 T. Lazaroff, 'Legal Report on Outposts Recommends Authorization', *The Jerusalem Post*, 7 September 2012, available at www.jpost.com/Diplomacy-and-Politics/Legal-report-on-outposts-recommends-authorization (visited 5 January 2017).

91 The Levy Commission Report, *The Legal Status of Building in Judea and Samaria* (Jerusalem, 2012) (translated by Regavim, 2014), at 8, available at http://israelipalestinian.procon.org/sourcefiles/The-Levy-Commission-Report-on-the-Legal-Status-of-Building-in-Judea-and-Samaria.pdf (visited 5 January 2017).

110 *Relinquishing control over territory*

is also contrary to the Israeli HCJ's reasoning in *Mara'abe v. The Prime Minister of Israel*:

> The Judea and Samaria areas are held by the State of Israel in belligerent occupation. The long arm of the state in the area is the military commander. He is not the sovereign in the territory held in belligerent occupation. [. . .] His power is granted him by public international law regarding belligerent occupation. The legal meaning of this view is twofold: first, Israeli law does not apply in these areas. They have not been "annexed" to Israel. Second, the legal regime which applies in these areas is determined by public international law regarding belligerent occupation.[92]

Be that as it may, on 13 September 1993, representatives of the government of Israel and the Palestinian Liberation Organization (PLO) signed the Declaration of Principles on Interim Self-Government Arrangements (Oslo I), followed on 28 September by the Israeli-Palestinian Interim Agreement (Oslo II).[93] The overall purpose of the latter was to transfer authority in the West Bank and the Gaza Strip to a Palestinian Council.[94] To do so, the West Bank was divided into three administrative zones: Area A (Palestinian towns), Area B (Palestinian villages and hamlets), and Area C (all the rest, including Israeli army bases and settlements).[95] The yet to be established Palestinian Council was to have maximum jurisdiction over areas A and B while in Area C Israel would transfer only "civil powers and responsibilities not relating to territory."[96] For Area A, Israel pledged to fully transfer authority to the Palestinian Council.[97] In Area B, while Israel envisaged the complete redeployment of its military forces, it would maintain "the overriding responsibility for security for the purpose of protecting Israelis and confronting the threat of Terrorism",[98] and Palestinians assumed the responsibility for public order only for Palestinians via forming their own police force,[99] subject however to Israeli restrictions.[100]

---

92 High Court of Justice, Israel (HCJ) 7957/04 Mara'abe v. the Prime Minister of Israel (Judgment of 21 June 2005) § 14; see also HCJ, Israel 9593/04 Rashed Morar, Head of Yanun Village Council and Others v. IDF Commander in Judea and Samaria (a petition, 26 June 2006) § 12.

93 Israeli-Palestinian 'Interim Agreement on the West Bank and the Gaza Strip' (Oslo II), 28 September 1995, available at www.mfa.gov.il/mfa/foreignpolicy/peace/guide/pages/the%20israeli-palestinian%20interim%20agreement.aspx (visited 5 January 2017).

94 Ibid., Preamble and Article 1.

95 E. Benvenisti, *The International Law of Occupation* (Oxford: Oxford University Press, 2012), at 210.

96 Israeli-Palestinian, 'Interim Agreement on the West Bank and the Gaza Strip' (Oslo II), *supra* note 93, Article XI (2.a and c)

97 Ibid., Article XIII (1).

98 Ibid., Article XIII (2.a).

99 Ibid., Article XIII (2.b)

100 Ibid., Article XIII (2.b.7). On the political effects, see for example A. Gross, *The Writing on the Wall: Rethinking the International Law of Occupation* (Cambridge: Cambridge University Press, 2017), at 203–204.

Relinquishing control over territory 111

The accord clearly set out the transfer of powers in Areas A and B, while provisions relating to Area C remained the vaguest in formulation. But how to interpret the transfer of "civil powers and responsibilities not relating to territory" to mean that occupation is over when in essence the management of *any* population is tied to the management of the territory on which it lives? For even if one argues that the right to education does not fall under powers relating to territory, school buildings still need to be located on a piece of land, and access thereto necessitates roads and supply lines etc. Furthermore, Oslo II does not really envisage anything with regards to the Israeli government giving up territorial control over Area C.[101] Still today, the Israeli military retains full authority over the development of that area, including control over the planning and zoning of houses, industrial zones, tourism sites, roads, and electricity lines.[102]

The clearest example of Israel's potential for regaining control and re-occupying a territory is Area A. For example, March and April 2002 saw suicide bomb attacks by Palestinian groups against Israelis increasing in frequency.[103] Subsequently, the Israeli Defence Force (IDF) twice entered Palestinian towns and villages in the West Bank, including areas under the administrative and security responsibility of the Palestinian Authority (i.e. Area A).[104] On 29 March, "Operation Defensive Shield" started with an incursion into Ramallah, the IDF seizing most of the buildings in the headquarters of Chairman Arafat; by 3 April, six of the largest cities in the West Bank and their surrounding towns, villages, and refugee camps were occupied by the IDF.[105]

The IDF announced the official end of the operation on 21 April, as they had withdrawn from Nablus and parts of Ramallah, while continuing negotiations to end the siege of the Church of the Nativity in Bethlehem.[106] Nevertheless, the IDF's withdrawal from Palestinian cities was not to pre-29 March positions, but rather to positions encircling these cities. The IDF continued its incursions into many of the Palestinian towns and cities from which it had withdrawn at the end of "Operation Defensive Shield". During each urban incursion, Israeli troops used tanks and armoured personnel carriers, and curfews on the civilian population were imposed.[107]

SC Resolution 1402, adopted one day after the start of "Operation Defensive Shield", called for the withdrawal of Israeli troops from Palestinian cities, including

---

101 See further HCJ, Israel 2164/09 *Yesh Din Volunteers for Human Rights et. al. v. Commander of the IDF Forces in the West Bank et. al.* (26 December 2011, Judgment), § 13: in this case Area C is classified by the HCJ to be under prolonged military occupation.

102 Middle East Quartet, *Report of the Middle East Quartet* (12 February 2016), at 5, available at www.un.org/News/dh/infocus/middle_east/Report-of-the-Middle-East-Quartet.pdf (visited 5 January 2017).

103 Report of the Secretary-General Prepared Pursuant to GA resolution ES-10/10 (Report on Jenin), *Illegal Israeli actions in Occupied East Jerusalem and the Rest of the Occupied Palestinian Territory*, GA (A/ES-10/186), 30 July 2002, § 14.

104 Ibid., § 14.

105 Ibid., § 23.

106 Ibid.

107 Ibid., § 24.

112   *Relinquishing control over territory*

Ramallah.[108] Even so, Israel possesses the potential to re-enter the West Bank at will. And even though, as a result of Oslo II, the Palestinians attained a certain level of autonomy, especially as regards urban dwellings (Area A), they remain "subject to overall Israeli belligerent occupation".[109] Vital aspects of territorial management (e.g. security) were de facto retained by the occupant. Israel also conducts hot pursuits of Palestinian fugitives wanted on security charges in Area A at will.[110]

3.4 Control retained over territory after withdrawal: Gaza

What happens when the occupant fully withdraws from the territory but manages to retain control in various forms and degrees over the territory and its inhabitants? How much and what kind of control is required for the retired occupying power to retain so that IHL (or some of its rules) remain applicable? Factual elements such as the continuation of hostilities or the exercise of some degree of authority by the local authorities or by foreign forces during or after a phasing-out period may complicate a classification of the situation pursuant to IHL,[111] especially if it is disputed that occupation continues. This section thus deals with an example where the occupying troops have withdrawn, yet retain elements of control over it from the outside. Such control varies not only in strength, but also as regards its aspects and the objects it is wielded over. What this section will strive to unpack is whether this type of control means a state is still considered to be an occupant for the purposes of IHL or whether there are at least certain functional obligations under GC IV.

The discussion relies heavily on the case of the Gaza Strip, from which Israel "disengaged" in 2005.[112] The language of the respective Cabinet Resolution insinuates that the vacated areas had been left under the Israeli military forces' control as exercised *peripherally*, that is via borderline control. In other words, control was retained over Gaza in the form of an Israeli military presence *on the border*, by setting up a security fence, controlling the airspace over and the sea off the Gaza Strip, and by reserving to itself the right to engage in self-defence at any time.[113]

But was occupation actually terminated by this disengagement plan?[114] The 2007 Human Rights Council Report of the Special Rapporteur on the situation

---

108 SC Res. 1402 (2002); see also SC Res. 1397 (2002).
109 Y. Dinstein, *The International Law of Belligerent Occupation*, *supra* note 45, at 17.
110 A. A. Amer, 'Does Israel Have Justification to Enter West Bank's Area A?', *Palestine Pulse*, 14 April 2016, available at www.al-monitor.com/pulse/originals/2016/04/israel-hot-pursuits-westbank-incursions-security-pa.html (visited 5 January 2017).
111 *31st International Conference of the Red Cross and Red Crescent, International Humanitarian Law and the Challenges of Contemporary Armed Conflicts*, *supra* note 2, at 27.
112 Israel Ministry of Foreign Affairs, Cabinet Resolution Regarding the Disengagement Plan, 6 June 2004, available at www.mfa.gov.il/MFA/ForeignPolicy/Peace/MFADocuments/Pages/Revised%20Disengagement%20Plan%206-June-2004.aspx (visited 5 January 2017).
113 Ibid.
114 I. Scobbie, 'Gaza', in E. Wilmshurst (ed.), *International Law and the Classification of the Conflicts* (Oxford: Oxford University Press, 2012) 280–315, at 296; see generally S. Bashi

Relinquishing control over territory 113

of human rights in the Palestinian territories occupied since 1967 considered that, while Israel withdrew its settlers and military from Gaza in August 2005, Israeli statements that this had ended the occupation of Gaza were "grossly inaccurate":

> Even before the commencement of "Operation Summer Rains" [in summer 2006], following the capture of Corporal Gilad Shalit, Gaza remained under the effective control of Israel. [. . .] Israel retained control of Gaza's air space, sea space and external borders, and the border crossings of Rafah (for persons) and Karni (for goods). [. . .] In effect, following Israel's withdrawal, Gaza became a sealed off, imprisoned and occupied territory.[115]

However, in the case of *Gaber Al-Bassiouni v. Prime Minister*, the Israeli Supreme Court found that Israel was no longer an occupant as it no longer had effective control over the events in the Gaza Strip since September 2005: its soldiers were not in the area permanently and it had no duty to look after the welfare of the residents of Gaza or to maintain public order there.[116]

But Israel's continued ability to make its authority felt in Gaza cannot be ignored either. Although Israel is not militarily present there, it can mobilise the IDF near the Gaza border in a short span of time.[117] Moreover, even after its disengagement from Gaza, Israel and Hamas remained involved in several armed conflicts. While it is impossible here to list all of them, the most significant ones include operations "Summer Rains" (2006), "Cast Lead" (2008–9), "Pillar of Defence" (2012), and "Protective Edge" (2014).[118] Regarding "Operation Cast Lead", which involved Israel's attempts to stop Hamas rockets being fired into Israel, the Goldstone Report commissioned by the UN Human Rights Council in 2009 observed that Israel's attacks were deliberately disproportionate and aimed to punish and terrorise Gaza's civilian population.[119] The report also

---

and K. Mann, 'Disengaged Occupiers: The Legal Status of Gaza', *Gisha*, January 2007, available at www.gisha.org/userfiles/file/Report%20for%20the%20website.pdf (visited 5 January 2017).

115 *Report of the Special Rapporteur on the Situation of Human Rights in the Palestinian Territories Occupied Since 1967*, Human Rights Council, A/HRC/4/17, 29 January 2007, § 6, at 7.

116 HCJ, Israel 9132/07 *Jaber Al-Bassiouni v. Prime Minister, Minister of Defence* (Judgment of 30 January 2008) § 12.

117 See *Report of the Independent Fact Finding Commission on Gaza: No Safe Place*, presented to the League of Arab States, 30 April 2009, available at www.tromso-gaza.no/090501ReportGaza.pdf (visited 5 January 2017) § 403 at 102–103.

118 J.-P. Filiu, *Gaza: A History* (Oxford: Oxford University Press, 2014), at 294ff. and 316ff.; see generally International Crisis Group, 'No Exit? Gaza & Israel Between Wars', Middle East Report Nr. 162, 26 August 2015, available at www.crisisgroup.org/middle-east-north-africa/eastern-mediterranean/israelpalestine/no-exit-gaza-israel-between-wars (visited 5 July 2017).

119 *Report of the United Nations Fact Finding Mission on the Gaza Conflict*, Human Rights Council, A/HRC/12/48, 25 September 2009, § 1690 at 525. However, Judge Goldstone later retracted some of those findings, particularly with regards to the intentional targeting of civilians by Israel. Nevertheless, his three co-panelists did not endorse his retraction;

114 *Relinquishing control over territory*

affirmed that Israel, beyond all doubt and at all times during the mission, had exercised effective control (OL) over the Gaza Strip and that the circumstances of this control meant that the territory had remained under Israeli occupation.[120]

During "Operation Pillar of Defence",[121] the Israeli Army did not re-enter the territory,[122] save for instances of incursions.[123] In 2014, the IDF launched "Operation Protective Edge", equally aiming at stopping Hamas rockets flying into Israel.[124] The operation resulted in seven weeks of heavy fighting, countless Hamas rockets and an IDF invasion, albeit brief,[125] to destroy 32 tunnels into Israeli territory.[126]

Israel also imposed a siege on Gaza after Hamas had come to power in June 2007, closing all border crossings between Israel and Gaza, thereby denying residents of Gaza almost every possibility of exit or entry, in addition to blocking

---

R. Goldstone, 'Reconsidering the Goldstone Report on Israel and War Crimes', *The Washington Post*, 1 April 2011, available at www.washingtonpost.com/opinions/reconsidering-the-goldstone-report-on-israel-and-war-crimes/2011/04/01/AFg111JC_story.html?utm_term=.e640fa9c296f, and H. Jilani, C. Chinkin, and D. Travers, 'Goldstone Report: Statement Issued by Members of UN Mission on Gaza War', *The Guardian*, 14 April 2011, available at www.theguardian.com/commentisfree/2011/apr/14/goldstone-report-statement-un-gaza (visited 5 January 2017).

120 *Report of the United Nations Fact Finding Mission on the Gaza Conflict, supra* note 199, § 276, at 73.

121 *Annual Report of the United Nations High Commissioner for Human Rights and Reports of the Office of the High Commissioner and the Secretary-General, Concerns Related to Adherence to International Human Rights and International Humanitarian Law in the Context of the Escalation Between the State of Israel, the De Facto Authorities in Gaza and Palestinian Armed Groups in Gaza that Occurred from 14 to 21 November 2012*, Human Rights Council, A/HRC/22/35/Add.1, 6 March 2013, 1–17, §32–33 at 11–12.

122 See also Israel Ministry of Foreign Affairs, *Operation Pillar of Defense: IDF Updates*, 22 November 2012, available at http://mfa.gov.il/MFA/ForeignPolicy/Terrorism/Palestinian/Pages/Operation_Pillar_of_Defense_Nov_2012-IDF_updates.aspx (visited 5 January 2017).

123 R. Ahren, 'Israel Says It "Fulfilled All Its Goals", While Hamas "Hails an Exceptional Victory"', *The Times of Israel*, 22 November 2012, available at www.timesofisrael.com/israel-says-it-fulfilled-all-its-goals-while-hamas-hails-an-exceptional-victory-pillar-of-defense-gaza/ (visited 5 January 2017).

124 Amnesty International, *Unlawful and Deadly Rocket and Mortar Attacks by Palestinian Armed Groups During the 2014 Gaza/Israel Conflict*, March 2015, 3–63, at 9, available at www.amnesty.org/en/documents/mde21/1178/2015/en/ (visited 5 January 2017); *Human Rights Situation in Palestine and Other Occupied Arab Territories*, UN Human Rights Council, A/HRC/29/52, 24 June 2015, at 6.

125 J. Rudoren and A. Barnard, 'Israeli Military Invades Gaza, With Sights Set on Hamas Operation', *The New York Times*, 17 July 2014, available at www.nytimes.com/2014/07/18/world/middleeast/israel-gaza-strip.html?_r=0 (visited 5 January 2017).

126 The Meir Amit Intelligence and Terrorism Information Centre at the Israeli Intelligence and Heritage Commemoration Centre, Operation Protective Edge – Update No. 21 (as of 12:00 Hours, 6 August 2014), available at www.terrorism-info.org.il/ (visited 5 January 2017); see also Amnesty International, *Israel/Gaza Operation Cast Lead: 22 Days of Death and Destruction*, 2009, at 6, available at www.refworld.org/docid/4a4db45a2.html (visited 5 January 2017).

Relinquishing control over territory 115

the import and exports of goods.[127] Already in 2009, the Goldstone Report had flagged that Israel exercised control from the borders, enabling it to determine the conditions of life within the Gaza Strip.[128]

In short, with the sole exception of the Rafah border crossing managed by Egypt,[129] Israeli military checkpoints control civilians going in and out of Gaza, not to mention fully controlling Gaza's maritime zone and airspace. According to the OCHA, access to basic healthcare, education, water, sanitation, and shelter remains severely restricted for Palestinians both in the Gaza Strip and the West Bank mainly due to the control that Israel keeps over the right to freedom of movement.[130]

It is of course perfectly legitimate for a state to control who crosses its borders. Nonetheless, with Israel the difficulty arises in its control over Gaza's civilian population and their movement, and particularly its control over Gaza's borders.[131] Let us assume that a student from Gaza is admitted for an LLM programme in

---

127 HaMoked and B'Tsalem, *So Near and Yet So Far*, January 2014, at 8, available at www.btselem.org/download/201401_so_near_and_yet_so_far_eng.pdf (visited 5 January 2017).

128 *Report of the United Nations Fact Finding Mission on the Gaza Conflict*, *supra* note 119, § 278, at 74; see generally *Report of the Committee of Independent Experts in International Humanitarian and Human Rights Laws to Monitor and Assess Any Domestic, Legal or Other Proceedings Undertaken by Both the Government of Israel and the Palestinian Side, in the Light of General Assembly Resolution 64/254, Including the Independence, Effectiveness, Genuineness of These Investigations and Their Conformity with International Standards*, Human Rights Council, A/HRC/15/50, 23 September 2010; *Report of the International Fact-Finding Mission to Investigate Violations of International Law, Including International Humanitarian and Human Rights Law, Resulting from the Israeli Attacks on the Flotilla of Ships Carrying Humanitarian Assistance*, Human Rights Council, A/HRC/15/21, 27 September 2010.

129 *Freedom of Movement, Human Rights Situation in the Occupied Palestinian Territory, Including East Jerusalem*, Report of the Secretary General to the UN Human Rights Council A/HRC/31/44 (February 2016), at 9, 11–12, and 14; *Israeli Practices Affecting the Human Rights of the Palestinian People in the Occupied Palestinian Territory, Including East Jerusalem*, Report of the Secretary General, A/70/421 (14 October 2015), at 7–8; see also 'Egypt Closes Rafah Border Crossing After 5 Day Opening', 20 November 2016, *Middle East Palestine PressTV*, available at www.presstv.ir/Detail/2016/11/20/494431/Gaza-Rafah-Israel-Egypt (visited 5 January 2017); 'Gaza: Hamas Says Rafah Crossing with Egypt to Briefly Reopen', 28 January 2019, *Aljazeera*, available at www.aljazeera.com/news/2019/01/gaza-hamas-rafah-crossing-egypt-briefly-reopen-190128201714989.html (visited 26 January 2020).

130 OCHA, *2015 Humanitarian Needs Overview OPT*, 2014, available at www.ochaopt.org/documents/hno2015_factsheet_final_november_2014.pdf (visited 5 January 2017), at 3; see also *Human Rights Situation in Palestine and Other Occupied Arab Territories*, UN Human Rights Council, A/HRC/29/52, 2015, at 4 and 17; *Freedom of Movement*, UN Human Rights Council, A/HRC/31/44, 20 January 2016, 1–16.

131 However, according to OCHA (OPT) data, in the year 2015 for instance barely 30,000 people in the whole year were allowed to cross the border at Rafah, down from 420,000 in 2012; see *Gaza Crossings: Movement of People and Goods, United Nations Office for the Coordination of Humanitarian Affairs: Occupied Palestinian Territory*, available at http://data.ochaopt.org/gazacrossing/index.aspx?id=2 (visited 5 January 2017).

116 *Relinquishing control over territory*

country X, but s/he cannot leave Gaza due to either Israeli or Egyptian control of the respective border crossings. In both cases, because such a control is beyond mere border control since it concerns the border between two other entities, Gaza and country X, it affects all the other rights that are accrued from the freedom of movement.[132] Even from the perspective of the Gaza Strip, the Rafah border crossing only offers a partial relief to this process as it is up to Egypt to decide when and for how long to open it.[133]

Therefore, Israel's cooperation with Egypt on border and security matters becomes poignant. The 1979 peace treaty between Israel and Egypt has been in place for more than 30 years.[134] Based on the Agreement on Movement and Access (AMA), it was agreed that the Rafah crossing would be operated by the Palestinian Authority on the Palestinian side and by Egypt on the Egyptian side. In fact, Rafah is the only crossing between the Gaza Strip and Egypt[135] and serves as a major route for Gaza Strip inhabitants to go abroad. The use of the Rafah crossing is restricted to Palestinian ID holders and exceptionally others, in agreed categories and with prior notification of Israel.[136]

However, after Hamas came to power in Gaza in June 2007, Israel announced the freezing of the Agreement on Movement and Access.[137] The Palestinian Authority for its part was unable to reach the crossing due to Hamas' control of the Gaza Strip. Israel objected to opening the crossing on the grounds it was unable to monitor the persons passing through, and Egypt too closed the border since it was impossible to implement the AMA.[138] On 2 June 2010, Egypt re-opened the Rafah crossing on its side of the border.[139]

132 Such rights are, for instance, the right to access to education and healthcare, the right to work, or the right to freedom of association.

133 For example, the Rafah crossing was closed by the Egyptian authorities in October 2014; see *Freedom of Movement*, UN Human Rights Council, A/HRC/31/44, 20 January 2016, at 9.

134 For example, Binyamin Ben-Eliezer, Israel's former Minister of Defence, qualified the relationship as follows: "Egypt is not only our closest friend in the region, the co-operation between us goes beyond the strategic." See I. Kershner, 'Israeli Concern for Peace Partner', *The Courier*, 27 January 2011, available at www.thecourier.com.au/story/915535/israeli-concern-for-peace-partner (visited 5 January 2017). Israeli-Egyptian cooperation on border control in 2014 was marked by Egypt blocking all regular movement of goods at the Rafah crossing and severely restricting the movement of people through the border; see Human Rights Watch, *World Report 2015: Israel Palestine, Events of 2014*, available at www. hrw.org/world-report/2015/country-chapters/israel/palestine (visited 10 June 2016).

135 Agreed Documents on Movement and Access from and to Gaza, Agreement on Movement and Access (AMA) and Agreed Principles for Rafah Crossing, 15 November 2005, all available at www.mfa.gov.il/mfa/foreignpolicy/peace/mfadocuments/pages/agreed%20documents%20on%20movement%20and%20access%20from%20and%20to%20gaza%2015-nov-2005.aspx (visited 5 January 2017).

136 Ibid.

137 See generally B'Tselem, *Gaza Strip, The Rafah Crossing*, 13 January 2016, available at www.btselem.org/gaza_strip/rafah_crossing (visited 5 January 2017).

138 Ibid.

139 See generally Gisha, *Gaza 2015: A Few Steps Forward and Several Steps Back*, April 2016, available at http://gisha.org/UserFiles/File/publications/2015_annual_summary/summary_en.pdf (visited 10 June 2016).

Yet the crossing cannot be used for goods[140] and, because Israel administers the Palestinian population registry, "Israel retains indirect control over the issuing of Palestinian passports, which are required for travel through Rafah."[141]

As already discussed in section 3.3, the West Bank too is under Israeli sway. Israel does not allow for free movement between Gaza and the West Bank, although constituting – in theory – one single entity. Its control over Palestinians' movement between Gaza and the West Bank limits their travel to "exceptional humanitarian cases".[142] Such a restriction gives rise to a "separation policy" fragmenting the Palestinian territory.[143]

Because IHL application is determined based on the facts on the ground, wielding control over most border crossings and the general life of the territory, declaring no-go areas within the Strip, and maintaining maritime and air control must not be dismissed lightly. The question that can now be asked is whether all these forms of control, taken together, amount to effective control (OL). While lacking the element of military presence on the ground, it could be argued that what has just been listed represents a developed version of effective control – more modern than that of Article 42 HR 1907, which in turn could be seen as a classic form of control tied to the physical presence of the hostile army in the territory (see Chapter 1).

In fact, the Gaza example demonstrates how this classical concept of effective control has considerably evolved due not least to the advancement of technology and states' military and technical capacities such as for example airborne surveillance and targeted killing through drones.[144] Thus, effective control (OL) can in principle be wielded by a military force without even being stationed on a territory, and not only over territory *stricto sensu* but on any number of things that would have the cumulative effect of hindering a new authority or the ousted sovereign to exercise effective control. For by definition, the effective control of the occupier includes the ability to impede anybody else to possess such control. Articles 42 and 55[145] HR 1907 (the latter regarding the occupant "only as

---

140 *Gisha*, 'The Gaza Cheat Sheet', 10 August 2016, available at www.gisha.org/UserFiles/File/publications/Info_Gaza_Eng.pdf (visited 5 January 2017).

141 Ibid.

142 S. Bashi and E. Diamond, *Separating Land, Separating People: Legal Analysis of Access of Restrictions Between Gaza and the West Bank* (Gisha, June 2015), at 5, available at http://gisha.org/UserFiles/File/publications/separating-land-separating-people/separating-land-separating-people-web-en.pdf (visited 5 January 2017).

143 Ibid., at 4–5; see also A. Khalil, *Family Unification of Residents in the Occupied Territory* (Italy: European University Institute, Robert Schuman Centre for Advanced Studies, 2009), 1–17.

144 A. Gross, *The Writing on the Wall*, *supra* note 100, at 246–247. Note that also in earlier times sieges were employed to conquer territory, whereas in the case of Gaza it arguably serves the purpose of putting political pressure on Hamas, see ibid., at 235 and 239.

145 Article 55 Regulations Concerning the Laws and Customs of War on Land (HR 1907): "The occupying State shall be regarded only as administrator and usufructuary of public buildings, real estate, forests, and agricultural estates belonging to the hostile State, and

118   *Relinquishing control over territory*

administrator and usufructuary of public buildings") as well as Article 47 GC IV imply the territory to be free from a hostile force's control so that a new power is elected or the ousted sovereign can return. Until the full transfer of control over the territory and its inhabitants has materialised, it will be problematic to accept the statement that occupation has ended. In addition, being fully in control of the territory presupposes that the entity in control has sovereignty over its internal affairs, *especially* via policing land, air, and adjacent sea.

Those who regard Gaza to be occupied suggest that the control exercised by Israel shows it never actually terminated its occupation.[146] Accordingly, effective control (OL) over Gaza is still exercised by the Israeli military and other relevant government agencies, the only difference being that it is exercised from *outside* the Strip. For most forms of control in an armed conflict context, especially for airspace, border, and maritime control, military forces are in fact used. Yet already Oppenheim was of the view that when the legitimate sovereign was hindered from exercising its powers, and the occupant able to assert its authority by establishing an administration over a territory, "it matters not with what means, and in what ways, his authority is exercised."[147] Being in control of the territory and its inhabitants indicates that one is sovereign in deciding over what to extend one's control.[148] Sovereignty in turn is born out of unobstructed self-determination:

> Setting imposed constitutionalism against the principle of self-determination presumes that 'among the inhabitants inter se' not only that some constitutional order persists but that sufficient constitutional order persists to permit an end of occupation.[149]

---

situated in the occupied country. It must safeguard the capital of these properties, and administer them in accordance with the rules of usufruct."

146 S. Darcy and J. Reynolds, 'An Enduring Occupation: The Status of the Gaza Strip from the Perspective of International Humanitarian Law', 15 *Journal of Conflict and Security Law* (2010) 211–243, at 235–243. See however S. Solomon, 'Occupied or Not: The Question of Gaza's Legal Status After Israeli Disengagement', 19 *Cardozo Journal of International and Comparative Law* (2011) 59–90, at 81–89.

147 L. Oppenheim, *International Law: A Treatise*, Vol. 2 (7th edn., London; New York: Longmans Green, 1952), at 435.

148 M. De Vattel, *The Law of Nations* (T & J. W. Johnson, Law Book Sellers, 1844), § 205, at 98–99: Discussing the establishment of the nation implied possessing control was an important factor: "When a nation takes possession of a country to which no prior owner can lay claim, it is considered as acquiring the empire or sovereignty over it at the same time with the dominion. For, since the nation is free and independent, it can have no intention, in settling in a country, to leave to others the right to command, or any of those rights that constitute sovereignty."

149 P. Stirk, *The Politics of Military Occupation* (Edinburgh: Edinburgh University Press, 2012), at 220; see also Y. Dinstein, *The International Law of Belligerent Occupation*, *supra* note 45, at 272: "In any event, any Occupying Power harboring the thought of prescription must today take into account the right of self-determination vested in the people inhabiting the occupied territory."

It is surely the case that Israel has lessened its control over Gaza, but neither Hamas nor Fatah have any full control. The Oslo Accords appear to have loosened selected restrictions on certain areas of governance, but they tightened Israel's control over others.[150] For instance, through the consensus provision in the joint committee system, Israel retains a veto over any law enacted; Israel's capacity or willingness to undermine Palestinian self-governance through military means has not ceased.[151]

At the same time, Israel is unable to ensure law and order in the Gaza Strip as provided by Article 43 HR 1907 because of tensions with Hamas. These tensions are not at bay and expound a certain complexity in themselves: Hamas continuously fires rockets from Gaza into Israel and, because of this, Israel may be viewed as not having effective control (OL) over Gaza – for if it had, it would be able to stop Hamas' actions – and therefore not being an occupant. This view may have gained further grounds ever since Israel militarily disengaged.

In sum, one consideration is that Israel's disengagement plan and its military withdrawal did not factually end its occupation of the Gaza Strip. It might have brought an end *nominally*, under Article 42 HR 1907, because the element of military presence on the territory vanished. Hence, Israel relinquishing effective control (OL) over the territory was seemingly satisfied. In reality, however, it is argued by the proponents of this view that the Israeli military simply relocated and redeployed, controlling the land parameters of Gaza from outside.[152] It also seems that the Israeli government never actually allowed the independent functioning of the territory, whereby key state managerial powers such as border control, maintaining a population registry, or checking the movement of persons and goods in and out of Gaza would be fully passed on to either Fatah, Hamas, or to any other political authority. What seems to have been created is a security envelope[153] in which Israel placed Gaza.

Scobbie views the situation in Gaza as an international armed conflict: "the occupation, and thus an international armed conflict, persists as the over-arching legal structure between Israel and Gaza, and in particular in relation to the obligations Israel owes to the Gazan population qua occupier."[154] At the same time, according to the author a *separate* conflict between Hamas and Israel exists. While primarily a NIAC, the conflict became international by the imposition of the blockade on Gaza on 3 January 2009 during "Operation Cast Lead".[155]

---

150 Democracy and Governance Programme, Middle East Project, *Occupation Colonialism, Apartheid?* (Human Sciences Research Council, May 2009), at 129, available at www. alhaq.org/attachments/article/236/Occupation_Colonialism_Apartheid-FullStudy.pdf (visited 5 January 2017).

151 Ibid.

152 S. Darcy and J. Reynolds, 'An Enduring Occupation', *supra* note 146, at 235.

153 G. Aronson, 'Issues Arising from the Implementation of Israel's Disengagement from the Gaza Strip', 34 *Journal of Palestine Studies* (2005) 49–63, at 57.

154 I. Scobbie, 'Gaza', *supra* note 114, at 300–301.

155 Ibid., at 301–302.

120   *Relinquishing control over territory*

Scobbie draws an analogy with declaring a blockade during a civil war: if a state proclaimed a blockade in relation to territory occupied by armed forces, this amounted to a recognition of the belligerent status of those forces, thus making the conflict an IAC.[156] Hence, according to Scobbie the conflict between Israel and Gaza (or between Israel and Hamas) should be classified as international,[157] and the occupation of Gaza has never factually ended.

However, according to my reflection, the occupation of Gaza by Israel has ended after Israel's disengagement; nevertheless, the latter's obligations under the GC IV functional application persist. While Chapter 4 provides a fuller discussion of the functional application of GC IV, it is necessary here to briefly apply it to the Gaza Strip.[158] As mentioned earlier, Israel continues to control the Strip through most of its land crossings, airspace, and territorial waters, carrying out incursions, declaring "no-go" zones, and controlling who may reside in the Strip. The characteristic feature of a functional application of the GC IV is that obligations under this instrument towards protected persons apply not only before the situation of occupation is established (during the invasion phase, for instance), but also when some elements of effective control (OL) are retained. Accordingly, the functional application of the GC IV is to be construed as comprising obligations that are proportionate to the (retained) control of the state whose armed forces are in the process of vacating or have already left the territory. In any case, the applicability of GC IV obligations would then depend on the retained functions as well as on the exercised level of control. Simultaneously, GC IV would not apply to those obligations that were already handed over, for instance to a local government.[159]

The GC IV therefore provides for *varying* levels of control that differ from Article 42 HR 1907, Common Article 2 GCs, and Article 1 AP I 1977. It is submitted that there can be full or partial control; this in turn has effects on the types of obligations pursuant to the GC IV. Such a view echoes the ICRC's standpoint regarding Gaza, considering Israel to be bound "by obligations under occupation law that are commensurate with the degree to which it exercises control".[160] More generally, *a functional ending of occupation* is conceptualised as follows: when foreign forces withdraw from occupied territory but nevertheless hold on to authority or other important governmental functions that were once performed by them, the law of occupation continues to apply within the territorial and functional limits of such authority.[161]

---

156 Ibid., at 304.

157 Ibid., at 305.

158 A. Gross, *The Writing on the Wall*, *supra* note 100, at 76: "a differentiated responsibility approach seeks to create responsibility in the exercise of power." Also ibid., at 213–214: "Israel's power to control people and goods entering and leaving Gaza entails responsibility for these crucial aspects of Gaza life. Israel, then, may not be bound by all the duties of an occupier but only by those where its own actions affect the life of Gaza's residents because control, as based on a functional analysis, gives rise to obligations."

159 T. Ferraro, *Expert Meeting*, *supra* note 3, at 31.

160 P. Maurer, 'Challenges to Humanitarian Action in Contemporary Conflicts: Israel, the Middle East and Beyond', 47 *Israel Law Review* (2014) 175–180, at 179.

161 ICRC, *International Humanitarian Law and the Challenges of Contemporary Armed Conflicts* (ICRC, October 2015), at 12.

Furthermore, according to the ICRC, despite the lack of physical presence by the occupant's army, retained authority may amount to effective control for the purposes of the law of occupation. It can thus prompt the continued application of the relevant provisions of IHL norms, implying that occupation is not fully over yet.[162]

The ICRC calls this the "functional approach" to the application of occupation law. In fact, technological and military developments made it possible to exercise effective control (OL) over a foreign territory without permanent and/or large-scale military presence. What should thus be considered instead is the *extent of authority retained* by foreign forces, as opposed to focusing exclusively on *the means* by which such authority is actually exercised.[163] The geographical proximity or even contiguity of two belligerent states further enables the remote (but territorially close) exercise of effective control (OL).[164]

A considerable specificity is discerned from the ICRC's stance on the functional ending of occupation. Yet, three additional points need to be made. First, the *territorial and functional limits* should be construed as exercising control over certain parts of the territory, with certain tasks performed for the purposes of controlling that very territory. Second, the military presence of the occupant's army is no longer a *sine qua non*, at least not in the understanding of GC IV. Third, a difficulty arises in measuring and ascertaining the extent of authority retained by the outside power. Put differently, how is one to prove that the retained authority indeed triggers GC IV obligations? This question should be answered by establishing whether the retained authority is debilitating for the local authorities, its inhabitants, or any other power: Nobody else should be able, because of such retained authority from the outside, to fully control the territory, to entirely discharge governmental functions, or to engage in other acts necessary for controlling the territory.

In the case of Gaza, the *extent of authority retained*, i.e. the intensity and degree of control retained by Israel from outside, may be termed *partial effective control* (OL) as neither Hamas, nor Fatah, nor any other power completely controls the Strip. Israel relinquished only some aspects of territorial control. Israel's military relocated from within Gaza to its outside but continues to control Gaza's borders by land, air, and sea, not to mention controlling civilian access to basic needs, e.g. restricting their freedom of movement in and out from the Strip, policing no-go zones, Gaza being dependent on Israeli electricity,[165] and checking the import of goods.

The notion of *partial effective control* (OL) thus finds its roots in the functional application of GC IV (dealt with more extensively in Chapter 4). Hence, Israel remains duty bound to discharge its obligations in Gaza, even if it refuses to be bound by the GC IV. According to the Israeli Supreme Court, Israel observes

---

162 Ibid.
163 Ibid.
164 Ibid.
165 HCJ, Israel, 9132/07 Jaber Al-Bassiouni v. Prime Minister, *supra* note 128, §12; HCJ, Israel 201/09 and 248/09 Physicians for Human Rights and Others v. Prime Minister of Israel et al., and Gisha Legal Centre for Freedom of Movement and Others v. Minister of Defense, HCJ (judgment of 19 January 2009) § 14.

122   *Relinquishing control over territory*

the humanitarian provisions of GC IV, and this for the purposes of the petition before them was "sufficient."[166] Israel's Supreme Court provided no further elaboration on why this was sufficient or in what way such sufficiency was manifest.

It follows that there may be at least three types of obligations a state could be bound by:[167]

1   *Ongoing obligations.* Here, there are two forms of obligations:

   (a) *full* ongoing obligations in case of full effective control (OL) exerted by the occupant over the territory (when the criteria of Article 42 HR 1907, Common Article 2 GCs, and Article 1 AP I 1977 are fully met; see Chapter 1), and
   (b) *partial* ongoing obligations, which stem from partial effective control (OL), that is obligations commensurate to the level of control retained – when the state does not have full effective control (OL) but nevertheless exercises control over the territory from the outside.

2   *Residual obligations.*[168] Even once occupation is over, i.e. when the former occupant does not have effective control (OL) over the territory anymore, some obligations such as the repatriation of POW[169] or civilian internees[170] still apply. After WWII, Russia for example did not repatriate all Japanese POWs and used them for forced labour in Siberia.[171]

---

166 HCJ, Israel, 769/02 Public Committee Against Torture v. Government (a petition, 14 December 2006) § 20.

167 On the issue of reparations in armed conflict, generally see B. Oswald and B. Wellington, 'Reparation for Violations in Armed Conflict and the Emerging Practice of Making Amends', in R. Livoja and T. McCormack (eds.), *Routledge Handbook of the Law of Armed Conflict* (Milton Park: Routledge, 2016) 520–537; Arts. 1, 28 and 31 of ILC Articles on Responsibility of States; Case Concerning *Gabčíkovo-Nagymaros Project (Hungary v. Slovakia)*, Judgment of 25 September 1997, §152, available at www.icj-cij.org/en/case/92; *Case Concerning Avena and Other Mexican Nationals (Mexico v. United States of America)*, Judgment of 31 March 2004, § 119–120, available at www.icj-cij.org/en/case/128; *Case Concerning Armed Activities on the Territory of the Congo (Democratic Republic of the Congo v. Uganda)*, Judgment of 19 December 2005, §§ 259–261, available at www.icj-cij.org/en/case/116 (all visited 15 July 2017).

168 On post-occupation duties more generally see A. Gross, *The Writing on the Wall*, *supra* note 100, at 220–224; B. Rubin, 'Disengagement from the Gaza Strip and Post Occupation Duties', 42 *Israel Law Review* (2009) 528–563, at 553.

169 With regards POW repatriation, Article 118 of GC III does not allow for repatriation if there is no orderly plan concluded by the parties to the conflict. In case there is no such plan, the detained power can draw one up, see S. Krähenmann, 'Protection of Prisoners in Armed Conflict', in D. Fleck (ed.), *The Handbook of International Humanitarian Law* (3rd edn., Oxford: Oxford University Press, 2013) 359–411, at 408.

170 Article 132 GC IV, Article 75 (3) AP I 1977; see generally H.-P. Gasser and K. Dörmann, 'Protection of the Civilian Population', in D. Fleck (ed.), *The Handbook of International Humanitarian Law* (3rd edn., Oxford: Oxford University Press, 2013) 231–320.

171 Memory of the Reconciliation of Asia Pacific, *Official Statements: Russia*, available at www.gwu.edu/~memory/data/government/russia_pow.html (visited 5 January 2017);

Relinquishing control over territory 123

3 *Obligations raised based on past violations.* Here, it is the responsibility of the former occupant to take certain actions that remains. While there are no ongoing obligations under IHL in this case, because of previous violations of IHL norms during occupation, there may still be a responsibility of the once occupant to take certain actions. SC Resolution N 687 for example reaffirmed that Iraq was "liable under international law for any direct loss, damage, including environmental damage and the depletion of natural resources, or injury to foreign Governments, nationals and corporations, as a result of Iraq's unlawful invasion and occupation of Kuwait."[172]

Chapter 4 will assess the functional application of GC IV in more detail through the concept of *partial ongoing obligations* of IHL. It will also look at IHRL application based on the level of control exercised by an occupant.

3.5 The ending of indirect (effective) control/occupation exercised by an intermediary

Chapter 2 defined indirect effective control, or occupation exercised by an intermediary. This section now considers how can it be determined that this type of occupation has ended.

The test for assessing whether occupation based on indirect effective control has come to an end differs from the one which establishes it. What should be recalled is that the relationship of overall control (SR/IHL) outlines[173] and devolves certain tasks from the intervening state to the local actors. For as long as such a relationship persists and the foreign state does not relinquish overall control (SR/IHL) over its proxy, the territory remains occupied. Kennan describes the relationship between the de facto authorities/armed groups and state A who wields overall control (SR/IHL) over them as follows:

> In internal matters, it has exactly the same independence as a dog on a leash. As long as the dog trots quietly and cheerfully at his master's side – and in

---

H. Kimura, *Distant Neighbours: Japanese-Russian Relations Under Gorbachov and Yeltsin* (New York: Routledge, 2000), at 164–166; see also Tokyo (District Court) Claims for Compensation for Forced Labor in Siberia, *Tomoya Kanbayashi et al. vs. Japan*, Judgment of 4 April 1989, available at www.icrc.org/ihl-nat.nsf/0/e9c4adb3e1d50d3ec 125708f004e3712/$FILE/Case%20Law%20-%20Kamibayashi%20-%20Japan.pdf (visited 5 January 2017).

172 SC Res. 687 (1991) § 16.

173 Such control may mean issuing tasks and directives for the territorial management and foreign policy, the third state's armed forces providing for the security of the borders and performing police functions for maintaining law and order, in addition to conducting detentions, catering for the civilians' humanitarian needs, financing and paying the wages not only of the proxy regime's members, but also of its governmental entities, in addition to having high-profile military officials holding decisive positions in the proxy administration.

124 *Relinquishing control over territory*

the same direction – he is quite free; if he starts out on any tangents of his own, he feels the pull at once.[174]

Establishing the end of occupation based on indirect effective control would thus firstly depend on the outside state giving up overall control (SR/IHL) over the de facto authorities/other organised armed groups, who would then cease to be its pawn and no longer act on its behalf. The entity's actions will no longer be attributed to the outside state. Until the sovereign state regains control over its territory militarily, by overpowering the armed group, or until through free and fair elections either the armed group, the de facto authority, or another entity becomes the legitimate government (see Chapter 3), there would be a situation of a NIAC, always provided the criteria of Common Article 3 GCs and AP II 1977 are met.[175]

The ending of occupation through indirect effective control may be also claimed by the occupant when setting up a new government or state. However, in this case occupation only ends if the new government is *not* a subordinate to the former occupant. By contrast, the approach of conventional IHL is that Article 47 GC IV makes the occupant duty bound by the GC IV as a whole even if it has made changes in the institutions or government structures of the occupied territory, concluded agreements with the authorities of the occupied territory, or annexed the whole or parts of the territory (see also Chapter 2). According to Pictet, concluding agreements with the occupied authorities is an especially "subtle" way to escape one's obligations under IHL, applying it to cases where the lawful authorities in the occupied territory have concluded a derogatory agreement with the occupying power as well as to cases where the occupant has installed and maintained a government regime.[176] In this vein, the spirit of Article 47 GC IV enables the continued application of the GC IV, affording protection notwithstanding any covert action the occupant might engage in.[177] Even

---

174 Kennan speaks about the so-called independent government of Slovakia under Axis domination just before WWII would commence; G. F. Kennan, *Report to the State Department on About 1 May 1939: From Prague After Munich* (Princeton, NJ: Princeton University Press, 1968), at 135.

175 On AP II 1977 and the element of the territorial control, see S. Sivakumaran, *The Law of Non-International Armed Conflict* (Oxford: Oxford University Press, 2012), at 185–187. The author in this regard notes, at 187: "The essential point is that it is the ability to carry out sustained and concerted military operations and to implement the Protocol that is crucial feature of the Protocol and not the quantum of territory controlled by the armed group. The territorial control is an enabling element for the operations and the implementation of the Protocol." Additionally, see D. Péclard and D. Mechoulan, *Rebel Governance and Politics of Civil War* (Bern: Swisspeace, 2015), at 5–32, available at www.files.ethz. ch/isn/191183/WP_1_2015.pdf (visited 5 January 2017); and see generally A. Arjona, N. Kasfir and Z. Mampilly (eds.), *Rebel Governance in Civil Wars* (New York: Cambridge University Press, 2015).

176 J. Pictet (ed.), *Commentary of 1958, supra* note 14, Article 47, at 274–275.

177 J. Grinion, 'The Geneva Conventions and the End of Occupation', in A. Clapham, P. Gaeta, and M. Sassòli (eds.), *The 1949 Geneva Conventions: A Commentary* (Oxford:

Relinquishing control over territory   125

the occupant declaring the formation of a new government does not mean that occupation is over.

The final way in which occupation based on indirect effective control can end is through the loss of effective control (OL) over territory by the armed group/de facto local authorities. Thus, while the outside state may continue to wield overall control (SR/IHL) over the group or entity, because the latter is – for whatever reason – not exercising territorial control anymore, occupation has ended.

3.6 Remaining based on a UN SC mandate

What is the relationship between the UN and the termination of occupation? This section starts with a more general question, namely whether the SC should at all be involved in categorising situations as IAC or NIAC. The analysis then covers two issues: the UN SC deciding the end of occupation, and UN endorsed control, i.e. an occupant remaining on the territory based on a UN SC resolution. The discussion there relies on the example of Iraq in 2003–2004 and UN SC Resolution 1546.

3.6.1 The UN SC

The SC is given primary responsibility by the UN Charter to maintain and re-establish international peace and security.[178] It is intended to operate as an efficient UN executive organ with assigned political functions[179] and consists of five permanent members with veto power – China, France, Russia, the UK, and the US – and ten other countries. Their decisions may be said to be based on political benefits as opposed to the objective criteria relating to non-compliance.[180] The SC acts under Chapters 6 and 7 of the UN Charter, determining the existence of any threat to peace, breach of peace, or act of aggression (Article 39

Oxford University Press, 2015) 1575–1596, at 1587. See also Y. Dinstein, 'The Dilemmas Relating to Legislation Under Article 43 of the Hague Regulations, and Peace-Building', *International Humanitarian Law Research Initiative* (2004) 1–12, at 10, available at https://www.hpcrresearch.org/sites/default/files/publications/dinstein.pdf (visited 5 May 2020).

178 R. Kolb, *An Introduction to the Law of the United Nations* (Portland, OR: Hart Publishing, 2008), at 133; M. N. Shaw, *International Law* (6th edn., Cambridge: Cambridge University Press, 2012), at 1206; see generally V. Gowlland-Debbas (ed.), *National Implementation of United Nations Sanctions* (Leiden: Martinus Nijhoff Publishers, 2004).

179 See *Case Concerning Military and Paramilitary Activities in and Against Nicaragua* (Jurisdiction) (Nicaragua v. USA), Judgment of 26 November 1984, § 94–95, available at www.icj-cij.org/en/case/70 (visited 15 July 2017).

180 M. Sassòli and Y. Issar, 'Challenges to International Humanitarian Law', in A. von Arnauld et al. (eds.), *100 Years of Peace Through Law: Past and Future* (Berlin: Duncker and Humbolt, 2015) 181–235, at 213; see additionally H. Kelsen, *Collective Security Under International Law* (5th edn., Clark, NJ: The Law Book Exchange, 2009), at 39–49.

126 *Relinquishing control over territory*

UN Charter);[181] it makes recommendations or decides what measures are needed pursuant to Articles 41 and 42 of the UN Charter to maintain or restore international peace and security (see also Chapter 1, section 3).[182]

The SC's interaction with international law is two-dimensional. The first dimension is represented by those SC resolutions wherein its support for the validity and enforcement of relevant international norms and instruments is advanced – such as subscribing to and upholding the non-interference in internal affairs or respect for humanitarian law and human rights.[183] The second dimension is represented by resolutions via which the SC purports to impact, qualify, or modify legal positions under international law.[184] The impact of SC resolutions is most salient in combination with Articles 103 and 25 UN Charter.[185] Yet the resolutions cannot override the *jus cogens* norms of international law; in fact, any "SC decision in conflict with a norm of *jus cogens* must necessarily be without effect".[186]

In general, UN SC resolutions can entail three types of legal effects: (1) creating obligations, rights, and powers (substantive effects); (2) making determinations of facts (something that is true) on legal situations and/or stating that certain obligations were violated, thus triggering the substantive effect (causative effect); and (3) prescribing how and when the substantive effects operate (modal effect).[187] As will be seen, the capacity of the UN SC to determine facts on legal situations and whether certain obligations were violated is of great importance. The UN SC has also opined on the formation of new states or delineated the territorial boundaries of states in the context of an armed conflict. It is, however,

---

181 D. Akande, 'The International Court of Justice and the Security Council: The Political Organs of the United Nations', 46 *International and Comparative Law Quarterly* (1997) 309–343, at 314–315.

182 Article 39, UN Charter; V. Gowlland-Debbas, 'Security Council Enforcement Action and Issues of State Responsibility', 43 *International and Comparative Law Quarterly* (1994) 55–98, at 61–72; V. Gowlland-Debbas, *Collective Responses to Illegal Acts in International Law: United Nations Action in the Question of Southern Rhodesia* (Dordrecht: Martinus Nijhoff Publishers, 1990), at 437–441 and 459–460.

183 A. Orakhelashvili, 'The Acts of the Security Council: Meaning and Standards of Review', in A. von Bogdandy and R. Wolfrum (eds.), 11 *Max Planck Yearbook of United Nations Law* (2007) 143–195, at 145.

184 Ibid.

185 *Questions of Interpretation and Application of the 1971 Montreal Convention Arising from the Arial Incident at Lockerbie* (Libyan Arab Jamahiriya v. USA), provisional measures order of 14 April 1992, §§ 39–42, available at www.icj-cij.org/en/case/89 (visited 15 July 2017).

186 D. Akande, 'The International Court of Justice', *supra* note 181, at 322; *Case Concerning Application of the Convention on the Prevention and Punishment of the Crime of Genocide (Bosnia and Herzegovina v. Yugoslavia 1993)*, request for the indication of provisional measures, order of 8 April 1993, provisions m and o at 6, and Separate Opinion of Judge Lauterpacht, §§ 98–104, both available at www.icj-cij.org/en/case/91 (visited 15 July 2017); H. Cuyckens, *Revisiting the Law of Occupation*, *supra* note 1, at 65.

187 M. Divac Oberg, 'The Legal Effects of Resolutions of the UN Security Council and General Assembly in the Jurisprudence of ICJ', 16 *European Journal of International Law* (2006) 879–906, at 881–882.

debatable whether the SC has a right to abrogate, delineate, or alter *titles* to territory:

> The Security Council might, [. . .] order occupation of a country in order to restore peace and security, but it could not thereby or as part of the operation, abrogate or alter territorial rights. [. . .] It was to keep the Peace that the SC was set up not to change world order.[188]

The UN SC's capacity can be inferred from the wording of Article 41 of the Charter, which grants the SC exceptionally broad powers in order to maintain peace and security.[189] Based on Chapter 7 and with the aim of strengthening international peace, certain SC resolutions have declared regimes as violating norms of non-discrimination on the grounds of race with regards to not recognising the declaration of independence of Southern Rhodesia.[190] The SC has also pronounced itself on the boundaries of contested territories, thus overlooking the principle of the territorial integrity of states and altering territorial boundaries, for instance in the Iraq-Kuwait Boundary Demarcation Resolution (where the SC demanded that Iraq and Kuwait respected the inviolability of the boundaries and allocated islands as per the 'Agreed Minutes Between the State of Kuwait Regarding the Restoration of Friendly Relations, Recognition and Related Matters'[191]) and on the partition of Palestine (implementation of the GA resolution).[192]

Poignant in all these resolutions is that the UN SC usually avoids categorising armed conflicts as either IACs or NIACs and uses general terms, for instance "conflict" or "parties to the conflict". Sometimes the existence of an armed conflict is merely implied by the text of the resolution. The SC also does not employ factual tests of IHL or cite the Nicaragua or Tadić cases to arrive at the conclusion that there is a NIAC or IAC. In this manner, the resolution on the situation in Darfur employed the term "parties to the conflict";[193] the resolution regarding Syria called for all parties in Syria "including the opposition, immediately to cease all armed violence in all its forms";[194] and in the case of Ukraine, the SC

---

188 *Legal Consequences for States of the Continued Presence of South Africa in Namibia (South West Africa) Notwithstanding Security Council Resolution 276 (1970)*, Dissenting Opinion of Sir Judge Gerald Fitzmaurice Namibia Advisory Opinion, § 115, available at www.icj-cij. org/en/case/53 (visited 15 July 2017).

189 M. Goodwin, 'From Province to Protectorate to State: Sovereignty Lost, Sovereignty Gained?', in J. Summers (ed.), *Kosovo: A Precedent?* (Leiden: Martinus Nijhoff Publishers, 2011) 87–108, at 99–102; *Reparation for Injuries Suffered in the Service of the United Nations*, Advisory Opinion of 11 April 1949, § 182–184, available at www.icj-cij.org/en/ case/4 (visited 15 July 2017).

190 SC Res. 216 (1965); SC Res. 217 (1965).

191 SC Res. 687 (1991).

192 GA Res. 181 (II), 29 November 1947, SC Res. 42 (1948); M. Goodwin, 'From Province to Protectorate to State', *supra* note 189, at 100.

193 SC Res. 1593 (2005).

194 SC Res. 2042 (2012).

128   *Relinquishing control over territory*

expressed its grave concern at "the tragic events and violence in eastern regions of Ukraine".[195] What can also be observed is that when it comes to identifying situations as military occupation, the SC has indeed explicitly and directly employed this term. Thus, the UN SC resolution on Namibia considered the "continued occupation of Namibia by the government of South Africa" as a defiance of relevant resolutions of the UN and the UN Charter.[196] With regards to Israel, the SC explicitly referred to it as an occupant and deemed the Palestinian territories and parts of other Arab states occupied since 1967.[197] Finally, in the context of the Nagorno Karabakh conflict, the SC adopted at least four resolutions in 1993 considering the Azerbaijani territories to be occupied by Armenian forces.[198]

Not all the resolutions relating to occupation, however, employ this term – especially not when the political interests of one of the permanent members are at stake. For instance, in the case of Georgia, Russia blocked a draft resolution concerning the 2008 August war which called on it to immediately withdraw from Georgian territories.[199] The formulation of "the territorial integrity of Georgia within its internationally recognized borders" was also rejected, Russia regarding this principle to be obsolete since the Moscow-backed breakaway regions Abkhazia and South Ossetia would refuse to be part of Georgia.[200]

While the capacity of the UN SC to deem and proclaim a situation of occupation to be over is discussed next, the broader topic of the SC determining that armed conflicts have come to an end from the perspective of IHL lies outside the scope of this book.

3.6.2. *Iraq and UN SC 1546*

There was no dispute that, between April 2003 and 28 June 2004, Iraq was occupied.[201] In Resolution 1546, the UN SC welcomed the fact that

---

195 SC Res. 2202 (2015).
196 SC Res. 276 (1970).
197 SC Res. 446 (1979).
198 SC Res. 822 (1993), SC Res. 853 (1993), SC Res. 874 (1993), SC Res. 844 (1993). See also V. Koutroulis, *Le début et la fin de l'application du droit de l'occupation* (Paris: Pedone, 2010), at 97–121, where the author argues that facts on the ground remain decisive to qualify the situation as one of military occupation. Moreover, a UN SC resolution affirming a situation of military occupation despite factual evidence to the contrary would be considered ultra vires.
199 'Russia Blocks Draft Security Council Resolution on Georgia Crisis', *CBC News*, 20 August 2008, available at www.cbc.ca/news/world/russia-blocks-draft-security-council-resolution-on-georgia-crisis-1.725452 (visited 5 January 2017).
200 'Russia Blocks U.N. Security Council Draft on Georgia', *UNIAN*, 20 August 2008, available at www.unian.info/world/138913-russia-blocks-un-security-council-draft-on-georgia. html (visited 5 January 2017); UN SC Press Release, 'Security Council Holds Third Emergency Meeting as South Ossetia Conflict Intensifies, Expands to Other Parts of Georgia (SC 9419)', 10 August 2008, available at www.un.org/press/en/2008/sc9419.doc.htm (visited 5 January 2017).
201 A. Roberts, 'The End of Occupation: Iraq 2004', 54 *International and Comparative Law Quarterly* (2005) 27–48, at 30.

the occupation would end at a certain point in time by "looking forward to the end of the occupation and the assumption of full responsibility and authority by a fully sovereign and independent Interim Government of Iraq by 30 June 2004."[202] Yet, something is amiss in the SC's stance, for one ought to question whether the situation after 30 June 2004 is equivalent to the assumption of full authority by the Iraqi government. That is, was the CPA's effective control (OL) over Iraq, including its internal affairs, genuinely relinquished?

As pointed out by Roberts, Resolution 1546 mentions "sovereignty" eight times.[203] However, the question remains whether the new government of Iraq was indeed sovereign. Roberts views sovereignty to mean "the idea of a situation in which there is a centre of decision-making power over a specific territory, not subject to a higher sovereign."[204] This would, in essence, also mean that the government ensures by itself the security of its territory, in addition to having a parliament, which incidentally was not at that time elected in Iraq. Moreover, for its survival and security the Iraqi government clearly depended on foreign assistance and military presence. Attention should also be paid to the operative paragraph of Resolution 1546, where the UN SC, while endorsing the formation of the new Iraqi government, at the same time keeps it on a tight leash in terms of its future actions: The SC

> endorses the formation of a sovereign Interim Government of Iraq, as presented on 1 June 2004, which will assume full responsibility and authority by 30 June 2004 for governing Iraq *while refraining from taking any actions affecting Iraq's destiny* beyond the limited interim period until an elected Transitional Government of Iraq assumes office as envisaged in paragraph four below.[205]

This temporal constraint on the substance of possible decisions taken by the interim government violates the very idea of a sovereign government, which as just stated implies the absence of any higher authority. A second point concerns the establishment of the MNF, composed of the same forces that were previously occupants, tasked to ensure security and to fight the remaining enemies in addition to conducting internments.

Stating that the Iraqi occupation was in fact never over, based on Resolution 1546, can be challenged by arguing that the MNF's presence in Iraq was requested by the new Iraqi government. Like the word "sovereignty", the word "request" is equally used quite frequently throughout Resolution 1546. This is suggestive of the SC's attempts to justify the presence of the MNF and possibly

---

202 SC Res. 1546 (2004).
203 A. Roberts, 'The End of Occupation', *supra* note 201, at 39.
204 Ibid.
205 Ibid., at 42 (emphasis added).

130 *Relinquishing control over territory*

restore the good name of the US and its Coalition. Hence, the MNF was mandated to

> have the authority to take all necessary measures to contribute to the maintenance of security and stability in Iraq [. . .] inter alia, the Iraqi request for the continued presence of the multinational force and setting out its tasks, including by preventing and deterring terrorism.[206]

Contributing to the "maintenance of security and stability" with "all necessary measures" can encompass numerous tasks. In turn, discharging these tasks is based on a tight and thorough control of territory. In fact, the MNF's outlined duties mirror the language of Article 43 HR 1907, save for the fact that the SC decreed occupation would end.[207]

In other words, the SC declared Iraq to be no longer occupied and then established the MNF with functions akin to those of an occupying army. In this context, Schmitt argues that a non-international conflict predated the transfer of sovereignty of 28 June, and that armed conflicts may be horizontally mixed, that is a NIAC and an IAC might coexist.[208] Furthermore, there was no situation of occupation after the SC's actions. Roberts, on the other hand, considers this to be the case, since while "clearly not a case of an occupation coming to an end when an occupying power withdraws from the territory [. . .] 28 June 2004 marks an important stage on the road to the full resumption of Iraqi sovereignty, not arrival at that destination."[209]

So, did the occupation of Iraq continue even after the SC had declared it to have ended, under its own sanctioned effective control (OL) as exerted by the MNF? To answer this it should be assessed whether effective control (OL) over territory was fully passed on to the new Iraqi government and whether the presence of the MNF was requested by the latter without third-party intervention. That the Iraqi government unaffectedly consented to such a presence in this regard is germane. If either of the two criteria had been established, the occupation would indeed have been over. Yet the factual circumstances in the case of Iraq suggest otherwise. The tasks the MNF was expected to carry out at that time also have to be taken into account. For as long as the coalition forces were engaged in combat to extinguish pockets of resistance as well as "exercising at least some administrative authority in certain areas of Iraq, the occupation has come to a close only 'notionally'."[210] So when the occupation of Iraq was formally declared to be over, *neither* of the two conditions had in fact materialised to

---

206 SC Res. 1546 (2004) § 10; on conducting detentions, see B. J. Bill, 'Detention Operations in Iraq: A View from the Ground', in R. A. Pedrozo (ed.), *The War in Iraq: A Legal Analysis* (Newport, RI: Naval War College, 2010) 411–455.
207 Article 43 Regulations Concerning the Laws and Customs of War on Land (HR 1907).
208 M. N. Schmitt, 'Iraq (2003 Onwards)', in E. Wilmshurst (ed.), *International Law and the Classification of the Armed Conflicts* (Oxford: Oxford University Press, 2012) 356–386, at 371–372.
209 A. Roberts, 'The End of Occupation', *supra* note 201, at 46.
210 Y. Dinstein, *The International Law of Belligerent Occupation*, *supra* note 45, at 273.

Relinquishing control over territory 131

substantiate the SC's position: neither was effective control (OL) over territory and its inhabitants relinquished, nor did an actual transfer of governing authority to the Iraqis take place.[211]

The case of Iraq thus provides an example of UN SC endorsed effective control (OL) of territory. The SC's previous account of adopting resolutions on various armed conflicts suggests that such a phenomenon has emerged gradually, commencing with the SC *not* endorsing effective control (OL) over certain territories. The SC, for example, demanded the withdrawal of South Africa from Namibia.[212] Resolution 276 (1970) declared the continued presence of South African officials to be illegal, in addition to pronouncing South Africa's occupation of Namibia to have grave consequences for the rights and interests of the people there.[213] The language of this resolution submits that the UN did not endorse South African control of the territory. The ICJ in the Namibia Advisory Opinion also found that while the General Assembly had the power to terminate a mandate, the withdrawal of the illegal administration could only have been enforced by the SC through a binding resolution.[214] As seen, the SC dealt similarly with the Kuwait crisis of 1990.[215] SC Resolution 678, adopted after Iraq had invaded and occupied Kuwait, authorised all UN member states cooperating with the government of Kuwait to use "all necessary means" to ensure that Iraq would withdraw.[216] Similarly, NATO's intervention in Kosovo – not authorised by the SC – culminated in the SC adopting Resolution 1244 (1999), approving the international security presence in Kosovo.[217] This can be interpreted as a retrospective approval of the use of force against (the former) Yugoslavia, in addition to raising wider issues of *jus ad bellum* outside the scope of this book. It also reveals the SC developing a notion of SC-endorsed effective control (OL) over territory exercised by foreign states, coalitions thereof, or international organisations. Such points are again a matter of *jus ad bellum*, i.e. whether occupation X has come about through lawful or unlawful use of force. However, this needs to be kept apart from establishing the de facto existence of occupation (see Chapter 1, section 2).

In sum, no matter if the SC does or does not endorse the existence or termination of military occupation, the tests for determining the beginning and ending of territorial control for the purposes of military occupation remain based on

---

211 E. Benvenisti, *The International Law of Occupation*, *supra* note 95, at 255.

212 See SC Res. 385 (1976); SC Res. 435 (1978); C. Thornberry, 'Namibia', in D. M. Malone (ed.), *The UN Security Council: From the Cold War to the 21st Century* (London: Lynne Rienner Publishers, 2004), 407–436.

213 SC Res. 276 (1970).

214 E. de Wet, *The Chapter 7 Powers of the United Nations Security Council* (Oxford: Hart Publishing, 2004), at 35.

215 On the Iraqi-Kuwait crisis generally, see *supra* note 70; also K. Manusama, *The United Nations Security Council in the Post-Cold War Era* (Leiden: Martinus Nijhoff Publishers, 2006), at 62–75.

216 SC Res 678 (1990) §2; see also SC Res. 660 (1990) § 2.

217 SC Res. 1244 (1999) § 5, § 8 and § 19.

132 *Relinquishing control over territory*

facts.[218] In other words, the SC dealing with the legality of attained control does not change the fact that one is in effective control (OL) of a given territory and hence an occupant. Resolution 1546 overrides the rules of IHL under Article 103 UN Charter, which is regrettable and a dangerous precedent in itself. To make the application of IHL conditional on criteria related to the desired legitimacy of the new government and to the needs of a US administration distorts the separation between *jus ad bellum* and *jus in bello* rules.[219] Resolution 1546 is the only one of this kind in the record of the SC,[220] and is unlikely to be repeated anytime soon, most probably due to the veto power vested with the SC's permanent members and their politically dominant interests.[221]

Conclusion

This chapter has identified the test for assessing the end of control over territory for the purposes of determining the end of military occupation. It can now be concluded that occupation has ended if at least *one* of the following three conditions is met:

1 State A's military forces are no longer physically present on the territory (they have either willfully left the territory or been forcefully ejected);
2 State A's military forces are not in a position to or willfully do not exercise authority over the total or parts of the territory of state B anymore; or
3 State A's military forces are no longer hostile to state B, as the latter has consented to their presence.[222]

The transfer of effective control (OL) over the territory and its inhabitants may also serve as an indicator that occupation has terminated. However, such a transfer should not be bogus and the previous occupant should not interfere with the governmental functions of the new power. Only such non-interference would confirm that the former occupant has actually terminated its own effective control (OL) over the territory.

The previously provided test does not seem to present any difficulty. However, the ending of contemporary military occupations may not be assessed so easily. This is so either because the occupant's forces have physically left the territory but retain elements of control from the outside (as in the case of Gaza); the occupying state has set up a puppet regime, or uses an armed group over which it

---

218 H. Cuyckens, *Revisiting the Law of Occupation, supra* note 1, at 59–60.
219 M. Sassòli, 'Legislation and Maintenance of Public Order and Civil Life by Occupying Powers', 16 *European Journal of International Law* (2005) 661–694, at 684.
220 Y. Dinstein, *The International Law of Belligerent Occupation, supra* note 45, at 273.
221 M. Sassòli and Y. Issar, 'Challenges to International Humanitarian Law', *supra* note 180, at 213.
222 See also V. Koutroulis, *Le début et la fin de l'application du droit de l'occupation, supra* note 198, at 191.

wields overall control (SR/IHL), which in turn exercises effective control (OL) over territory (see also Chapter 2); or because the UN SC precipitately declares the end of occupation. Thus, at least six forms of relinquishing control over territory have been identified: the complete end of control over territory, the temporary or partial loss of control over parts of the territory, the potential for regaining control, control retained after withdrawal, the ending of indirect effective control, and remaining based on a UN SC mandate.

Through an analysis of the case of Gaza, this chapter also revealed that relinquishing effective control (OL) over territory does not (fully) discharge the (former) occupant from its obligations under GC IV 1949. Under a functional approach, GC IV obligations apply not only in times of military occupation, but also before occupation materialises as well as after it has ceased. More particularly, state obligations are retained commensurate to the level of control still exercised by the outside state. However, the functional application of GC IV should not be taken to mean that military occupation as such persists. The three types of obligations the outside power could continue to be bound by are: ongoing obligations, with two subtypes: (a) full ongoing obligations in case of full effective control (OL) exerted by the occupant over the territory, and (b) partial ongoing obligations which flow from partial effective control (OL); residual obligations; and obligations based on past violations.

Lastly, the UN SC declaring a situation of occupation to be over was addressed and certain concerns were voiced in this regard. In this context, the facts on the ground have to be assessed impartially and their interpretation should be devoid of political considerations, e.g. the attempt to clear certain states from pejorative and unpalatable terms such as "unlawful invader" or "occupant".[223]

---

223 Another question is whether the UN SC can be 'a modulator' of occupation law so to "better suit the specificities of the occupation at hand, as long as the limits imposed by the peremptory norms are respected." See further H. Cuyckens, *Revisiting the Law of Occupation*, *supra* note 1, at 241. This question, while certainly related to the issues discussed here lies, however outside the scope of the present book.

4 The effect of control on substantive obligations

1. Introduction

This final chapter examines the occupant's substantive obligations in view of IHL and IHRL, triggered based on the level of control exerted by a state at a specific point in time, i.e. in a concrete situation. Under IHL, a state may exercise control either over territory, in light of Article 42 HR 1907, Common Article 2 GCs, and Article 1 AP I 1977. A state can wield control also over persons, pursuant to Article 4 GC IV. In other words, a state may also exercise a type of control that does not amount to a situation of military occupation, for example during the invasion phase.[1] Furthermore, it may also retreat from the territory or lose swathes of it fully, temporarily, or partially (see Chapter 3).

At the same time, this chapter investigates whether occupation law and IHRL share a common test for triggering obligations. It will be seen that while the control tests for occupation law and for IHRL's extraterritorial application are based on common elements (control over persons and control over territory), important differences still remain. Military occupation's test for effective control (OL) automatically triggers human rights obligations,[2] since when a state's military force asserts effective control (OL) over a foreign territory, it automatically assumes the responsibility for what previously rested under the ousted sovereign's control. However, control for human rights purposes does not automatically make a state an occupant.

---

1 M. Sassòli, 'A Plea in Defence of Pictet and the Inhabitants of Territories Under Invasion: The Case for the Applicability of the Fourth Geneva Convention During the Invasion Phase', 94 *International Review of the Red Cross* (2012) 42–50, at 43.
2 N. Lubell, 'Human Rights Obligations in Military Occupation', 94 *International Review of the Red Cross* (2012) 317–337, at 334; see however Court of Appeal (Civil Division), R (on the Application of Mazin Mumaa Galteh Al-Skeini and Others) v. Secretary of State for Defence [2005] EWCA Civ 1609 (leading judgment by Lord Justice Brooke), § 127.

2. The occupying power's substantive obligations from the perspective of IHL

While IHRL primarily articulates the rights of persons (emphasising individual rights),[3] IHL establishes the obligations of states with regards to extending protection to those concerned as well as defining what states can or cannot do whilst at war. An occupying power's substantive obligations in IHL are not as extensive as in IHRL and can be divided into obligations vis-à-vis the displaced sovereign and those towards civilians. An occupant's substantive obligations include for instance, the respect of private and public property – it can generally not be destructed by the occupant and private property may be confiscated under local legislation only.[4] As regards the welfare of the civilian population, GC IV lists rights, from the provision of food supplies and hygiene to the running of hospitals, the internment and welfare of civilians, in addition to classifying torture and inhumane treatment as grave breaches of the GCs.[5] To better understand a state's substantive obligations, the threshold of control contained in GC IV needs further probing.

---

3 C. Lekha Sriam, O. Martin-Ortega and J. Herman, *War, Conflicts and Human Rights: Theory and Practice* (2nd edn., New York: Routledge, 2014), at 51.

4 M. Sassòli, A. A. Bouvier, and A. Quintin, *How Does Law Protect in War?*, Vol. 1 (3rd edn., Geneva: ICRC, 2011), at 231; Articles 46 and 55 HR 1907; Article 53, GC IV 1949; Practice Relating to Rule 51, Public and Private Property in Occupied Territory, Section B: Immovable Public Property in Occupied Territory, Customary IHL, available at https://ihl-databases.icrc.org/customary-ihl/eng/docs/v2_rul_rule51_sectionb (visited 29 January 2017); Y. Arai-Takahashi, 'Protection of Private Property', in A. Clapham, P. Gaeta and M. Sassòli (eds.), *The 1949 Geneva Conventions: A Commentary* (Oxford: Oxford University Press, 2015) 1515–1534, at 1522–1527; A. Van Engeland, 'Protection of Public Property', in A. Clapham, P. Gaeta, and M. Sassòli (eds.), *The 1949 Geneva Conventions: A Commentary* (Oxford: Oxford University Press, 2015) 1535–1550, at 1541–1548; D. Dam-de Jong, *International Law and Governance of Natural Resources in Conflict and Post-Conflict Situations* (Cambridge: Cambridge University Press, 2015), at 217, at 243.

5 H.-P. Gasser and K. Dörmann, 'Protection of the Civilian Population', in D. Fleck (ed.), *The Handbook of International Humanitarian Law* (3rd edn., Oxford: Oxford University Press, 2014) 231–320, at 234–235; see also *Report of the Special Rapporteur on the Situation of Human Rights in the Palestinian Territories Occupied Since 1967*, UN Doc. A/HRC/25/67, 13 January 2014, § 55, at 16, § 62–63, at 17, and § 78, at 20; S. Sivakumaran, 'Torture in International Human Rights and International Humanitarian Law: The Actor and the Ad Hoc Tribunals', 18 *Leiden Journal of International Law* (2005) 541–556, at 553–555; L. D. Beck and S. Vité, 'International Humanitarian Law and Human Rights Law', 293 *International Review of the Red Cross* (1993), available at www.icrc.org/eng/resources/documents/article/other/57jmrt.htm (visited 29 January 2017); H.-J. Heintze, 'On the Relationship Between Human Rights Protection and International Humanitarian Law', 856 *International Review of the Red Cross* (2004) 789–813, at 798–811; see generally R. Kolb, 'Human Rights and Humanitarian Law', *Max Planck Encyclopaedia of Public International Law* (2013), §1–44, available at http://opil.ouplaw.com/view/10.1093/law:epil/9780199231690/law-9780199231690-e811?prd=EPIL (visited 29 January 2017).

136   *The effect of control on substantive obligations*

2.1 Forms and degrees of control in GC IV

Control can be wielded not only over territory, but also over persons, thereby enhancing the applicability of GC IV as opposed to Article 42 HR 1907. According to Sassòli, the "concept of control could be interpreted in a functional way, with a different threshold for different rules",[6] meaning that while a situation may not amount to occupation, some rules from GC IV would still be applicable: pursuant to a functional understanding of occupation, a territory that was invaded could already be occupied for the purpose of Article 49 GC IV (prohibiting deportation), but not occupied for the purpose of the applicability of Article 50 (on education).[7]

A significant difference can be identified in the GC IV and HR 1907 application thresholds. GC IV centres on the protection of civilians, possessing a lower threshold of application. That is, as soon as protected persons find themselves in the "hands of a Party to the conflict or Occupying Power", GC IV starts to apply. On the other hand, Article 42 HR 1907, which establishes authority over territory (effective control (OL)) and the powers and obligations of the occupant along with its relationship with the ousted sovereign, contains more stringent application criteria (see Chapter 1). Therefore, the difference lies not only in the *aim* of the two instruments, but also in the *application thresholds*, although both potentially concern the same situation, namely military occupation (see also Chapters 1 and 3).

The application of GC IV is much broader than one may think: "The present Convention shall apply from the outset of any conflict or occupation mentioned in Article 2."[8] Insofar as individuals are concerned, Pictet reasoned that GC IV application did not depend on the existence of military occupation within the meaning of Article 42 HR 1907: the relations between the civilians living on a territory and troops advancing into that territory, whether fighting or not, were ruled by GC IV; no intermediary period existed between the invasion phase and the inauguration of a stable regime of occupation.[9]

In other words, already during the enemy forces' invasion phase, GC IV "should be applied as soon as troops are in foreign territory and in contact with the civilian population there"[10] – including to a certain extent the provisions of GC IV Part III, Section III, on occupied territories.[11] This means that "the

---

6 M. Sassòli, 'A Plea in Defence of Pictet and the Inhabitants of Territories Under Invasion', *supra* note 1, at 43.

7 Ibid., at 49.

8 Article 6, Convention (IV) Relative to the Protection of Civilian Persons in Time of War Geneva, 12 August 1949.

9 J. Pictet (ed.), *Commentary of 1958, Convention (IV) Relative to the Protection of Civilian Persons in Time of War Geneva, 12 August 1949*, Article 6 (Geneva: ICRC, 1958), at 60.

10 Ibid., at 59.

11 See *Eritrea-Ethiopia Claims Commission – Partial Award: Western Front, Aerial Bombardment and Related Claims – Eritrea's Claims 1, 3, 5, 9–13, 14, 21, 25 and 26*

The effect of control on substantive obligations   137

applicability of the Fourth Geneva Convention during the invasion phase would be based on effective control over persons rather than on effective control over foreign territory (or parts of it)."[12]

Pictet's theory was termed as the "functional" beginning of belligerent occupation.[13] It is, however, submitted that this term, and even the general idea of the functional application, is too vague as it does not clearly convey the mode and boundaries of GC IV's application. What does "functional" really mean? The conventional understanding of that word relates to the way in which something works or operates.[14] In essence, a situational and a functional application both lead to the same result: whatever is functional is to be considered practical as opposed to decorative. Consequently, it is applicable to various situations. A more adequate term would, therefore, be a "situational application", as GC IV itself (in common Article 2 and Article 6) envisages various situations: armed conflict, invasion, or occupation. This consideration flows from the fact that as soon as a soldier encounters a person in *any* of these situations, GC IV applies, placing that person under GC IV protection.

Grasping Pictet's theory therefore is dependent upon drawing a sharp line between the invasion phase and actual occupation. The difference between the two is that an invasion does not hinge on the concept of effective control (OL) as envisaged by Article 42 HR 1907; whether an invasion progresses into occupation is a factual matter. The former implies a military operation while the latter signifies the exercise of governmental authority to the exclusion of the established government.[15]

(19 December 2005) § 27, available at http://legal.un.org/riaa/cases/vol_XXVI/291-349.pdf (visited 29 January 2017); see also A. Gross, *The Writing on the Wall: Rethinking the International Law of Occupation* (Cambridge: Cambridge University Press, 2017), at 75–78; see also G. H. Aldrich, 'The Work of the Eritrea-Ethiopia Claims Commission', 6 *Yearbook of International Humanitarian Law* (2003) 435–442, at 440.

12 T. Ferraro (ed.), *Expert Meeting Occupation and Other Forms of Administration of Foreign Territory* (Geneva: ICRC, 2012), at 25.

13 M. Siegrist, *The Functional Beginning of Belligerent Occupation* (Geneva: Graduate Institute Publications, 2010), at 26–28.

14 Oxford Dictionary definition of 'functional' in English, available at https://en.oxforddictionaries.com/definition/functional (visited 29 January 2017).

15 US Tribunal at Nuremberg, Hostages Trial, Law Reports of Trial of War Criminals, Vol. III, UN War Crimes Commission, 1949, London, at 55–56. Also: "This presupposes the destruction of organised resistance and the establishment of an administration to preserve law and order. To the extent that the occupant's control is maintained and that of the civil government eliminated, the area will be said to be occupied" (USA v. Wilhelm List et al., Law Reports of Trials of War Criminals, Vol. VIII, UN War Crimes Commission, London, 1949, at 56.). Similarly, in case N 45 12, the Permanent Military Tribunal at Dijon, when applying Article 2 of the HR 1907, stated that "any part of territory in which the occupant has been deprived of actual means for carrying out *normal* administration by the presence of opposing military forces, would not have the status of 'occupied' territory within the terms of articles 2 and 42 of the Hague Regulations. The fact that other parts of the occupied country as a whole, are under effective enemy occupation, would not affect this situation"; see trial of Carl Bauer, Ernst Schrameck, and Herbert Falten, *Law Reports of Trials of War Criminals,*

138 *The effect of control on substantive obligations*

Yet the question remains as to what law is applicable during the invasion phase. Such an inquiry is further complicated by the exercise of identifying when invasion is transformed into occupation. The transition from invasion into occupation may be gradual and murky.[16] At the same time, if a situation of occupation coincides with clashes with a resistance movement, or with a combat situation between the ousted sovereign and the occupant, it is only logical that in such circumstances the rules of conduct of hostilities apply next to the corpus of occupation law (see also Chapter 3, section 2.3), as "the law of occupation and the law of hostilities are not mutually exclusive, but may apply in parallel to different activities occurring within the same territory at the same time."[17] In this context, Article 4 GC IV states that

> persons protected by the Convention are those who, at a given moment and in any manner whatsoever, find themselves in case of a conflict or occupation, in the hands of a party to the conflict or Occupying Power of which they are not nationals.[18]

Here, the French text uses "*au pouvoir*", which literally translates as "in the power of", or also under the control. The wording "in the hands of" is explained by Pictet to be "used in an extremely general sense",[19] meaning that a person is on territory under the control of the concerned state.[20]

Furthermore, the wording "at any given moment and in any manner whatsoever" is intended to ensure that "all situations and cases were covered."[21] It should, nevertheless, not be forgotten that Article 4 GC IV does not stretch its application to situations of hostilities, which are regulated by the rules spelled out in HR 1907 and AP I 1977. The ICTY, in Naletilić and referring to GC IV, also considered that the "application of the law of occupation to the civilian population differs from its application under Article 42 of the 1907 Hague

---

UN War Crimes Commission, Vol. VIII, London, 1949, at 18; also L. Oppenheim, *International Law: A Treatise*, Vol. 2 (7th edn., London; New York: Longmans Green, 1952), at 207; Y. Dinstein, *The International Law of Belligerent Occupation* (Cambridge: Cambridge University Press, 2009), at 38; and R. Kolb and S. Vité, *Le droit de l'occupation militaire* (Geneva: Bruylant, 2009), at 138–139.

16 However, see *US Department of Defense Law of War Manual* (General Counsel of the Department of Defense, June 2015), at 741.

17 N. Melzer, *Targeted Killing in International Law* (Oxford: Oxford University Press, 2008), at 157.

18 Article 4 Convention (IV) relative to the Protection of Civilian Persons in Time of War Geneva, 12 August 1949; M. Siegrist, *The Functional Beginning of Belligerent Occupation*, *supra* note 13, at 24 and 27.

19 J. Pictet, *Commentary of 1958*, *supra* note 9, Article 4, at 47.

20 Ibid; see also N. Nishat, 'The Structure of Geneva Convention IV and the Resulting Gaps in that Convention', in A. Clapham, P. Gaeta, and M. Sassòli (eds.), *The 1949 Geneva Conventions: A Commentary* (Oxford: Oxford University Press, 2015) 1069–1087, at 1073–1075 and 1077–1078.

21 J. Pictet, Commentary of 1958, *supra* note 9, Article 4, at 47.

Regulations".[22] The ICTY Trial Chamber further noted that the application of the law of occupation,

> as it affects "individuals" as civilians protected under Geneva Convention IV, does not require that the occupying power have actual authority. For the purposes of those individuals' rights, a state of occupation exists upon their falling into "the hands of the occupying power." Otherwise civilians would be left, during an intermediate period, with less protection than that attached to them once occupation is established.[23]

This would then hold true "regardless of the stage of hostilities" and there would be no need to establish occupation as defined by Article 42 HR 1907.[24] The ICTY Trial Chamber therefore formulated two legal tests, both sharing the element of control but exercised over different objects: control over territory and control over people. Through both, occupation law then applies:

> Consequently, the Chamber will have recourse to different legal tests to determine whether the law of occupation applies, depending on whether it is dealing with individuals or with property and other matters. In the present case, it finds that the forcible transfer [. . .] and the unlawful labour [. . .] of civilians were prohibited from the moment that they fell into the hands of the opposing power, regardless of the stage of the hostilities.[25]

However, not everybody agrees with Pictet's approach. Zwanenburg, for example, cautions that Pictet's theory may lead to a scenario "in which the determination whether a person is a 'protected person' is conflated with the test for determining whether there is an occupation."[26] The present writer has also advanced that the criteria of Article 42 HR 1907 continue to live within Common Article 2 GCs and Article 1 AP I 1977 (see Chapters 1, 2, and 3). However, the structure of Common Article 2.2. GCs and Articles 4 and 6(1) GC IV, as well as the object and purpose of GC IV, all point towards a *situational* application of the Convention. Bothe, too, considers Pictet's theory an "oversimplification"[27] since as "an invading army advances, fighting its way into foreign territory, a situation of control is not established immediately"[28] and in that stage of the armed conflict,

---

22 Judgment, *Naletilić and Martinović* (IT-98–34-T), Trial Chamber, 31 March 2003, § 219.
23 Ibid., § 221.
24 Ibid.
25 Ibid., § 122.
26 M. Zwanenburg, 'Challenging the Pictet Theory', 885 *International Review of the Red Cross* (2012) 30–36, at 33.
27 M. Bothe, 'Effective Control During Invasion: A Practical View on the Application Threshold of the Law of Occupation', 885 *International Review of the Red Cross* (2012) 37–41, at 38.
28 Ibid., at 39.

140 *The effect of control on substantive obligations*

the invading force does not yet have the duty of an occupant to see to the welfare of the local population.[29]

It is submitted that precisely here the issue of different degrees of control and the ensuing different obligations come into play: different obligations start at different times, depending on the degree and type of control exerted by the invading force or the occupant in a concrete situation. In other words: on a sliding scale of obligations relative to the degree of control, obligations to abstain would be applicable as soon as the conduct they outlaw materialises, while obligations to provide and guarantee would apply only at a later stage.[30]

This later stage would be constituted by a situation of military occupation under Article 42 HR 1907 and Common Article 2 GCs, while the earlier stage describes the invasion scenario set forth by Bothe. Therefore, obligations contained in certain rules apply if they are materially possible to be carried out, while others do not apply because the means to carry them out do not exist (yet).[31]

What is more, disregarding the potential and adjustability afforded by GC IV, along with Pictet's theory, would run contrary to the logic and spirit of IHL. If the threshold of effective control (OL) over territory from Article 42 HR 1907 is narrowly applied to GC IV, then a gap is created as in several scenarios (such as during invasions), persons protected under GC IV risk being left outside the safeguards of IHL. Put differently, different situations entail different forms of control, which in turn lead to different obligations. The provisions related to the law of military occupation as well as GC IV start to apply as soon as protected persons fall into the hands of a party to the conflict, even if there is no military occupation *stricto sensu*. It is, therefore, put forward that due to humanitarian reasons and based on the general spirit of IHL, GC IV has a more flexible understanding of control and applies to different situations. To the term "functional applicability", "situational" should however be preferred so as to avoid confusion in the application of the law and make it easier to comprehend its intentions and usage. This term also more clearly conveys the *ratione materiae* of IHL.

GC IV, in consequence, affords the most favourable and practicable protection to civilians and comes forward with a very adaptable application: a "different threshold for different rules."[32] While a given situation might not directly present itself as one of occupation, some rules from GC IV become applicable already in the invasion phase, the purpose being to enhance and reinforce the protection of civilians.

---

29 Ibid.

30 M. Sassòli, 'A Plea in Defence of Pictet and the Inhabitants of Territories Under Invasion', *supra* note 1, at 49. See also M. Siegrist, *The Functional Beginning of Belligerent Occupation*, *supra* note 13, at 27.

31 T. Ferraro, *Expert Meeting*, *supra* note 12, at 25.

32 M. Sassòli, 'A Plea in Defence of Pictet and the Inhabitants of Territories Under Invasion', *supra* note 1, at 43.

2.2 State obligations during the temporary or partial loss of control over territory

When the occupying power loses its effective control (OL) over the territory and cannot regain it, IHL rules on occupation law will no longer apply. However, when the occupying power loses effective control (OL) over the territory only temporarily or partially, territory is not automatically free from being occupied (see Chapter 3), nor do the IHL rules of military occupation cease instantly. Local resistance does not preclude the applicability of the law of occupation either.[33] The main aspect here is that the occupying power eventually re-establishes its authority over the territory.[34] While trying to reclaim its power, the state will not be practically able to meet the threshold of the HR 1907 (for example due to hostilities between the occupant and its adversaries). However, based on the situational application of GC IV, it must live up to those obligations that are commensurate to the level of control exercised in a concrete situation. GC IV applicability is instrumental when the state loses effective control (OL) over territory either fully or temporarily. The control thresholds in GC IV, which are based on the ability of a state to exercise control at a specific point in time (a certain situation triggering a specific obligation), thus determines its obligations.

The question then is which articles operate when a state either completely or temporarily lost effective control (OL) over territory and when a group of its soldiers encounters some farmers and detains them on security grounds? Under GC IV, the farmers would be entitled to the immediate protection of Article 27, which safeguards their honour and family rights, religious convictions, manners and customs, and their right to be humanely treated at all times. Article 27 GC IV, therefore, applies in all circumstances. The GC IV Commentary also advocates that this article's application has to be understood broadly,[35] encompassing all possible scenarios, including those in which the occupant has either fully, temporarily, or partially lost control over territory. Such a modus operandi is for instance shown by Articles 28–34 and 13–26 GC IV.

Difficulties nonetheless arise when the armed forces are confronted with a demand for ensuring *all* the rights contained in GC IV, as not all of them may be provided for.[36] For example, Article 24 regulates child welfare and may be difficult to implement once an occupant's effective control (OL) over the territory has been challenged by local resistance. It is thought that Article 24 GC IV requires uninterrupted effective control (OL) over territory, as opposed to Article 18, which is designated for the protection of civilian hospitals caring for

---

33 H.-P. Gasser and K. Dörmann, 'Protection of the Civilian Population', *supra* note 5, at 273.
34 UK Ministry of Defence, *The Manual of the Law of Armed Conflict* (Oxford: Oxford University Press, 2004), § 11.7.1, at 277.
35 J. Pictet, *Commentary of 1958*, *supra* note 9, Article 27, at 199–207.
36 H.-P. Gasser and K. Dörmann, 'Protection of the Civilian Population', *supra* note 5, at 274.

142 *The effect of control on substantive obligations*

wounded, sick and maternity cases.[37] It follows that certain GC IV rights are adaptable to the occupant's level of control, while some others have to be provided for even if the occupant's effective control (OL) over territory is challenged or has to be secured anew.

3. Is control construed the same way in IHRL and occupation law?

Examples of substantive rights under IHRL, to name just a few, are the rights to life, to a fair trial, to freedom of speech, or to freedom of movement, all enshrined in the cohort of human rights treaties concluded on an international level.[38] These instruments permit persons to live in freedom and dignity.[39] States are the duty bearers bound by them;[40] they need to ensure the enshrined rights not only to their citizens, but also to whomever is present on their territory.[41] While the overall responsibility for the protection of human rights rests with states, regional and international bodies exercise a supervisory role over how the former fulfil their obligations.[42]

In turn, the extraterritorial application of IHRL – regardless of the various wordings of human rights treaties such as the ECHR, ICCPR, or the American Convention on Human Rights – rests on one key element: "exercise of jurisdiction".[43] In other words, all IHRL instruments base their applicability on

---

37 M. -Skuza, 'Hospitals', in A. Clapham, P. Gaeta, and M. Sassòli (eds.), *The 1949 Geneva Conventions: A Commentary* (Oxford: Oxford University Press, 2015) 207–229, at 210–212 and 218. See additionally Article 19, GC IV 1949.

38 C. Tomuschat, *Human Rights* (3rd edn., Oxford: Oxford University Press, 2014), at 112.

39 Ibid.; see also R. Provost, *International Human Rights and Humanitarian Law* (Cambridge: Cambridge University Press, 2003), at 43–49.

40 C. Tomuschat, *Human Rights, supra* note 38, at 119. Under international law, states become bound by treaties only through acceptance (VCLT Article 11), that is the state has to ratify the treaty. On the issues of prevention of human rights violations, see generally C. Bourloyannis-Vrailas and L.-A. Sicilianos (eds.), *The Prevention of Human Rights Violations* (Leiden: Brill/Martinus Nijhoff Publishers, 2001).

41 W. Mansell and K. Openshaw, *International Law: A Critical Introduction* (Oxford: Hart Publishing, 2013), at 47–48.

42 R. K. M. Smith, *International Human Rights* (2nd edn., Oxford: Oxford University Press, 2005), at 173.

43 T. Ruys and S. Verhoeven, 'DRC v. Uganda: The Applicability of International Humanitarian Law and Human Rights Law in Occupied Territories', in R. Arnold and N. Quénvet (eds.), *International Humanitarian Law and Human Rights Law: Towards a New Merger in International Law* (Leiden: Martinus Nijhoff Publishers, 2008) 155–195, at 174; I. Brownlie, *Principles of Public International Law* (7th edn., Oxford: Oxford University Press, 2008), at 299; A. Cassese, *International Law* (2nd edn., Oxford: Oxford University Press, 2005), at 386; M. J. Dennis, 'Application of Human Rights Treaties Extraterritorially in Times of Armed Conflict and Military Occupation', 99 *American Journal of International Law* (2005) 119–141, at 122; D. McGoldrick, 'Extraterritorial Application of the International Covenant on Civil and Political Rights', in F. Coomans and M. T. Kamminga (eds.), *Extraterritorial Application of Human Rights*

a state exercising control over an individual (personal connection) and over territory (spatial connection).[44] The level of control needed to be exerted for the purposes of the spatial connection, based on the practice of Human Rights Committee, the ECtHR, and the Inter-American Commission of Human Rights, is that of effective control (*effective control* (IHRL)). However, with regards to the personal connection, the adjective "effective" has not been used.[45]

The UN Secretary General rejected a narrow application of human rights by stating that they "apply always and everywhere".[46] Nevertheless, it remains to be ascertained whether IHRL also applies in times of military occupation and on what basis. Does it apply *because of* occupation or despite? This issue is far from clear and its explanation has been somewhat avoided by the ICJ, its dicta only remarking IHRL to be applicable in times of armed conflict, including situations of military occupation.[47] The ECtHR, on the other hand, purported to shed

---

Treaties (Antwerp; Oxford: Intersentia, 2004) 41–72, at 49. T. Meron, 'The 1994 U.S Action in Haiti: Extraterritoriality of Human Rights Treaties', 89 *American Journal of International Law* (1995) 78–82, at 82; M. Scheinin, 'Extraterritorial Effect of the International Covenant on Civil and Political Rights', in F. Coomans and M. Kamminga (eds.), *Extraterritorial Application of Human Rights Treaties* (Antwerp; Oxford: Intersentia, June 2004) 73–83, at 77–78; see additionally on the issue of the *espace juridique* S. Miller, 'Revisiting Extraterritorial Jurisdiction: A Territorial Justification for Extraterritorial Jurisdiction Under the European Convention', 20 *The European Journal of International Law* (2009) 1223–1246, at 1235–1236; M. Milanović, 'Al-Skeini and Al-Jedda in Strasbourg', 23 *The European Journal of International Law* (2012) 121–139, at 125–129; C. Ryngaert, 'Clarifying the Extraterritorial Application of the European Convention on Human Rights', 28 *Utrecht Journal of International and European Law* (2012) 57–60, at 58–59. Regarding case law, see *M. v. Denmark*, ECtHR (1992) (App. no 17392/90) (complaint against Danish diplomatic authorities); Banković et al. v. Belgium et al., ECtHR (Grand Chamber Decision as to the Admissibility of) (2001) (App. no. 52207/99) §73; Al-Skeini and Others v. Secretary for Defence (2004) EWHC 2911, 14 December 2004, § 270; Al-Skeini and Others v. Secretary of State for Defence (2005) EWCA Civ 1609, Court of Appeal, 21 December 2005, §§ 13–28, §§ 48–136; House of Lords Al-Skeini and Others (Respondents) v. Secretary of State for Defence (Appellant); Al-Skeini and Others (Appellants) v. Secretary of State for Defence (Respondent) (2007) UKHL 26, 13 June 2007, § 109; M. Milanović, *Extraterritorial Application of Human Rights Treaties: Law, Principles, and Policy* (Oxford: Oxford University Press, 2011), at 11–39; K. Da Costa, *The Extraterritorial Application of Selected Human Rights Treaties* (Leiden: Martinus Nijhoff Publishers, 2013), at 128–181.

44 R. Wilde, 'Triggering State Obligations Extraterritorially: The Spatial Test in Certain Human Rights Treaties', 2 *Israel Law Review* (2007) 503–526, at 508.

45 However, see C. Droege, 'The Interplay Between International Humanitarian Law and International Human Rights Law in Situations of Armed Conflict', 2 *Israel Law Review* (2007) 310–355, at 325.

46 *Respect for Human Rights in Armed Conflict, Report of the Secretary General*, UN DOC. A/8052 (1970) § 25.

47 See *Case Concerning Legality of the Threat or Use of Nuclear Weapons*, Advisory Opinion of 8 July 1996, § 24–25, available at www.icj-cij.org/en/case/95; *Legal Consequences of the Construction of a Wall in the Occupied Palestinian Territory*, Advisory Opinion of 9 July 2004, § 106–114 available at www.icj-cij.org/en/case/131; *Case Concerning Armed Activities on the Territory of the Congo (Democratic Republic of the Congo v. Uganda)*,

144 *The effect of control on substantive obligations*

light on the matter in its case law, albeit with shortcomings addressed on the pages to come.

The following question is thus posed: during military occupation, do IHRL obligations arise based on the same test and in par with military occupation? Or are they founded on a different test?[48]

3.1 Authority and control over individuals

The extraterritorial applicability of IHRL instruments and state extraterritorial jurisdiction arise when a state agent exerts authority and control over individuals, including such cases as abduction, detention, or any form of ill-treatment of a person. State agents can exercise control over persons both in peacetime and during armed conflicts, including situations of military occupation. While this aspect has been extensively covered by the ECtHR, what has not been elaborated upon is the impact of and the relationship this trigger of jurisdiction has with occupation law. In *Al-Skeini v. UK*, the ECtHR referred to "state agent authority and control" in the following way:

> whenever the State through its agents exercises control and authority over an individual, and thus jurisdiction, the State is under an obligation under Article 1 [of the ECHR] to secure to that individual the rights and freedoms under section 1 of the convention that are relevant to the situation of that individual.[49]

A breakdown of this relationship as explained by the court is displayed in Figure 4.1.

The level of control needed to be exerted by the state agent over an individual – which would then give rise to that state's jurisdiction under the ECHR – does however not clearly emerge from the rendered passage. In Öcalan, the ECtHR described the required level of control as follows: "the applicant was effectively under Turkish authority and therefore within jurisdiction of that State [. . .] forced to return to Turkey by Turkish officials and was under their authority and control following his arrest and return to Turkey."[50] In *Issa and Others v. Turkey*, which concerned the activity of a state's armed forces, the ECtHR noted that a state could also be held accountable under the ECHR for

---

Judgment of 19 December 2005, § 178–180, available at www.icj-cij.org/en/case/116 (all visited 15 July 2017).

48 F. J. Hampson, 'The Relationship Between International Humanitarian Law and Human Rights Law from the Perspective of a Human Rights Treaty Body', 871 *International Review of the Red Cross* (2008) 549–572, at 567: "Is the test for occupation the same under IHL and human rights law?". See also M. Milanović, *Extraterritorial Application of Human Rights Treaties, supra* note 43, at 141–142 and 147.

49 Al-Skeini and Others v. the United Kingdom, ECtHR (2011) (App. No. 55721/07) § 137.

50 Öcalan v. Turkey Judgment, ECtHR (2005) (App. no. 46221/99) § 91;

The effect of control on substantive obligations   145

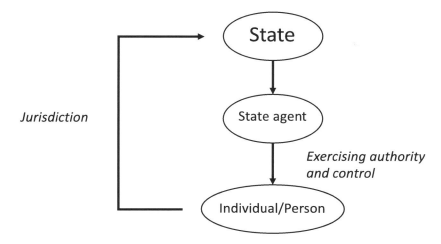

Figure 4.1 State agent authority and control over persons/individuals (ECtHR)

violations of the rights of persons "who are in the territory of another State but who are found to be under the former *State's authority and control through its agents* operating – whether lawfully or unlawfully – in the latter State."[51] This can, but does not have to, mean that there is a military occupation or a situation of armed conflict. In Al-Saadoon and Mufdhi, within a military occupation context, and having stated that "during the first months of the applicants' detention the United Kingdom was an occupying power in Iraq",[52] the ECtHR in its decision of admissibility maintained that "given the total and exclusive *de facto*, and subsequently also *de jure*, control exercised by the United Kingdom authorities *over the premises in question* [a prison], the individuals detained there, including the applicants, were within the United Kingdom's jurisdiction."[53] Finally, *Medvedyev and Others v. France* considered that the applicants were under French jurisdiction for the purposes of the ECHR because the French agents had "exercised full and exclusive control over the *Winner* and its crew" from the time the ship and the crew were intercepted in international waters, "in a continuous and uninterrupted manner until they were tried in France".[54] In all these cases, state agents were responsible for discharging a state's obligations under the ECHR.

51 Issa and Others v. Turkey, ECtHR (2005) (App. no. 31821/96) § 71; emphasis added.
52 Al-Saadoon and Mufdhi v. United Kingdom, ECtHR (2009) (App. no. 61498/08) § 87.
53 Ibid., § 88.
54 Medvedyev and Others v. France, ECtHR (App. no. 3394/03) (2010) § 67.

146 *The effect of control on substantive obligations*

It thus appears that the ECtHR does not consider jurisdiction to be arising solely from control exercised by a state over buildings, aircrafts, or ships in which individuals are held. In such cases, what is decisive "is the exercise of the physical power and control over the person in question."[55] In turn, exercising physical power over a person implies that this person is not at full liberty over his own physical situation. What is more, this form of control also always results in *specific* control over a person's ability to enjoy *specific* rights. However, control over specific rights does not necessarily result in full physical control over the person: for example, in the case of *Solomou and Others v. Turkey*, the ECtHR found the Turkish agents to have violated the applicant's right to life without however having had full physical control over him. In fact, had they exerted such full physical control, Solomou would never have been able to climb the flagpole to begin with.[56]

The analysis of the ECtHR's case law takes yet another interesting turn with *Jaloud v. The Netherlands*. The complaint in Jaloud was brought by an Iraqi national whose son met his death on 24 April 2004 at a checkpoint in Iraq through shots fired by Dutch troops.[57] The applicant contended that the investigation into the death of his son had been inadequate and that the Netherlands had violated their procedural obligations under Article 2 ECHR. The Netherlands, on the other hand, argued that the deceased did not fall under their jurisdiction within the meaning of Article 1 ECHR and that they did not consider themselves to be an occupant in terms of IHL.[58] Only the UK and the US were occupying powers, as designated by UN SC Resolution 1483.[59] For that reason, the Netherlands had not assumed any public powers in Iraq normally exercised by the sovereign government.[60] The Court, however, noted that for the purposes of establishing jurisdiction, it only took into account the factual context and the relevant rules of international law.[61] Regarding jurisdiction, the ECtHR further opined that

> the status of "occupying power" within the meaning of Article 42 of the Hague Regulations, or lack of it, is not *per se* determinative. Although it found that concept relevant in *Al-Skeini* [. . .] and in *Al-Jedda v. the United Kingdom* [. . .] the Court did not need to have recourse to it in finding that the responsibility of Turkey was engaged in respect of events in northern Cyprus [. . .] or that of Russia in respect of the situation in Moldovan territory east of the Dniester.[62]

As already explained in Chapter 2, what the Court found in the Northern Cyprus and Transdniestrian cases amounted to effective overall control and decisive

---

55 Al-Skeini and Others v. the United Kingdom, *supra* note 49, § 136.
56 Solomou and Others v. Turkey, ECtHR (App. no. 36832/97) (2008) § 71, § 75 and § 79.
57 Jaloud v. the Netherlands, ECtHR (App. no. 47708/08) (2014) §§ 10–38.
58 Ibid.
59 Ibid., § 113.
60 Ibid., § 114.
61 Ibid., § 141.
62 Ibid., § 142.

influence. In Jaloud, however, the Court crafted a *new* basis for jurisdiction based on "persons passing through a checkpoint": Jaloud died when the vehicle in which he sat was fired upon while passing through a checkpoint operated by personnel under the command and supervision of a Netherlands Royal Army officer. The Court therefore was satisfied that the respondent exercised its "jurisdiction" within the limits of its SFIR mission and for the purpose of asserting authority and control over persons passing through the checkpoint.[63] The Court thus found Dutch jurisdiction under Article 1 ECHR to be given because Mr. Jaloud came within the sphere of authority and control established by the checkpoint. The Court did not directly consider the concerned state to be an occupant, although it referred to UN SC Resolution 1483. The open question now is whether jurisdiction is only triggered by setting up a checkpoint during military occupation, or also regardless of it.[64] While in theory a checkpoint can be set up anytime and anywhere, it is of course very improbable that a state enters the territory of another state solely for that purpose. In practice, checkpoints will inevitably be connected to military occupations or at least ongoing armed conflicts.

At this point, it should be recalled that the key question here is what impact the *state agent authority and control over a person* test may have and how it can manifest itself in times of military occupation. What commonalities does it share with occupation law, and particularly with GC IV's threshold of control over protected persons? The key provision here is Article 4 GC IV.[65] In this Article, the main formulation points towards various contexts – "at a given moment and in any manner whatsoever find themselves, in case of a conflict or occupation, in the hands of a Party to the conflict or Occupying Power" – and insinuates that a person may be under the control of an adversary not only when placed in detention, but also when members of the armed forces are passing through a certain area.[66] Control over a person "in a territory that is not the invader's own must therefore be sufficient to trigger the application to that person of Convention IV's provisions applicable in occupied territories."[67] Figure 4.2 shows the operating mechanism that triggers the application of GC IV – be that during invasions, occupations, or armed conflicts more generally.

Concluding this section, both IHRL and IHL cognise control over persons. The *state agent authority and control over individuals* and *in the hands of* tests concern the same object – civilians – and the same subject – a representative of the state, namely its agents or members of its armed forces. Both IHRL and IHL

---

63 Ibid., § 152.
64 A. Sari, 'Untangling Extra-Territorial Jurisdiction from International Responsibility in Jaloud v. Netherlands: Old Problem, New Solutions?' 53 *Military Law and the Law of War Review* (2014) 287–318, at 296–302.
65 See J. Pictet, *Commentary of 1958, supra* note 9, Article 4, at 45–50.
66 T. Ferraro, *Expert Meeting, supra* note 12, at 25.
67 M. Sassòli, 'A Plea in Defence of Pictet and the Inhabitants of Territories Under Invasion', *supra* note 1, at 45.

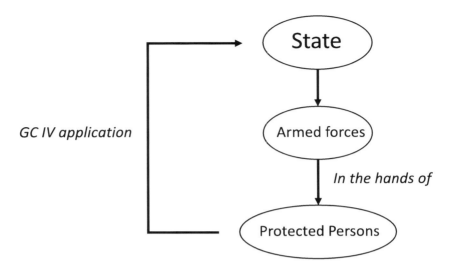

Figure 4.2 State obligations regarding protected persons (Article 4, GC IV 1949)

therefore ensure that persons' rights are protected when members of the armed forces or state agents more generally exercise control over them.[68]

3.2 Control over territory

In international law, it is primarily the state who controls the territory, irrespective of whether it has a title over it or whether its military presence there is lawful or not.[69] Due to such control, a state is responsible for what happens there. For example, in the Namibia case the ICJ viewed South Africa to be unlawfully occupying Namibia and accountable for any violations "of the rights of the people" of Namibia.[70] The fact that South Africa had no title to administering that territory did not release it from its obligations under international law, as the "physical control of a territory, and not sovereignty or legitimacy of the title, is the basis of

---

68 See J. Pictet, *Commentary of 1958*, *supra* note 9, Article 4, at 47.
69 See R. Wilde, 'Triggering State Obligations Extraterritorially', *supra* note 44, at 508–511; V. P. Tzevelekos, 'Reconstructing the Effective Control Criterion in Extraterritorial Human Rights Breaches: Direct Attribution of Wrongfulness, Due Diligence, and Concurrent Responsibility', 36 *Michigan Journal of International Law* (2014) 129–178, at 129–130.
70 *Legal Consequences for States of the Continued Presence of South Africa in Namibia (South West Africa) Notwithstanding Security Council Resolution 276 (1970)*, Advisory Opinion of 21 June 1971, § 118, available at www.icj-cij.org/en/case/53 (visited 29 January 2017).

State liability for acts affecting other States."[71] In short, a "state ought not to be able to escape from duties that befall it when it is acting in its own territory by 'relocating' its activity in some other territory".[72]

That IHRL can apply to military occupation "is now widely, but by no means universally, accepted."[73] Non-acceptance is principally demonstrated by states shunning their responsibilities for their extraterritorial actions under the respective conventions.[74] However, the ICJ in the Wall case found that IHRL instruments (such as the International Covenant on Economic, Social, and Cultural Rights/ICESCR, the International Covenant on Civil and Political Rights/ICCPR, and the Convention on the Rights of the Child) were applicable also in times of occupation. To reach such a conclusion, the Court had to determine whether these instruments were applicable only on the territory of state parties or whether they also applied outside of it – and if so, under what circumstances.[75]

The ICJ observed that while the jurisdiction of states was primarily territorial, it could sometimes subsist also outside the national territory of a state. Taking into consideration the object and purpose of the ICCPR, the latter would in fact apply during such cases.[76] To solidify its reasoning, the ICJ had recourse to the Human Rights Committee, subsequently basing its stance on the latter's analysis. The Human Rights Committee found the ICCPR to be applicable wherever a state exercised its jurisdiction on foreign territory. Here, jurisdiction is revealed to be synonymous to control. The Committee viewed the wording employed in Article 2 ICCPR as not intending to allow states to evade their obligations when they exercised jurisdiction outside their national domain.[77] During the preparation of its report to the Committee, Israel however advanced that "the Covenant and similar instruments did not directly apply to the current situation in the occupied territories".[78] The Human Rights Committee in its concluding

---

71 Ibid.
72 M. Koskenniemi, 'Occupation and Sovereignty – Still a Useful Distinction?' in O. Engdahl and P. Wrange (eds.), *Law at War: The Law As It Was and the Law As It Should Be* (Leiden; Boston: Martinus Nijhoff Publishers, 2008) 163–174, at 169.
73 A. Roberts, 'Transformative Military Occupation: Applying the Laws of War and Human Rights', in M. Schmitt and J. Pejic (eds.), *International Law and Armed Conflict: Exploring the Faultlines* (Leiden: Martinus Nijhoff Publishers, 2007) 439–495, at 458.
74 Israel, with regards to the application of the ICCPR in the occupied territories, considers "that the Convention, which is territorially bound, does not apply, nor was it intended to apply, to areas beyond a state's national territory." See *Human Rights Committee, Consideration of Reports Submitted by States Parties Under Article 40 of the Covenant Pursuant to the Optional Reporting Procedure, Fourth Periodic Report of States Parties Due in 2013*, Israel, CCPR/C/ISR/4, 12 December 2013, § 48.
75 *Legal Consequences of the Construction of a Wall in the Occupied Palestinian Territory, supra* note 47, § 107.
76 Ibid., § 109.
77 Ibid.
78 Ibid., § 110.

150 *The effect of control on substantive obligations*

observations expressed concern over such a stance and pointed "to the long-standing presence of Israel in [the occupied] territories, Israel's ambiguous attitude towards their future status, as well as the exercise of effective jurisdiction by Israeli security forces therein".[79] Moreover, it found the ICCPR to be applicable in the occupied territories "for all conduct by the State party's authorities or agents in those territories that affect the enjoyment of rights enshrined in the Covenant and fall within the ambit of State responsibility of Israel under the principles of public international law."[80] The ICESCR, too, was regarded by the ICJ to be applicable to the occupied territories.[81]

In advancing that the IHRL extraterritorial obligations of a state are also triggered in times of military occupation, the ICJ aligned itself with the Human Rights Committee's perception regarding the level of control. In the Wall Advisory Opinion, the Court considered extraterritorial jurisdiction to be arising based on the exercise of effective control (OL). The ICJ viewed Israel as an occupant because it subjected the territories to its territorial jurisdiction. In the exercise of the powers available to it on such a basis,[82] Israel was bound by the ICESCR as well as by the ICCPR. In the view of the ICJ, also the Convention on the Rights of the Child was applicable to Israeli policies.[83] Article 2 of that Convention provides that "State Parties shall respect and ensure the rights set forth in the [. . .] Convention to each child within their jurisdiction".[84] The ICJ thus viewed jurisdiction as extending to every child subject to Israel's effective control (OL), i.e. based on the territory Israel militarily occupied.[85]

Unlike in the Wall case, in *DRC v. Uganda* the ICJ only briefly considered the extraterritorial applicability of IHRL in times of military occupation. Before actually finding that IHRL was applicable to Ugandan actions, the Court firstly considered whether Uganda was an occupant for the purposes of IHL. The ICJ concluded that Uganda was indeed an occupying power in Ituri at the relevant time; it was therefore under an obligation according to Article 43 HR 1907 to take all the measures in its power to restore and ensure as far as possible public order and safety in the occupied area, as well as obliged to secure respect for the applicable rules of IHRL.[86]

---

79 Ibid.
80 Ibid.
81 Ibid., § 112.
82 Ibid., § 109 and § 112.
83 Ibid., § 113; see further *Defence for Children International Palestine, Shadow Report to the Fourth Periodic Report of Israel, Impact of Israeli Military Offensives in the Gaza Strip on Palestinian Children*, 112th Session of the Human Rights Committee, 7–31 October 2014, available at http://tbinternet.ohchr.org/Treaties/CCPR/Shared%20Documents/ISR/INT_CCPR_CSS_ISR_18223_E.pdf (visited 29 January 2017).
84 Article 2 Convention on the Rights of the Child (1990).
85 *Legal Consequences of the Construction of a Wall in the Occupied Palestinian Territory, supra* note 47, § 113.
86 *Case Concerning Armed Activities on the Territory of the Congo (Democratic Republic of the Congo v. Uganda), supra* note 47, § 178.

The effect of control on substantive obligations 151

For the ICJ, those obligations were due to Uganda being an occupant pursuant to IHL. Also, it had the general obligation flowing from IHL to take all the measures in its power to restore and ensure, as far as possible, public order and safety – this includes IHRL obligations. It is thus submitted that it was effective control (OL) over territory that gave rise to IHRL obligations. Moreover, in this case the Court even went further and considered IHRL, along with IHL, to give rise to a wider responsibility of the occupant, making it not only responsible for acts and omissions of its subordinates, but also for generally preventing *any* violations:

> Uganda's responsibility is engaged both for any acts of its military that violated its international obligations and for any lack of vigilance in preventing violations of human rights and international humanitarian law by other actors present in the occupied territory, including rebel groups acting on their own account.[87]

Consequently, in the Court's view Uganda possessed constant responsibility for all actions and omissions of its own military forces in the territory of the DRC "in breach of its obligations under the rules of international human rights law and international humanitarian law which are relevant and applicable in the specific situation."[88] Thus it appears as if in *DRC v. Uganda*, the ICJ tried to push ahead and touch a new frontier in the expansive applicability of IHRL instruments to an occupying power's actions. It unambiguously held that "international human rights instruments are applicable in respect of acts done by a state in the exercise of its jurisdiction outside its own territory, particularly in occupied territories".[89] The ICJ also attempted to identify the basis for the application of IHRL during a military occupation: based on the analysis just presented, the trigger for this applicability is identical to the test that determines the existence of military occupation as such, i.e. effective control (OL). The Human Rights Committee, too, conceptualises a state exercising effective control over another state's territory as the trigger for the ICCPR's extraterritorial application.[90]

A different term is used by the ECtHR, which coined the term *effective overall control*, addressed already in Chapter 2 for the purposes of establishing proxy occupation. Can this test be regarded as the ECtHR's own threshold of applying human rights in situations of military occupation? Like the ICJ, the ECtHR considers the jurisdiction of a state to be stretching primarily over its own territory (territorial principle). It also contemplates state jurisdiction to arise in times of military occupation and, more generally, when a state acts extraterritorially,

---

87 Ibid., § 179.
88 Ibid., § 180.
89 Ibid., § 216.
90 *General Comment 31, Nature of the General Legal Obligation on States Parties to the Covenant*, Human Rights Committee, UN Doc. CCPR/C/21/Rev.1/Add.13, 2004, § 10; emphasis added.

152 *The effect of control on substantive obligations*

thereby hindering the respective state to absolve itself from responsibility arising under the ECHR.[91] The ECtHR introduced the *effective overall control* test when dealing with the Turkish occupation of Northern Cyprus and in cases involving Transdniestria. However, the Strasbourg Court has not specified the exact meaning of this test.

Tomuschat observes that the ECtHR's *effective overall control* is used for establishing military occupations.[92] According to this author, the criterion applied both to the Turkish occupation of Northern Cyprus and Russian support for the insurgents in the Transdniestrian part of Moldova, but not to the short-term Turkish operation in Northern Iraq.[93] However, the purpose of the ECtHR was not to qualify the situation as an occupation or not, but to determine the application of the ECHR to the Turkish and Russian governments, respectively. In the preliminary objections phase of *Loizidou v. Turkey*, the ECtHR employed the term "effective control over territory" (without the word "overall") as understood in military occupation.[94] Already then, the ECtHR seemed to contemplate not only classic situations of occupation as envisaged by Article 42 HR 1907, but also situations where the effective control of a state was wielded via subordinate military administrations (see also Chapter 2, section 3).[95] In other words, although this passage suggests that various forms of military occupation exist, they still give rise to the IHRL obligations of a state under the ECtHR on the grounds of exercising effective control (OL) over territory. In the later stage of the Loizidou case, notably in the judgment, the ECtHR seems to have gone even one step further in resorting to a different threshold for the application of the ECHR. It inserted the word "overall" after "effective", resulting in a threshold of *effective overall control*. As already pointed out, the ECtHR did not provide an explanation, nor did it qualify the situation there as one of occupation. Instead, the ECtHR centred on the general applicability of the ECHR:

> It is not necessary to determine whether, as the applicant and the Government of Cyprus have suggested, Turkey actually exercises detailed control over the policies and actions of the authorities of the 'TRNC'. It is obvious from the large number of troops engaged in active duties in Northern Cyprus [. . .] that her army exercises *effective overall control* over that part of the island. Such control, according to the relevant test and in the circumstances of the

---

91 L. Zwaak, 'General Survey of the European Convention', in P. van Dijk, F. van Hoof, A. van Rijn, and L. Zwaak (eds.), *Theory and Practice of the European Convention on Human Rights* (4th edn., Antwerp; Oxford: Intersentia, 2006) 1–93, at 19–22.

92 C. Tomuschat, *Human Rights, supra* note 38, at 99.

93 Ibid.

94 Loizidou v. Turkey (Preliminary Objections), ECtHR (1995) (App. no. 15318/89) § 62–64. Note: SC Res. 541 (1983) considered the attempt to create the TRNC as invalid, and SC Res. 550 (1984) explicitly referred to Northern Cyprus as the "Occupied part of the Republic of Cyprus".

95 Ibid.

The effect of control on substantive obligations 153

case, entails her responsibility for the policies and actions of the 'TRNC'. [. . .] Those affected by such policies or actions therefore come within the 'jurisdiction' of Turkey.[96]

In Chapter 2, it was argued that effective overall control and indirect effective control concern the same aspects and possess the same content, namely a state purporting to conceal its effective control (OL) over territory via overall control (SR/IHL) over an intermediary. The key questions to be addressed now are the circumstances and effect of such control on a state's substantive obligations.

In Issa, the ECtHR used a structural analysis of existing case law: state military action, whether lawful or unlawful, giving rise to effective control (OL) over territory, and the obligation to provide in such an area the rights enshrined in the ECHR, stemming from the fact of such control – whether exercised directly, through its armed forces, or through a subordinate local administration.[97] This time, the Court seemed to acknowledge that effective control (OL) over territory as understood in occupation law triggers the application of IHRL: even if a state does not have its forces stationed on every square meter of a territory, because it has effective control (OL) over the territory in question it is generally responsible under the ECHR for the territories. Issa thus reads:

> It is not necessary to determine whether a Contracting Party actually exercises detailed control over the policies and actions of the authorities in the area situated outside its national territory, since *even overall control* of the area may engage the responsibility of the Contracting Party concerned.[98]

Pursuant to such a reasoning, the Court appears not to exclude the possibility that, as a consequence of Turkish military action, Turkey could be considered to have exercised, temporarily at least, *effective overall control* of a particular portion of the territory of Northern Iraq. But still the Court appears to have showed caution and did not open the door for a laxer interpretation of that threshold. It consequently required factual evidence of Turkish military action. If there had been a sufficient factual basis proving this, and if the victims had been in the specific area, it would have followed that they were within the jurisdiction of Turkey.[99] In the end, however, the ECtHR did not establish that Turkey had exercised *effective overall control* over Northern Iraq. Also, according to the Court the situation there differed from Northern Cyprus as adjudicated in the *Loizidou v. Turkey*

---

96 Loizidou v. Turkey, ECtHR (1996) (App. no. 15318/89) § 56. Note: The test of effective overall control was used in Djavit v. Turkey, ECtHR (2003) (App. no. 25781/94) §21–23; Cyprus v. Turkey, ECtHR (2001) (App. no. 25781/94) § 77. However, see Adali v. Turkey, ECtHR (2005) (App. no. 38187/97); Demades v. Turkey, ECtHR (2008) (App. no. 16219/90).
97 Issa and Others v. Turkey, *supra* note 51, § 69.
98 Ibid., § 70 (emphasis added).
99 Ibid., § 74.

154 *The effect of control on substantive obligations*

and *Cyprus v. Turkey* cases.[100] This stance was however not followed by further clarifications.

In the more recent case of *Al-Skeini and Others v. UK*, the UK argued that the acts in question took place in southern Iraq, outside its jurisdiction under Article 1 ECHR; the sole exception being the killing of the sixth applicant's son, which occurred in a British military prison over which the UK admitted to have had jurisdiction.[101] In the UK government's submission the fact that, between May 2003 and June 2004 it was an occupying power within the meaning of the HR 1907, did not give rise to the UK's obligation to secure the rights enshrined in the ECHR to the inhabitants of south-east Iraq.[102] The ECtHR subsequently took into consideration the territorial principle, state agent authority and control, and effective control over an area of the ECHR to trigger the jurisdiction of the Convention. For the purposes of this book, particular attention has to be paid to the way the ECtHR approached the understanding of *effective overall control* over territory. While the Court did not mention *effective overall control* explicitly, it mentioned the idea implicitly in § 138 by referencing to its previous case law of Loizidou, *Cyprus v. Turkey*, Banković, and Ilaşcu – but not to Issa. In fact, upon further examination of the judgment, in § 139 the ECtHR seems to offer two separate tests: one modelled on the reading of Article 42 HR 1907, the other on the understanding of *overall control*, thereby resembling the reasoning employed in Tadić, Loizidou, and Ilaşcu:

> It is a question of fact whether a Contracting State exercises effective control over an area outside its own territory. In determining whether effective control exists, the Court will primarily have reference to the strength of the State's military presence in the area. [. . .] Other indicators may also be relevant, such as the extent to which its military, economic and political support for the local subordinate administration provides it with influence and control over the region.[103]

In determining whether the UK had jurisdiction over any of the deceased, the ECtHR did not base its reasoning on the effective overall control test. After all, it considered the UK to be an occupying power, alongside the US, within the meaning of Article 42 HR 1907,[104] including the time frame of the CPA up until the formation of the sovereign interim government of Iraq (SC Res. 1546) and, in the event, occupation coming to an end on 28 June 2004 (see also Chapter 3, section 3.6.2). Based on such events, and particularly

---

100 Ibid., § 75.
101 Al-Skeini and Others v. the United Kingdom, *supra* note 49, § 101, see also § 111–112.
102 Ibid., § 114.
103 Ibid., § 139.
104 Ibid., § 143.

following the removal of the Baath regime and until the accession of the Iraqi interim government, the UK (with the US) assumed the exercise of some of the public powers in Iraq that were normally exercised by a sovereign government. Furthermore, the ECtHR established a jurisdictional link between the UK and the deceased family members of the applicants on the basis of the fact that the UK

> assumed the authority and responsibility for the maintenance of security in south-east Iraq. In these exceptional circumstances [. . .] the United Kingdom, through its soldiers engaged in security operations in Basra during the period in question, exercised authority and control over individuals killed in the course of such security operations.[105]

The given quotation is, however, not clear: is the ECtHR referring to the state agent authority and control test over individuals or control over an area? It commences with control over the area ("south-east Iraq"), but the next sentence refers to control over individuals. There is thus a concoction[106] of the two tests; which one the Court relies on for its analysis is unclear. Furthermore, in *Hassan v. UK*, the ECtHR advanced that because the UK had assumed authority for the maintenance of security in south-east Iraq, it was unnecessary to establish whether jurisdiction also arose on the ground that the UK was in effective military control there during that period.[107]

An additional confusion is thus created by the attempt of separating the action of *assuming authority for the maintenance of security* from the act of *effective military control*: does the former not relate to effective control (OL) pursuant to Article 42 HR 1907, which in turn enables the application of Article 43 of the same instrument? In Hassan, the Court did not find it necessary to decide whether the UK was in effective control (OL) of the area during the relevant period, as UK jurisdiction over Mr. Hassan, according to the Court, arose on a different ground:

> Following his capture by British troops early in the morning of 23 April 2003, until he was admitted to Camp Bucca later that afternoon, Tarek Hassan was within the physical power and control of the United Kingdom soldiers and therefore fell within United Kingdom Jurisdiction.[108]

The stance of the Court suggests that *assuming authority for the maintenance of security* constitutes a different threshold and is not part and parcel of military occupation. In other words, a situation of military occupation is different

---

105 Ibid., § 149.
106 N. Lubell, 'Human Rights Obligations in Military Occupation', *supra* note 2, at 321.
107 Hassan v. the United Kingdom, ECtHR (2014) (App. no. 29750/09) § 75.
108 Ibid., § 76.

156 *The effect of control on substantive obligations*

from a state *assuming authority for the maintenance of security*. Evidently, with such a dictum the Court blurs the lines of the ECHR's extraterritorial application during military occupations, when assuming authority for the maintenance of security is an integral task of the state's armed forces – if not the sole, considering that the occupying power's own security has to be ensured and maintained, too. Or did the Court view *assuming authority for the maintenance of security* to be a part of armed conflicts, short of military occupation, that is when fighting is ongoing and the invading state still attempting to establish its effective control (OL) over territory? In Iraq, 23 April 2003 was not regarded as falling within the period of military occupation, which started only on 1 May 2003.[109]

What Hassan may in fact be advancing – and what the ECtHR should have made clear – is that during military operations, in case someone is detained on a military base, the ECHR applies because of the physical power and control the invading soldiers of a state party to the ECHR exercise over the person in the material time. This case thus shows the fine line that separates state jurisdiction based on control over territory from that based purely on control over persons (see section 3.1). In other words, although at the end of the day the UK troops exercised "physical power and control" over Mr. Hassan, such a state of affairs was only possible because of the territorial control exercised by the British troops at that time and in that area (army patrol, capture, and detention).

Now what does all this mean? On what basis is IHRL triggered in times of military occupation properly – does human rights law have its own applicability trigger in this particular setting? Unfortunately, the ECtHR's recent case of *Chiragov and Others v. Armenia* further obstructs an answer to these questions. The most notable discrepancies are detected in the wording used with regards to the test of effective control (OL) over territory during military occupation. The case concerned six Azerbaijani nationals who claimed they had been prevented from returning to the district of Lachin in territory occupied by Armenia, thus not being able to enjoy their property located on that territory, nor having received any fitting compensation.[110] The Court had to determine whether Armenia had exercised, and continued to exercise, effective control over the mentioned territories and whether, based on such a control, it could be held answerable for the alleged violations.[111]

To determine whether Armenia had jurisdiction over these territories, it was necessary to establish whether Armenia exercised effective control (OL) over Nagorno Karabakh and the surrounding territories.[112] It should be observed that the word *overall* is not included, since the Court seems to introduce other

---

109 Ibid., § 75.
110 Chiragov and Others v. Armenia, ECtHR (2015) (App. no. 13216/05) § 1, § 3.
111 Ibid., § 169.
112 Ibid., § 170.

criteria for establishing Armenian responsibility. The ECtHR consequently concluded that

> the Republic of Armenia, from the early days of the Nagorno-Karabakh conflict, has had a significant and decisive influence over the "NKR", that the two entities are highly integrated in virtually all important matters and that this situation persists to this day. In other words, the "NKR" and its administration survives by virtue of the military, political, financial and other support given to it by Armenia which, consequently, exercises effective control over Nagorno-Karabakh and the surrounding territories, including the district of Lachin. The matters complained of therefore come within the jurisdiction of Armenia for the purposes of Article 1 of the Convention.[113]

The ECtHR again fuses language from Loizidou and the cases concerning Transdniestria; however, this time it more visibly employs the effective control (OL) threshold from Article 42 HR 1907 for establishing Armenian responsibility.[114] According to Judge Motoc's concurring opinion, in Chiragov the ECtHR raised the threshold of effective control compared to earlier cases such as Loizidou.[115] It seems that this was due to the fact that the Court considered the elements of military presence, a high integration of the two entities, and financial support all at the same time. However, according to the Judge, the Court did not "consider it necessary to draw a distinction between effective control and the type of control that it had established in the case of Ilaşcu".[116] The Court employs the words "a significant and decisive influence over the 'NKR'", used also in the cases of Ilaşcu and Catan. Chiragov can be comprehended in such a way that the ECtHR attempts to more lucidly formulate its own understanding of effective control (OL) for the purposes of establishing not only a situation of military occupation, but also the ECHR's application. The Court uses the element of military presence from Article 42 HR 1907, along with the elements of overall control (SR/IHL), such as the Armenian government extending financial and military support to the Nagorno Karabakh de facto entity. Hence, effective control in the understanding of the Court comprises military presence, high political integration of the entities, and significant financial support extended from one to the other.

Another possible route through which the Court could have approached this case would have been to employ Article 4 ILC Articles on Responsibility of States.[117] Based on this, and on the available facts at hand as reproduced earlier

---

113 Ibid., § 186.
114 Ibid., § 187.
115 Chiragov and Others v. Armenia Judgment – Separate Opinions, Concurring Opinion of Judge Motoc, § 84.
116 Ibid.
117 See, however, the Dissenting Opinion of Judge Gyulumyan, who calls for Article 8 of the ILC Articles on Responsibility of States to have been employed; Chiragov

158 *The effect of control on substantive obligations*

(especially the NKR being "highly integrated in virtually all important matters" with Armenia), the Court could have eventually regarded the de facto authorities of the region, i.e. the NKR, as Armenia's de facto organ, triggering thereby the responsibility and jurisdiction of Armenia proper.

Similarly so in another case, *Sargsyan v. Azerbaijan*, where the applicant was an Armenian national bringing a case against Azerbaijan, alleging the denial of his right to return to the village of Gulistan, thus having no access to his property and the graves of his relatives.[118] The applicant claimed violations of Article 1 Protocol I and Article 8 ECHR, whereas Azerbaijan argued that because of the circumstances it was "unable to exercise its legitimate authority" over the village of Gulistan.[119] Gulistan is in fact situated on the front line between Azerbaijan and the NKR, and was at that time short of civilian inhabitants, in addition to being heavily mined.[120] The ECtHR noted that because Gulistan is located on the internationally recognised territory of Azerbaijan, the presumption of Azeri jurisdiction applied.[121] To assess whether Gulistan was occupied, the Court resorted to Article 42 HR 1907 and concluded that this was not the case, since the effective control of foreign forces over that territory would require their presence there.[122] This led the Court to conclude that the facts out of which the violations had arisen were within the jurisdiction of Azerbaijan, hence dismissing the respondent government's objections, activating its responsibility under the ECHR, and absolving Armenia.[123]

What is especially noteworthy is that in its reasoning the Court used Article 42 HR 1907, thereby sidestepping its usual formulations of *effective overall control* and *decisive influence*. This may be due to the fact that the case was concerned with ruling *out* the jurisdiction of a respondent government over *own* territory, instead of establishing it extraterritorially. Also, while historically the ECtHR has hardly ever referred to IHL, it can be observed that this practice is slowly changing.

The ECtHR, nevertheless, displays no consistency in its usage of the tests of *effective control (OL)*, *effective overall control*, or *decisive influence* (see also Chapter 2). The question then is why the ECtHR keeps shifting between these formulations, not to mention having more clearly employed Article 42 HR 1907 in two of its recent cases as just illustrated. Providing explanations and achieving and maintaining consistency in the usage of these tests would help to clearly identify the required threshold that gives rise to the application of the ECHR.[124]

---

and Others v. Armenia Judgment – Separate Opinions, Dissenting Opinion of Judge Gyulumyan, § 86.

118 Sargsyan v. Azerbaijan, ECtHR (2015) (App. no. 40167/06) § 3.

119 Ibid., § 123 and § 145.

120 Ibid., § 137 and § 233.

121 Ibid., § 139.

122 Ibid., § 144; see also § 142.

123 Ibid., § 151.

124 For alternative views, which consider 'effective overall control' to be a general territorial test, see C. Droege, 'The Interplay Between International Humanitarian Law and International Human Rights Law', *supra* note 45, at 328–330; W. Kälin and J. Künzli, *The Law*

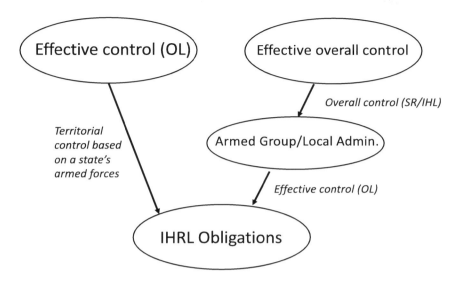

Figure 4.3 Territorial control and IHRL obligations

To conclude this section, in case a state is a military occupant, the threshold of effective control (OL) over territory alone would suffice to give rise to the application of IHRL: once occupation is established, "the full spectrum" of IHRL is applicable.[125] By contrast, the *effective overall control test* may be conceptualised as a two-tiered test, where overall control (SR/IHL) over a group or entity gives rise to effective control (OL) over the territory (see also Chapter 2). Both types of control require a state to fully ensure the application of *all* the human rights enshrined in the ECHR (and/or other instruments of IHRL of which the state is a member) and demand that the state lives up to its duties across the entire territory under its control. Figure 4.3 shows how these two tests operate.

3.3 Degrees of IHRL obligations according to specific contexts

Our interim conclusion is that control for human rights purposes can be construed in two ways, separating control over territory from control over persons. With control over territory, there seems to be an automatic applicability of

---

of *International Human Rights Protection* (Oxford: Oxford University Press, 2009), at 136–137.
125 D. Murray et al., *Practitioners' Guide to Human Rights Law in Armed Conflict* (Oxford: Oxford University Press, 2016), at 70; see also *Case Concerning Armed Activities in the Territory of the Congo (Democratic Republic of the Congo v. Uganda)*, supra note 47, § 178.

160   *The effect of control on substantive obligations*

human rights law. Still, the question is: how does one determine the existence of control for human rights purposes? Similarly, control over persons directly (e.g. patrolling, security operations, or holding a person in custody) also entails certain IHRL obligations. Such obligations include treating the person humanely, i.e. not inflicting torture or arbitrarily depriving them of their life. In other words, a state agent would have control over certain rights.

This interpretation allows us to view control in IHRL disjunctively: control over territory and control over persons. In the latter case, control widens its reach by the mere fact that IHRL is applicable to various situations: persons may be affected by it during peacetime, in situations of riots or sporadic acts of violence, or during armed conflicts, including military occupation. Such an interpretation seems to be more flexible in allowing the state to fulfil certain human rights obligations, especially because, in IHRL, if the state is exercising control over X (e.g. the right to life), this does not automatically mean that it also has control over Y (e.g. the right to education).[126] Hence, control in IHRL may differ in its degrees as to the actual provision of human rights. IHRL obligations apply insofar as control is exerted, but their nature and scope is determined by the level of control demonstrated by a state in a specific context: *full* state control entails full state obligations, *partial* state control only entails partial obligations. On the other hand, one could also question whether under occupation the exact same human rights standards have to be provided, given that although exercising effective control (OL), the state is still dealing with and present on *alien* territory.[127]

But just because a state may not have complete control does not mean that it possesses none.[128] This point was made clear in Ilaşcu, when the ECtHR considered that Russia and Moldova did not have the same amount of obligations; instead it divided ECHR obligations and attributed them to each state according to its ability to exercise territorial control. For Moldova, the ECtHR considered that

> even in the absence of effective control over the Transdniestrian region, Moldova still has a *positive obligation* under Article 1 of the Convention to take the diplomatic, economic, judicial or other measures *that it is in its power to take* and are in accordance with international law to secure to the applicants the rights guaranteed by the Convention.[129]

---

126 F. Hampson and N. Lubell, *Georgia v. Russia* (II) 38263/08, Amicus Curiae Brief of the Human Rights Centre, University of Essex, § 4, at 2, available at http:// repository.essex.ac.uk/9689/1/hampson-lubell-georgia-russia-amicus-01062014. pdf (visited 29 January 2017).

127 N. Lubell, 'Applicability of Human Rights Law in Situations of Occupation', in *Current Challenges to the Law of Military Occupation* (34 Proceedings of the Bruges Collegium, 2006) 50–56, at 55.

128 F. Hampson and N. Lubell, *Georgia v. Russia*, *supra* note 126, § 4, at 2.

129 *Ilaşcu and Others v. Moldova and Russia* (2004) (Application no. 48787/99) § 331 (emphasis added); in § 352, the ECtHR concluded that "Moldova's responsibility could be engaged under the Convention on account of its failure to discharge its positive obligations

The effect of control on substantive obligations   161

Limited and tailored state responsibility under IHRL also played a role in *Sargsyan v. Azerbaijan*, when the ECtHR portioned responsibility according to Azerbaijan's exercised level of control over the village of Gulistan.[130] Apportioned responsibility in turn may be construed as giving rise to IHRL jurisdiction on a sliding scale, i.e. resembling a cause and effect understanding of control.[131] Thus, fully ensuring all obligations in times of military occupation may be problematic due to a number of reasons: the state's effective control (OL) of the entire territory may be challenged by an insurgency, or the state may not possess the means and ability to ensure certain rights. The UK Court of Appeal, for example, in deciding the Al-Skeini case, found that

> it is quite impossible to hold that the UK, although an occupying power for the purposes of the Hague Regulations and Geneva IV, was in effective control of Basrah City for the purposes of ECHR jurisprudence at the material time. If it had been, it would have been obliged, pursuant to the Banković judgment, to secure to everyone in Basrah City the rights and freedoms guaranteed by the ECHR.[132]

Hampson also considers that, in Al-Skeini, the English courts determined territory could be occupied for the purposes of IHL, but not occupied for the purposes of IHRL, as they read the ECtHR case law to require the *full* respect of the ECHR in occupied territory but that providing this full respect was unrealistic in southern Iraq.[133] The UK stance on the indivisibility of Convention rights, however, has been superseded in a more recent case, *Smith v. Ministry of Defence*, where Lord Hope advanced that:

> The concept of dividing and tailoring goes hand in hand with the principle that extra-territorial jurisdiction can exist whenever a state through its agents

---

with regard to the acts complained of which occurred after May 2001." See also Ivanţoc and Others v. Moldova and Russia, ECtHR (2011) (App. no. 23687/05) §§ 118–120; Catan and Others v. Moldova and Russia, ECtHR (2012) (Apps. nos. 43370/04, 8252/05 and 18454/06) §§ 121–122; A. Gioia, 'The Role of the European Court of Human Rights in Monitoring Compliance With Humanitarian Law in Armed Conflict', in O. Ben-Naftali (ed.), *International Humanitarian Law and International Human Rights Law* (Oxford: Oxford University Press, 2011), 201–249, at 208; see also B. Hofstötter, 'European Court of Human Rights: Positive Obligations in E. and Others v. United Kingdom', 2 *International Journal of Constitutional Law* (2004) 525–534, at 527–534.

130 Sargsyan v. Azerbaijan, *supra* note 118, § 140, § 143 and § 151.

131 R. Wilde, 'Triggering State Obligations Extraterritorially', *supra* note 44, at 524.

132 The UK Court of Appeal Judgment, Case No: C1/2005/0461, C1/2005/0461B, 21 December 2005, Lord Justice Brooke LJ, § 124.

133 F. Hampson, 'The Scope of the Extra-Territorial Applicability of International Human Rights Law', in G. Gilbert, F. Hampson, and C. Sandoval (eds.), *The Delivery of Human Rights: Essays in Honour of Professor Sir Nigel Rodley* (New York: Routledge, 2011) 157–182, at 180. See also D. McGoldrick, 'Human Rights and Humanitarian Law in the UK Courts', 40 *Israel Law Review* (2007) 527–562, at 527.

162 *The effect of control on substantive obligations*

exercises authority and control over an individual. The court need not now concern itself with the question whether the state is in a position to guarantee Convention rights to that individual other than those it is said to have breached.[134]

In view of avoiding unrealistic expectations and ensuring the protection of victims, it is certainly worthwhile to divide and tailor a state's IHRL obligations according to specific situations and/or based on the degree of control that a state is exercising in a material time and place.[135]

4. A contextual approach to state obligations

Neither IHL nor IHRL explicitly provide an explanation of what contextual obligations could be. Lubell considers the contextual approach to IHRL to mean two things: firstly, that during military occupation context affects the *content* of obligations ("their mode of application"); secondly, that outside of military occupation context determines *which* obligations apply ("their applicability").[136] In the latter case, this reasoning closely follows the state agent authority and control test outlined earlier (section 3.1), namely that the state must ensure "those rights that the state agents have the power to control in the circumstances".[137] In the former case, although in principle a state must guarantee *all* human rights when being a military occupant, specific circumstances – like the security being volatile or the state lacking access to certain areas – might obstruct the state from providing them.[138] In both cases, the IHRL obligations of a state thus hinge on the precise level and type of control exerted in a particular context.

In IHRL, control can be exercised during various situations – be that in peacetime or during riots, internal disturbances, and armed conflicts, including a state's military invasion and occupation. As already stated, the level of control on which this branch rests its application is effective control exercised over individuals or territory. A contextual (or situational) approach to IHRL obligations may be helpful especially when a state has not fully established control over territory as envisaged by Article 42 HR 1907 and/or merely maintains a certain level of control over the lives of civilians residing on a territory. Let us for a

---

134 UK Supreme Court Judgment, [2013] UKSC 41, 19 June 2013, Lord Hope, § 49. For possible ramifications of this, see I. Scobbie, 'Human Rights Protection During Armed Conflict: What, When and For Whom?' in E. de Wet and J. Kleffner (eds.), *Convergence and Conflicts of Human Rights and International Humanitarian Law in Military Operations* (Pretoria: Pretoria University Law Press, 2014) 1–17, at 11–17.

135 F. Hampson, 'The Scope', *supra* note 133, at 180; see also M. Sassòli, 'The Role of Human Rights and International Humanitarian Law in Types of Armed Conflicts', in O. Ben Naftali (ed.), *International Humanitarian Law and International Human Rights Law* (Oxford: Oxford University Press, 2011) 34–94, at 65–66.

136 N. Lubell, 'Human Rights Obligations in Military Occupation', *supra* note 2, at 323–324.

137 Ibid., at 323.

138 Ibid., at 324.

The effect of control on substantive obligations   163

moment consider that there is no occupation of Gaza and that the Israeli army is not stationed inside Gaza *stricto sensu*; consequently, Israel is not exercising effective control (OL). However, Israel controls all the *ins* and *outs* of Gaza (see Chapter 3, section 3.4) and governs the basic aspects of daily life there, such as providing electricity and ensuring the flow of food and other supplies, as well as collecting taxes. What law applies in this case and under which law may Israel be held answerable for its actions?

Following the contextual approach, Israel would have IHRL obligations towards the population of Gaza in relation to those rights that are in its power to ensure, such as rights related to border crossing and freedom of movement. Israel would, therefore, not have *all* the human rights obligations vis-à-vis Gaza's population, also because a certain level of control over the daily life of the territory is exercised by the rivalling Hamas government. Put differently, Israel is responsible merely for those violations that are within its power to control. This way, it appears that there may be *something else* in IHRL that allows to contemplate certain types of control that do not just correspond to the obvious tests of control that trigger a state's full extraterritorial jurisdiction. Indeed, there may be a level of control that entails only *some* obligations of the state under IHRL. Through this, IHRL can render a state responsible for certain violations stemming from the concrete situation under its control. In the provided example, Israel could thus be held responsible for violating any rights which in a given moment its agents were actually able to infringe upon.

In the same vein, Fraenkel thinks that an international bill of rights should apply in times of military occupation "at least after the purely military phase of the occupation has ended".[139] Fraenkel's words suggest that the occupant has to have the ability to discharge and provide for the rights guaranteed under the IHRL instruments and not be asked impossible requests that it simply cannot implement. In Al-Skeini, Lord Justice Sedley considered that while the occupant is not the guarantor of human rights, it just has to *do all it can* at the material time.[140]

---

139 E. Fraenkel, *Military Occupation and the Rule of Law* (New York: Oxford University Press, 1944), at 205–206.

140 *Al-Skeini v. Secretary of State for Defence* (2005) EWCA 1609 (Civ.) § 196–197 (Lord Justice Sedley); emphasis added. See also G. Verdirame, 'Human Rights Law in Wartime: A Framework for Analysis', 6 *European Human Rights Law Review* (2008) 689–705, at 693: "In applying human rights, we should not persuade ourselves that a human rights-compliant war is ever a possibility. This is one of those situations where the law is mandatory, but full respect of it is an impossibility. Different degrees of inobservance are however possible: some states will violate human rights less than others in war, and it is entirely appropriate that human rights NGOs, or human rights courts when seized of these cases, should assess the various instances of non-compliance with human rights standards despite their axiomatic unattainability in wartime. Moreover, while there is insoluble conflict between war and human rights, no such conflict exists with international humanitarian law: premised on a more pragmatic balance between norm and fact, the obligations

164   *The effect of control on substantive obligations*

In Sassòli's opinion, a functional approach to the application of the ECHR is equally practicable, that is "distinguishing the degree of control necessary according to the right protected."[141] While such a sliding scale approach was rejected by the ECtHR in Banković,[142] according to that scholar

> This functional approach would . . . mean that international forces have to respect the right to life of a person simply by omitting to attack that person as soon as those forces could affect that right by their attack. On the other hand, it is only while they physically detain a person that they would have to respect the procedural guarantees inherent in the right to personal freedom.[143]

Yet the terms functional application and responsibility arising on a "sliding scale" seem rather vague, not clearly conveying and delineating the scope, reach and anticipated result of the application of the ECHR. The term "situational application" appears more practice-oriented, as it defines a concrete situation necessitating a concrete obligation in light of IHRL.

Reverting back to IHL, let us consider a situation where effective control (OL) is not secured over the entire territory, e.g. being an occupant of state B's western part but not of its east. Now it is possible, due to the volatility of the situation, that not all IHL rights are provided for by the occupant. Would the military traversing state B's east be obligated to ensure law and order under Article 43 HR 1907 when they come across a group of civilians beating up a lone man, who subsequently dies?[144] Would they be required merely to stop the beating or also to set up a fair trial? How far do the state's obligations extend under IHL? Again, the point of the offered example is that the precise obligations of a state may be assessed pursuant to the level of control it exercises on the ground at a specific point in time. Fully established control over territory would signify full obligations, albeit with possible variation on the delivery mode, while partially established control (e.g. encountering resistance) activates specific obligations only.

For the purpose of summarising the provided tests triggering the application of IHRL and IHL obligations, it may be seen that the test of effective control (IHRL) over persons' particular rights and the test of the situational application of the GC IV are equivalent, since both deal with *specific rights* (such as Article 24 GC IV ensuring child welfare; Article 75 AP I 1977 enshrining fundamental guarantees; or Article 2 ECHR dealing with the right to life) of *specific persons* (civilians, protected persons, and individuals under the jurisdiction of a state party to the ECHR) at a *specific point in time* (for example during invasions, occupations or insurrections).

---

  international humanitarian law imposes and the rights its confers are always fully attainable in armed conflict."

141 M. Sassòli, 'The Role of Human Rights', *supra* note 135, at 65.

142 Banković and Others v. Belgium and Others, ECtHR (2001) (Decision as to the Admissibility) (App. no. 52207/99) § 74–76.

143 M. Sassòli, 'The Role of Human Rights', *supra* note 135, at 65–66.

144 F. Hampson and N. Lubell, *Georgia v. Russia*, *supra* note 126, at 4 (§ 11).

The effect of control on substantive obligations 165

There are three aspects to such a situational application of the ECHR and for that matter to a state's situational obligations. First, there is a particular right enshrined in the ECHR that is applicable to a certain situation. Second, the situation arises against the backdrop of a certain threshold of control that the state is exercising at the material time. That threshold of control is the benchmark for whether the state can provide the fulfilment of a right or not. Third, while concrete situations determine a state's ability to control, the latter in turn commands the feasibility of ensuring a specific right. Therefore, not all situations of military occupation may be of the same kind. As much as armed conflict scenarios can have different dynamics, with setbacks and advancements often intertwined, so may different occupying states face different insurgencies while purporting to establish effective control (OL) over territory, while others still secure effective control (OL) over territory instantly. Here, the all-or-nothing approach to applying IHRL instruments would have a pernicious effect on those who necessitate protection and release a state from its obligations, arguing that because it was not in the position to provide some obligations, it had to ensure none. Thus, and as shown in Figure 4.4, the tests of control in occupation law and IHRL can lead to different substantive obligations.

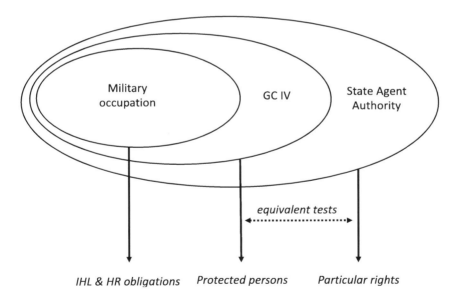

Figure 4.4 GC IV situational application and control (IHRL) over persons' particular rights

Note: The circles display the scope of application of the tests in different scenarios: anytime (including peacetime, armed conflict, invasion, and occupation), armed conflicts (including invasion and military occupation), and military occupation alone.

166 *The effect of control on substantive obligations*

5. IHL and IHRL inter-application

The final issue to be dealt with is whether occupation law overrides human rights law or the other way around; or if the two are complementary in light of contextual/situational obligations.

In the eighteenth century, the law of war began to pay attention to humanitarian considerations, which also constitute the essence of human rights.[145] Pictet famously remarked that "Humanitarian Law comprises two branches: the law of war and the law of human rights."[146] While the two fields are interrelated, they are also distinct, however much they share the same origin: they both stem from the need "to protect the individual against those who would crush them."[147] The ICJ has addressed the inter-application of IHRL and IHL in three of its landmark cases, namely those on Nuclear Weapons, the Wall, and the *DRC v. Uganda*. In the first two, the ICJ accorded IHL the status of *lex specialis*.[148] Notably in the Wall case, the Court spelled out three modes of the inter-application of IHL and IHRL:

> some rights may be exclusively matters of international humanitarian law; others may be exclusively matters of human rights law; yet others may be matters of both these branches of international law. In order to answer the question put to it, the Court will have to take into consideration both these branches of international law, namely human rights law and, as lex specialis, international humanitarian law.[149]

However, in *DRC v. Uganda* the ICJ abandoned the *lex specialis* principle and instead forged "a complementary approach to the concurrent application of" IHRL and IHL.[150]

The nature of IHRL is such that it applies also during peacetime and to everyone, containing no special categories of persons. IHL, on the other hand,

---

145 G. I. A. D. Draper, 'The Relationship Between the Human Rights Regime and the Law of Armed Conflicts', 1 *Israel Yearbook on Human Rights* (1971) 191–207, at 191.

146 J. Pictet, *Humanitarian Law and the Protection of the War Victims* (A. W. Sijthoff-Leyden: Henry Dunant Institute Geneva, 1975), at 14. However, see K. Suter, 'An Inquiry into the Meaning of the Phrase "Human Rights in Armed Conflicts"', 15 *Military Law and Law of War Review* (1976) 393–439, at 397–402.

147 J. Pictet, *Humanitarian Law*, *supra* note 146, at 15.

148 *Case Concerning Legality of the Threat or Use of Nuclear Weapons*, *supra* note 47, § 25; *Legal Consequences of the Construction of a Wall in the Occupied Palestinian Territory*, *supra* note 47, § 106; see also W. Jenks, 'The Conflict of Law-Making Treaties', 30 *British Yearbook of International Law* (1953) 401–453, at 446.

149 *Legal Consequences of the Construction of a Wall in the Occupied Palestinian Territory*, *supra* note 47, § 106.

150 N. Lubell and N. Prud'homme, 'Impact of Human Rights Law', in R. Liivoja and T. McCormarck (eds.), *Routledge Handbook of the Law of Armed Conflict* (London; New York: Routledge, 2016) 106–120, at 117.

differentiates between own and enemy civilians (protected persons) as well as combatants (and POWs), primarily cognising these two statuses. Nevertheless, a tendency transpires that the provisions of the GCs are not only considered as obligations to be discharged by the high contracting parties, but also as individual rights of protected persons:[151] Buergenthal views IHL as "the human rights component of the law of war",[152] whereas Draper considers the essential nexus between IHL and IHRL to be "that the former is an essential part of the latter", i.e. the law of war being a derogation from the normal regime of human rights.[153] Some even argue that IHL is a branch of IHRL, as it strives to retain a "modicum of civilization amid the worst of all cataclysms human communities can experience",[154] i.e. in times of war.

Legally speaking, however, it is IHL that came first. Generally, both branches extend their protection to persons. Suffice it to mention Article 75 AP I 1977, which conveys and expresses some major human rights principles,[155] and the fact that IHL enshrines the Martens Clause (the "principles of humanity" and "dictates of the public conscience").[156] Nonetheless, when it comes to applying the two branches in actual armed conflicts, their norms may either overlap or clash. That is, if the issue of child education has to be assessed during military occupation, IHRL appears to be better at supplementing the IHL of occupation law, as it provides the occupant with much more detailed guidance regarding educational policies,[157] in addition to the mere access to and provision of food as

---

151 See generally D. Schindler, 'The International Committee of the Red Cross and Human Rights', 208 *International Review of the Red Cross* (1979), available at www.icrc.org/eng/resources/documents/article/other/57jm9z.htm (visited 29 January 2017).

152 T. Buergenthal, *Public International Law in a Nutshell* (2nd edn., St Paul, MN: West Publishing, 1990), at 142.

153 G. I. A. D. Draper, 'The Relationship Between the Human Rights Regime', *supra* note 145, at 206.

154 C. Tomuschat, *Human Rights Between Idealism and Realism* (2nd edn., Oxford: Oxford University Press, 2010), at 292.

155 J. K. Kleffner, 'Scope of Application of International Humanitarian Law', in D. Fleck (ed.), *The Handbook of International Humanitarian Law* (3rd edn., Oxford: Oxford University Press, 2014) 43–78, at 72.

156 On the Martens Clause, the International Law Commission stated that "even in cases not covered by specific international agreements, civilians and combatants remain under the protection and authority of the principles of international law derived from established custom, from the principles of humanity and from the dictates of public conscience." See *Report of the International Law Commission on the Work of Its Forty-sixth Session, 2 May–22 July 1994*, UN GAOR A/49/10, at 317; R. Giladi, 'The Enactment of Irony: Reflections on the Origins of the Martens Clause (Comments)', 25 *European Journal of International Law* (2014) 847–870, 850–868; A. Cassese, 'The Martens Clause: Half a Loaf or Simply Pie in the Sky', 11 *European Journal of International Law* (2000) 187–216, at 193–198.

157 *Substantive Issues Arising in the Implementation of the International Covenant on Economic, Social and Cultural Rights (General Comment 11)*, UN Committee on Economic, Social and Cultural Rights, UN Doc. E/C. 12/1994/4, 10 May 1999, § 6, § 9.

168 *The effect of control on substantive obligations*

per GC IV.[158] Yet the occupant may not be in a position to ensure such a right instantly, nor ensure all the rights on the entire territory it controls (see previous section). IHL, in turn, is better able to deal with POWs who do not possess the same degree of individual freedom as those arrested and jailed in peacetime.

The best approach to be adopted, therefore, appears to be one that is geared towards *interaction* between the two branches rather than substitution or simple addition.[159] *Addition* would mean that in any situation, obligations, and rights stemming from both branches apply concomitantly. For instance, the right to life would have to be guaranteed next to the application of the principles of distinction, proportionality, and precautions in attack as enshrined in IHL.[160] However, the right to life has to be viewed through the lens of IHL and its relevant rules.[161] *Substitution*, in turn, would mean one or the other branch applies. Thus, in our example the state would either have to give precedence to the right to life or to IHL rules governing its conduct. But the case law as well as the legal doctrine have by now established that IHRL obligations need to be ensured whenever a state exercises jurisdiction, even during armed conflict and/or extraterritorially (see also section 3 above).[162]

Since neither addition nor substitution are feasible, the only solution therefore is *interaction*, which means that rules from one branch inform the precise application of rules from the other. This can work in both directions: either an IHL rule is used to specify an IHRL rule, or an IHRL rule is employed to interpret an IHL rule. For example, even where the judicial guarantees of IHL are much more precise, such as Article 105 GC III on bringing POWs before a court, the case law of the human rights bodies should be evoked "to know what details must be given and when those details may be modified."[163] Since the protective provisions of IHL rights are non-derogable,[164] reference should be made not only to the non-derogable core of human rights guarantees but to their entirety, taking into account the fact that IHRL adapts more flexibly to a specific situation.[165]

---

158 Article 55 GC IV 1949; see C. McCarthy, 'Human Rights Standards During Military Occupation', in R. Arnold and N. Quénivet (eds.), *International Humanitarian Law and Human Rights Law* (Leiden; Boston: Martinus Nijhoff Publishers, 2008) 121–132, at 127–132.

159 T. Meron, 'Convergence of International Humanitarian Law and Human Rights Law', in D. Warner (ed.), *Human Rights and Humanitarian Law: The Quest for Universality* (The Hague: Martinus Nijhoff Publishers, 1997), 97–105, at 100.

160 *Case of the Santo Domingo Massacre v. Colombia*, Preliminary Objections, Merits and Reparations, IACtHR, judgment of 30 November 2012, § 211–30; see also *Isayeva, Yusupova and Bazayeva v. Russia*, ECtHR (2005) (Apps. Nos. 57947/00, 57948/00 and 57949/00) §174–200.

161 *Case Concerning Legality of the Threat or Use of Nuclear Weapons*, *supra* note 47; Arts. 50–52, AP I 1977.

162 N. Lubell and N. Prud'homme, 'Impact of Human Rights Law', *supra* note 150, at 112.

163 M. Sassòli, 'The Role of Human Rights', *supra* note 135, at 74.

164 Ibid., at 75.

165 Ibid.

The question at this juncture, however, is: what is the primary and what is the secondary legal framework to begin with?[166] Jenks for example argues that the laws of war have to be viewed as the *lex specialis* in relation to instruments defining peacetime norms concerning the same subjects.[167] Sassòli and Olson, on the other hand, break that principle down to the level of rules, preferring the more special rule closer to a particular subject matter and taking better account of the contextual uniqueness.[168]

But the *lex specialis* nature of IHL has also been looked at more critically.[169] It was proposed to forsake seeing it "as a sort of magical, two-word explanation of the relationship between"[170] IHL and IHRL; a tool that was nothing more than "a sub-species of harmonious interpretation, a method of norm conflict avoidance",[171] assisting in the interpretation of general terms and standards in either IHL or IHRL by referencing more specific norms from the other branch.[172]

Two frameworks that apply to different situations and which are constructed in two different ways have also been outlined. First, under the "active hostilities framework", IHL provides the primary point of reference and IHRL is applied in its context. Second, under the "security operations framework", IHRL provides the primary point of reference and IHL is applied in its context, in turn.[173] The "active hostilities framework" applies whenever there is active fighting, both in IACs and NIACs.[174] The "security operations framework" applies to situations of the nature of law enforcement, including situations of occupation,[175] traditional law enforcement operations during an IAC,[176] as well as low-intensity fighting in a NIAC.[177]

Turning to situations of military occupation, this means that "the content of the occupying power's international human rights law obligations in relation to the administration of the occupied territory are determined by the framework of

---

166 E. De Vattel, *The Law of Nations* (Philadelphia, PA: T. & J. W. Johnson, 1844), § 316 at 272.
167 W. Jenks, 'The Conflict of Law-Making Treaties', *supra* note 148, at 446.
168 M. Sassòli and L. M. Olson, 'The Legal Relationship Between International Humanitarian Law and Human Rights Law Where It Matters: Admissible Killing and Internment of Fighters in Non-International Armed Conflict', 871 *International Review of the Red Cross* (2008) 599–627, at 603–604.
169 M. Milanović, 'Norm Conflicts, International Humanitarian Law, and Human Rights Law', in O. Ben-Naftali (ed.), *International Humanitarian Law and Human Rights Law* (Oxford: Oxford University Press, 2011) 95–125.
170 Ibid., at 98.
171 Ibid., at 115.
172 Ibid., at 116.
173 D. Murray et al., *Practitioners' Guide to Human Rights Law in Armed Conflict*, *supra* note 125, at 88.
174 Ibid., at 90.
175 Ibid., at 91.
176 Ibid., at 93.
177 Ibid., at 98.

170 *The effect of control on substantive obligations*

permissible activity established by the law of armed conflict".[178] More specifically, an occupant "may impose certain restrictions on movement, association, and assembly" because although the respective rights are guaranteed by IHRL, the IHL obligation to provide public order and civil life may be a reason to restrict them.[179] Similarly, the right to manifest one's religion or belief may be restricted provided the principles of legality, necessity, and proportionality are adhered to.[180]

In short, IHL and IHRL should not be construed as barriers for one another, least of all in times of occupation. Both IHL and IHRL norms may operate individually, with each branch capable of providing standards for the assessment of state action.[181] However, the most promising way forward seems to be to further specify their interplay and work towards their complementary application.[182]

Conclusion

This chapter has shown that both IHL and IHRL obligations can be triggered by control over persons and/or territory. Regarding the former, Article 4 GC IV and its formulation "in the hands of" were found to be equivalent to IHRL's "state agent authority and control" test, which in turn triggers state jurisdiction. A state agent may also be in a position to exercise control over and thus be held liable for breaching a person's *particular* right, such as the right to life in the case of Mr. Solomou.[183] However, while there may be GC IV obligations arising already during invasion, what is needed for establishing occupation is effective control (OL) over territory (see also Chapter 1). In other words, GC IV obligations may exist before the actual beginning of occupation.

Yet, to determine *which* obligations a state has to abide by, a situational approach to IHRL, as manifested in the state agent authority test, essentially relies on specific control exercised by state agents over specific individuals. For example, when a person is passing through a checkpoint or held in a detention centre, the obligations to secure the right to life and freedom of movement exist. This means that the obligations of states apply insofar as authority and control is exercised by a state's armed forces/agents, and their nature and scope is proportional to the level of control.[184]

---

178 Ibid., at 238.

179 Ibid., at 244–245.

180 Ibid., at 248–249.

181 A. Orakhelashvili, 'The Interaction Between Human Rights and Humanitarian Law: Fragmentation, Conflict, Parallelism, or Convergence', 19 *The European Journal of International Law* (2008) 161–182, at 168.

182 N. Lubell and N. Prud'homme, 'Impact of Human Rights Law', *supra* note 150, at 120.

183 Solomou and Others v. Turkey, *supra* note 56, § 79; Ergi v. Turkey, ECtHR (1998) (App. no. 66/1997/850/1057) § 25 and §§ 81–82.

184 R. Wilde, 'Triggering State Obligations Extraterritorially', *supra* note 44, at 524. The author bases this test on Banković v. Belgium, ECtHR, *supra* note 142, § 75.

The effect of control on substantive obligations   171

This chapter also found that effective control (OL) over territory gives rise to IHRL obligations, either directly (in the case of military occupation) or indirectly, through effective overall control. Nevertheless, even when a state's military forces assert effective control (OL) over a foreign territory, not all IHRL obligations may actually have to be provided to the fullest extent, but the state should do all it can.

Finally, that in situations of military occupation only IHL should apply would undermine the rationale and idea of the inter-applicability of the two branches. The principle of *inter arma enim silent leges* (the laws fall mute in times of war) can now be considered obsolete, as both IHL and IHRL are very much vocal about and capable of rendering the required protection to those in need even during a conflict. However, their precise interplay and suitable interaction in a particular situation must be determined on a case-by-case basis.

Conclusion

When a state is militarily present on another state's territory without the latter's consent and yet argues that it does not occupy that state's territory, it will most likely not abide by the IHL norms relating to situations of military occupation. This deprives civilians living on that territory of the pertinent and timely protection envisaged by occupation law. The state in question may argue that its military presence does not amount to a situation of occupation there, either because it does not exercise sufficient control over territory, or because it has obtained consent to its presence by the de facto local authorities. Given such a possibility, this book has endeavoured to unravel the notion of control for the purposes of rendering a state an occupant. It also offered alternatives to this status, still making the state bound by IHL norms. More specifically, the book has not only identified the importance of control for the purposes of military occupation, but also tried to present different forms of control and their impact on state obligations during and outside of military occupations.

Before summarising the book's main findings, it should be recalled that different forms of control are used by different branches of international law for different purposes. In the law of state responsibility, complete dependency (SR), effective control (SR), and overall control (SR) are used to establish a state's responsibility for the actions of its de jure and de facto organs. By contrast, international criminal law conceives of effective control (ICL) over subordinates as command responsibility in both a military and civilian hierarchy. In international human rights law, in turn, the extraterritorial application is determined by effective control over territory (IHRL), state agent authority and control over persons/individuals, or effective overall control. Finally, international humanitarian law employs overall control (IHL) to establish the involvement of a foreign state in prima facie non-international armed conflicts (see Introduction) and effective control (OL) for considering a territory occupied. Figure 5.1 maps all these branches and their respective usages of control conclusively.

Building on this, Chapter 1 has identified a clear test for establishing control over territory for the purposes of military occupation in IHL. The formulation

Conclusion 173

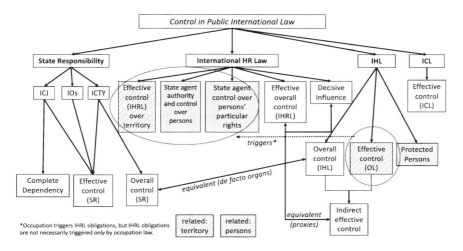

Figure 5.1 Control in public international law

"*actually placed under the authority*" of Article 42 HR 1907 is to mean effective control (OL). Multinational forces' control over territory (including UN operations) show there can also be more than one occupant. In fact, the UN may also be regarded as an occupant, depending on whether it exercises effective control (OL) over territory or not. The responsibility of the UN or the troop-contributing state can then be established by examining whether effective control (SR) over a given act is exercised pursuant to Article 7 ILC Draft Articles on the Responsibility of International Organisations (see also left-hand side of Figure 5.1).

Moving on to more complex manifestations of control, Chapter 2 has deciphered the concept of *indirect effective control*, which gives rise to situations of military occupation by an intermediary. This type of control consists of overall control (SR/IHL) and effective control (OL) and was shown to be equivalent to the notion of effective overall control (IHRL; see also Figure 5.1). The notion of decisive influence was also inspected. It was concluded that it amounted to a situation of occupation where state A exercised crucial, critical power and hence overall control (SR/IHL) over an armed group/de facto authority X in state B who in turn had effective control (OL) over territory. Finally, it was argued that IHL possessed its own mechanism of control that can be used to render a prima facie NIAC as an IAC, useful for determining proxy occupations. Thus, Article 4 A2 GC III and Article 29 GC IV comprise a threshold of control that corresponds to that of overall control (SR/IHL).

Chapter 3 dealt with relinquishing control over territory, thus establishing a test for occupation ending. Because determining the end of occupation is at

174 Conclusion

variance with assessing its beginning, occupation has ended if at least *one* of the following three conditions is met:

1. State A's military forces are no longer *physically present* on the territory, that is they have either wilfully left the territory or have been forcefully ejected;
2. State A's military forces are not in a position to or wilfully do not *exercise authority* over the total territory of state B or parts thereof anymore; or
3. State A's military forces are no longer *hostile* to state B, which is the case only if their presence has been consented to by the legitimate government of the latter.

Furthermore, at least six forms of relinquishing control over territory were identified and discussed: the complete end of control over territory, temporary and partial loss of control over parts of a territory, the potential for regaining control, control retained over territory after withdrawal, the ending of indirect (effective) control (i.e. of occupation exercised by an intermediary), and remaining on the basis of a UN SC mandate. It was also argued that relinquishing control over territory would not instantaneously release the former occupant from its obligations, especially not from those of GC IV. Instead, the (former) occupant's obligations are retained commensurate to the level of control still exercised by the state at a material time. A situation of occupation declared to be over by the SC was approached with concern, however, as when embarking on this exercise the facts on the ground have to be assessed impartially and independently of the (political) views of the SC and its members.

Finally, Chapter 4 has analysed the effect of control on a state's substantive obligations. It was put forth that in times of military occupation, IHRL obligations apply fully because effective control (OL) triggers state jurisdiction (see also Figure 5.1). The ECtHR's and the ICJ's dicta also indicate the occupation test of effective control over territory as understood in Article 42 HR 1907, Common Article 2 GCs, and Article 1 AP I 1977 to automatically activate human rights obligations. In other words, a state military force establishing effective control (OL) over a territory automatically assumes the general responsibility over that territory which formerly lay with the (now expelled or incapacitated) sovereign. However, both IHL and IHRL can also give rise to a state's situational obligations because both branches may apply pursuant to a state's control at a material time, i.e. in conformity with the level of control exercised not only over territory but also over persons/individuals. Thus, in IHL already during the invasion phase some of the provisions of GC IV benefiting protected persons apply. In IHRL, in turn, it is the state agent authority and control test which establishes a state's responsibility either over persons or persons' particular rights, e.g. the right to life.

In showing the anatomy of the effective control test which determines the beginning and end of situations of occupation, this book has made a

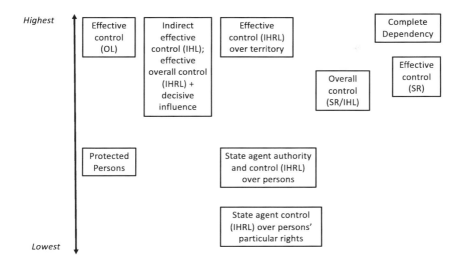

Figure 5.2 Degrees of control

contribution to the understanding and application of IHL in times of military occupation. Chapters 2, 3, and 4 in particular have demonstrated that in present-day occupations, control occurs in different forms and variations. The polymorphic features of occupation can be seen in the way that states establish control over territory either directly or indirectly, and in the manner in which they retain, relinquish, or regain it. This book also evidenced that control found in GC IV affords the most favourable and practicable protection to civilians and comes forward with a very adaptable application. This means that while a given situation might not directly present itself as one of occupation, some rules from GC IV apply nonetheless with the view of enhancing and reinforcing the protection of civilians.

Now, where does all this leave us? IHL is very well able to cope with contemporary situations of military occupation, despite states refusing to assume the responsibilities of an occupant. This means that IHL, notwithstanding its unclear wording concerning military occupation, *does* and *will not* let states evade their obligations. In other words, even if a state claims that it is not supporting an armed group against another state, IHL will still engage its responsibility provided it can be shown it exercises overall control (SR/IHL) over the armed group.

In fact, occupation law understands effective control (OL) in a both restrictive and flexible way. While Article 42 HR 1907 can be regarded as a legal straightjacket in that its application criteria are very strict, the provisions

176 *Conclusion*

contained in GC IV, notably Article 4, are triggered by a laxer understanding of control, namely one for which control over persons is sufficient. More generally, Figure 5.2 shows all the mentioned notions and types of control arranged by their degrees. It emerges that control over persons' particular rights (IHRL) requires the lowest degree of control; at the other end of the spectrum we can place complete dependency (SR) as well as effective control (IHRL) and effective control (OL) over territory.

It is hoped that the analyses contained in this work contribute to providing clarity in debates surrounding the concept of military occupation and the role of control. The overall idea this book has tried to re-enforce is that no one should be left outside the protection of IHL.[1]

---

1 Reports and Documents, 'International Humanitarian Law and the Challenges of Contemporary Armed Conflicts: Document Prepared by the International Committee of the Red Cross for the 30th International Conference of the Red Cross and Red Crescent, Geneva, Switzerland, 26–30 November 2007', 86 *International Review of the Red Cross* (2007) 719–757, at 727.

Bibliography

1. Primary sources

International treaties and instruments

American Convention on Human Rights (22 November 1969), entry into force 18 July 1978.

Charter of the United Nations (26 June 1945), entry into force 24 October 1945.

Convention on the Rights of the Child (20 November 1989), entry into force 2 September 1990.

Geneva Convention for the Amelioration of the Condition of the Wounded and Sick in Armed Forces in the Field (12 August 1949), entry into force 21 October 1950.

Geneva Convention for the Amelioration of the Condition of Wounded, Sick and Shipwrecked Members of Armed Forces at Sea (12 August 1949), entry into force 21 October 1950.

Geneva Convention Relative to the Protection of Civilian Persons in Time of War (12 August 1949), entry into force 21 October 1950.

Geneva Convention Relative to the Treatment of Prisoners of War (12 August 1949), entry into force 21 October 1950.

International Covenant on Civil and Political Rights (16 December 1966), entry into force 23 March 1976.

International Covenant on Economic, Social and Cultural Rights (16 December 1966), entry into force 3 January 1976.

Protocol Additional to the Geneva Conventions of 12 August 1949, And Relating to the Protection of Victims of International Armed Conflicts (Protocol I) (8 June 1977), entry into force 7 December 1978.

Protocol Additional to the Geneva Conventions of 12 August 1949, And Relating to the Protection of Victims of Non-International Armed Conflicts (Protocol II) (8 June 1977), entry into force 7 December 1978.

Regulations Annexed to the Hague Convention (IV) Respecting the Laws and Customs of War on Land (18 October 1907), entry into force 26 January 1910.

Rome Statute of the International Criminal Court, entry into force 1 July 2002.

Vienna Convention on the Law of Treaties (23 May 1969), entry into force 27 January 1980.

178   *Bibliography*

UN reports

Annual Report of the United Nations High Commissioner for Human Rights and reports of the Office of the High Commissioner and the Secretary-General, *Concerns Related to Adherence to International Human Rights and International Humanitarian Law in the Context of the Escalation Between the State of Israel, the De Facto Authorities in Gaza and Palestinian Armed Groups in Gaza That Occurred from 14 to 21 November 2012*, Human Rights Council, A/HRC/22/35/Add.1, 6 March 2013.

Freedom of Movement, Human Rights Situation in the Occupied Palestinian Territory, Including East Jerusalem, Report of the Secretary General to the UN Human Rights Council, A/HRC/31/44, February 2016.

Freedom of Movement, UN Human Rights Council, A/HRC/31/44, 20 January 2016.

Gaja, G., *Eighth Report on the Responsibility of International Organisations*, A/CN.4/640, 14 March 2011.

Human Rights Committee, *Consideration of Reports Submitted by States Parties Under Article 40 of the Covenant Pursuant to the Optional Reporting Procedure, Fourth Periodic Report of States Parties Due in 2013, Israel*, CCPR/C/ISR/4, 12 December 2013.

Human Rights Situation in Palestine and Other Occupied Arab Territories, UN Human Rights Council, A/HRC/29/52, 24 June 2015.

Israeli Practices Affecting the Human Rights of the Palestinian People in the Occupied Palestinian Territory, Including East Jerusalem, Report of the Secretary General, A/70/421, 14 October 2015.

Israeli Settlements in the Occupied Palestinian Territory, Including East Jerusalem, and the Occupied Syrian Golan, A/71/355, 24 August 2016.

Kälin, W., *Report On the Situation of Human Rights in Kuwait Under Iraqi Occupation*, UN Commission on Human Rights, EC/N 4/1992/26, 16 January 1992, available at http://hr-travaux.law.virginia.edu/content/report-situation-human-rights-kuwait-under-iraqi-occupation-prepared-walter-kälin-special (visited 5 January 2017).

OCHA, *2015 Humanitarian Needs Overview OPT*, 2014.

Peace and Security Section (in cooperation with the Department of Peacekeeping Operations), Middle East UNEF-1, Completed Peacekeeping Operations, 2003, available at www.un.org/en/peacekeeping/missions/past/unef1backgr2.html (visited 5 December 2016).

Report of the Committee of Independent Experts in International Humanitarian and Human Rights Laws to Monitor and Assess Any Domestic, Legal or Other Proceedings Undertaken by Both the Government of Israel and the Palestinian Side, in the Light of General Assembly Resolution 64/254, Including the Independence, Effectiveness, Genuineness of These Investigations and Their Conformity With International Standards, Human Rights Council, A/HRC/15/50, 23 September 2010.

Report of the International Fact-Finding Mission to Investigate Violations of International Law, Including International Humanitarian and Human Rights Law, Resulting from the Israeli Attacks on the Flotilla of Ships Carrying Humanitarian Assistance, Human Rights Council, A/HRC/15/21, 27 September 2010.

Report of the International Law Commission on the Work of Its Forty-sixth Session, A/49/10, 2 May – 22 July 1994.

Report of the Secretary General on the United Nations Interim Administration Mission in Kosovo, S/2008/354, 12 June 2008.

Report of the Secretary-General on the Situation Concerning Western Sahara, S/2015/246, 10 April 2015.

Report of the Secretary-General on the Situation Concerning Western Sahara, S/2016/355, 19 April 2016.

Report of the Secretary-General on the Situation Concerning Western Sahara, UN SC S/2019/787, 2 October 2019.

Report of the Secretary-General prepared pursuant to GA resolution ES-10/10 (Report on Jenin), *Illegal Israeli Actions in Occupied East Jerusalem and the Rest of the Occupied Palestinian Territory*, A/ES-10/186, 30 July 2002.

Report of the Special Rapporteur on the Situation of Human Rights in the Palestinian Territories Occupied Since 1967, Human Rights Council, A/HRC/4/17, 29 January 2007.

Report of the Special Rapporteur on the Situation of Human Rights in the Palestinian Territories Occupied Since 1967, UN Doc. A/HRC/25/67, 13 January 2014.

Report of the United Nations Fact Finding Mission on the Gaza Conflict, Human Rights Council, A/HRC/12/48, 25 September 2009.

Respect for Human Rights in Armed Conflict, Report of the Secretary General, A/8052, 9 December 1970.

UN human rights committee concluding observations

Defence for Children International Palestine, *Shadow Report to the Fourth Periodic Report of Israel, Impact of Israeli Military Offensives in the Gaza Strip on Palestinian Children*, 112th Session of the Human Rights Committee, 7–31 October 2014.

Israel, CCPR/C/79/Add.93, 18 August 1998.

Israel, CCPR/C/ISR/CO13, 29 July 2010.

Russian Federation, CCPR/C/RUS/CO/7, 28 April 2015.

Uganda, CCPR/CO/80/UGA, 4 May 2004.

UN commission on human rights

Human Rights Resolution 2005/8: *Human Rights in the Occupied Syrian Golan*, E/CN.4/RES/2005/8, 14 April 2005.

Other international organisations

31st International Conference of the Red Cross and Red Crescent, International Humanitarian Law and the Challenges of Contemporary Armed Conflicts (EN 31IC/11/5.1.2), 28 November–1 December 2011, ICRC Report, available at https://app.icrc.org/e-briefing/new-tech-modern-battlefield/media/documents/4-international-humanitarian-law-and-the-challenges-of-contemporary-armed-conflicts.pdf (visited 5 January 2017).

Amnesty International, *Israel and the Occupied Palestinian Territories, 2015/2016 Annual Report*, available at www.amnesty.org/en/countries/middle-east-and-north-africa/israel-and-occupied-palestinian-territories/report-israel-and-occupied-palestinian-territories/ (visited 5 January 2017).

Amnesty International, *Israel/Gaza Operation Cast Lead: 22 Days of Death and Destruction*, 2009, available at www.refworld.org/docid/4a4db45a2.html (visited 5 January 2017).

Amnesty International, *Unlawful and Deadly Rocket and Mortar Attacks by Palestinian Armed Groups During the 2014 Gaza/Israel Conflict*, March 2015,

180 *Bibliography*

available at www.amnesty.org/en/documents/mde21/1178/2015/en/ (visited 5 January 2017).

Council of Europe and the Conflict in Georgia, CM/Del/Dec(2017)1285/2.1, 1285th Meeting, 3 May 2017, available at https://search.coe.int/cm/Pages/result_details.aspx?ObjectID=090000168070ec0b (visited 5 May 2017).

Council of Europe, Consolidated Report on the Conflict in Georgia (October 2017-March 2018), 11 April 2018, available at https://rm.coe.int/consolidated-report-on-the-conflict-in-georgia-october-2017-march-2018/16807b81cc (visited 20 December 2019).

Human Rights Watch, *Azerbaijan: Seven Years of Conflict in Nagorno Karabakh*, 8 December 1994, available at www.hrw.org/sites/default/files/reports/AZER%20Conflict%20in%20N-K%20Dec94.pdf (visited 3 January 2017).

Human Rights Watch, *Off Target: The Conduct of the War and Civilian Casualties in Iraq* (section: Synopsis of the Air War), December 2003, available at www.hrw.org/reports/2003/usa1203/index.htm (visited 5 December 2016).

Human Rights Watch, *World Report 1989, Afghanistan*, available at www.hrw.org/reports/1989/WR89/Afghanis.htm#TopOfPage (visited 5 January 2017).

Human Rights Watch, *World Report 2015: Israel Palestine, Events of 2014*, available at www.hrw.org/world-report/2015/country-chapters/israel/palestine (visited 10 June 2016).

Human Rights Watch Report, *Violent Response, US Army in al-Fallujah*, 16 June 2003, available at www.hrw.org/report/2003/06/16/violent-response/us-army-al-falluja (visited 5 January 2017).

Human Rights Watch Report, *War or Peace? Human Rights and Russian Military Involvement in the 'Near Abroad'*, 1 December 1993, available at www.hrw.org/legacy/reports/1993/russia/ (visited 3 January 2017).

ICRC, *Contemporary Challenges to IHL – Occupation: Overview*, available at www.icrc.org/eng/war-and-law/contemporary-challenges-for-ihl/occupation/overview-occupation.htm (visited 27 April 2014).

ICRC, *International Humanitarian Law and the Challenges of Contemporary Armed Conflicts*, October 2015.

ICRC, *Multinational Forces (Overview)*, 29 October 2010, available at www.icrc.org/eng/war-and-law/contemporary-challenges-for-ihl/multinational-forces/overview-multinational-forces.htm (visited 5 December 2016).

ICRC, *Occupation and International Humanitarian Law: Questions and Answers*, Resource Centre, 4 August 2008, available at www.icrc.org/eng/resources/documents/misc/634kfc.htm (visited 5 December 2016).

ICRC, *Violence and the Use of Force* (Geneva: ICRC, July 2011).

Independent International Fact-Finding Mission on the Conflict in Georgia, Vol. II (September 2009), available at www.mpil.de/files/pdf4/IIFFMCG_Volume_II1.pdf (visited 3 January 2017).

Reports and Documents, 'International Humanitarian Law and the Challenges of Contemporary Armed Conflicts Document Prepared by the International Committee of the Red Cross for the 30th International Conference of the Red Cross and Red Crescent, Geneva, Switzerland, 26–30 November 2007', 86 *International Review of the Red Cross* (2007).

Western Sahara Remains on the UN Listing as a Non-Self-Governing Territory Since 1963, available at www.un.org/en/decolonization/pdf/Western%20Sahara%202015%20profile_15Dec2015.pdf (visited 5 January 2017).

Bibliography 181

Regional organisations

League of Arab States, *Report of the Independent Fact Finding Commission on Gaza: No Safe Place*, 30 April 2009, available at www.tromso-gaza.no/090501ReportGaza.pdf (visited 5 January 2017).

Non-governmental organisation reports

B'Tselem, *Gaza Strip, The Rafah Crossing*, 13 January 2016, available at www.btselem.org/gaza_strip/rafah_crossing (visited 5 January 2017).

B'Tsalem – The Israeli Information Center for Human Rights in the Occupied Territories, *47 Years of Temporary Occupation*, available at www.btselem.org/download/201406_47_year_long_temporary_occupation_eng.pdf (visited 5 January 2017).

Chatham House, *International Law Discussion Group on Legal Responsibility of International Organisations in International Law*, 10 February 2011, available at www.chathamhouse.org/sites/files/chathamhouse/public/Research/International%20Law/il100211summary.pdf (visited 5 December 2016).

Gisha, *Gaza 2015: A Few Steps Forward and Several Steps Back*, April 2016, available at http://gisha.org/UserFiles/File/publications/2015_annual_summary/summary_en.pdf (visited 10 June 2016).

Gisha – Legal Centre for Freedom of Movement, 'Disengaged Occupiers: The Legal Status of Gaza', *Position Paper* (2007), available at www.gisha.org/userfiles/file/Report%20for%20the%20website.pdf (visited 3 December 2016).

HaMoked and B'Tsalem, *So Near and Yet So Far*, January 2014, available at www.btselem.org/download/201401_so_near_and_yet_so_far_eng.pdf (visited 5 January).

Human Sciences Research Council, *Occupation Colonialism, Apartheid?* May 2009, available at www.soas.ac.uk/lawpeacemideast/publications/file60532.pdf (visited 15 July 2017).

International Crisis Group, *No Exit? Gaza & Israel Between Wars*, August 2015, available at www.crisisgroup.org/middle-east-north-africa/eastern-mediterranean/israelpalestine/no-exit-gaza-israel-between-wars (visited 5 July 2017).

The Meir Amit Intelligence and Terrorism Information Centre at the Israeli Intelligence and Heritage Commemoration Centre, Operation Protective Edge – Update No. 21, available at www.terrorism-info.org.il/en/index.aspx (visited 15 July 2017).

Program on Humanitarian Policy and Conflict Research (Policy Brief), *Legal Aspects of Israel's Disengagement Plan under International Humanitarian Law*, Harvard University, 2010, available at http://hhi.harvard.edu/publications/legal-aspects-israels-disengagement-plan-under-international-humanitarian-law-ihl (visited 5 January 2017).

Historical sources

Actes de la Conférence de Bruxelles, 1874.

Correspondence Respecting the Proposed Conference at Brussels on the Rules of Military Warfare, United Kingdom Parliamentary Papers, Miscellaneous No. 1 (1875).

Declaration of Guidelines on the Recognition of New States in Eastern Europe and in the Former Soviet Union, 16 December 1991, available at www.dipublico.

182 Bibliography

org/100636/declaration-on-the-guidelines-on-the-recognition-of-new-states-in-eastern-europe-and-in-the-soviet-union-16-december-1991/(visited 3 January 2017).

The Draft Revised or New Conventions for the Protection of War Victims, XVII International Red Cross Conference, Stockholm, August 1948, available at www.loc.gov/rr/frd/Military_Law/pdf/RC_Draft-revised.pdf (visited 5 January 2017).

Final Record of the Diplomatic Conference of Geneva of 1949, Vol. II Section A (Bern: Federal Political Department, 1949).

Final Record of the Diplomatic Conference of Geneva of 1949, Vol. II Section B (Bern: Federal Political Department, 1949).

The Laws of War on Land, Oxford, 9 September 1880.

Memory of the Reconciliation of Asia Pacific, *Official Statements: Russia*, available at www.gwu.edu/~memory/data/government/russia_pow.html (visited 5 January 2017).

Official Records of the Diplomatic Conference on the Reaffirmation and Development of International Humanitarian Law Applicable in Armed Conflicts (Geneva 1974–1977), available at www.loc.gov/rr/frd/Military_Law/Geneva-Conventions_materials.html (visited 15 December 2016).

Project of an International Declaration concerning the Laws and Customs of War, Brussels, 27 August 1874, available at www.icrc.org/ihl/INTRO/135 (visited 3 December 2017).

Seventeenth International Red Cross Conference, Stockholm, August 1948, available at www.loc.gov/rr/frd/Military_Law/pdf/RC_XVIIth-RC-Conference.pdf (visited 3 December 2016).

Military manuals

Военная Оккупация, Законодательная база Российской Федерации, available at http://zakonbase.ru/dictJur/2587 (visited 3 December 2016).

Canada, *National Defence Joint Doctrine Manual* (B-GJ-005–104/FP-021) (Issued on Authority of the Chief of Defence Staff), 13 August 2001.

Canada, National Defence, *The Law of Armed Conflict at the Operational and Tactical Levels*, Office of the Judge Advocate General (2001).

République Française, Ministère de la Défense, *Manuel De Droit De Conflits Armés* (Ministère de la Défense, Edition, 2012), available at www.cicde.defense.gouv.fr/IMG/pdf/20130226_np_cicde_manuel-dca.pdf (visited 3 December 2016).

UK Ministry of Defence, *The Manual of the Law of Armed Conflict* (Oxford: Oxford University Press, 2004).

US Department of Army Joint Publication 3–16, *Multinational Operations*, 16 July 2013, available at www.fas.org/irp/doddir/dod/jp3-16.pdf.

The US Department of Defense Law of War Manual (Office of General Counsel Department of Defense, June 2015).

2. Secondary sources

Books, articles, and chapters

Abi-Saab, G., 'The 1977 Additional Protocols and General International Law: Some Preliminary Reflections', in A. J. M. Delissen and G. J. Tanja (eds.), *Humanitarian*

Law of Armed Conflict: Challenges Ahead (Dordrecht: Martinus Nijhoff Publishers, 1991) 115–126.

Akande, D., 'Classification of Armed Conflicts: Relevant Legal Concepts', in E. Wilmshurst (ed.), *International Law and Classification of Conflicts* (Oxford: Oxford University Press, 2012) 32–79.

Akande, D., 'The International Court of Justice and the Security Council: The Political Organs of the United Nations', 46 *International and Comparative Law Quarterly* (1997) 309–343.

Akram, S. M., and Lynk, M., 'Arab-Israeli Conflict', *Max Planck Encyclopedia of Public International Law* (2011), available at http://opil.ouplaw.com/view/10.1093/law:epil/9780199231690/law-9780199231690-e1246 (visited 5 January 2017).

Aldrich, G. H., 'The Work of the Eritrea-Ethiopia Claims Commission', 6 *Yearbook of International Humanitarian Law* (2003) 435–442.

Appel Graber, D., *The Development of the Law of Belligerent Occupation 1863–1914: A Historical Survey* (New York: Colombia University Press, 1949).

Arai-Takahashi, Y., 'Protection of Private Property', in A. Clapham, P. Gaeta, and M. Sassòli (eds.), *The 1949 Geneva Conventions: A Commentary* (Oxford: Oxford University Press, 2015) 1515–1534.

Arai Takahashi, Y., *The Law of Belligerent Occupation: Continuity and Change in International Humanitarian Law* (Leiden; Boston: Martinus Nijhoff Publishers, 2009).

Arimatsu, L., 'The Democratic Republic of the Congo, 1993–2010', in E. Wilmshurst (ed.), *International Law and the Classification of Conflicts* (Oxford: Oxford University Press, 2012) 146–203.

Arjona, A., Kasfir, N., and Mampilly, Z. (eds.), *Rebel Governance in Civil Wars* (New York: Cambridge University Press, 2015).

Aronson, G., 'Issues Arising from the Implementation of Israel's Disengagement from the Gaza Strip', 34 *Journal of Palestine Studies* (2005) 49–63.

Atkin, N., *Pétain* (New York: Routledge, 2014).

Bartels, R., 'Timelines, Borderlines and Conflicts', 873 *International Review of the Red Cross* (2009) 35–67.

Bashi, S., and Diamond, E., 'Separating Land, Separating People: Legal Analysis of Access of Restrictions Between Gaza and the West Bank', *Gisha*, June 2015, available at http://gisha.org/UserFiles/File/publications/separating-land-separating-people/separating-land-separating-people-web-en.pdf (visited 5 January 2017).

Bashi, S., and Mann, K., 'Disengaged Occupiers: The Legal Status of Gaza', *Gisha*, January 2007, available at www.gisha.org/userfiles/file/Report%20for%20the%20website.pdf (visited 5 January 2017).

Baty, T., 'So-called "De facto Recognition"', 5 *Yale Law Journal* (1922) 469–488.

Beck, L. D., and Vité, S., 'International Humanitarian Law and Human Rights Law', 293 *International Review of the Red Cross* (1993), available at www.icrc.org/eng/resources/documents/article/other/57jmrt.htm (visited 29 January 2017).

Beevor, A., *The Second World War* (London: Phoenix, 2013).

Bellal, A. (ed.), *The War Report: Armed Conflict in 2014* (Oxford: Oxford University Press, 2015).

Ben-Naftali, O., '"A La Recherche Du Temps Perdu": Rethinking Article 6 of the Fourth Geneva Convention in the Light of the Legal Consequences of the Construction of a Wall in the Occupied Palestinian Territory Advisory Opinion', 38 *Israel Law Review* (2005) 211–229.

184 *Bibliography*

Ben-Naftali, O., Gross, A. M., and Michaeli, K., 'Illegal Occupation: Framing the Occupied Palestinian Territory', 23 *Berkley Journal of International Law* (2005) 551–614.

Benvenisti, E., 'Occupation Pacific', *Max Planck Encyclopedia of Public International Law* (2009), available at http://opil.ouplaw.com/view/10.1093/law:epil/9780199231690/law-9780199231690-e360?prd=EPIL (visited 5 December 2016).

Benvenisti, E., *The International Law of Occupation* (Oxford: Oxford University Press, 2013).

Benvenisti, E., 'The Law on the Unilateral Termination of Occupation', 93 *Tel Aviv University Law Faculty Papers* (2008) 1–12, available at http://law.bepress.com/cgi/viewcontent.cgi?article=1099&context=taulwps (visited 5 January 2017).

Bhuta, N., 'The Role International Actors Other Than States Can Play in the New World Order', in A. Cassese (ed.), *Realising Utopia: The Future of International Law* (Oxford: Oxford University Press, 2012) 61–75.

Bill, B. J., 'Detention Operations in Iraq: A View from the Ground', in R. A. Pedrozo (ed.), *The War in Iraq: A Legal Analysis* (Newport, RI: Naval War College, 2010) 411–455.

Bing Jia, B., 'The Doctrine of Command Responsibility in International Law with Emphasis on Liability for Failure to Punish', XLV *Netherlands International Law Review* (1998).

Birkhimer, W. E., *Military Government and Martial Law* (Kansas City, MO: Franklin Hudson Publishing Company, 1914).

Blum, Y. Z., 'The Missing Reversioner: Reflections on the Status of Judea and Samaria', 3 *Israel Law Review* (1968) 279–301.

Bogdanos, M., and Patrick, W., *Thieves of Baghdad* (New York: Bloomsbury, 2005).

Borgen, C. J., 'States and International Law: The Problems of Self-Determination, Secession, and Recognition', in B. Cali (ed.), *International Law for International Relations* (Oxford: Oxford University Press, 2009) 191–212.

Bothe, M., 'Effective Control During Invasion: A Practical View on the Application Threshold of the Law of Occupation', 885 *International Review of the Red Cross* (2012) 37–41.

Bothe, M., 'Occupation, Belligerent', in R. Bernhardt (ed.), Vol. 3 *Encyclopedia of Public International Law* (Amsterdam: Elsevier, 1997) 763–768.

Bourloyannis-Vrailas, C., and Sicilianos, L.-A. (eds.), *The Prevention of Human Rights Violations* (Leiden: Martinus Nijhoff Publishers, 2001).

Bowring, B., 'Transnistria', in C. Walter, A. von Ungern-Sternberg, and K. Abushov (eds.), *Self-Determination and Secession in International Law* (Oxford: Oxford University Press, 2014) 157-174.

Brown, J., *The Proceedings of the Hague Conference, Translation of the Official Texts: The Conference of 1899* (Oxford: Oxford University Press, 1920).

Brownlie, I., *International Law* (Oxford: Oxford University Press, 2008).

Brownlie, I., *System of the Law of Nations State Responsibility* (Oxford: Clarendon Press, 1983).

Bruderlein, C., 'Protection, Occupation and International Humanitarian Law in the Occupied Palestinian Territory: A Critical Appraisal', 28 *Humanitarian Exchange* (Humanitarian Practice Network) (2004) 5–9.

Buchheit, L. C., *Secession: The Legitimacy of Self-Determination* (New Haven, CT: Yale University Press, 1978).

Bibliography 185

Buergenthal, T., *Public International Law in a Nutshell* (2nd edn., St Paul, MN: West Publishing, 1990).

Buerger, F. M., 'Analysis of UN Peacekeeping in Cambodia', Naval War College, November 1994, available at www.dtic.mil/dtic/tr/fulltext/u2/a283479.pdf (visited 5 December 2016).

Carcano, A., *Transformation of Occupied Territory in International Law* (Leiden: Brill/Martinus Nijhoff Publishers, 2015).

Casey-Maslen, S. (ed.), *The War Report 2012* (Oxford: Oxford University Press, 2013).

Cassese, A., *International Law* (2nd edn., Oxford: Oxford University Press, 2005).

Cassese, A., 'The Martens Clause: Half a Loaf or Simply Pie in the Sky', 11 *European Journal of International Law* (2000) 187–216.

Cassese, A., 'The Nicaragua and Tadić Tests Revisited in Light of the ICJ Judgment on Genocide in Bosnia', 18 *The European Journal of International Law* (2007) 649–668.

Condorelli, L., and Kress, C., 'Rules of Attribution: General Considerations', in J. Crawford et al. (eds.), *The Law of International Responsibility* (Oxford: Oxford University Press, 2010) 221–236.

Coomans, F., and Kaminga, M. T., 'Comparative Introductory Comments on the Extraterritorial Application of Human Rights Treaties', in F. Coomans and M. T. Kamminga (eds.), *Extraterritorial Application of Human Rights Treaties* (Antwerp; Oxford: Intersentia, 2004) 1–7.

Cordovez, D., and Harrison, S. S., *Out of Afghanistan: The Inside Story of the Soviet Withdrawal* (New York: Oxford University Press, 1995).

Crawford, J., *The International Law Commission's Articles on State Responsibility: Introduction, Text and Commentaries* (Cambridge: Cambridge University Press, 2005).

Crawford, J., and Olleson, S., 'The Nature and Forms of International Responsibility', in M. D. Evans (ed.), *International Law* (Oxford: Oxford University Press, 2010) 441–471.

Cuyckens, H., *Revisiting the Law of Occupation* (Leiden: Brill/Mrtinus Nijhoff Publishers, 2018).

Da Costa, K., *The Extraterritorial Application of Selected Human Rights Treaties* (Leiden: Martinus Nijhoff Publishers, 2013).

Darcy, S., *Judges, Law and War: The Judicial Development of International Humanitarian Law* (Cambridge: Cambridge University Press, 2014).

Darcy, S., and Reynolds, J., 'An Enduring Occupation: The Status of the Gaza Strip from the Perspective of International Humanitarian Law', 15 *Journal of Conflict and Security Law* (2010) 211–243.

De Hoogh, A. J. J., 'Articles 4 and 8 of the 2001 ILC Articles on State Responsibility, The Tadić Case and Attribution Acts of Bosnian Serb Authorities to the Federal Republic of Yugoslavia', 72 *British Yearbook of International Law* (2001) 255–292.

Del Mar, K., 'The Requirement of "Belonging" Under International Humanitarian Law', 21 *The European Journal of International Law* (2010) 105–124.

Dennis, M. J., 'Application of Human Rights Treaties Extraterritoriality in Times of Armed Conflict and Military Occupation', 99 *American Journal of International Law* (2005) 119–141.

De Vattel, M., *The Law of Nations* (T & J.W. Johnson, Law Book Sellers, 1844).

de Wet, E., *The Chapter 7 Powers of the United Nations Security Council* (Oxford: Hart Publishing, 2004).

186 *Bibliography*

Diehl, P. F., *Peace Operations* (London: Policy Press, 2008).

Dinstein, Y., *Non-International Armed Conflicts in International Law* (Cambridge: Cambridge University Press, 2014).

Dinstein, Y., 'The Dilemmas Relating to Legislation under Article 43 of the Hague Regulations, and Peace-Building', *International Humanitarian Law Research Initiative* (2004) 1–12.

Dinstein, Y., *The International Law of Belligerent Occupation* (Cambridge: Cambridge University Press, 2009).

Dinstein, Y., *War, Aggression and Self-Defence* (5th edn., Cambridge: Cambridge University Press, 2011).

Divac Oberg, M., 'The Legal Effects of Resolutions of the UN Security Council and General Assembly in the Jurisprudence of ICJ', 16 *European Journal of International Law* (2006) 879–906.

Dominicé, C., 'The Secession of the Canton of Jura in Switzerland', in M. G. Kohen (ed.), *Secession: International Law Perspectives* (Cambridge: Cambridge University Press, 2006) 453–469.

Dörmann, K., and Colassis, L., 'International Humanitarian Law in the Iraq Conflict', 47 *German Yearbook of International Law* (2004) 293–342.

Draper, G. I. A. D., 'The Relationship Between the Human Rights Regime and the Law of Armed Conflicts', 1 *Israel Yearbook on Human Rights* (1971) 191–207.

Droege, C., 'The Interplay Between International Humanitarian Law and International Human Rights Law in Situations of Armed Conflict', 2 *Israel Law Review* (2007) 310–355.

Durand, Y., *Le Nouvel ordre européen nazi, 1938–1945* (Paris: Éditions Complexe, 1990).

Emanuelli, C., *Les Actions Militaires de l'Onu et le Droit International Humanitaire* (Montreal: Wilson et Lafleur Itée, 1995).

Europa Publications (ed.), *The Territories of Russian Federation 2016* (17th edn., London: Routledge, 2016).

Feifer, G., *The Great Gamble: The Soviet War in Afghanistan* (New York: Harper Perennial, 2009).

Ferraro, T., 'Determining the Beginning and End of an Occupation Under International Humanitarian Law', 94 *International Review of the Red Cross* (2012) 133–163.

Ferraro, T., *Expert Meeting Occupation and Other Forms of Administration of Foreign Territory* (Geneva: ICRC, 2012).

Ferraro, T., 'The Applicability and Application of International Humanitarian Law to Multinational Forces', 95 *International Review of the Red Cross* (2013) 561–612.

Ferraro, T., 'The Applicability of the Law of Occupation to Peace Forces', in G. L. Beruto (ed.), *International Humanitarian Law, Human Rights and Peace Operations* (International Institute of Humanitarian Law, San Remo, 4–6 September 2008) 133–167.

Ferraro, T., 'The ICRC's Legal Position on the Notion of Armed Conflict Involving Foreign Intervention and on Determining the IHL Applicable to This Type of Conflict', 97 *International Review of the Red Cross* (2015) 1227–1252.

Ferraro, T., and Cameron, L., 'Article 2: Application of the Convention', in ICRC (ed.), *Commentary on the First Geneva Convention* (Cambridge: Cambridge University Press, 2016) 68–125.

Filiu, J.-P., *Gaza: A History* (Oxford: Oxford University Press, 2014).

Bibliography 187

Foulk, V. L., *The Battle for Fallujah* (Jefferson, NC: McFarland and Company, 2007).

Fox, G., 'Transformative Occupation and the Unilateralist Impulse', 94 *International Review of the Red Cross* (2012) 237–266.

Fraenkel, E., *Military Occupation and the Rule of Law* (New York: Oxford University Press, 1944).

Frowein, J. A., 'De facto Regime', *Max Planck Encyclopedia of Public International Law* (2013) available at http://opil.ouplaw.com/view/10.1093/law:epil/9780199231690/law-9780199231690-e1395 (visited 3 January 2017).

Gaggioli, G. (ed.), *The Use of Force in Armed Conflicts* (Geneva: ICRC, 2013).

Gal, T., 'Unexplored Outcomes of Tadić, Applicability of the Law of Occupation to War by Proxy', 12 *Journal of International Criminal Justice* (2014) 59–80.

Gasser, H.-P., 'From Military Intervention to Occupation of Territory: New Relevance of International Law of Occupation', in H. Fischer et al. (eds.), *Krisensicherung und Humanitärer Schutz – Crisis Management and Humanitarian Protection: Festschrift für Dieter Fleck* (Berlin: Berliner Wissenschafts-Verlag, 2004) 139–159.

Gasser, H.-P., 'Internationalised Non-International Armed Conflicts: Case Studies of Afghanistan, Kampuchea and Lebanon', 33 *The American University Law Review* (1983) 145–161.

Gasser, H.-P., and Dörmann, K., 'Protection of the Civilian Population', in D. Fleck (ed.), *The Handbook of International Humanitarian Law* (3rd edn., Oxford: Oxford University Press, 2014) 231–320.

Giladi, R., 'The Enactment of Irony: Reflections on the Origins of the Martens Clause (comments)', 25 *European Journal of International Law* (2014) 847–870.

Gill, T. D., 'Legal Characterisation and Basis for Enforcement Operations and Peace Enforcement Operations Under the Charter', in T. D. Gill and D. Fleck (eds.), *The Handbook of the International Law of Military Operations* (2nd edn., Oxford: Oxford University Press, 2015) 95–109.

Gioia, A., 'The Role of the European Court of Human Rights in Monitoring Compliance With Humanitarian Law in Armed Conflict', in O. Ben-Naftali (ed.), *International Humanitarian Law and International Human Rights Law* (Oxford: Oxford University Press, 2011) 201–249.

Goldman, R. K., 'Extraterritorial Application of the Human Rights to Life and Personal Liberty, Including Habeas Corpus, During Situations of Armed Conflict', in R. Kolb and G. Gaggioli (eds.), *Research Handbook on Human Rights and Humanitarian Law* (London: Edward Elgar Publishing, 2013) 104–124.

Goodwin, M., 'From Province to Protectorate to State: Sovereignty Lost, Sovereignty Gained?' in J. Summers (ed.), *Kosovo: A Precedent?* (Leiden: Martinus Nijhoff Publishers, 2011) 87–108.

Gowlland-Debbas, V., *Collective Responses to Illegal Acts in International Law: United Nations Action in the Question of Southern Rhodesia* (Dordrecht: Martinus Nijhoff Publishers, 1990).

Gowlland-Debbas, V. (ed.), *National Implementation of United Nations Sanctions* (The Hague; Leiden: Martinus Nijhoff Publishers, 2004).

Gowlland-Debbas, V., 'Security Council Enforcement Action and Issues of State Responsibility', 43 *International and Comparative Law Quarterly* (1994) 55–98.

Greenwood, C., 'Customary Law Status of the 1977 Geneva Protocols', in A. J. M. Delissen and G. J. Tanja (eds.), *Humanitarian Law of Armed Conflict: Challenges Ahead* (Dordrecht: Martinus Nijhoff Publishers, 1991) 93–114.

188   Bibliography

Greenwood, C., 'International Humanitarian Law and the Tadic Case', 7 *The European Journal of International Law* (1996) 265–283.

Greenwood, C., 'International Humanitarian Law and United Nations Military Operations', 1 *Yearbook of International Humanitarian Law* (1998) 3–34.

Grinion, J., 'The Geneva Conventions and the End of Occupation', in A. Clapham, P. Gaeta and M. Sassòli (eds.), *The 1949 Geneva Conventions: A Commentary* (Oxford: Oxford University Press, 2015) 1575–1596.

Gross, A., *The Writing on the Wall: Rethinking the International Law of Occupation* (Cambridge: Cambridge University Press, 2017).

Hall, W. E., *A Treatise on International Law* (Oxford: The Clarendon Press, 1924).

Hampson, F., 'The Scope of the Extra-Territorial Applicability of International Human Rights Law', in G. Gilbert, F. Hampson and C. Sandoval (eds.), *The Delivery of Human Rights: Essays in Honour of Professor Sir Nigel Rodley* (New York: Routledge, 2011) 157–182.

Hampson, F., and Lubell, N., *Georgia v. Russia* (II) 38263/08, Amicus Curiae Brief of the Human Rights Centre, University of Essex, available at http://repository. essex.ac.uk/9689/1/hampson-lubell-georgia-russia-amicus-01062014.pdf (visited 29 January 2017).

Hampson, F. J., 'Afghanistan 2001–2010', in E. Wilmshurst (ed.), *International Law and Classification of Conflicts* (Oxford: Oxford University Press, 2012) 242–279.

Hampson, F. J., 'The Relationship Between International Humanitarian Law and Human Rights Law from the Perspective of a Human Rights Treaty Body', 871 *International Review of the Red Cross* (2008) 549–572.

Hassan, H. A., *The Iraqi Invasion of Kuwait* (Sterling, VA: Pluto Press, 1999).

Heintze, H.-J., 'On the Relationship Between Human Rights Protection and International Humanitarian Law', 856 *International Review of the Red Cross* (2004) 789–813.

Higgins, R., 'A Babel of Judicial Voices', 55 *The International and Comparative Law Quarterly* (2006) 791–804.

Hinsley, F. H., *Sovereignty* (Cambridge: Cambridge University Press, 1986).

Hirsch, M., Housen-Couriel, D., and Lapidoth, R., *Whither Jerusalem* (The Hague: Martinus Nijhoff Publishers, 1995).

Hoffmeister, F., 'Case Study on Cyprus', in A. von Arnauld, N. Matz-Lück, and K. Odendhal (eds.), *100 Years of Peace Through Law: Past and Future* (Berlin: Duncker and Humbolt, 2015) 113–131.

Hofmann, R., 'Annexation', *Max Planck Encyclopedia of Public International Law* (2013), available at http://opil.ouplaw.com/view/10.1093/law:epil/9780199231690/law-9780199231690-e1376?prd=EPIL (visited 3 January 2017).

Hofstotter, B., 'European Court of Human Rights: Positive Obligations in E. and Others v. United Kingdom', 2 *International Journal of Constitutional Law* (2004) 525–534.

Holliday, J., *Middle East Security Report: The Struggle for Syria in 2011* (Institute for the Study of War, December 2011).

Hull, W. I., *The Two Hague Conferences* (Boston: Ginn and Company, 1908).

Imseis, A., 'Critical Reflections on the International Humanitarian Aspects of the ICJ Wall Advisory Opinion', 99 *The American Journal of International Law* (2005) 102–118.

James, C., *An Universal Military Dictionary* (4th edn., London: T. Egerton, 1816).

Jenks, W., 'The Conflict of Law-making Treaties', 30 *British Yearbook of International Law* (1953) 401–453.

Jennings, I., *The Approach to Self-Government* (Cambridge: Cambridge University Press, 1958).

Jong Dam-de, D., *International Law and Governance of Natural Resources in Conflict and Post-Conflict Situations* (Cambridge: Cambridge University Press, 2015).

Kälin, W., and Künzli, J., *The Law of International Human Rights Protection* (Oxford: Oxford University Press, 2009).

Kelly, M. J., 'Iraq and the Law of Occupation: New Tests for an Old Law', in Vol. 6 *Yearbook of International Humanitarian Law* (The Hague: T.M.C. Asser Press, 2003) 127–165.

Kelly, M. J., *Restoring and Maintaining Order in Complex Peace Operations* (The Hague: Kluwer Law International, 1999).

Kelsen, H., *Collective Security Under International Law* (5th edn., Clark, NJ: The Law Book Exchange, 2009).

Kennan, G. F., *Report to the State Department on About 1 May 1939, From Prague After Munich* (Princeton, NJ: Princeton University Press, 1968).

Khalil, A., *Family Unification of Residents in the Occupied Territory* (Italy: European University Institute, Robert Schuman Centre for Advanced Studies, 2009).

Kimura, H., *Distant Neighbours: Japanese-Russian Relations Under Gorbachov and Yeltsin* (New York: Routledge, 2000).

Kirss, K., 'Role of the International Court of Justice: Example of the Genocide Case', 3 *ACTA SOCIETATIS MARTENSIS* (2007/2008) 143–164.

Klappe, B. F., 'The Law of International Peace Operations', in D. Fleck (ed.), *The Handbook of International Humanitarian Law* (3rd edn., Oxford: Oxford University Press, 2014) 611–646.

Kleffner, J. K., 'Scope of Application of International Humanitarian Law', in D. Fleck (ed.), *The Handbook of International Humanitarian Law* (3rd edn., Oxford: Oxford University Press, 2014) 43–78.

Kolb, R., *An Introduction to the Law of the United Nations* (Portland, OR: Hart Publishing, 2008).

Kolb, R., 'Human Rights and Humanitarian Law', *Max Planck Encyclopaedia of Public International Law* (2013), available at http://opil.ouplaw.com/view/10.1093/law:epil/9780199231690/law-9780199231690-e811?prd=EPIL (visited 29 January 2017).

Kolb, R., *Theory of International Law* (Bloomsbury: Hart Publishing, 2016).

Kolb, R., and Hyde, R., *An Introduction to the International Law of the Armed Conflict* (Oxford; Portland, OR: Heart Publishing, 2008).

Kolb, R., and Vité, S., *Le droit de l'occupation militaire: perspectives historiques et enjeux juridiques actueles* (Bruxelles: Bruylant, 2009).

Koskenniemi, M., 'Occupation and Sovereignty – Still a Useful Distinction?' in O. Engdahl and P. Wrange (eds.), *Law at War: The Law As It Was and the Law As It Should Be* (Leiden; Boston: Martinus Nijhoff Publishers, 2008) 163–174.

Koskenniemi, M., and Leino, P., 'Fragmentation of International Law? Postmodern Anxieties', 15 *Leiden Journal of International Law* (2002) 553–579.

Kostiner, J., *Conflict and Cooperation in the Gulf Region* (Wiesbaden: VS Verlag für Sozialwissenschaften, 2009).

Koutroulis, V., *Le début et la fin de l'application du droit de l'occupation* (Paris: Pedone, 2010).

190   *Bibliography*

Krähenmann, S., 'Protection of Prisoner in Armed Conflict', in D. Fleck (ed.), *The Handbook of International Humanitarian Law* (3rd edn., Oxford: Oxford University Press, 2013) 359–411.

Kress, C., 'L'Organe de facto en droit international public: réflexions sur l'imputation à l'état de l'acte d'un particulier à la lumière des développements récents', 105 *Revue Générale de Droit International Public* (2001) 93–144.

Krüger, H., 'Nagorno-Karabakh', in C. Walter, A. von Ungern-Sternberg, and K. Abushov (eds.), *Self-Determination and Secession in International Law* (Oxford: Oxford University Press, 2014) 214-232.

Krüger, H., *The Nagorno Karabakh Conflict: A Legal Analysis* (Heidelberg: Springer, 2010).

Labuda, P. I., 'Peacekeeping and Peace Enforcement', *Max Planck Encyclopedia of Public International Law* (2015), available at https://opil.ouplaw.com/view/10.1093/law:epil/9780199231690/law-9780199231690-e364 (visited 8 February 2020).

Lauterpacht, E., *Jerusalem and the Holy Places* (London: The Anglo-Israeli Association, London, 1968, reprinted in 1980).

Lavoyer, J.-P., 'Jus in Bello: Occupation Law and the War in Iraq', 98 *Proceedings of the American Society of International Law* (2004) 117–124.

Leigh, M., 'Yeager v. Islamic Republic of Iran', 82 *American Journal of International Law* (1988) 353–362.

Lekha Sriam, C., Martin-Ortega, O., and Herman, J., *War, Conflicts and Human Rights: Theory and Practice* (2nd edn., New York: Routledge, 2014).

Longobardo, M., *The Use of Armed Force in Occupied Territory* (Cambridge: Cambridge University Press, 2018).

Lowry, R. S., *The Gulf War Chronicles* (New York: iUniverse Inc., 2003).

Lubell, N., 'Applicability of Human Rights Law in Situations of Occupation', in *Current Challenges to the Law of Military Occupation* (34 Proceedings of the Bruges Collegium, 2006) 50–56.

Lubell, N., 'Challenges in Applying Human Rights Law to Armed Conflict', 87 *International Review of the Red Cross* (2005) 737–753.

Lubell, N., 'Human Rights Obligations in Military Occupation', 94 *International Review of the Red Cross* (2012) 317–337.

Lubell, N., 'Parallel Application of International Humanitarian Law and International Human Rights Law: An Examination of the Debate', 40 *Israel Law Review* (2007) 648–660.

Lubell, N., and Prud'homme, N., 'Impact of Human Rights Law', in R. Liivoja and T. McCormarck (eds.), *Routledge Handbook of the Law of Armed Conflict* (London; New York: Routledge, 2016) 106–120.

Mačák, K., *Internationalised Armed Conflicts in International Law* (Oxford: Oxford University Press, 2018).

Maine, H. S., *International Law* (Boston: Elibron Classics, Adamant Media Corporation, 2005).

Malanczuck, P., *Akehurst's Modern Introduction to International Law* (7th edn., London: Routledge, 2004).

Manusama, K., *The United Nations Security Council in the Post-Cold War Era* (Leiden: Martinus Nijhoff Publishers, 2006).

Marek, K., *Identity and Continuity of States in Public International Law* (Genève: Droz, 1968).

Martel, W. C., *Victory in War* (Cambridge: Cambridge University Press, 2007).

Maryan Green, N. A., *International Law, Law of Peace* (London: Macdonald and Evans, 1982).

Maurer, P., 'Challenges to Humanitarian Action in Contemporary Conflicts: Israel, the Middle East and Beyond', 47 *Israel Law Review* (2014) 175–180.

Mazower, M., *Griechenland unter Hitler* (Frankfurt am Main: S. Fischer, 2016).

McCarthy, C., 'Human Rights Standards During Military Occupation', in R. Arnold and N. Quénivet (eds.), *International Humanitarian Law and Human Rights Law* (Leiden; Boston: Martinus Nijhoff Publishers, 2008) 121–132.

McGoldrick, D., 'Extraterritorial Application of the International Covenant on Civil and Political rights', in F. Coomans and M. T. Kamminga (eds.), *Extraterritorial Application of Human Rights Treaties* (Antwerp; Oxford: Intersentia, 2004) 41–72.

Meller, S. E., 'The Kosovo Case: An Argument for a Remedial Declaration of Independence', 40 *Georgia Journal of International and Comparative Law* (2012) 834–866.

Melnyk, A. Y., 'Nagorny-Karabakh', *Max Planck Encyclopedia of Public International Law* (2013), available at http://opil.ouplaw.com/view/10.1093/law:epil/9780199231690/law-9780199231690-e2073?prd=EPIL (visited 3 January 2017).

Melzer, N., *Interpretative Guidance on the Notion of Direct Participation in Hostilities Under International Humanitarian Law* (Geneva: ICRC, May 2009).

Melzer, N., *Targeted Killing in International Law* (Oxford: Oxford University Press, 2008).

Meron, T., 'Classification of Armed Conflict in the Former Yugoslavia: Nicaragua's Fallout', 92 *The American Journal of International Law* (1998) 236–242.

Meron, T., 'Convergence of International Humanitarian Law and Human Rights Law', in D. Warner (ed.), *Human Rights and Humanitarian Law: The Quest for Universality* (The Hague: Martinus Nijhoff Publishers, 1997) 97–105.

Meron, T., *Human Rights and Humanitarian Norms as Customary Law* (Oxford: Oxford University Press, 1989).

Meron, T., 'The 1994 U.S Action in Haiti: Extraterritoriality of Human Rights Treaties', 89 *American Journal of International Law* (1995) 78–82.

Messineo, F., 'Attribution of Conduct', in A. Nollkaemper and I. Plakokefalos (eds.), *Principles of Shared Responsibility in International Law* (Cambridge: Cambridge University Press, 2014) 60–97.

Mettraux, G., *The Law of Command Responsibility* (Oxford; New York: Oxford University Press, 2009).

Milano, E., 'The Non-Recognition of Russia's Annexation of Crimea: Three Different Legal Approaches and One Unanswered Question', *Questions of International Law* (2014), available at www.qil-qdi.org/the-non-recognition-of-russias-annexation-of-crimea-three-different-legal-approaches-and-one-unanswered-question/ (visited 3 January 2017).

Milanović, M., 'Al-Skeini and Al-Jedda in Strasbourg', 23 *The European Journal of International Law* (2012) 121–139.

Milanović, M., *Extraterritorial Application of Human Rights Treaties: Law, Principles, and Policy* (Oxford: Oxford University Press, 2011).

Milanović, M., 'From Compromise to Principle: Clarifying the Concept of State Jurisdiction in Human Rights Treaties', 8 *Human Rights Law Review* (2008) 411–448.

192   Bibliography

Milanović, M., 'Norm Conflicts, International Humanitarian Law, and Human Rights Law', in O. Ben-Naftali (ed.), *International Humanitarian Law and Human Rights Law* (Oxford: Oxford University Press, 2011) 95–125.

Milanović, M., and Hadzi-Vidanovic, V., 'A Taxonomy of Armed Conflict', in N. White and C. Henderson (eds.), *Research Handbook on International Conflict and Security Law: Jus ad Bellum, Jus in Bello and Jus Post Bellum* (London: Edward Elgar Publishing, 2013) 256–314.

Miller, S., 'Revisiting Extraterritorial Jurisdiction: A Territorial Justification for Extraterritorial Jurisdiction Under the European Convention', 20 *The European Journal of International Law* (2009) 1223–1246.

Mirzayev, F., 'Abkhazia', in C. Walter, A. von Ungern-Sternberg, and K. Abushov (eds.), *Self-Determination and Secession in International Law* (Oxford: Oxford University Press, 2014) 191-213.

Moir, L., *The Law of Internal Armed Conflict* (Cambridge: Cambridge University Press, 2002).

Momtaz, D., 'Attribution of Conduct to the State: State Organs and Entities Empowered to Exercise Elements of Governmental Authority', in J. Crawford et al. (eds.), *The Law of International Responsibility* (Oxford: Oxford University Press, 2010) 237–246.

Montejo, B., 'The Notion of "Effective Control" Under the Articles on the Responsibility of International Organisations', in M. Ragazzi (ed.), *Responsibility of International Organisations* (Leiden: Martinus Nijhoff Publishers, 2013) 389-404.

Murphy, R., *UN Peacekeeping in Lebanon, Somalia and Kosovo* (Cambridge: Cambridge University Press, 2007).

Murray, D. et al., *Practitioner's Guide to Human Rights Law in Armed Conflict* (Oxford: Oxford University Press, 2016).

Nijman, J., *The Concept of International Legal Personality: An Inquiry into History and Theory of International Law* (The Hague: T.M.C. Asser Press, 2004).

Nishat, N. 'The Structure of Geneva Convention IV and the Resulting Gaps in that Convention', in A. Clapham, P. Gaeta and M. Sassòli (eds.), *The 1949 Geneva Conventions: A Commentary* (Oxford: Oxford University Press, 2015) 1069–1087.

Nolte, G., 'Intervention by Invitation', *Max Planck Encyclopedia of Public International Law* (2010), available at http://opil.ouplaw.com/view/10.1093/law:epil/9780199231690/law-9780199231690-e1702?prd=EPIL (visited 3 January 2017).

O'Boyle, M., 'The European Convention on Human Rights and Extraterritorial Jurisdiction: A Comment on Life After Banković', in F. Coomans and M. T. Kamminga (eds.), *Extraterritorial Application of Human Rights Treaties* (Antwerp; Oxford: Intersentia, 2004) 125–140.

Oppenheim, L., *International Law, A Treatise* (Vol. 1 of 2) (London; New York: Longmans Green, 1921).

Oppenheim, L., 'The Legal Relations Between and Occupying Power and the Inhabitants', 33 *The Law Quarterly Review* (1917) 363–370.

Orakhelashvili, A., 'Human Rights Protection During Extra-territorial Military Operations: Perspectives on International and English Law', in N. White and C. Henderson (eds.), *Research Handbook on International Conflict and Security Law: Jus ad Bellum, Jus in Bello and Jus Post Bellum* (London: Edward Elgar Publishing, 2013) 598–637.

Bibliography   193

Orakhelashvili, A., 'The Acts of the Security Council: Meaning and Standards of Review', in A. von Bogdandy and R. Wolfrum (eds.), 11 *Max Planck Yearbook of United Nations Law* (2007) 143–195.

Orakhelashvili, A., 'The Interaction Between Human Rights and Humanitarian Law: Fragmentation, Conflict, Parallelism, or Convergence', 19 *The European Journal of International Law* (2008) 161–182.

Oswald, B., and Wellington, B., 'Reparation for Violations in Armed Conflict and the Emerging Practice of Making Amends', in R. Livoja and T. McCormack (eds.), *Routledge Handbook of the Law of Armed Conflict* (Milton Park: Routledge, 2016) 520–537.

Palchetti, P., 'De Facto Organs of a State', *Max Planck Encyclopedia of Public International Law* (2010), available at http://opil.ouplaw.com/view/10.1093/law:epil/9780199231690/law-9780199231690-e1394?prd=EPIL (visited 2 December 2016).

Palchetti, P., 'The Allocation of Responsibility for Internationally Wrongful Acts Committed in the Course of Multinational Operations', 95 *International Review of the Red Cross* (2013) 727–742.

Péclard, D., and Mechoulan, D., *Rebel Governance and Politics of Civil War* (Bern: Swisspeace, 2015).

Pegg, S., *International Society and the De Facto State* (Brookfield, VT: Ashgate, 1998).

Pejic, E., 'Status of Armed Conflicts', in E. Wilmshurst and S. Breau (eds.), *Perspectives on the ICRC Study on Customary International Humanitarian Law* (Cambridge: Cambridge University Press, 2007) 77–100.

Pellet, A., 'The Definition of Responsibility in International Law', in J. Crawford, A. Pellet and S. Olleson (eds.), *The Law of International Responsibility* (Oxford: Oxford University Press, 2010) 3–16.

Peters, A., 'The Crimean Vote of March 2014 as an Abuse of the Institution of the Territorial Referendum', in C. Calliess (ed.), *Staat und Mensch im Kontext des Völker- und Europarechts: Liber Amicorum für Torsten Stein* (Baden-Baden: Nomos, 2015) 255–280.

Picciotti, R. A., 'Problems of Occupied Nations After the Termination of Occupation', 33 *Military Law Review* (1966) 25–57.

Pictet, J. (ed.), *Commentary of 1958, Convention (IV) Relative to the Protection of Civilian Persons in Time of War Geneva, 12 August 1949* (Geneva: ICRC, 1958).

Pictet, J., *Humanitarian Law and the Protection of the War Victims* (A. W. Sijthoff-Leyden: Henry Dunant Institute Geneva, 1975).

Pocar, F., 'To What Extent Is Protocol I Customary International Law?', 78 *International Law Studies* (2002) 337–351.

Pomerance, M., *Self-Determination in Law and Practice* (The Hague: Martinus Nijhoff Publishers, 1982).

Provost, R., *International Human Rights and Humanitarian Law* (Cambridge: Cambridge University Press, 2003).

Ratner, S. R., 'Foreign Occupation and International Territorial Administration: The Challenges of Convergence', *The European Journal of International Law* (2005) 695–719.

Roberts, A., 'Prolonged Military Occupation: The Israeli-Occupied Territories since 1967', 84 *The American Journal of International Law* (1990) 44–103.

Roberts, A., 'The End of Occupation: Iraq', 54 *International and Comparative Law Quarterly* (2005) 27–48.

194 *Bibliography*

Roberts, A., 'What Is Military Occupation?', 55 *British Yearbook of International Law* (1984) 249–305.

Roberts, A., 'Transformative Military Occupation: Applying the Laws of War and Human Rights', in M. Schmitt and J. Pejic (eds.), *International Law and Armed Conflict: Exploring the Faultlines* (Leiden: Martinus Nijhoff Publishers, 2007) 439–495.

Roberts, A., and Sivakumaran, S., 'Law Making by Non-State Actors: Engaging Armed Groups in the Creation of International Humanitarian Law', 37 *Yale Journal of International Law* (2012) 108–152.

Ronen, Y., 'A Century of the Law of Occupation', 17 *Yearbook of International Humanitarian Law* (The Hague: T.M.C. Asser Press, 2014) 169–186.

Ronen, Y., 'Post-Occupation Law', in C. Stahn, J. S. Easterday and J. Iverson (eds.), *Jus Post Bellum* (Oxford: Oxford University Press, 2014) 428–446.

Ronen, Y., 'Superior Responsibility of Civilians for International Crimes Committed in Civilian Settings', 43 *Vanderbilt Journal of Transnational Law* (2010) 314–356.

Rosenne, S., *The International Law Commission's Draft Articles on State Responsibility* (Dordrecht: Martinus Nijhoff Publishers, 1991).

Rubin, B., 'Israel/Occupied Territories', *Max Planck Encyclopedia of Public International Law* (2009), available at http://opil.ouplaw.com/view/10.1093/law: epil/9780199231690/law-9780199231690-e1301 (visited 15 January 2017).

Ruys, T., *Armed Attack and Article 51 UN Charter: Evolutions of Customary Law and Practice* (Cambridge: Cambridge University Press, 2010).

Ruys, T., and Verhoven, S., 'DRC v. Uganda: The Applicability of International Humanitarian Law and Human Rights Law in Occupied Territories', in R. Arnold and N. Quénivet (eds.), *International Humanitarian Law and Human Rights Law* (Leiden: Martinus Nijhoff Publishers, 2008) 155–195.

Ryngaert, C., 'Clarifying the Extraterritorial Application of the European Convention on Human Rights', 28 *Utrecht Journal of International and European Law* (2012) 57–60.

Sandoz, Y., Swinarski, C., and Zimmerman, B. (eds.), *Commentary on the Additional Protocols of 8 June 1977 to the Geneva Conventions of 12 August 1949* (ICRC: Martinus Nijhoff Publishers, 1987).

Sari, A., 'Untangling Extra-Territorial Jurisdiction from International Responsibility in Jaloud v. Netherlands: Old Problem, New Solutions?' 53 *Military Law and the Law of War Review* (2014) 287–318.

Sassòli, M., 'A Plea in Defence of Pictet and the Inhabitants of Territories Under Invasion: The Case for the Applicability of the Fourth Geneva Convention During the Invasion Phase', 94 *International Review of the Red Cross* (2012) 42–50.

Sassòli, M., 'Legislation and Maintenance of Public Order and Civil Life by Occupying Powers', 16 *The European Journal of International Law* (2005) 661–694.

Sassòli, M., 'Taking Armed Groups Seriously: Ways to Improve Their Compliance with International Humanitarian Law', 1 *Journal of International Humanitarian Legal Studies* (2010) 5–51.

Sassòli, M., 'The Concept and the Beginning of Occupation', in A. Clapham, P. Gaeta and M. Sassòli (eds.), *The 1949 Geneva Conventions: A Commentary* (Oxford: Oxford University Press, 2015) 1390–1419.

Sassòli, M., 'The Role of Human Rights and International Humanitarian Law in Types of Armed Conflicts', in O. Ben-Naftali (ed.), *International Humanitarian Law and International Human Rights Law* (Oxford: Oxford University Press, 2011) 34–94.

Sassòli, M., and Bouvier, A. A., *How Does Law Protect in War?* (2nd edn., Geneva: ICRC, 2006).

Sassòli, M., Bouvier, A. A., and Quintin, A., *How Does Law Protect in War?* (3rd edn., Geneva: ICRC, 2011).

Sassòli, M., and Issar, Y., 'Challenges to International Humanitarian Law', in A. von Arnauld et al. (eds.), *100 Years of Peace Through Law: Past and Future* (Berlin: Duncker and Humbolt, 2015) 181–235.

Sassòli, M., and Olson, L. M., 'The Judgment of the ICTY Appeals Chamber on the Merits in the Tadic Case', 839 *International Review of the Red Cross* (2000) 733–769.

Sassòli, M., and Olson, L. M., 'The Legal Relationship Between International Humanitarian Law and Human Rights Law Where It Matters: Admissible Killing and Internment of Fighters in Non-International Armed Conflict', 871 *International Review of the Red Cross* (2008) 599–627.

Saul, M., 'The Normative Status of Self-Determination in International Law: A Formula for Uncertainty in the Scope and Content of the Right?' 11 *Human Rights Law Review*, 609–644.

Schabas, W. A., *International Criminal Law* (4th edn., Cambridge: Cambridge University Press, 2012).

Scheinin, M., 'Extraterritorial Effect of the International Covenant on Civil and Political Rights', in F. Coomans and M. Kamminga (eds.), *Extraterritorial Application of Human Rights Treaties* (Antwerp; Oxford: Intersentia, June 2004) 73–83.

Schindler, D., *The Different Types of Armed Conflicts According to the Geneva Conventions and Protocols* (The Netherlands: Sijthoff and Noordhoof, 1979).

Schindler, D., 'The International Committee of the Red Cross and Human Rights', 208 *International Review of the Red Cross* (1979), available at www.icrc.org/eng/resources/documents/article/other/57jm9z.htm (visited 29 January 2017).

Schmalenbach, K., 'International Responsibility for Humanitarian Law Violations by Armed Groups', in H. Krieger (ed.), *Inducing Compliance with International Humanitarian Law* (Cambridge: Cambridge University Press, 2015) 470–503.

Schmitt, M. N., 'Iraq (2003 Onwards)', in E. Wilmshurst (ed.), *International Law and the Classification of Conflicts* (Oxford: Oxford University Press, 2012) 356–386.

Schoiswhol, M., 'De facto Regimes and Human Rights Obligations – The Twilight Zone of Public International Law', 6 *Austrian Review of International and European Law* (2001) 45–90.

Schwarzenberger, G., *The Law of Armed Conflict (International Law as Applied by International Courts and Tribunals)* (London: Stevens & Sons, 1968).

Scobbie, I., 'Gaza', in E. Wilmshurst (ed.), *International Law and the Classification of the Conflicts* (Oxford: Oxford University Press, 2012) 280–315.

Scobbie, I., 'Human Rights Protection During Armed Conflict: What, When and for Whom?' in E. de Wet and J. Kleffner (eds.), *Convergence and Conflicts of Human Rights and International Humanitarian Law in Military Operations* (Pretoria: Pretoria University Law Press, 2014) 1–17.

Scobbie, I., 'International Law and the Prolonged Occupation of Palestine', United Nations Roundtable on Legal Aspects of the Question of Palestine the Hague (20–22 May 2015), available at http://papers.ssrn.com/sol3/papers.cfm?abstract_id=2611130 (visited 5 January 2017).

Scobbie, I., and Hibbin, S., *The Israeli-Palestine Conflict in International Law: Territorial Issues* (The U.S./Middle East Project, 2009).

196 *Bibliography*

Senese, S., 'External and Internal Self-Determination', 16 *Social Justice* (Human Rights and Social Rights: Views) (1989) 19–25.

Shaw, M. N., *International Law* (Cambridge: Cambridge University Press, 2008).

Shraga, D., 'Military Occupation and UN transitional Administrations: The Analogy and Its Limitations', in M. G. Cohen (ed.), *Promoting Justice, Human Rights and Conflict Resolution Through International Law: Liber Amicorum* (Leiden: Martinus Nijhoff Publishers, 2007) 479–498.

Shraga, D., 'The United Nations as an Actor Bound by International Humanitarian Law', 5(2) *International Peacekeeping* (1998) 64–81.

Shraga, D., and Zacklin, R., 'L'applicabilité du DIH aux Opérations de Maintien de la Paix de Nations Unies: Questions Conceptuelles et Pratiques', in *Symposium sur l'action humanitaire et les opérations de maintien de la paix*, Rapport, CICR Genève, 1995.

Siegrist, M., *The Functional Beginning of Belligerent Occupation* (Geneva: The Graduate Institute Publications, 2011).

Simma, B., 'Universality of International Law from the Perspective of Practitioner', 20 *The European Journal of International Law* (2009) 265–297.

Sivakumaran, S., *The Law of Non-International Armed Conflict* (Oxford: Oxford University Press, 2012).

Sivakumaran, S., 'Torture in International Human Rights and International Humanitarian Law: The Actor and the Ad Hoc Tribunals', 18 *Leiden Journal of International Law* (2005) 541–556.

Skoutaris, N., *The Cyprus Issue: The Four Freedoms in a Member State under Siege* (Oxford; Portland, OR: Hart Publishing, 2011).

Skuza, -M., 'Hospitals', in A. Clapham, P. Gaeta and M. Sassòli (eds.), *The 1949 Geneva Conventions: A Commentary* (Oxford: Oxford University Press, 2015) 207–229.

Smith, R. K. M., *International Human Rights* (2nd edn., Oxford: Oxford University Press, 2005).

Snyder, T. D., *Bloodlands: Europe Between Hitler and Stalin* (New York: Basic Books, 2012).

Solomon, S., 'Occupied or Not: The Question of Gaza's Legal Status After Israeli Disengagement', 19 *Cardozo Journal of International and Comparative Law* (2011) 59–90.

Spinedi, M., 'On the Non-Attribution of the Bosnian Serbs' Conduct to Serbia', 5 *Journal of International Criminal Justice* (2007) 829–838.

Stahn, C., *The Law and Practice of International Territorial Administration* (Cambridge: Cambridge University Press, 2008).

Stirk, P. M. R., *The Politics of Military Occupation* (Edinburgh: Edinburgh University Press, 2012).

Summers, J., *Peoples and International Law* (2nd edn., Leiden: Brill/Martinus Nijhoff Publishers, 2013).

Suter, K., 'An Inquiry into the Meaning of the Phrase "Human Rights in Armed Conflicts"', 15 *Military Law and Law of War Review* (1976) 393–439.

Talmon, S., 'The Duty Not to Recognise as Lawful a Situation Created by the Illegal Use of Force or Other Serious Breaches of a Jus Cogens Obligation: An Obligation Without Real Substance?' in C. Tomuschat and J.-M. Thouvenin (eds.), *The Fundamental Rules of the International Legal Order Jus Cogens and Obligations Erga Omnes* (Leiden: Brill/Martinus Nijhoff Publishers, 2006) 99–125.

Talmon, S., 'The Various Control Tests in the Law of State Responsibility and the Responsibility of Outside Powers for Acts of Secessionist', *Legal Research Paper Series*, University of Oxford (May 2009) 1–21.

Thornberry, C., 'Namibia', in D. M. Malone (ed.), *The UN Security Council From the Cold War to the 21st Century* (London: Lynne Rienner Publishers, 2004) 407–436.

Thürer, D., 'The Failed State and International Law', 836 *International Review of The Red Cross* (1999), available at www.icrc.org/eng/resources/documents/article/other/57jq6u.htm (visited 3 January 2017).

Thürer, D., and Burri, T., 'Self-Determination', *Max Planck Encyclopedia of Public International Law* (2008), available at http://opil.ouplaw.com/view/10.1093/law:epil/9780199231690/law-9780199231690-e873 (visited 6 December 2017);

Tomuschat, C., *Human Rights* (3rd edn., Oxford: Oxford University Press, 2014).

Tomuschat, C., *Human Rights Between Idealism and Realism* (2nd edn., Oxford: Oxford University Press, 2010).

Tzevelekos, V. P., 'Reconstructing the Effective Control Criterion in Extraterritorial Human Rights Breaches: Direct Attribution of Wrongfulness, Due Diligence, and Concurrent Responsibility', 36 *Michigan Journal of International Law* (2014) 129–178.

van der Heijden, I., 'Other Issues Relating to the Treatment of Civilians in Enemy Hands', in A. Clapham, P. Gaeta, and M. Sassòli (eds.), *The 1949 Geneva Conventions (A Commentary)* (Oxford: Oxford University Press, 2015), 1241–1268.

van Engeland, A., 'Protection of Public Property', in A. Clapham, P. Gaeta and M. Sassòli (eds.), *The 1949 Geneva Conventions: A Commentary* (Oxford: Oxford University Press, 2015) 1535–1550.

van Essen, J., 'De Facto Regimes in International Law', 28(74) *Merkourios – Utrecht Journal of International and European Law* (2012) 31–49.

Verdirame, G., 'Human Rights Law in Wartime: A Framework for Analysis', 6 *European Human Rights Law Review* (2008) 689–705.

Verhoeven, S., 'International and Non-International Armed Conflicts', *Institute for International Law*, Working Paper No. 107, K.U. Leuven Faculty of Law (2007) 3–22.

Vetter, G. R., 'Command Responsibility of Non-Military Superiors in the International Criminal Court', 25 *The Yale Journal of International Law* (2000) 90–143.

Vité, S., 'L'applicabilité du droit de l'occupation militaire aux opérations des organisations internationales', in *Current Challenges to the Law of Occupation, Proceedings of the Bruges Colloquium*, 20–21 October 2005, 93–100.

Vité, S., 'Typology of Armed Conflicts in International Humanitarian Law: Legal Concepts and Actual Situations', 91 *International Review of the Red Cross* (2009) 69–94.

von Clausewitz, C., *On War* (translated by Col. J. John Graham; London: N. Trübner, 1873).

Walter, C., 'Postscript: Self-Determination, Secession, and the Crimean Crisis 2014', in C. Walter, A. von Ungern-Sternberg, and K. Abushov (eds.), *Self-Determination and Secession in International Law* (Oxford: Oxford University Press, 2014) 293–331.

Waters, C., 'South Ossetia', in C. Walter, A. von Ungern-Sternberg, and K. Abushov (eds.), *Self-Determination and Secession in International Law* (Oxford: Oxford University Press, 2014) 175-190.

198 *Bibliography*

Watts, A., 'Heads of State', *Max Planck Encyclopaedia of Public International Law* (2010), available at http://opil.ouplaw.com/view/10.1093/law:epil/9780199231690/law-9780199231690-e1418 (visited 5 December 2016).

Watts, S., 'Who Is a Prisoner of War?' in A. Clapham, P. Gaeta, and M. Sassòli (eds.), *The 1949 Geneva Conventions: A Commentary* (Oxford: Oxford University Press, 2015) 890–910.

Wilde, R., *International Territorial Administration: How Trusteeship and the Civilising Mission Never Went Away* (Oxford: Oxford University Press, 2008).

Wilde, R., 'Triggering State Obligations Extraterritorially: The Spatial Test in Certain Human Rights Treaties', 40 *Israel Law Review* (2007) 503–526.

Williamson, J. A., 'Some Considerations on Command Responsibility and Criminal Liability', 90 *International Review of the Red Cross* (2008) 303–317.

Wills, S., 'Occupation Law and Multi-National Operations: Problems and Perspectives', 77 *British Year Book of International Law* (2006) 256–332.

Wilson, H., *International Law and the Use of Force by National Liberation Movements* (Oxford: Clarendon Press, 1988).

Zegveld, L., *Accountability of Armed Opposition Groups in International Law* (Cambridge: Cambridge University Press, 2002).

Zwaak, L., 'General Survey of the European Convention', in P. van Dijk, F. van Hoof, A. van Rijn, and L. Zwaak (eds.), *Theory and Practice of the European Convention on Human Rights* (4th edn., Antwerp; Oxford: Intersentia, 2006) 1–93.

Zwanenburg, M., 'Challenging the Pictet Theory', 885 *International Review of the Red Cross* (2012) 30–36.

Zwanenburg, M., 'United Nations and International Humanitarian Law', *Max Planck Encyclopedia of Public International Law* (2015), available at http://opil.ouplaw.com/view/10.1093/law:epil/9780199231690/law-9780199231690-e1675 (visited 5 December 2016).

Internet and media sources

Agence France-Presse, 'Vladimir Putin Describes Secret Meeting When Russia Decided to Seize Crimea', *Agence France-Presse/The Guardian*, 9 March 2015, at www.theguardian.com/world/2015/mar/09/vladimir-putin-describes-secret-meeting-when-russia-decided-to-seize-crimea (visited 3 January 2017).

Ahren, R., 'Israel Says It "Fulfilled All Its Goals", While Hamas "Hails an Exceptional Victory"', *The Times of Israel*, 22 November 2012, at www.timesofisrael.com/israel-says-it-fulfilled-all-its-goals-while-hamas-hails-an-exceptional-victory-pillar-of-defense-gaza/ (visited 5 January 2017); April 2016, at www.al-monitor.com/pulse/originals/2016/04/israel-hot-pursuits-westbank-incursions-security-pa.html (visited 5 January 2017).

Amer, A. A., 'Does Israel Have Justification to Enter West Bank's Area A?', *Palestine Pulse*, 14, at www.al-monitor.com/pulse/originals/2016/04/israel-hotpursuits-westbank-incursions-security-pa.html (visited 5 January 2017).

Aristotelous, A., 'What Will Be the Strategy of Akinci?' *Cyprus Centre for Strategic Studies*, 8 May 2015, at http://strategy-cy.com/ccss/index.php/el/anaysis-gr/item/276-pia-stratigiki-tha-akoloyuesei-o-akinci-watill-be-the-strategy-of-acinci (visited 3 January 2017).

Artman, V. M., 'Annexation by Passport (Opinion)', *Aljazeera America*, 14 March 2014, at http://america.aljazeera.com/opinions/2014/3/ukraine-russia-crimea passportizationcitizenship.html (visited 3 January 2017).

Bibliography 199

CBC News, 'Russia Blocks Draft Security Council Resolution on Georgia Crisis', *CBC News*, 20 August 2008, at www.cbc.ca/news/world/russia-blocks-draft-security-council-resolution-on-georgia-crisis-1.725452 (visited 5 January 2017).

Civil.Ge, 'Moscow, Sokhumi Sign Treaty on "Alliance and Strategic Partnership"', *Civil.Ge*, 24 November 2014, at www.civil.ge/eng/article.php?id=27845 (visited 3 January 2017).

de Carbonnel, A., 'How the Separatists Delivered Crimea to Moscow', *Reuters*, 12 March 2014, at www.reuters.com/article/us-ukraine-crisis-russia-aksyonov-insigh-idUSBREA2B13M20140312 (visited 3 January 2017).

Emmott, R., 'Putin warns Ukraine Against Implementing EU Deal Letter', *Reuters*, 23 September 2014, at www.reuters.com/article/us-ukraine-crisis-trade-idUSKCN0HI1T820140923 (visited 3 January 2017).

Evripidou, S., 'Turkish Troop Numbers Upped in North', *Cyprus Mail*, 2 July 2013, at http://cyprus-mail.com/2013/07/03/turkish-troop-numbers-upped-in-north/ (visited 3 January 2017).

Fisher, I., 'US Troops Fire on Iraqi Protestors, Leaving 15 Dead', *The New York Times*, 29 April 2003, at www.nytimes.com/2003/04/29/international/worldspecial/29CND-IRAQ.html?pagewanted=all (visited 5 January 2017).

Goldberg, J., 'The West Bank: If It's Not Occupation, Then What Is It?' *The Atlantic*, 9 July 2012, at www.theatlantic.com/international/archive/2012/07/the-west-bank-if-its-not-occupation-then-what-is-it/259562/ (visited 5 January 2017).

Goldstone, R., 'Reconsidering the Goldstone Report on Israel and War Crimes', *The Washington Post*, 1 April 2011, at www.washingtonpost.com/opinions/reconsidering-the-goldstone-report-on-israel-and-war-crimes/2011/04/01/AFg111JC_story.html?utm_term=.e640fa9c296f (visited 3 January 2017).

Hardin, L., and Walker, S., 'Flight MH17 Downed by Russian-Built Missile Dutch Investigators Say', *The Guardian*, 13 October 2015, at www.theguardian.com/world/2015/oct/13/mh17-crash-report-plane-partially-reconstruced-blames-buk-missile-strike (visited 3 January 2017).

The Iraq Museum, *About the Museum*, at www.iraqmuseum.org/pages/about-the-museum/ (visited 5 December 2016).

Jilani, H., Chinkin, C., and Travers, D., 'Goldstone Report: Statement Issued by Members of UN Mission on Gaza War', *The Guardian*, 14 April 2011, at www.theguardian.com/commentisfree/2011/apr/14/goldstone-report-statement-un-gaza (visited 5 January 2017).

Кавказский Узел, Договор между Российской Федерацией и Республикой Южная Осетия о союзничестве и интеграции: www.kavkaz-uzel.ru/articles/259096/ (visited 3 January 2017).

Kershner, I., 'Israeli Concern for Peace Partner', *The Courier*, 27 January 2011, at www.thecourier.com.au/story/915535/israeli-concern-for-peace-partner/ (visited 5 January 2017).

Lazaroff, T., 'Legal Report on Outposts Recommends Authorization', *The Jerusalem Post*, 7 September 2012, at www.jpost.com/Diplomacy-and-Politics/Legal-report-on-outposts-recommends-authorization (visited 5 January 2017).

Malling, J., 'The Value of a Frozen Conflict', *Le Monde Diplomatique*, March 2015, at http://mondediplo.com/2015/03/04transnistria (visited 3 January 2017).

McElroy, D., 'South Ossetia Police Tell Georgians to Take a Russian Passport, or Leave Their Home', *The Telegraph*, 30 August 2008, at www.telegraph.co.uk/news/worldnews/europe/georgia/2651836/South-Ossetian-police-tell-Georgians-to-take-a-Russian-passport-or-leave-their-homes.html (visited 3 January 2017).

200 Bibliography

Millward, D., 'MH17: Russian Separatist Leader Sued for $900 Million by Crash Victims', *The Telegraph*, 16 July 2015, at www.telegraph.co.uk/news/worldnews/europe/ukraine/11742865/MH-17-Russian-separatist-leader-sued-for-900-million-by-crash-victims.html (visited 3 January 2017).

The New York Times, 'The Fall of Baghdad', *The New York Times*, 10 April 2003, at www.nytimes.com/2003/04/10/opinion/the-fall-of-baghdad.html (visited 5 December 2016).

Nikolsky, A., 'Putin Signed Order Appointing Aksyanov as Interim Head of Crimea', *Russian News Agency*, 15 April 2014, at http://tass.ru/en/russia/727839 (visited 3 January 2017).

Phillips, D. L., 'Implementation Review: Six Point Ceasefire Agreement Between Russia and Georgia', *The National Committee on American Foreign Policy*, 10 August 2011, at www.ncafp.org/2016/wp-content/uploads/2011/08/implementation-review-russia-and-georgia-aug2011.pdf (visited 3 January 2017)

President of Georgia, 'Statement on Signing the So-Called "Treaty on Alliance and Integration" Between the Russian Federation and the Occupational Regime of Tskhinvali', at www.president.gov.ge/en/PressOffice/News?9351 (visited 3 January 2017).

PressTV, 'Egypt Closes Rafah Border Crossing After 5 Day Opening', *Middle East Palestine PressTV*, 20 November 2016, at www.presstv.ir/Detail/2016/11/20/494431/Gaza-Rafah-Israel-Egypt (visited 5 January 2017).

Radio Free Europe, 'Leaked MH17 Draft Report Blames Pro-Russian Rebels', *Radio Free Europe*, at www.rferl.org/content/mh17-draft-report-points-to-pro-russian-rebels-ukraine/27130860.html (visited 3 January 2017).

Radio Free Europe, 'Tensions Rise in Georgia's Breakaway Regions', *Radio Free Europe*, 26 August 2013, at www.rferl.org/a/georgia-breakaway-abkhazia-south-ossetia/25086522.html (visited 3 January 2017).

Radio Svaboda, 'Prime Minister of Crimea Declared Crimea Would Support New Elected Ukrainian President', *Radio Svaboda*, 24 February 2014, at https://web.archive.org/web/20140224032704/www.radiosvoboda.org/content/article/25274524.html (visited 3 January 2017).

Rudoren, J., and Barnard, A., 'Israeli Military Invades Gaza, with Sights Set on Hamas Operation', *The New York Times*, 17 July 2014, at www.nytimes.com/2014/07/18/world/middleeast/israel-gaza-strip.html?_r=0 (visited 5 January 2017).

Sassòli, M., 'Protection of Civilians in the Mandates of Military Operations: Legal and Operation Considerations: Interview', *Professionals in Humanitarian Assistance*, 21 January 2015, at https://phap.org/thematic-notes/2015/january/interview-prof-marco-Sassòli- - -protection-civilians-mandates-military-op (visited 5 December 2016).

Shevchenko, V., 'BBC Monitoring "Little Green Men" or "Russian Invaders"', *BBC*, 11 March 2014, at www.bbc.com/news/world-europe-26532154 (visited 3 January 2017).

Swaine, J., 'Russia and Georgia "Agree in Principle" to Nicolas Sarkozy Backed Peace Plan', *The Telegraph*, 13 August 2008, at www.telegraph.co.uk/news/worldnews/europe/georgia/2550129/Russia-and-Georgia-agree-in-principle-to-Nicolas-Sarkozy-backed-peace-plan.html (visited 5 December 2016).

Taştekin, F., 'Northern Cyprus Demands Respect from Turkey', *Turkey Pulse*, 28 April 2015, at www.al-monitor.com/pulse/originals/2015/04/turkey-greece-cypriot-baby-grow-up.html# (visited 3 January 2017).

The Telegraph, 'Ukraine Says It Will Not Fight Russia over Crimea', *The Telegraph*, 12 March 2014, at www.telegraph.co.uk/news/worldnews/europe/ukraine/10692122/Ukraine-says-will-not-fight-Russia-over-Crimea.html (visited 3 December 2016).

Ukraynskaya Pravda, 'У парламенті Криму заявили, що не планують відділятись від України' ('Crimean Parliament Stated They Did Not Plan to Separate from Ukraine'), *Ukraynskaya Pravda*, at www.pravda.com.ua/news/2014/02/26/7016360/ (visited 3 January 2017).

UNIAN, 'Russia Blocks U.N. Security Council Draft on Georgia', 20 August 2008, at www.unian.info/world/138913-russia-blocks-un-security-council-draft-on-georgia.html (visited 5 January 2017).

UN SC Press Release, 'Security Council Holds Third Emergency Meeting as South Ossetia Conflict Intensifies, Expands to Other Parts of Georgia' (SC 9419), 10 August 2008, at www.un.org/press/en/2008/sc9419.doc.htm (visited 5 January 2017).

Voltaire Network, *Declaration of Independence of the Autonomous Republic of Crimea and Sevastopol*, 11 March 2014, at www.voltairenet.org/article182723.html (visited 3 January 2017).

Table of cases

1. International tribunals

International Court of Justice (ICJ)

Accordance of International Law of the Unilateral Declaration of Independence in Respect of Kosovo, Advisory Opinion, 22 July 2010, available at www.icj-cij.org/en/case/141 (visited 15 July 2017).

Application of the International Convention for the Suppression of the Financing of Terrorism and of the International Convention on the Elimination of all Forms of Racial Discrimination (Ukraine v. Russian Federation), Order of 19 April 2017, available at www.icj-cij.org/files/case-related/166/166-20170419-ORD-01-00-EN.pdf (visited 4 April 2019).

Application of the International Convention for the Suppression of the Financing of Terrorism and of the International Convention on the Elimination of All Forms of Racial Discrimination (Ukraine v. Russian Federation), Judgment 8 November 2019, available at https://www.icj-cij.org/files/case-related/166/166-20191108-JUD-01-00-EN.pdf (visited 1 June 2020).

Case Concerning Application of the Convention on the Prevention and Punishment of the Crime of Genocide (Bosnia and Herzegovina v. Serbia and Montenegro), Judgment of 26 February 2007, available at www.icj-cij.org/files/case-related/91/091-20070226-JUD-01-00-EN.pdf (visited 15 July 2017).

Case Concerning Application of the Convention on the Prevention and Punishment of the Crime of Genocide (Bosnia and Herzegovina v. Yugoslavia 1993), Request for the Indication of Provisional Measures, Order of 8 April 1993, available at www.icj-cij.org/en/case/91 (visited 15 July 2017).

Case Concerning Armed Activities on the Territory of the Congo (Democratic Republic of the Congo v. Uganda), Judgment of 19 December 2005, available at www.icj-cij.org/en/case/116 (visited 15 July 2017).

Case Concerning Avena and Other Mexican Nationals (Mexico v. United States of America), Judgment of 31 March 2004, available at www.icj-cij.org/en/case/128 (visited 15 July 2017).

Case Concerning East Timor (Portugal v. Australia), Judgment of 30 June 1995, available at www.icj-cij.org/en/case/84 (visited 5 December 2017).

Case Concerning Gabčíkovo-Nagymaros Project (Hungary v. Slovakia), Judgment of 25 September 1997, available at www.icj-cij.org/en/case/92 (visited 15 July 2017).

Case Concerning Legal Consequences of the Construction of a Wall in the Occupied Palestinian Territory, Advisory Opinion, 9 July 2004, available at www.icj-cij.org/en/case/131 (visited 15 July 2017).

Table of cases   203

Case Concerning Legality of the Threat or Use of Nuclear Weapons, Advisory Opinion of 8 July 1996, available at www.icj-cij.org/en/case/95 (visited 15 July 2017).

Case Concerning Military and Paramilitary activities in and Against Nicaragua (Jurisdiction) (Nicaragua v. USA), Judgment of 26 November 1984, available at www.icj-cij.org/en/case/70 (visited 15 July 2017).

Legal Consequences of the Separation of the Chagos Archipelago from Mauritius in 1965, Advisory Opinion, 25 February 2019, available at www.icj-cij.org/files/case-related/169/169-20190225-01-00-EN.pdf (visited 4 April 2019).

Legal Consequences for States of the Continued Presence South Africa in Namibia (South West Africa) Notwithstanding Security Council Resolution (276) (1970), Advisory Opinion of 21 June 1971, available at www.icj-cij.org/en/case/53 (visited 15 July 2017).

Questions of Interpretation and Application of the 1971 Montreal Convention arising from the Arial Incident at Lockerbie (Libyan Arab Jamahiriya v. USA), Provisional Measures Order of 14 April 1992, available at www.icj-cij.org/en/case/89 (visited 15 July 2017).

Reparation for Injuries Suffered in the Service of the United Nations, Advisory Opinion of 11 April 1949, available at www.icj-cij.org/en/case/4 (visited 15 July 2017).

Western Sahara, Advisory Opinion of 16 October 1975, available at www.icj-cij.org/en/case/61 (visited 15 July 2017).

International Criminal Court (ICC)

The Prosecutor v. Jean-Pierre Bemba Gombo (ICC-01/05–01/08), Pre-Trial Chamber II, 15 June 2009.

The Prosecutor v. Jean-Pierre Bemba Gombo (ICC-01/05–01/08 66/364), Trial Chamber III, 21 March 2016.

International Criminal Tribunal for the Former Yugoslavia (ICTY)

Judgment, *Aleksovski* (IT-95–14/1-T), Trial Chamber, 25 June 1999.

Judgment, *Blaškić* (IT-95–14-IT), Trial Chamber, 3 March 2000.

Judgment, *Delalić, Mucić, Delić and Landžo (Celebici Case)* (IT-96–21-A), Appeals Chamber, 20 February 2001.

Judgment, *Hadžihasanović* (IT-01–47-A), Appeals Chamber, 22 April 2008.

Judgment, *Halilović* (IT-01–48-A), Appeals Chamber, 16 October 2007.

Judgment, *Kordić and Čerkez* (IT-95–14/2-T), Trial Chamber, 26 February 2001.

Judgment, *Kunarac* (IT-96–23-T and IT-96–23/1-T), Trial Chamber, 22 February 2001.

Judgment, *Naletilić and Martinović* (IT-98–34-T), Trial Chamber, 31 March 2003.

Judgment, *Orić* (IT-03–68-A), Appeals Chamber, 3 July 2008.

Judgment, *Perišić* (IT-04–81-T), Trial Chamber, 6 September 2011.

Judgment, *Prlić et al.* (IT-04–74-A), Appeals Chamber, 29 November 2017.

Judgment, *Tadić* (IT-94–1-A), Appeals Chamber, 15 July 1999.

International Criminal Tribunal for Rwanda (ICTR)

Judgment, *Akayesu* (ICTR-96–4-T), Trial Chamber, 2 September 1998.

Judgment, *Bagilishema* (ICTR-95–1A-A), Appeals Chamber, 3 July 2002.

204   Table of cases

Judgment, *Bagosora et al.* (ICTR-98–41-T) Trial Chamber I, 18 December 2008.
Judgment, *Gacumbitsi* (ICTR-2001–64-A), Appeals Chamber, 7 July 2006.
Judgment, *Kajelijeli* (ICTR-98–44A-A), Appeals Chamber, 23 May 2005.
Judgment, *Kajelijeli* (ICTR-98–44A-T), Trial Chamber, 1 December 2003.
Judgment, *Kayishema* (ICTR-95–1-T), Trial Chamber, 21 May 1999.
Judgment, *Musema* (ICTR-96–13-A), Trial Chamber, 27 January 2000.
Judgment, *Nahimana* (ICTR-99–52-A), Appeals Chamber, 28 November 2007.

Special Court for Sierra Leone

Judgment, *Brima et al.* (SCSL-04–16-T), Trial Chamber, 20 June 2007.
Judgment, *Fofana and Kondewa* (SCSL-04–14-T), Trial Chamber, 2 August 2007.

International military tribunals on WWII

France et al. v. Göring et al. (1946) 22 IMT 203, 13 ILR 203.
High Command Trial, *The United States of America v. Wilhelm von Leeb et al.*, Judgment of 27 October 1948, US Military Tribunal Nuremberg, available at http://werle.rewi.hu-berlin.de/High%20Command%20Case.pdf (visited 2 December 2016).
Hostages Case, US Military Tribunal, Judgment of 19 February 1948, Nuremberg.
Josef Altstötter et al., US Military Tribunal Nuremberg (the Justice Cases), Judgment of 4 December 1947, available at http://werle.rewi.hu-berlin.de/Justice%20Case%20Judgment.pdf (visited 2 December 2016).
Trial of Wilhelm List et al., United States Military Tribunal Nuremberg, 8 July 1947 to 19 February 1948 (Case No. 47) at 71, available at www.loc.gov/rr/frd/Military_Law/pdf/Law-Reports_Vol-8.pdf (visited 2 December 2016).

European Commission on Human Rights

Cyprus v. Turkey (App. nos. 6780/74 and 6950/75), decision of 26 May 1975 on the admissibility of the applications.
Sanchez Ramirez v. France (App. no. 28780/95), decision of 24 June 1996 on the admissibility of the application.

European Court of Human Rights (ECtHR)

Adali v. Turkey, ECtHR (2005) (App. no. 38187/97).
Al-Jedda v. United Kingdom, ECtHR (2011) (App. no. 27021/08).
Al-Saadoon and Mufdhi v. United Kingdom, ECtHR (2009) (App. no. 61498/08).
Al-Skeini and Others v. the United Kingdom, ECtHR (2011) (App. no. 55721/07).
Andreau v. Turkey, ECtHR (2009) (App. no. 45653/99).
Banković et al. v. Belgium et al., ECtHR (2001) (Grand Chamber Decision as to the Admissibility of) (App. no. 52207/99).
Catan and Others v. the Republic of Moldova and Russia, ECtHR (2012) (App. nos. 43370/04, 8252/05 and 18454/06).
Chiragov and Others v. Armenia, ECtHR (2015) (App. no 13216/05).
Cyprus v. Turkey, ECtHR (2001) (25781/94).
Demades v. Turkey, ECtHR (2003) (App. no. 16219/90).

Table of cases 205

Djavit v. Turkey, ECtHR (2003) (Appl. no. 25781/94).
Drozd and Janousek v. France and Spain, ECtHR (1992) (App. no. 12747/87).
Ergi v. Turkey, ECtHR (1998) (App. no. 66/1997/850/1057).
Hassan v. the United Kingdom, ECtHR (2014) (App. no. 29750/09).
Ilaşcu and Others v. Moldova and Russia, ECtHR (2004) (App. no. 48787/99).
Issa and Others v. Turkey, ECtHR (2004) (App. no 31821/96).
Isaak v. Turkey, ECtHR (2008) (App. no. 44587/98).
Ivanţoc and Others v. Moldova and Russia, ECtHR (2011) (App. no. 23687/05).
Jaloud v. The Netherlands, ECtHR (2014) (App. no. 47708/08).
Loizidou v. Turkey, ECtHR (Judgment) (1996) (App. no. 15318/89).
Loizidou v. Turkey, ECtHR (Preliminary Objections) (1995) (App. no. 15318/89).
M. v. Denmark, ECtHR (1992) (App. no 17392/90).
Medvedyev and Others v. France, ECtHR (2010) (App. no. 3394/03).
Mozer v. the Republic of Moldova and Russia, ECtHR (2016) (App. No. 11138/10).
Nada v. Switzerland, ECtHR (2012) (App. no. 10593/08).
Öcalan v. Turkey, ECtHR (2005) (App. no. 46221/99).
Pad and Others v. Turkey, ECtHR (2007) (App. no. 60167/00) (as to the admissibility of application).
Sargsyan v. Azerbaijan, ECtHR (2015) (App. no. 40167/06).
Solomou and Others v. Turkey, ECtHR (2008) (App. no. 36832/97).

UN Human Rights Committee

Chitat Ng v. Canada, Communication No 469/1991, UN Doc. CCPR/C/49/D/469/1991 (1994).
Kindler v. Canada, Communication No 470/1991, UN Doc. CCPR/C/48/D/470/1991 (1993).
Lilian Celiberti de Casariego v. Uruguay, Communication No. 56/1979, UN Doc. CCPR/C/OP/1 (1984).
Mabel Pereira Montero v. Uruguay, Communication No. 106/1981, UN Doc. CCPR/C/OP/2 (1990).
Sergio Euben Lopez Burgos v. Uruguay, Communication No. 12/52, UN Doc. A/36/40 (1981).

Inter-American Commission on Human Rights

Alejandre Jr and Others v. Republica de Cuba (Brothers to the Rescue) 11.589, Report no. 86/99 OEA (1999).
Coard vs. United States, 10.951, Report no. 109/99 (1999).
Franklin Guillermo Aisalla Molina (Ecuador v. Colombia), Report no. 112/10 (2011).
Precautionary Measure 259/02 – Detainees Held by the United States in Guantanamo Bay, Cuba (13 March 2002).

Inter-American Court of Human Rights

Case of the Santo Domingo Massacre v. Colombia, Preliminary Objections, Merits and Reparations, IACtHR, Judgment of 30 November 2012.
State Obligations in Relation to the Environment in the Context of the Protection and Guarantee of the Rights to Life and to Personal Integrity: Interpretation and Scope of

206 *Table of cases*

Articles 4(1) and 5(1) in Relation to Articles 1(1) and 2 of the American Convention on Human Rights, IACtHR, Advisory Opinion of 15 November 2017.

Eritrea-Ethiopia Claims Commission

Eritrea-Ethiopia Claims Commission – Partial Award: Western Front, Aerial Bombardment and Related Claims – Eritrea's Claims 1, 3, 5, 9–13, 14, 21, 25 and 26 (19 December 2005).

Iran-United States Claims Tribunal

Yeager v. Islamic Republic of Iran (1987), Iran-United States Claims Tribunal Reports, Vol. 17 (Cambridge: Grotius, 1988).

2. UN resolutions

Security council

42 (1948)
216 (1965)
217 (1965)
242 (1967)
276 (1970)
385 (1976)
446 (1976)
435 (1978)
465 (1980)
478 (1980)
484 (1980)
541 (1983)
550 (1984)
660 (1990)
662 (1990)
678 (1990)
687 (1991)
690 (1991)
745 (1992)
822 (1993)
844 (1993)
853 (1993)
874 (1993)
884 (1993)
1244 (1999)
1327 (2000)
1397 (2002)
1402 (2002)
1483 (2003)
1546 (2004)
1593 (2005)

2042 (2012)
2202 (2015)
2334 (2016)

General assembly

181 (II), 29 November 1947
2145 (XXI), 27 October 1966
62/243, 14 March 2008
62/249, 15 May 2008
68/262, 27 March 2014

3. National courts

Canada

Reference re Secession of Quebec, Supreme Court of Canada (1998) 2. SCR 217, 1998 CanLII 793 (SCC)

Belgium

Cour Militaire Belge, Jugement Concernant des Violations du Droit Humanitaire Commises en Somalie et au Rwanda, Nr. 54 A.R. 1997, 20 Novembre 1997, *Journal des Tribunaux*, 14 Avril 1998.

Greece

Judgment, *In re G.* (Criminal Court of Heraklion) (Crete) (1943–1945) 12 AD 437 Case No 151.

Israel

High Court of Justice, Israel 102/82, *Tsemel v. Minister of Defence*, 37 (3), P.D. (1983).

High Court of Justice, Israel 7957/04, *Mara'abe v. the Prime Minister of Israel* (judgment of 21 June 2005).

High Court of Justice, Israel 9593/04, *Rashed Morar, Head of Yanun Village Council and Others v. IDF Commander in Judea and Samaria* (a petition, 26 June 2006).

High Court of Justice, Israel 769/02, *Public Committee Against Torture v. Government* (a petition, 14 December 2006).

High Court of Justice, Israel 9132/07, *Jaber Al-Bassiouni v. Prime Minister, Minister of Defence* (Judgment of 30 January 2008).

High Court of Justice, Israel 201/09 and 248/09, *Physicians for Human Rights and Others v. Prime Minister of Israel et al., and Gisha Legal Centre for Freedom of Movement and Others v. Minister of Defense* (Judgment of 19 January 2009).

High Court of Justice, Israel 2164/09, *Yesh Din Volunteers for Human Rights, et. al. v. Commander of the IDF Forces in the West Bank, et. al.* (Judgment of 26 December 2011).

208 *Table of cases*

Japan

Tokyo (District Court) Claims for Compensation for Forced Labor in Siberia, *Tomoya Kanbayashi et al. vs. Japan*, Judgment of 4 April 1989.

United States Military Commission

Trial of General Tomoyuki Yamashita (Case No. 21) (IV Law Reports of Trials of War Criminals, United States Military Commission, Manila, 8th October–7th December, 1945), available at www.loc.gov/rr/frd/Military_Law/pdf/Law-Reports_Vol-4.pdf (visited 2 December 2016).

United Kingdom

Al-Skeini and Others v. Secretary for Defence [2004] EWHC 2911.
Al-Skeini and Others (Appellants) v. Secretary of State for Defence (Respondent) [2007] UKHL 26.
R (on the Application of Al-Jedda) (FC) (Appellant) v. Secretary of State For Defence (Respondent), Opinion of Lord Bingham of Cornhill, House of Lords, Session 2007–08, on appeal from [2006] EWCA Civ 327.
R (on the Application of Mazin Mumaa Galteh Al-Skeini and Others) v. Secretary of State for Defence [2005] EWCA Civ 1609 (leading judgment by Lord Justice Brooke).
Smith and Others (FC) (Appellants) v. The Ministry of Defence (Respondent) [2013] UKSC 41.

The Netherlands

The Hague Court of Appeal, *Nuhanović v. Netherlands*, Appeal Judgment, 5 July 2011, ILDC 1742 (NL 2011).

4. Other relevant documents

National legislation

Coalition Provisional Authority Regulation Number 1.
Constitution of the Crimean Republic, 11 April 2014.
Constitution of the Russian Federation of 1993, as amended by 21 March 2014.
Constitution of Ukraine of 1996 (amended by 21 February 2014).
Israel Ministry of Foreign Affairs, The Cabinet Resolution Regarding the Disengagement Plan, 6 June 2004.
Israel Military Order No. 947 Concerning the Establishment of a Civilian Administration (Judea and Samaria).

Laws on admitting Crimea and Sevastopol to the Russian Federation, 21 March 2014

One Hundred Fifteenth Congress of the United States of America, An Act, H.R. 244, Occupation of the Georgian Territories of Abkhazia and Tskhinvali Region/South Ossetia.

The Military Doctrine of the Republic of Armenia, Preface, Ministry of Defence of Armenia, 2015.

National commissions

The Levy Commission Report, *The Legal Status of Building in Judea and Samaria* (Jerusalem, 2012).

Agreements and peace plans

Agreed Documents on Movement and Access from and to Gaza, Agreement on Movement and Access (AMA) and Agreed Principles for Rafah Crossing, 15 November 2005.

Georgia: The 6 Point Plan, 14 August 2008, Embassy of France in Washington DC, 8 September 2008.

Israeli-Palestinian 'Interim Agreement on the West Bank and the Gaza Strip' (Oslo II), 28 September 1995.

Index

Note: page numbers in *italic* indicate a figure. Page numbers followed by 'n' indicate a note.

Abizaid, John 107
Abkhazia 70–72, 81
access to occupied territory 19
actual control 32–35, 36, 104
Additional Protocol I of 1977 (AP I 1977) 13; Article 1 2, 21, 23–24, 45, 95, 105, 134, 139, 158; Article 3 100–102; Article 74 95; Article 75 167
Additional Protocol II of 1977 (AP II 1977) 43n177, 124
Afghanistan 105
Agreement on Movement and Access (AMA) 116
Akande, D. 85
Al-Jedda v. United Kingdom 49
Al-Saadoon and Mufdhi v. United Kingdom 145
Al-Skeini and Others v. UK 144, 154–155, 163
annexation and occupation, interrelationship between 72–74
Armed Activities on the Territory of Congo 29
armed groups, control over 53, 55–57, 123–124; Article 4 GC III 83–86, *85*; Article 29 GC IV 86–87; control of Uganda over MLC 59–61, *60*; critical appraisal 61–65; Croatia and Croatian Defence Council 57–59, *59*; territorial aspirations 56–57
armed resistance: and effective control 26; fighting on behalf of party of conflict 83, 84; occupation without 22; and temporary loss of control over parts of territory 107

Armenia 74–75, 156–158
authority 19, 25, 37; ability of enemy foreign forces to exert 33, 34; assuming for maintenance of security 155–156; and control 2, 14–15; and control retained over territory after withdrawal 113, 118, 120–121; and ending of occupation 91–92, 102, 103, 104, 108; exercising 16, 25, 26, 27, 32, 33–34, 91–92, 103, 137; extent of 121; of occupying power, beginning of 37–38; over individuals, and IHRL applicability 144–148, *145*; sharing of 34–35; substitution of 25, 27, 33; ultimate control and authority 9, 48–50
Azerbaijan 74–75, 158, 161

Ben-Naftali, O. 100n47
Benvenisti, E. 31, 54, 64–65
Bingham, Lord 49
Blaškić case 57, 58
Bosnia-Herzegovina conflict 10n26
Bothe, M. 139, 140
Bowring, B. 77
Bremer, Paul 107
Brussels Declaration of 1874 14–15, 91–92
Buergenthal, T. 167

Canadian Military Manual 102
Catan and Others v. the Republic of Moldova and Russia 76
Chiragov and Others v. Armenia 156
civilian population, exercising authority over 26

Index 211

Coalition Provisional Authority (CPA) 39, 40, 129

coerced consent 30

complete dependency 3–4, 9–10; control over armed groups 60, 61; control over de facto authorities 81–82

complete end of control over territory 105

conduct of hostilities model 96, 96n27, 96n29, 97, 138

Congo Liberation Movement (MLC), control of Uganda over 59–61, *60*

consent 172; absence of 30–32, 45; control over de facto authorities 78–81; and effective control 29–32; and end of military occupation 103–104, 108, 130; forms of 30; peacekeeping *v.* peace-enforcement 43; and UN multinational force deployment 42, 44–45

Convention on the Rights of the Child 150

Convention (IV) Respecting the Laws and Customs of War on Land and Its Annex: Regulations Concerning the Laws and Customs of War on Land *see* Hague Regulations 1907 (HR 1907)

Crimea 67–68; Russian occupation of 22, 34, 36, 74

Croatian Defence Council (HVO), control of Croatia over 57–59, *59*

Cyprus 68–70, 77, 82

Cyprus v. Turkey 70

Czechoslovakia 22

decisive influence 4, 55, 75, 76–78, *78*, 88–89, 158, 173

de facto authorities, control over 53, 55–57, 66–67, 123–124; and annexation 73–74; Crimea 67–68; critical appraisal 81–83; Cyprus 68–70, 77, 82; decisive influence 75, 76–78, *78*; Georgia 70–72, 74; military presence and consent 78–81; Moldova 75–76, 77; Nagorno Karabakh 74–75

de facto regimes 66

de facto states 66–67

degrees of control 136–140, *175*; *see also* level of control for establishing occupation

Democratic Republic of Congo (DRC) v. Uganda 29, 31–32, 33n112, 59–61, 150–151, 166

Draper, G. I. A. D. 167

duration of occupation 16, 92, 94, 98, 101

effective control 7n16, 13, 17, 20, 25–27, 52, 173; actual *v.* potential control 32–35; and annexation 73; and Common Article 2 GCs 22; consent 29–32; control over armed groups 60, 61, 62, 63, 65, 88; control over de facto authorities 73, 75, 76, 77, 82; control retained over territory after withdrawal 117, 118, 119, 121; and decisive influence 77; and end of military occupation 101, 102, 103, 106, 125, 130–131, 132; exercising authority 25, 26, 27; explicit criteria 24; former occupant's military capacity to re-assert 108; and general close of military operations 95; implicit criteria 24–25; and intermediary occupation 54, 88, 173; intermittent 63; international criminal law 5, 172; international human rights law 6, 143, 164; joint and shared control 38–52; law of state responsibility 7, 9–11, 36, 48, 50, 54, 60, 61; military presence 28–29; MNF control over territory 39–41; over persons 136, 137, 162, 164; over territory 151, 152, 153, 154, 156, 157, 158, 159, 161, 162, 164; and proxy occupation 64–65; and public order and safety 26–27; for qualifying situation as occupation 35–38; responsibility of UN and troop-contributing states 46–52; and state responsibility 63, 64; and substantive obligations 134, 141–142; transfer of 102; UN operations 41–46, 173; UNSC endorsed 131

effective overall control 7, 69–70, 146, 151–154, 159

effectivity 15, 37, 91

Egypt 42, 115, 116

engineered consent 30

European Convention on Human Rights (ECHR) 152–153, 156, 160,

212 Index

161, 164; Article 1 76, 146, 147, 160; Article 2 146; Article 8 158; situational application of 165
European Court of Human Rights (ECtHR) 50–51, 143–144, 174; authority and control over individuals 144–146, *145*; control over territory 151–155, 156–158, 160, 161; decisive influence 4, 55, 75, 76–78, *78*; effective overall control 7, 69–70, 82, 151–154, 159; ultimate control and authority 9, 48–50
external self-determination 80, 81

Ferraro, T. 42, 54
Fourth Geneva Convention (GC IV 1949) 38, 53, 65, 98, 120, 121–122, 135; application threshold 136; Article 4 8, 134, 138, 139, 147, 170, 176; Article 6 93, 94, 95–100, 100n47; Article 6(1) 139; Article 6(3) 34, 98; Article 24 141; Article 27 141; Article 29 53, 86–87, 173; Article 47 34, 35, 73–74, 118, 124; Article 49 136; Article 50 34, 35, 136; Article 55 35; Article 56 34, 35; forms and degrees of control in 136–140; and relinquishing control over territory 93–95, 141; situational application of 137, 139, 140, 141, 164, *165*
Fraenkel, E. 163
freedom of movement 115, 116–117
full ongoing obligations 122
functional application of state obligations 38, 120–121, 133, 136, 137, 140, 164

Gaber Al-Bassiouni v. Prime Minister 113
Gaja, G. 48
Gaza Strip 28, 112–123, 163
Gbagbo, Laurent 66
Geneva Conventions of 1949 (GCs 1949) 13, 133; and Article 1 AP I 1977 23; Common Article 2 2, 21–22, 42, 43, 45, 95, 101, 105, 107, 134, 139, 140; Common Article 3 42, 43, 124; grave breaches 57, 84, 135
Georgia 70–72, 74
Girkin, Igor 63
Gisha 28

Goldstone Report 113–114, 115

Hague Conferences 17–20, 92
Hague Court of Appeal 50
Hague Regulations 1907 (HR 1907) 13, 53; application threshold 136; Article 2 137n15; Article 42 2, 20–21, 22, 24–25, 29, 30, 32, 33, 36, 43, 45, 52, 95, 97, 101, 102–103, 105, 117, 119, 134, 136, 137, 139, 140, 152, 154, 155, 157, 158, 172, 175; Article 43 26, 38, 97, 119, 130, 150, 155, 164; Article 55 117–118n145
Hamas 113–114, 116, 119, 163
Hassan v. UK 155–156
Hope, Lord 161–162
horizontal sharing of authority 34
hostilities: active hostilities framework 169; conduct of hostilities model 96, 96n27, 96n29, 97, 138; and effective control 22; termination of 95–98, 99
Human Rights Committee 143, 149–150, 151

Ilaşcu and Others v. Moldova and Russia 76, 157, 160
ILC Articles on Responsibility of States for Internationally Wrongful Acts (2001): Article 4 3–4, 60, 61, 81, 86, 157–158; Article 5 60; Article 8 7–8, 61, 86
ILC Articles on the Responsibility of International Organisations 49, 52; Article 4 56; Article 7 7, 46, 49, 50, 52, 173; Article 17.2 7, 49
Imseis, A. 99
indirect effective control *see* intermediary, occupation by
Inter-American Commission of Human Rights 143
intermediary, occupation by 53, 54, 173; allegiance of agents to occupying power 87; armed groups, control over 55–65; de facto authorities, control over 55–57, 66–83; ending of 123–125; indirect effective control 11, 53, 55, *59*, 67, 70, 74, 78, 81, 87–88, *88*, 173; members of party to conflict 83–86, *85*; potentiality of Article 29 GC IV 86–87; subordinate governments, control over 55–57
internal self-determination 79–80

Index 213

international armed conflicts (IACs) 1, 10n26, 45, 54, 127; active hostilities framework and security operations framework 169; Belgian peacekeeping actions in Somalia 41–42; classification of NIACs as 10, 54, 65, 86, 173; conduct of hostilities 96; Gaza–Israel conflict as 119–120; in Iraq 130; and NIACs, coexistence of 130

International Committee of the Red Cross (ICRC) 13, 34, 40, 45, 70, 77, 120–121

International Convention for the Suppression of the Financing of Terrorism of 9 December 1999 (ICSFT) 63–64n46

International Convention on the Elimination of All Forms of Racial Discrimination of 21 December 1965 (CERD) 63n46

International Court of Justice (ICJ) 3, 7, 10, 37, 109n85, 143, 174; on annexation 73; on applicability of IHRL instruments 149, 150–151; on control over armed groups 59–61; on inter-application of IHRL and IHL 166; interpretation of Article 6 GC IV 99; on military presence 29, 32; Namibia Advisory Opinion 131; on self-determination 80n140; on substitution of authority 33

International Covenant on Civil and Political Rights (ICCPR) 149, 150, 151

International Covenant on Economic, Social and Cultural Rights (ICESCR) 150

international criminal law (ICL) 3, 5, 172

International Criminal Tribunal for the Former Yugoslavia (ICTY) 3, 10, 10n26, 35–36; on application of occupation law 138–139; on belonging to party to conflict 84; effective control 7; overall control test 7, 8n21, 56, 57–59, 62; on relationship between de facto organs/agents and foreign power 57

International Declaration Concerning the Laws and Customs of War *see* Brussels Declaration of 1874

international humanitarian law (IHL) 1, 3, 11, 90, 172, 174, 175; and IHRL, inter-application 166–170; *lex specialis* nature of 169; members of party to conflict 83–86, *85*; overall control test 7–8, 8n21, 10, 11, 36, 53, 54, 56, 57–59, 64, 87–88, *88*, 123–124, 123n173, 173; perspective, of substantive obligations 135–142; potentiality of Article 29 GC IV 86–87

international human rights law (IHRL) 3, 134, 135, 172, 174; authority and control over individuals 144–148, *145*, 160; construal of control in 142–162; contextual approach to 162–165; control over territory 148–160, *159*; degrees of obligations according to specific contexts 159–162; effective control 6, 143, 164; effective overall control 7, 151–154, 159; exercise of jurisdiction 142–143; and IHRL, inter-application 166–170

International Law Commission 167n156

International Law Institute 16

international territorial administration 44

invasion phase: applicability of GC IV during 136–137, 147; substantive obligations during 38, 134, 136–137, 139–140; transition into occupation 138

Iraq, US invasion of: effective control 37, 38; multinational force 38, 39, 129–130; sovereignty of new government 129; temporary loss of control over parts of territory 106–107; and UNSC Resolution 1546 128–132

Iraq-Kuwait Boundary Demarcation Resolution 127

Israel 36; control over Gaza Strip 28, 112–123, 163; occupation of West Bank 108–112; Wall case 29, 73, 99, 109n85, 149–150

Israeli Defence Force (IDF) 111, 113, 114

Issa and Others v. Turkey 144–145, 153

Ivorian election crisis (2011) 66

Jaloud v. The Netherlands 146

Jenks, W. 169

Jomini, Antoine-Henri 16

214   Index

jurisdiction: authority and control over individuals 144, 145, 146–147; control over territory 149–150, 151–153, 154, 155, 156, 158; and extraterritorial application of IHRL 142–143; and intermediary occupation 76, 82, 83
jus ad bellum 42, 44, 131, 132
jus in bello 42, 44, 54, 132

Kennan, G. F. 124n174
Kooijmans, Pieter 33
Kosovo: independent statehood of 66, 80; NATO's intervention in 131
Kuwait, Iraqi invasion of 38–39, 131

law enforcement model 96, 96n29, 97
law of state responsibility (SR) 3, 11, 51, 172; attribution mechanism in 10n26; complete dependency 3–4, 9–10, 61, 81–82; effective control 7, 9–11, 36, 48, 50, 54, 60, 61; overall control test 7–8, 8n21, 10, 36, 53, 54, 56, 57–59, 64, 87–88, *88*, 123–124, 123n173, 173; total control 4, 56
legal authorities, status of 19
level of control for establishing occupation 2, 13; Article 1 AP I 1977 23–24; Article 42 HR 1907 20–21, 22, 24–25; Brussels conference 14–16; Common Article 2 GCs 21–22; Hague Conference 17–20; Oxford Manual of 1880 16–17; *see also* effective control
Levy, Edmond 109
Levy Report 109
lex specialis principle 166, 169
lines of communication 18, 92
Loizidou v. Turkey 69, 70, 152–153
long arm occupation 53
Lubell, N. 162

McDonald, Gabrielle Kirk 86
Manual of the Laws and Customs of War at Oxford (1880) *see* Oxford Manual of 1880
Mara'abe v. The Prime Minister of Israel 110
Martens Clause 167, 167n156
Medvedyev and Others v. France 145
Melzer, N. 84
MH17 flight, downing of 63–64

military manuals 33, 102
military operations, general close of: armed group not affiliated with state 97; and Article 6 GC IV 95–100; conduct of hostilities model 96, 96n27, 96n29, 97; law enforcement model 96, 96n29, 97; one-year rule 93, 94, 98
Military Order No. 947 (Israel) 36
military presence 18, 172; and absence of consent 30; and control over de facto authorities 78–81; and control over territory after withdrawal 112; and effective control 28–29; and end of military occupation 103, 104, 105
militias 83–84
Mirzayev, F. 77
missing reversioner theory 109
Moldavian Republic of Transdniestria (MRT) 75–76, 77, *78*, 152, 160
Moldova 75–76, 77, 160
Motoc, Iulia Antoanella 156
Mozer v. the Republic of Moldova and Russia 76
multinational force (MNF): control exercised by 38, 39–41, 173; UN operations 41–46, 173; US invasion of Iraq 38, 39, 129–130

Nada v. Switzerland 50–51
Nagorno Karabakh 74–75, 156–158
Naletilić and Martinović case 58, 138
Namibia, South African occupation of 32, 131, 148–149
NATO 9, 48, 131
Nazi Germany 55
Netanyahu, Benjamin 109
non-international armed conflicts (NIACs) 1, 7, 11; active hostilities framework and security operations framework 169; and armed groups 53, 54; and conduct of hostilities 96, 97; and IACs, coexistence of 130; as IACs, classification 10, 54, 65, 86, 173; in Iraq 130; overall control test 62–63
normative control 7, 49–50
Northern Cyprus *see* Turkish Republic of Northern Cyprus (TRNC)
Nuclear Weapons case 166
Nuhanović v. Netherlands 50

Öcalan v. Turkey Judgment 144
Olson, L. M. 169

ongoing obligations 122
Operation Cast Lead 113, 119
Operation Defensive Shield 111
Operation Phantom Fury 107
Operation Pillar of Defence 114
Operation Protective Edge 114
Operation Vigilant Resolve 107
Oppenheim, L. 118
Oslo I Accord 110, 119
Oslo II Accord 110–111, 119
Ouattara, Alassane 66
overall control test 7–8, 8n21, 10, 11,
    36, 49, 53; for conflict classification
    62; control over armed groups
    57–59, 62, 64, 65; control over de
    facto authorities 69, 75, 82; and
    decisive influence 77; and end of
    occupation 123, 123n173, 124,
    125; and intermediary occupation
    54, 56, 57, 87–88, 88, 123,
    123n173, 173; members of party to
    conflict 85–86; state responsibility
    62, 64
Oxford Manual of 1880 16–17, 92

pacific occupation 31
Palchetti, P. 49
Palestinian Liberation Organization
    (PLO) 110
paramilitary groups 83–84
partial effective control 121
partial loss of control over parts of
    territory 106–107, 141–142
partial ongoing obligations 122
past violations, obligations raised based
    on 123
peacekeeping: operations, UN 41–46,
    173; troop-contributing states,
    attribution of responsibility to 47; v.
    peace enforcement 43–44
Pétain, Philippe 55
Pictet, Jean 21–22, 74, 84, 86, 87, 94,
    124, 136, 137, 166
Pilloud, Claude 98, 100
potential control 32–35, 36, 104
potential for regaining control 108–112
Prlić et al. case 58
protected persons 8, 86; and annexation
    73; control over 40–41; and
    relinquishing control over territory
    94–95, 120; state obligations
    regarding 136, 138, 139, 140, 148,
    167

protection gap 33, 35, 65, 86, 87
Protocol Additional to the Geneva
    Conventions of 12 August 1949, and
    relating to the Protection of Victims
    of International Armed Conflicts of
    8 June 1977 see Additional Protocol
    I of 1977 (AP I 1977)
proxy occupation 33, 63, 64–65, 74,
    82, 89
puppet governments 55–56, 81, 104

Rajić, Ivica 57
relinquishing control over territory
    90–91, 173–174; Article 3 AP I 1977
    100–102; Article 6 GC IV and
    general close of military operations
    95–100; Brussels Declaration of 1874
    91–92; complete end of control over
    territory 105; control retained over
    territory after withdrawal 112–123;
    functional ending of occupation
    120–121, 133; and GC IV 93–95;
    Hague Conferences 92; Iraq and
    UNSC Resolution 1546 128–132;
    legal history 91–104; level of control
    for ending occupation 102–103;
    needed test for 102–103; occupation
    by intermediary 123–125; one-year
    rule 93, 94, 98; potential for regaining
    control 108–112; temporary/partial
    loss of control over parts of territory
    106–107; UN Security Council
    125–128
remote control 28
residual obligations 93, 122
respect of private and public property 135
Revolutionary United Front (Sierra
    Leone) 54
right to life 146, 164, 167
Roberts, A. 129, 130
Rumsfeld, Donald 107
Russia 122; and Crimea 22, 34, 36,
    67–68; and Georgia 70–72, 74; and
    Moldova 75–76, 77, 160
Russian-Georgian war (2008) 31, 71,
    128

Sargsyan v. Azerbaijan 158, 161
Sarkozy, Nicolas 31, 71
Sassòli, M. 29–30, 54, 58, 64–65, 82,
    136, 164, 169
Schmitt, M. N. 38, 130
Scobbie, I. 119–120

216 *Index*

Sedley, Lord Justice 163
self-defence, UN MNF use of force in 42
self-determination 23, 79–81, 80n140,
118
Shraga, D. 42
Six-Day War (1967) 108
Smith v. Ministry of Defence 161–162
Solomou and Others v. Turkey 146
Somalia, Belgian peacekeeping actions
in 41–42
South Africa, occupation of Namibia 32,
131, 148–149
Southern Rhodesia 127
South Ossetia 70–72
South West Africa 32
Soviet Union 105
Special Court of Sierra Leone 54
state agent authority and control test 8,
144–145, *145*, 147, 155, 162, 170
status of forces agreement (SOFA) 42
status of mission agreement (SOMA) 42
subordinate governments, control over
55–57
substantive obligations 134, 174;
assuming for maintenance of security
155–156; authority and control
over individuals 144–148, *145*, 160;
contextual approach to 162–165;
control over territory 148–160,
159; degrees of IHRL obligations
according to specific contexts
159–162; and effective overall
control 151–154, 159; forms
and degrees of control in GC IV
136–140; functional application 38,
120–121, 133, 136, 137, 140, 164;
IHL and IHRL inter-application
166–170; from IHL perspective
135–142; sliding scale approach 140,
161, 164; specific rights, control over
146, 164; during temporary/partial
loss of control over parts of territory
141–142

Tadić case 56, 57, 62, 65, 83, 86
temporary loss of control over parts of
territory 106–107, 141–142
Third Geneva Convention (GC III):
Article 4 53, 83–86, *85*, 173; Article
105 168; Article 118 99
Tomuschat, C. 152
total control 4, 56

Transdniestria 75–76, 77, *78*, 152, 160
Treaty on Alliance and Integration,
Russia–South Ossetia 72
Treaty on Alliance and Strategic
Partnership, Russia–Abkhazia 72
Tsemel v. Minister of Defence 35
Turkish Republic of Northern Cyprus
(TRNC) 68–70, 82, 152–153

Uganda Peoples' Defence Forces
(UPDF) 60
UK Court of Appeal 161
ultimate control and authority 9,
48–50
UN Charter 125; Article 2.4 72; Article
25 126; Article 41 126, 127; Article
42 126; Article 103 126, 132
UN General Assembly (GA) 32,
75, 131; Resolution 68/262 68;
Resolution 2145 (XXI) (1966) 32
United Kingdom 97; and invasion of
Iraq 39, 40, 49, 145, 154–155; UK
Military Manual 33, 102
United Nations (UN) 1; attribution of
responsibility to 46–52; operations
38–39, 41–46, 173; peace-
enforcement *v.* peacekeeping 43–44
United Nations Office for the
Coordination of Humanitarian
Affairs (OCHA) 115
UN Security Council (UNSC) 9,
38–39, 75, 133; avoidance of
categorization of armed conflicts
127–128; and end of occupation
125–132; interaction with
international law 126; Resolution
242 108; Resolution 276 131;
Resolution 678 131; Resolution
687 123; Resolution 1244 48, 131;
Resolution 1327 45; Resolution
1402 111; Resolution 1483 39,
40, 146, 147; Resolution 1546
128–132; resolutions, legal effects
of 126
uprisings 15, 91–92, 106
use of force 1, 28, 30, 42, 54, 131
US Law of War Manual 33, 102

vertical sharing of authority 34–35
Vienna Convention on the Law of
Treaties (VCLT): Article 32 13, 91;
Article 52 30–31

Wall case 29, 73, 99, 109n85, 149–150, 166
Warsaw Ghetto 106
welcomed consent 30
West Bank 108–112, 117
Western Sahara 30
Wilde, R. 44

withdrawal, control retained over territory after 112–123
World War II (WWII) 21, 22, 55, 106

Zacklin, R. 42
Zwanenburg, M. 139

Printed in the United States
By Bookmasters